Telling Science Stori

MW00804313

A practical manual for anyone who wants to turn scientific facts into gripping science stories, this book provides an overview of story elements and structure, guidance on where to locate them in scientific papers and a step-by-step guide to applying storytelling techniques to writing about science.

In this book, Martin W. Angler outlines basic storytelling elements to show how and where fledgling science storytellers can find them in scientific output. Journalistic techniques like selection through news values and narrative interviews are covered in dedicated chapters. A variety of writing techniques and approaches are presented as a way of framing science stories in ways that are informative and compelling in different media – from short films to news articles. Practical examples, selected interviews and case studies complement each chapter, with exercises and experimentation suggestions included for deeper understanding. Review questions at the end of each chapter cement the newly gained knowledge to make sure readers absorb it, with links to articles and online tools inviting further reading.

A valuable resource for students of journalism and science communication, as well as professional journalists, scientists and scientists-in-training who want to engage with the public or simply improve their journal papers. This book is a one-stop shop on science storytelling with a clear focus on providing practical techniques and advice on how to thrive as science writers and communicate science in all of its complexity.

Martin W. Angler is a science journalist, storyteller and science blog editor with a background in technology and journalism. His pieces have appeared in major UK, US, German, Italian and Swiss outlets. When Martin's not writing, he runs workshops on science blogging, social media and storytelling.

Telling Science Stories

Reporting, Crafting and Editing for Journalists and Scientists

Martin W. Angler

Routledge
Taylor & Francis Group

LONDON AND NEW YORK

First published 2020
by Routledge
2 Park Square, Milton Park, Abingdon, Oxon OX14 4RN

and by Routledge
52 Vanderbilt Avenue, New York, NY 10017

Routledge is an imprint of the Taylor & Francis Group, an informa business

British Library Cataloguing in Publication Data
A catalogue record for this book is available from the British Library

Library of Congress Cataloging-in-Publication Data
Names: Angler, Martin W., author.
Title: Telling science stories : reporting, crafting and editing
for journalists and scientists / Martin W. Angler.
Description: London ; New York : Routledge, 2020. |
Includes bibliographical references and index.
Identifiers: LCCN 2019050425 (print) | LCCN 2019050426 (ebook) |
Subjects: LCSH: Science journalism. | Science news. |
Journalism--Technique.
Classification: LCC PN4784.T3 A54 2020 (print) |
LCC PN4784.T3 (ebook) |
DDC 070.4/495--dc23
LC record available at https://lccn.loc.gov/2019050425
LC ebook record available at https://lccn.loc.gov/2019050426

ISBN: 978-1-138-49056-7 (hbk)
ISBN: 978-1-138-49059-8 (pbk)
ISBN: 978-1-351-03510-1 (ebk)

Typeset in Baskerville
by Taylor & Francis Books

To Katharina

Contents

3   Discovering Science Stories   50

4   Narrative Structure   77

5   Story Formulas   105

6   Language and Style   133

Figures

Acknowledgments

This book survived three relationships and nearly its author. I reckon thanks are in order. Friends old and new: Philipp Volgger, Katia Cont, Jon Tennant, Marija Tošić, Valentine Delattre, Choesang Tenzin, Kerstin Wonisch, Barbara Ebner, Simone Treibenreif, Michelle Rufaro Maziwisa and Sigrid Hechensteiner, for all your love, patience and time. You kept me sane. Bünz, this includes you. At Routledge: my editors Margaret Farrelly and Jennifer Vennall, for believing in this project, for your trust, patience and professionalism. At Edinburgh Napier University: my mentors Rachel Younger and Simon Pia, for all your inspiration, for your fantastic programme and for all those recommendation letters. You're the reason I'm writing books. Many thanks to Amanda Gefter, Giorgia Guglielmi, Jack Hart, Francesca Scandellari, Erin Barker, Tullio Rossi, Stephanie J. Green, Kirsten Grorud-Colvert and Heather Mannix for your wonderful contributions to my book. Now it's also yours.

Foreword

Writing is a journey, like most good stories. You should have a goal (people often call this "something to say") that adds value for either very specific people or for the entire society. A universal truth, your theme, shines through your writing. Sometimes, this happens at the beginning, before you even start structuring your story. Sometimes, it will emerge while you're writing the story. Along the road, you'll find many obstacles. You'll be daunted by empty pages, you'll be annoyed by ideas you'll find hard to connect and you'll struggle to find balance between your day-to-day-life and your identity as a writer. All of that is normal. Critics may or may not like what you write, but that too is part of the game. In fact, the clearer your writing, the more you'll provide them with a target. But if you stick to it, if you come up with a reporting and writing plan, and if you sit through it, you'll end up having written something. To get there, as every story's protagonist, you have to be focused and active. There is nothing worse than being passive, both in real life and in writing. It'll get your nowhere. So be active and seize the opportune moment. Grab Caerus, the Roman god of opportunity, by the lock of hair on his forehead before he's gone. Two more considerations about him. First, Caerus embodies achieving the aim by recognising the right opportunities. Second, you know who fell in love with Caerus? Fortuna, the goddess of fortune and the personification of luck.

> That's probably just a ponderous way to say:
> Don't dawdle.
> Just write.

1   Introduction

What you will learn in this chapter:

- Does science need story?
- Your brain on story
- The power of three
- Scientist or storyteller?
- Storytelling in scientific writing
- Ethical considerations
- Case study: A science story

These are the heydays of science journalism. People love to read about new discoveries, profiles of famous scientists and researchers who go on lifelong quests to save the world from terrible diseases. Science stories have made it to the front pages of the *New York Times* and the likes (alright, not every day, but at least sometimes). Science is hugely popular in the media, and there is a reason for that: the powerful combination of narratives and hard scientific facts. In school lessons, kids allegedly struggle to focus for more than a quarter of an hour. Attention spans are highly debated. Some claim they are as low as seven (goldfish-ish) and twelve seconds. But then again, have you seen anyone with trouble focusing in the movie theatre? Or reading a book? Quite the contrary. Binge-watching is on the rise among college students (Panda & Pandey 2017). Everybody loves stories. We're wired to love stories. We learn through stories. Our society passes on knowledge through stories. We experience catharsis through stories. We connect with strangers through stories. Because stories are inherently persuasive, they are so powerful. Facts and figures? Less so. But that doesn't mean that storytelling and science are mutually exclusive. And it doesn't mean science is boring and story is not. In fact, it turns out that combining the two is a powerful combination. This is the best weapon we have in the fight against fake news these days. Fake news are stories without facts. Facts without story are boring. What we need is science stories that combine both and we will win.

So, welcome to this book on science and story! I have one goal and one goal only. To bring together the seemingly contrasting worlds of science and story. Throughout this book, we'll have a look at how you can apply various fiction writing techniques to tell science stories that stick. Some of them have already been used to tell science stories for lay audiences, some have been used in scientific manuscripts. And others are purely experimental. Before we dig into the craft of science stories, let's have a look at why the techniques work. You, I and everybody else are story junkies, like it or not. They just work. And when we consume stories, we absorb new information, combine it with our existing knowledge and blend them together into a new state of knowledge. That's how we learn. That's how science works, too. So here's already our first overlap between science and real life. So let's look at what makes us tick and how our brains process stories. That is why one of the first sections covers the brain science aspects, where I'm trying to give you a few biological and psychological reasons for why we crave stories.

Journalists have long discovered the potential of wrapping dry facts into stories using literary techniques. They deliver fact-checked true stories to their audience that read like pieces of fiction. The movement started in the 1950s (most prominently Rodolfo Walsh, who is also considered the founder of investigative journalism), took off in the 1960s (Truman Capote with "In Cold Blood") and was redefined in the 1970s, where Tom Wolfe wrote his seminal manifest "The New Journalism". That's a long time, and creative nonfiction, as narrative journalism is often called, has undergone several evolutionary steps. Also, it has always faced criticism. Some of this criticism is about ethics. Well-told stories are incredibly persuasive. Politicians use them to push their agendas, marketers use them to make us buy their products and yes, even scientists and journalists misuse them to make their points. The most important external driving factor is money. Thus, I've decided to dedicate one section of this chapter to address the ethics of narratives.

This chapter also contains two sections dedicated to the seemingly everlasting fight between scientists who refuse the application of storytelling techniques and storytellers who claim scientists can't get their science across. Both camps are right in some ways, but they can be reconciled. You'll find a section that addresses the criticism against storytelling in journalism, and it will also expand on a few specific debates on science storytelling. Does science need story? You bet. We'll rebut much of the criticism by pointing out the many misconceptions of using narrative techniques in science. To be clear, not only do we need science writers who can employ literary techniques, we also need an increasing number of scientists that can convey their science to a large audience. That's why initiatives like *Story Collider* (I've included a lovely conversation about it in the chapter on screenwriting) are so important, because they get the scientists out of the labs and onto the stage. Actually, theatrical techniques in conveying science is a thing. A big thing. Dissemination of scientific results is part of the scientific method. But why should it stop at submitting scientific papers? That's one-way communication, and that's not how the real world works. Studies show that dialogue is how we assimilate knowledge. Science journalists do a great job at making science accessible, but the general public still finds a lot of scientific advances fishy, to say the least. It just lacks trust. More than ever, scientists appear to inhabit their ivory towers and talk condescendingly to the rest of the world. And I do get the public. I've worked with many scientists over the years. Most were fun to work with and curious to experiment with language and story. But some are not, no offense. The only thing they are interested in is their academic profile. The way things run now, that means a high impact factor (wrong) and a high h-index. It just makes it easier to compare your… achievements. If you are a scientist reading this book, you might find some of the techniques shown in this book are not only for the popular divulgation of your work but also for improving your papers. This, in turn, adds the benefit that the journalists out there will have a much easier time grasping your paper's gist and limitations and hence make fewer mistakes when writing about your work.

Woah, this sounds like a bit of a heavy introduction, but it really isn't. We'll also have a bit of fun looking at the rule of threes, one of the fundamental rules in fiction and nonfiction persuasive writing. The structures of some literary masterpieces are built in threes, jokes are delivered in threes and marketers like Apple Inc. praise their products in triplets. The sentence you just read came in threes. Once we're done with the threes, we'll examine an award-winning, masterfully written *Nautilus* science piece, "The Man Who Tried to Redeem The World", which portraits a science protagonist on his journey through personal and professional woes. It's a tragedy. You all know what a tragedy looks and feels like. You all know what a good story is once it's in front of you. Call it gut feeling or innate knowledge or story genetics. Story is best learnt through looking at some practical examples, that's why Amanda Gefter shares with us the elements she focused on when writing her tragic story on Walter Pitts. Don't worry if you've never heard of these elements. Just absorb them and enjoy the story. In the next chapter, we'll have a closer look at story elements, and throughout the book, we'll zero in on the different storytelling elements and techniques. Once you've read through it, you'll be able to apply the techniques to tell stories about science. These techniques will also help you to omit whatever is irrelevant. Let's go!

Does science need story?

Yes it does. First, it needs stories as a research tool. Narratives play a role as a qualitative research methodology, for example in the social sciences. Narratives also play a role in medicine, where both medical staff and patients tell their stories. Rita Charon, who is both an internist and a literary scholar, runs a narrative medicine division at Columbia University. Later in this book, we'll take another look at Charon's efforts. Psychology uses narratives (both as a research method and as a form of therapy). Education analyses narratives and employs them to understand how children and adolescents learn. In higher education, researchers use PhD students' narratives to determine why some of them drop out of their programmes. During the interviews, they ask the students to list the high and low points on their journeys. On top of that, students also drew their journeys, and the researchers also analysed academic narratives (McAlpine 2016).

We'll see a number of other ways science can profit from storytelling methods. For example, writing papers (or at least abstracts) using narrative techniques should become a no-brainer whenever possible. Not all studies and disciplines equally lend themselves to storytelling. But when you apply those techniques (like identifying a character, plot points, scene-setting, using dialogue and many more of the elements you'll see in the next chapter), your study would definitely improve. Stories make it easy to pick up new information and integrate it with what you already know. It's a natural way to learn and stay focused. So why not use that? Arguments against using storytelling techniques often include that scientific papers are primarily written for scientific peers. That's both true and false. First argument: they're written for scientific peers. But peers are also humans, with the same brain structures and functions. Why not rivet their attention a little longer? Although peers may be from the same discipline, they perhaps specialise in different areas of expertise. Second, it's not just peers who read scientific publications. Think about science journalists who read the papers. Think about how often they misreport facts and, for example, imply causality when there is merely a correlation that emerges from the data analysis. Like everything (and especially story), science is subject to *change*. Why should scientific publishing be an exception? The current format (IMRAD) has its merits, but it's not a block of marble. In fact, scientific publishing is only 350 years old, and quality-assuring (at least in an ideal world) concepts like peer review are even younger. So dare to use narratives in scientific publishing if your material lends itself to storytelling. Indeed, science and story influence each other mutually, as literary scholar Jonathan Gottschall writes in his book "The Storytelling Animal". He points out an important aspect:

> Science, I argue, can help us make sense of storytelling. But some say that science is a grand story (albeit with hypothesis testing) that emerges from our need to make sense of the world. The storylike character of science is most obvious when it deals with origins: of the universe, of life, of storytelling itself.
> (Gottschall 2012:49)

Stories help us make sense of the world. As you'll see throughout this book, this sounds true in many ways. If you've ever wandered through a cemetery, how many epitaphs have you encountered that contain some sort of variation of "why"? Death often seems random and strikes us out of the blue. But us humans, we can't deal well with random events, we need to make sense of them. We need to put them in order. We need to find reasons. That is why cause and effect structures are one of the most powerful tools in storytelling. Studies show that we can't just observe two separate events happen one after another and think they are independent. We just naturally infer they are related.

This includes journalism. Not just science journalism but any kind of journalism can benefit from applying storytelling methods, and be it only specific story elements (as opposed to always writing full stories that contain all storytelling elements – that's usually not necessary to turn dry journalism into compelling reads). Investigative journalist Mark Lee Hunter writes that in regular, fast-paced news journalism, dramatic structure is not happening, and it doesn't have to. News is continuous, so it doesn't need an end. But in investigative journalism, the impact of the story depends directly on the dramatic structure you choose for your story. It is you, the reporter, who offers the story's conclusion.

The problem with science is that it is intrinsically boring. Wait, that came out wrong. Let me rephrase. Science in itself is not boring. The way it is being communicated is most often boring. It is either too specific – think jargon-packed five-liners as headlines aka journal paper titles; or it is too vague – think impalpable abstract words. How many people of the general public read journal papers? Not many. Probably nobody. Even science journalists repeatedly fail to read the papers in their entirety and just try to extract the elements they are specifically looking for in order to craft their stories. Whatever we read about science, it's pre-selected, filtered and hence biased. In more general terms, internet activist Eli Pariser called this effect the "filter bubble". Information is tailored to our demographic profile and to the interests we implicitly or explicitly declare on online platform. But in contrast to the scientific communication provided by many scientists, 30-second-long online videos (or a couple of minutes, at most) take off and go viral. Why is that? Because they tell a story. Have a look at one of the videos *National Geographic* or *BBC Earth* post on Facebook regularly. That's the stuff people share and tell their friends about. Because they're stories. So yes, science can use storytelling techniques and still remain accurate. And no, it cannot afford to just communicate the bare figures if it wants to engage the general public.

Sara ElShafie, a biologist and PhD candidate at the University of California, Berkeley, has done something remarkable: she contacted Pixar Animation Studios and teamed up with a few of their collaborators to find out how scientists can use the animators' storytelling techniques to convey their research. In order to make people care about science, it must achieve meaningfulness, which is best done through storytelling (ElShafie 2018). Storytelling also involves emotions, and if the audience remains emotionless, it won't care. So that's probably the main issue with science communication: everybody tries to be objective, but that objectivity is boring. Objectivity is emotionless. Objectivity doesn't take sides. In contrast, story does take a side. Story evokes emotions. Story is personal and accessible. Most importantly, story adds meaning through theme, that's the universal truth of each story that connects the audience members among each other. And it makes the audience connect with the story. In contrast to the Carl Sagan accusations, academics who engage in public outreach are often more productive than others. Successful public outreach paves the way for funding, broader public acceptance (which, don't forget that, provides the foundation for science-friendly politics as well as the taxpayers' money needed to actually conduct research):

> Scientists who communicate effectively with the public can promote broader support for the sciences, encourage greater funding of research, increase the influence of science on public policy, and inspire tomorrow's scholars to join the scientific ranks. For these and many other reasons, one could argue that it is in the interest of all scientists that they and their colleagues engage in "outreach" to promote broader science literacy and knowledge.
>
> (Blanton & Ikizer 2019:155)

In an op-ed for *The Guardian*, linguistics Professor Nick Enfield points out that scientists are also human beings and thus subject to the same physiological and psychological restrictions and abilities as everybody else: "Bugs in our reasoning from the confirmation bias to the gambler's fallacy make our natural thought processes deeply subjective and partial" (Enfield 2018). He also claims that even if a fully objective scientist existed, she would still have to deal with an audience who is not. Instead, that audience expects stories. Story adds meaning. But without interpretation, the bare facts are meaningless. This is what people often ask when facts are just presented as list: So what? What do you want to tell me? And that is what storytelling is: to add meaning (Enfield 2018). He finds clear words for whether storytelling and science go together or not:

> It is our responsibility to become at least literate, if not masterly, in storytelling about our work. Our audiences need stories. So we must tell the right stories about our findings, if we are going to treat those findings with the respect they need.
>
> (Enfield 2018)

Why does the audience "need" storytelling? Because our brain reacts to stories on a physiological and psychological level. When we consume stories, this reaction connects us among each other, and it connects us with the storyteller and the story. It's powerful on so many levels. As neuroscientist Antonio Damasio found out, all decisions we take are emotional, not rational. Let that sink in. All of them. There's no need to fight our penchant for story and emotions. All we can do is understand them and tap into them when we tell our own stories. That's why we'll now have a look at how we're wired for story.

Your brain on story

Not everybody can write a good story right away, but everybody instantly understands if a story she's watching, reading or listening to is good or sucks. If need be, we'd walk out of movies (Cron 2012). But figuring out what exactly drags us into a story is not so easy. That's not our fault. Good stories immerse us so deeply into them that we become part of them. We live the story. Our brains are sponges that soak up new information through stories. Good stories involve emotions, and emotions cunningly bypass cognition – they physically find shortcuts into our brain stem, prompting us to respond emotionally before that information could pass any of our brain's rational filters. It's just a shortcut into a more primordial circuit of our brain. That is the reason why a social media story evokes an emotion, people start commenting, liking and disliking without having read the story behind the post. This is also the reason why scientists cannot convince anti-vaxxers, flat-earthers and climate change deniers by just countering stories with facts. You can't beat story. Instead, science should employ stories to evoke strong emotions while telling factual, true stories. In order to do that, it first has to understand how the brain processes stories.

One explanation is chemistry, or better: hormones and neurotransmitters. Stories cause physiological changes in the brain. Hormones are released into the brain and our blood stream and change how we think and behave. What do sex and stories have in common? Both release the neurotransmitter dopamine. Dopamine plays a role in both addiction and pleasure. A disturbed dopamine release mechanism is associated with mental illnesses like depression and schizophrenia. Whether you enjoy an orgasm or a story, dopamine is released. So it's rather fitting that the highest dopamine release occurs during story climaxes as well as sexual climaxes, orgasms. Another hormone plays a role too. Does a good story excite you? If so, that's the stress hormone cortisol being released into your blood stream. High cortisol levels are not exactly a good thing, as they are known to cause cardiovascular diseases. Worst case, you end up having a stroke or a heart attack. But at a moderate level, cholesterol heightens our attention, which makes us more receptive for new information. But the real poster child of storytelling hormones is oxytocin, which we'll see in a minute.

One of storytelling's secrets is involving the audience actively. Give them two plus two, and they'll add it up by themselves. That's essentially what Pixar's master storyteller Andrew Stanton calls "the unifying theory of two plus two". You can do that in two ways. Give readers enough details to imagine a scene or character, but don't describe it fully. Instead, readers have to use their imagination to fill in the details from their own experiences and memories. In terms of arts: you draw, but you don't paint. You just provide guides and line drawings with indications for how we as readers should fill them in. The audience's mind fleshes out the rest. Stories rule our lives. We form memories by fictionalising facts. The way we talk to friends and family is dominated by stories (Gottschall 2012).

When we interact with friends, family, our children, during physical contact and when we're having sex, another neurotransmitter is released. It's called oxytocin, and the media often call it "the love hormone." Oxytocin is synthesized in the hypothalamus, an almond-sized brain region of the limbic system that steers hunger, sex drive and fear. Also, oxytocin plays a role in trust and storytelling. You can measure its levels in the blood and derive the brain's current oxytocin levels from those measurements.

That's what neuroeconomist Paul Zak did. His team showed two factual videos to an audience. The first video shows a father whose two-year-old son is dying of terminal brain cancer. The story is tense and has a dramatic arc. In the second video, the same father and son are seen, but this time as zoo-goers, not mentioning the illness the boy suffers from. After the first experiment, the audience had heightened levels of stress hormone cortisol and the happymaker oxytocin, but remarkably, the audience wanted to send money to the characters in the video. They reported feeling increased empathy. After watching the zoo video, nothing happened. No extra cortisol and oxytocin, no perceived increased empathy (Zak 2015). Fittingly, oxytocin is also called a "prosocial" hormone. Zak ran more experiments, administering oxytocin in a double-blinded study to participants in one group and placebos in another. Donations rose by 56 per cent in those who had received the actual oxytocin. Zak found more than an empathic response. He also leveraged what psycholinguists coined "narrative transportation", that is when the audience gets so deeply immersed into a story that they won't even notice how deeply they're in. In fact, our brains on story suppress the basic needs, like eating. That is why oxytocin is actually being used to treat obese patients (Lawson 2017). Other studies have shown that you can use the hormone to replace the need for eating (too much) by the need to have sex. Oxytocin is released when we console each other and when mothers breastfeed their children. It triggers empathy, which in turn triggers post-story actions. So how can you trigger empathy as a writer and release oxytocin into your audience's brain? One way is to balance admirable traits and forgivable flaws in your characters (ElShafie 2018).

Have you ever read a novel that you couldn't possibly put down if you tried? You just need to know what happens next. You don't just root for the protagonist, you *are* her. That's narrative transportation, and there are two phenomena that evoke it: empathy and mental imagery. Empathy helps you detach from your own, physical world (Van Laer *et al.* 2013). It's the viscerality component good stories evoke. Strong, three-dimensional or rounded characters. What also helps you beam yourself into a scene is mental imagery. This is often a stylistic question. Vivid description and sensory language prompt the audience to let mental images pop up as they consume stories. That means using words that appeal to our senses of vision, audition, olfaction (smell) and somatosensation (touch). This technique cuts both ways. German reporter Claas Relotius was known for transporting his readers into his feature stories by vividly drawing on music: in one of his stories, he describes how a lonely child walks down a street, singing a sad song. In another story, he describes how a CD player in a hospital corridor plays the same song over and over again. None of that ever happened. In December 2018 another journalist discovered that he had fabricated most of his sensory descriptions, invented characters and entire stories. Description alone is not sufficient to fully immerse a reader into a story, it also needs plot (Van Laer *et al.* 2013) that is a logical, cause and effect-like sequence of events. Plot is what makes you turn page after page and wonder what comes next. Once you have returned from being transported into the narrative world (it does not really make a difference whether it's a fiction or nonfiction story), you return changed. In fact, the narrative transportation effect causes persuasion. There are two different types of persuasion: first, analytical persuasion, which is the type of persuasion that happens when you read or watch bits of information that make it obvious they want to persuade you. It's information that persuades you of something because you find it logical. It just makes sense. This includes many nonfiction works, like "science books, news reports and speeches" (Van Laer 2013:800). The second type of persuasion is narrative persuasion. Its effects last longer. They are often stories whose primary purpose is to entertain, not persuade, like novels, short stories and movies. Narrative persuasion lasts longer than the rational one. Van Laer, a consumer research professor, distinguishes between "story" as the product of a storyteller, and a narrative, which is what the story receiver consumes. His team identifies a number of factors that influence transportation, and this is a lightly edited summary of their hypotheses:

1   **Storytellers**: the more stories have characters with whom story receivers can identify, a plot that story receivers can imagine, and verisimilitude ("lifelikeness"), the more narrative transportation increases.

2   **Story receivers**: the more story receivers are familiar with a story topic, pay attention to a story, possess transportability, are young, are educated, and are female, the more narrative transportation increases.

Now for the interesting part: the consequences after readers have been beamed into stories and returned from them:

1   **Consequences**: the more narrative transportation increases, the more story-consistent affective responses increase, critical thoughts decrease, narrative thoughts increase, story-consistent beliefs increase, story-consistent attitudes increase, and story-consistent intentions increase.

The viscerality of stories, that is how we live through stories and experience them as if we were the protagonists, is key to understanding how they affect us. Neuroscientists from the Washington University in St. Louis have shown using neuroimaging techniques (essentially taking fMRI pictures) that our brain activates the same regions regardless of whether we are reading a word that describes an action (say, score a goal) and actually carrying out that very action. This is also true of watching movies, where motoric regions and sensory neurons fire whenever we watch close-ups of hands and faces – and the same goes for the brain regions that handle auditory and visual information (Speer *et al.* 2009). That's not all: they found that readers simulate situations that are similar to recalling actual memories or simulating possible, future situations. This link between sensory and motoric actions while experiencing stories may indicate that our cognition is very much grounded in real-world experiences: "Language may have adopted this general mechanism over the course of human evolution to allow individuals to communicate experiences efficiently and vividly" (Speer *et al.* 2009:998).

A Princeton University neuroscientific team also used brain scans (fMRI images) to analyse how our brains react while experiencing stories. So we are actually wired for story. There's no escaping it. We even have a tendency to come up with stories for random phenomena, as the famous 1944 Heider and Simmel experiment has shown (Muurlink & McAllister 2015). We try to put in order what is chaotic. John Yorke notes this in his brilliant storytelling book *Into the Woods* (Yorke 2013).

Yorke is right. For example, stories synchronise our brain waves. Neuroscientist Uri Hasson and his team ran a number of experiments to find out how (you'll read more about the experiments in the next section). What he found is that the brain waves of the audience synchronise among each other when watching the same story. Their brain waves also synchronise with the storyteller as she recounts it. And Hasson also found that it's important that the story has meaning. Just listening to the same words does synchronise certain parts of the brain, like the auditory cortex. But the synchronisation goes really deep and affects the most areas when the audience watches or hears a story that has the same meaning. This phenomenon even crosses language barriers. If you translate the same story into another language, say, from English to Russian, and let two persons listen to the story but in different languages, their brain waves will still synchronise (Hasson 2016).

The claim that stories are a way to put a chaotic world in order is not just a claim. In fact, we're wired to perceive events. Psychologists have found that we cannot perceive separately occurring events that happen one after another, as independent events. Much rather, we would interpret them as being connected (Ladouceur, Paquet & Dubé 1996). This is a frequent problem with fake news, as you'll see later on in this chapter. In 1944, Austrian and German psychologists Fritz Heider and Marianne Simmel ran an experiment, showing an animation of random geometrical shapes like triangles, dots and lines to study participants. Whoever watched the animation would attribute feelings and motives to those inanimate objects (Heider & Simmel 1944). We just need to make sense of the world and put chaos into order. This works also visually. For example, in Gestalt psychology's reification. When we see disparate objects, our visual system completes illusory contours.

The power of three

Three is the magic number of storytelling, as we will see throughout this book. Dante's masterpiece, the Divine Comedy, teems with threes: its narrative is structured as a journey through three different locations, hell, purgatory and heaven (the three cantiche). Dante subdivided each cantica into 33 canti. Each canto consists of tercets, or lines of three. Three was Dante's magical number, but he was not alone. Apple uses the rule of three to enumerate its "awesome" new features, like the "thinner, lighter and faster" iPad in 2011. Or when Steve Jobs announced the first iPhone in 2007, he called it an iPod, a phone and an internet communicator (the unification of all three of them was the actual iPhone). *Game of Thrones* loves to deliver lines of three, like this, from the second episode of the fourth season: "She's sullen and stubborn and sinful." Not only is the line delivered in a sequence of three words but also an alliteration, so almost every word starts with the same letter. Quite memorable. Jokes? Many good jokes are structured in threes. Most fairy tales are structured in threes. Two failed attempts and a third provides the solution to the initial problem. Think about the three little pigs. Two die, the third is smart enough to build a brick house.

In storytelling, the number three is crucial as a structural element. In Aristotle's seminal book on dramatic theory, "Poetics", he introduces a three-part structure, which he calls a "whole action" that consists of a beginning, a middle and an end. To date, many dramatics use the same idea of dramatic structure as a foundation for their own structures, for example dividing the structure into story setup, confrontation and story resolution. Or thesis, antithesis and synthesis, as in the Hegelian dialectic. But back to Aristotle: in "Poetics", he analysed the structure of the Greek tragedy and found three stages that have to occur in a dramatic work. They are "peripeteia" (the reversal of fortune; in tragedies, that means a shift from fortune to misfortune, that's a plot twist), "anagnorisis" (recognition, a major revelation or epiphany, the protagonist gains knowledge), which eventually leads to "pathos" (suffering, pain and death on stage). In going through all three stages, pity and fear is evoked in the spectators, purifying them of emotions in an act called "catharsis". Each tragedy is kicked off by a mistake the protagonist commits, out of hubris or imprudence. In modern story speak, this is called the inciting incident.

Three-act structure is screenwriters' counterpart of this dramatic structure, often attributed to screenwriting teacher Syd Field, and "it's a model that lies behind all modern mainstream film and TV narratives" (Yorke 2013:26). Act one, act two, act three, divided by two turning points (the inciting incident and the crisis). Yorke argues that we cannot possibly escape this structure, and even some writers who dismiss it still unconsciously use this structure in writing their pieces. Our method of making sense of the world is the tripartite dialectical method that consists of thesis, antithesis and synthesis. *Thesis* is the story setup, which includes establishing a protagonist, *antithesis* is the protagonist's confrontation with her adversary, and *synthesis* is the assimilation of newly gained knowledge, causing growth and change. In screenwriting speak, this structure looks like this (Yorke 2013:26):

- Act One: establish a flawed character
- Act Two: confront them with their opposite
- Act Three: synthesise the two to achieve balance

Acts are units of action that depend on a character's desire. Like entire plays and stories, they can be subdivided into beginnings, middles and ends. Dialectic in the sense of thesis-antithesis-synthesis is often attributed to German philosopher Hegel, but in reality he did neither coin nor use the term; that was his fellow philosopher Fichte. The dialectic does not explain why an antithesis exists to counter the thesis. But Hegel came up with a similar construct, abstract-negative-concrete, and in addition he hinted at the existence of the antithesis (negative) due to the thesis (abstract) being incomplete and not concrete enough to be proven. You can see this in action in pretty much every horror film. A protagonist with a shortcoming (thesis) meets his adversary (monster, killer, antithesis). The monster most often embodies the protagonist's shortcoming, forcing her to confront it. Take the 1995 psychological thriller *Copycat* starring Sigourney Weaver. The protagonist's flaw is agoraphobia, she can't leave her apartment. Her adversary is a serial killer, and as you can guess, she is forced to leave her apartment at some point in order to eventually beat the killer. Story is exposure therapy.

> The dialectic pattern – thesis/antithesis/synthesis – is at the heart of the way we perceive the world; and it's a really useful way to look at structure. A character is flawed, an inciting incident throws them into a world that represents everything they are not, and in the darkness of that forest, old and new integrate to achieve a balance.
>
> (Yorke 2013:29)

TV series differ from typical stories in that the character does not change at the end. In that case, synthesis simply means fending off the antithesis. Famous playwright and writing teacher Lajos Egri was also known for advocating and using the dialectic method, most prominently in his seminal book *The Art of Dramatic Writing*. He adds another important element to it: the premise. The premise is the story's purpose, often called theme or main idea. Every good story has a premise, in fiction and in non-fiction. It is the golden thread that runs through a story, the moral of the story, or it's take-home message. "Every play must have a well-formulated premise." (Egri 1946:6) and "a good premise is a thumbnail synopsis of your play. He presents lots of examples, like "Great love even defies death" as the underlying premise of *Romeo and Juliet*. Egri defines how a well-formulated premise should look, and it's a tripartite structure, consisting of character, conflict and resolution. The premise author has to take a side and make it clear what he champions, Egri argues. Otherwise the premise is dull. Before we stray too far from factual storytelling: it is not hard to spot how the Hegelian dialectic can be at least in part likened to the scientific method. The formulation of a thesis, the formulation of the null hypothesis as its antithesis and the eventual synthesis that corresponds to the results and makes sense of the initial knowledge, presents the new findings, synthesises them and comes up with new knowledge that changes the status quo.

Scientist or storyteller?

Let's apply the Hegelian dialectic to an evergreen problem: science has all the facts, all the figures (at least, ideally), but it can't dissuade the general public from believing fake science news that are mere fictional stories. If science is the thesis with a flaw (it can't persuade as well as narrative), and if story is its antithesis (not facts but powerful narrative persuasion), then synthesising them could yield the best of both worlds. The persuasiveness of stories that are rooted in scientific facts. Let's try and formulate this as a premise: *Storytelling leads to better science communication.* Or, to frame it differently: *Science storytelling destroys fake news.*

What could be our premise for such a bold claim? *Science, when told with the persuasiveness of stories, beats fake news.*

Infections with the human papillomavirus (HPV) can increase the risk of getting certain cancer types. Ask actor and cunnilinguist Michael Douglas, who contracted HPV from his muff-diving activities and unfortunately got throat cancer as the probable consequence (Ball 2013). But there's good news. First, Douglas fully recovered. Second, since then, he has been speaking out on the issue to raise awareness. And yet, HPV is an under-perceived risk. It's a personal story from a celebrity, which can be much more powerful than just presenting bare facts. Xiaoli Nan *et al.* (2015) discovered in their study that statistics alone can't raise enough awareness in people and an increased perceived risk of HPV. This hardly comes as a surprise. They also tried narratives, but, and that is a bit of a surprise, neither did the narratives alone increase the awareness of the perceived HPV risk (although first-person narratives worked better than their third-person counterparts). So what did the trick? The combination between statistics and narrative! Science and story.

It is not exactly an equally balanced combination: if narrative and facts sat on opposing sides of a seesaw, it would tip in favour of the narrative. In fact, narrative would weigh twice as much, as Dahlstrom and Ho (2018) show.

Scientists and storytellers alike are quite aware of the power of narrative. But while the former find that it's dangerous, the latter obviously champion it. Scientists frequently argue that storytelling methods water down science's accuracy. They fear for their objective slant. In contrast, storytellers counter-argue that scientists reject telling stories. Both are right, and both are wrong. Scientists enjoy stories, just like everyone else. They are humans and not objective, just like everyone else. Storytellers often have no idea how science works and start bashing against scientists for not conveying their science better. And because life is neither black nor white, sometimes you find hybrid species: the scientist-turned-storyteller (or vice versa). One such example is Randy Olson, a former professor of marine biology and now documentary filmmaker.

Olson has written books with telling titles like *Don't Be Such a Scientist* and *Houston: We Have a Narrative*. In his books, Olson points out that science without creativity is "dull", while science without discipline and rigorosity is "dangerous" (Olson 2018). So both are needed. I second that: science and the right amount of storytelling complement each other. If I didn't believe that, why would I write this book? Olson's personal journey features lots of story elements. After graduating from an Ivy League university, he achieved tenure as a marine biology professor. He used to make short videos based on his research. One day, he quit his university job and moved to California where he attended film school. He came across some powerful storytelling techniques and systematically applied them to his documentary films. That's why some of them were well received.

Olson clearly addresses scientists, pointing out that many are not natural storytellers. I love clarity (it's my favourite part of the ABCs of journalism), but I do also believe that every now and then, Olson strikes a bit of an offensive note when coming up with statements like this:

> Truth teller is a valiant role, and I am in no way saying scientists shouldn't play it. [...] But in the end ... it's just not a very likeable trait. Nobody likes a party pooper. So the question is whether there are ways to play the scientist role without being the negating, annoying, no-fun voice.
>
> (Olson 2018:130)

He writes that scientists are too condescending and have a "negating role: the designated driver, remaining sober amid the fantasy-blinded townspeople". Come on. The irony is that Olson becomes a bit of a party pooper and wisenheimer himself in talking down to them. He talks in the same way to scientists as he claims they talk to the general public. It's like mom saying smoking is bad while a cigarette dangles from her mouth (damn, that's actually my mom). It's hard to imagine how you can convince anybody to change by just offending them, no matter if you mean well or not. So, what happened is that several academics took offense (no shit) and spoke out against his insults. Also, this is hardly constructive. For example, physiologist and science writer Bethany Brookshire points that out in her review of Olson's book *Don't Be SUCH A Scientist* (the first edition), where she writes that Olson tells his readers what not to do (like: don't fixate on facts, don't stick to sound bites). Her point is not that scientists don't need storytelling skills. On the contrary, she fully agrees that they need to become better science storytellers. But she doubts that an insulting book with little constructive advice will do the trick. Also, much of his advice boils down to be more like Carl Sagan or at least adopt some of his techniques (Brookshire 2009). Another of Olson's critics is palaeontologist and science writer Brian Switek. He writes that Olson's book, like part of his documentary filmmaking work, is incoherent. Switek particularly dislikes Olson's habit of stereotyping scientists. Indeed, Switek seems to have more of a problem with Olson's own documentary storytelling skills than with his attitude of being condescending towards scientists (Switek 2009).

But yeah, scientists love to argue over storytelling. If you're a scientist who advocates using storytelling techniques to convey science, your professional life doesn't get easier. One popular debate arose in 2013, when Yarden Katz from Harvard Medical School published an article against storytelling in science in *Nature Methods*. He argues that science should not be molded into predefined story structures, providing seemingly satisfactory ends to a scientific reality that just looks different. He says science is just not a single, easy-to-tell story with a beginning, middle and end; much rather, he told me in an interview a couple of years ago, science is a journey that sometimes lasts for years or even decades. Molding scientific projects into stories hence simply doesn't justice to their complexity. Katz' criticism was a response to an article published by Alberto Cairo and Martin Krzywinski, who had argued that story arcs can be used to better present data in papers' figures. I asked Katz and Cairo for commentary and published their responses in my previous book. It seems their points of view are still irreconcilable. Interestingly, Cairo is not a story-in-science advocate but points out that he is actually sick and tired of magazine stories that sport "story" leads (Angler 2017). As you can see, it's also a matter of personal taste. So, can scientists be storytellers? Absolutely. They already are. Everybody is. Can scientists still be rigorous about their work? Of course they can. The tension between scientists and storytellers is neither new nor surprising. In fact, conflict is one of the fundamental elements of story, and life. There will always be friction between the two. Ideally, the scientists (thesis) critically discuss and argue the pros and cons of storytelling with storytellers (antithesis), before distilling the best of the two worlds, compensating for each other's flaws and transforming the science journey into a winning combination for everybody (synthesis). Now, how's that for a dialectic story approach?

Storytelling in scientific writing

You might think that telling stories to a lay audience is all I'm going to address. No. Scientific writing can employ storytelling techniques, too. That doesn't mean scientists should lump their facts into some tight story corset. But if they write about their scientific findings in an accessible way, not only will it be clearer to peers from the same field, but their articles are also more likely to get picked up by the media, while those journalists who read it are less likely to misinterpret your findings and their implications. In facts, in climate change, narratives can increase the citation frequency (Hillier, Kelly & Klinger 2016).

The debate is still hot. In a blog post, Yarden Katz (2018) rebuts an opinion piece that linguist Nick Enfield published in *The Guardian*. Enfield advocates that scientists develop storytelling skills, or at least understand them. He cites Katz' previous work, but Katz feels misinterpreted. He clarifies that storytellers' advice to scientist is often laced with "neoliberal logic according to which the 'best' scientists are the most popular, based on citation metrics and media success. This approach also caters to the alliance between glamour scientific journals and mainstream media outlets" (Katz 2018). Katz has got a point there. Catering to scientific journals' style and content requests introduces bias in research. You'll read a bit more about that in this book's appendix.

But Enfield isn't alone in proposing using storytelling elements in scientific writing. For example, David Torres of Purdue University recommends Cohen's four storytelling elements. You can use them to craft powerful anecdotes that people can use to convey science (Torres & Pruim 2019 drawing on Cohen 2011):

1 **Setting**: time and place, only relevant details
2 **Character**: individuals who breathe life into a story
3 **Plot**: sequence in which the events unfold
4 **Moral**: the lesson the author wants to convey

These are essential elements of a story (in later chapters, we'll call "moral" differently). Most magazine features start with a human touch, zooming in on a character's situation. Good articles have structure and a take-home message, some universal truth that you learn from the story. They change your state of knowledge. What's astonishing is that most scientists are trained to eliminate every trace of humanity from their paper. They strip it from every personal pronoun and replace active with passive voice. "John did A." becomes "A was done". No wonder that the passive voice is badly received by readers. It yanks the characters out of every story. Sure, science well done seeks truth. But science is neither neutral nor objective. It's a human enterprise. It's a business machinery. It deals with a lot of money, so it's manipulated and flawed. So why pry out the human factor of science?

Torres and Pruim (2019) champion storytelling methods in scientific writing, as they believe our democracy will only function if all members and groups have the same level of understanding scientific discoveries. Incidentally, that is also very much in the spirit of Open Access! Also, scientific discoveries don't just impact the researchers' peers but all of society. Thus, it's only fair that they get to understand it, too. Except, there is no "they". We're all part of society, scientists and not. Think about it. To increase the common understanding of science, Torres and Pruim (2019) recommend using anecdotes, which they write are vignettesque, isolated events that contain the same storytelling elements as a full narrative.

But research papers' manuscripts run longer than typical anecdotes. That's why Anna Clemens, a materials scientist and a science journalist, recommends identifying the six plot elements (character, setting, tension, action, climax, resolution) and "three other story essentials" (main theme, chronology) of your research work and outlining your paper according to them. She mentions a study that found people remembered nouns better when they didn't just come as random enumerations but as stories that glued the nouns together (Clemens 2018). This technique is not new. Take memory sport. Some people use similar techniques to remember large numbers using random images of objects, or even sequences of plain numbers to which the athlete assigns images of objects to remember them. Then she links those images together by crafting a story. For example, "an elephant walks into a bar and kicks out a dog but then buys it a sunflower to console it". This method is known as mnemonic link system, or chain method. Stories enable us to remember complex, otherwise unconnected facts by simply taking unordered, chaotic information and putting it in order. That makes it a bit simpler to understand what rivets readers to the page (no matter if they read fiction or a scientific paper): a logical flow from argument A to argument B to argument C, until the end of your piece. It's structure, and if arguments or events are connected by cause and effect-relationships, then they become all the more memorable.

Clemens is an advocate of using storytelling methods in writing research manuscripts. For developing a scientific story, she likens the plot elements to certain elements of the manuscript. The main character is your study subject, be it a disease or a theory or a document. The setting, then, is your study's background – you point out the state of the art, and voilà, there is your introduction. Next, she recommends putting in tension by pointing out what the problem is. Also, you should point out why all previous research hasn't solved the problem (Clemens 2018). This is also what molecular biologists James Watson and Francis Crick did in their famous 1953 DNA paper. Clemens indeed recommends pointing out the problem as a narrative technique, and she also mentions using adversative conjunctions such as "but". Next, Clemens recommends you start with the action, embodied by plots, schemes and interpretations, which are your findings. At the end, that is in the results section, you should come full circle (sorry for the truism, really) and address the problem: have you solved it? No? Why not? And finally, your paper's discussion section will address future research you recommend be carried out, and the implications of your findings. This section corresponds to the resolution in drama (Clemens 2018). On a smaller scale, Clemens also advocates using storytelling techniques to write scientific abstracts (based on *Nature*'s submission guidelines). I've put a link to her recommendations in this chapter's "Links" section.

But not everybody is as convinced as Clemens. Lawrence Rajendran, a professor in systems and cell biology at the University of Zurich, is not quite a champion of storytelling techniques in scientific writing.

"The need to publish 'sexy' scientific stories has become more important than a solid, standalone observation in many fields. Plus, the science publishing system exerts enormous pressure on scientists to turn simple – sometimes powerful – observations into flashy stories, and since universities and funding agencies judge researchers on their publishing record, we have no choice but to oblige. Storytelling has thus become the prevailing paradigm of scientific publishing" (Weilenmann & Rajendran 2018:45).

Rajendran therefore has built the platform *ScienceMatters.io*, which encourages the submission of single observations, hypotheses and data separately, effectively splitting apart full papers and avoiding the spinning of fully story yarns. Rajendran is also an advocate of using blockchain in science and hence predicts the absence of academic publishers by 2030, after having been replaced by a peer-to-peer exchange in research and the publication process being fueled by semi-automated blockchain-based transactions. That's a long shot. But do you see what's going on here? It's everlasting tension between scientists and storytellers. Protagonist and antagonist. Thesis and antithesis. In terms of storytelling, that's fantastic. But what stands in the way of reaching synthesis is also a set of ethical considerations. Let's have a look.

Ethical considerations

When you tell science stories, you face a choice. Do you tell only the facts without employing storytelling techniques? Or do you wrap the facts into a story and choose and order that story's events? In the former case, you risk that nobody understands what you're talking about. If you don't reduce jargon and present scientific information as a sort of a logically connected narrative sequence of events, apart from your scientific peers nobody will understand you. In the latter case, if you do tell science stories, you might fear unfairly influencing your audience. Before we look into this seeming dilemma, let's make a few things clear. Science is not an objective endeavour. Much criticism on science storytelling revolves around the selection of events and facts that you present those in a specific order to your audience, for maximum persuasive effect. But that's not where science starts becoming biased. That starts way before. In choosing which studies to cite, which work to draw upon, scientists are already being selective, long before the public outreach starts. Journals introduce bias by putting focus on specific topics. If those journals are high-profile publications, which means they have a high impact factor (IF), then authors are likely to conduct and eventually submit research that caters to those topics. Other topics don't stand a chance against this machinery. Also, science is done by humans. Humans are driven by many needs (which we'll see in the next chapter). Social status, power and money are some of these drivers. They are also the reasons why scientists deceive, fabricate data or kill themselves.

My point is: using storytelling to convey science is a tradeoff. Not always will scientists have a complete narrative arc to tell. Not always is a story format the most suitable way to describe a scientific project. On the other hand, if science actively forgoes storytelling techniques, does it do society a service? Think about fake news. Fake newsers use storytelling techniques, and quite efficiently so. They draw on our perception of events and the fact that we connect them. They present non-existent facts and make sure we drink the Flavor Aid. That's not a new thing and can't be solely blamed on technology like social media. For example, in the 1958 "documentary" titled "White Wilderness", Walt Disney Productions showed how

Lemmings commit suicide by leaping off a cliff, into the sea. In reality, they don't. The filmmakers fabricated the scenes, shoving the lemmings off the cliff. The narrator adds an element of mystery in telling the audience that an unknown compulsion, a hysteria is driving them, a voice that forces them to move on and on. (Woodford 2003). That was 61 years ago. Once a rumor is out in the world, there's almost nothing that can stop it. Several researchers have debunked this myth, but most people still believe lemmings are suicidal.

This is one of the harmless scientific myths. The on-going debate about the non-existent link between vaccines and developing autism is an example of the power of narratives. Former physician Andrew Wakefield is the man behind the myth. He wrote a paper in 1998 in the *Lancet* in which he wrongly established a link between MMR (measles, mumps, rubella) vaccines and developing autism (Kolodziejski 2014). It took the *Lancet* twelve years to retract the study. Wakefield still defends his unsubstantiated point of view at anti-vaxxer rallies. There is still no scientific evidence the two phenomena are related, but the web is awash with powerful narratives involving "case studies" that imply they are. Those accounts are often narrated by affected parents. For example, the case of Ian Gromowski, a baby boy who developed life-threatening symptoms after getting a Hepatitis B shot at eight days old. Look closely. It says "after", not "because". That's a difference. But on the web, Ian's parents' blog post went viral (Shelby & Ernst 2013). That's because anecdotal evidence has power. It makes people assume that two events that occur in a temporal sequence are actually causally connected. That's wrong, and there's even a name for it: "post hoc ergo propter hoc" fallacy.

I'm inclined to intuitively argue that in times of post-truth, scientists need to reach out and weigh in on burning issues. In doing so, they need to be persuasive. This sounds like a bold statement, but think about the sheer volume. It's impossible to moderate the amount of fake news, scientific myths and misinformation that floods the web. The absolute number of Facebook posts per day has risen to a whopping 90,000 (Peters 2018), while Twitter users post 500 million tweets per day. That's 6,000 tweets per second (Cooper 2019). You don't have to be a mathematician to understand that it's impossible for a team of human moderators to fact-check and categorise this much information. Promising algorithms are underway, but so far they haven't been able to stop the spread of misinformation. That's why I would argue that scientists should draw on persuasion techniques to produce better, more graspable stories and shift the good story-bad story ratio more to the left side. But the ethical discourse is a bit more complex. Communication science has understood that the deficit model doesn't work: the model is an assumption that the general public is averse to science because it doesn't know enough about it, so science communication should fill that gap. A variation of this model built in the 1980s in the UK is called Public Understanding of Science (PUS). A more interactive model is public engagement in science and technology (PEST). It does the opposite: instead of trying to mute controversies, it sees them as a necessary part of the democratic process. Science communication's purpose is to ease the discussion about the pros and cons of science- and technology-influenced policies. Scientists can take four different roles in this process (Dahlstrom & Ho 2012, citing Pielke):

1   **Pure scientists** just focus on their scientific work and avoid commenting on policy.
2   **Science arbiters** respond to scientific questions but do not give recommendations on how to fix issues.
3   **Issue advocates** recommend policy actions. In doing so, they take sides and limit policy options.
4   **Honest brokers** comment on existing policy options and propose new ones. In doing so, they open up policy options.

Pielke names a fifth, unethical role scientists can assume. When they hide their advocacy behind a science façade, they become *stealth issue advocates*.

Dahlstrom argues that one of the determining factors is purpose. Why do you communicate science? Do you want to simply reduce controversy, like in the PUS model? Or do you want to stir public debates and discussions about scientific risks and benefits, like in the PEST model? Dahlstrom's premise is that narratives are inherently persuasive and hard to counter-argue. PUS-driven communicators might hence craft narratives that emphasise one side of an issue while omitting values that are the foundation of the other, opposing side. This can be done by selecting events that support the author's point. When confronted with such a piece, the audience then could easily be convinced to take the same side that the communicator has taken. In contrast, PEST-driven communication might leverage the same narrative mechanisms to a completely different end:

> Creating a narrative for these ends could involve selecting causal events that explain the factors underlying the science issue, portraying the events through a character neutral to the issue at hand or through multiple characters in order to represent multiple sides, and personifying the underlying social values that intersect with the issue. Such a narrative has the potential to engage a wider public in the debate, enhance understanding of the science, and create greater connections with existing knowledge.
>
> (Dahlstrom & Ho 2012)

Case study: a science story

So let's have a look at a real science story. Award-winning science writer Amanda Gefter was kind enough to write me how she came up with the story. Her story "The Man Who Tried to Redeem the World" won her the 2015 Kavli Science Journalism Silver Award in the Magazine category. If you haven't read the story, do it now. It spans about 5,000 words and is freely accessible online (you'll find a link to it in the "Links" section at the end of this chapter). Gefter's story is in many ways typical for award-winning (science) journalism stories: it follows a protagonist with a clear goal, facing obstacles, seemingly reaching his goal and, alas, a tragic ending. Much of it resembles the Greek tragedy Aristotle addressed in his book on dramatic structure, *Poetics*. The protagonist, Walter Pitts, has a flaw (actually, there are a few: he was a drinker and a runaway). After his inciting incident, Pitts gets thrown into the world of science, and, although unlikely to survive, he gets a taste of the high ranks of academia. He makes important discoveries in the fields of cybernetics and the precursors of artificial intelligence. Pitts stuns established experts and consequently gets offered a PhD in mathematics by his mentor Norbert Wiener. Then, another reversal of fortune: his mentor and father figure drops him like a hot potato. Depression sets in, and so does alcoholism. Pitts dies alone. Gefter uses a number of story elements, but she doesn't strictly employ all elements you would typically find in a fiction story (for example, there is no dialogue). That makes the story no less compelling. I've edited the interview for brevity and clarity (especially my questions).

Q: Did you consciously decide not to use dialogue and instead use direct speech?

> **A:** Since the whole story was based on historical documents (mostly letters), that's all I had to work with. But I was lucky in that the letters were extremely intimate and emotional, and gave a strong sense of the relationships among the characters. Honestly, it was such a powerful experience for me getting to read those primary sources – there's something incredibly intimate about holding and reading someone's private, handwritten letters – and I wanted to share that feeling with the reader if I could.

Q: The story's characters are three-dimensional. Did you look for specific traits to decide which ones would make it into your story?

> **A:** These particular characters were incredibly compelling and vivid, so I didn't have to do much work in that respect! McCulloch was a wild man, a brilliant, swashbuckling, bohemian poet. Marvin Minsky once said that even when McCulloch was speaking to a small group of people it was like he was talking to the whole world. So he was a great character, and there was something so sweet about seeing that kind of an intimidating, larger-than-life figure act so tenderly toward this sensitive young man, Walter Pitts. Pitts, in turn, was such an interesting combination because his genius made him the envy of every scientist who met him and yet he was such a fragile character, having been beaten by his father and having run away from home with nowhere to live. Wiener is a fascinating (and bizarre!) character, too, but less of that made it into the story. I had done a lot more character development for Wiener in an early draft, and Lettvin, too, but those ended up stealing too much focus away from the relationship between McCulloch and Pitts, which was the emotional heart of the story. I do wish I'd given a bit more character development to Wiener's wife, because a lot of readers reacted to that piece of the story, concerned that she was being treated as a kind of scapegoat or was unfairly maligned. In truth, she was a truly disturbed person – a Nazi sympathizer who kept copies of Hitler's *Mein Kampf* on her dresser. She was extremely paranoid, seeing sexual undertones in completely innocent situations. A few more sentences about her would have helped provide that context. I kept her out of the story because she was just there as a catalyst, and I didn't want to distract from the main narrative. But in retrospect I think the

lack of context did distract from the main narrative, because the reader had to stop and consider whether there was any merit to her story.

Q: Speaking of narrative: how did you structure your story?

A: I have a bad habit of always writing chronologically when really I should be writing narratively. Obviously chronology will always play a role in structure, but you have to think in terms of the story, and then use flashbacks and flashforwards when necessary. I learned a lot through the writing and editing of this piece, because my editor really showed me how to take a chronological story and restructure it to give it a strong narrative arc. I've taken that lesson with me, so now when I write, I'll write the first draft chronologically and then sit back, look at it, try to figure out the narrative arc and start rearranging accordingly. This story, in particular, was obviously a tragedy. So narratively speaking, it needed a strong optimistic rise to precede the fall. In an earlier draft, I introduced Pitts's struggle with depression in the midst of the rise, because that's when he wrote those letters to McCulloch, chronologically speaking. But my editor had the good sense to hold off on that and then tell it in flashback. That way, you have the rise before the fall and the whole story is more effective.

Q: Can you walk me through the most important plot points?

A: The first major plot point is the 12-year-old Pitts running away from his bullies and hiding in the library where he reads Russell and Whitehead's Principia. It couldn't be a more perfect anecdote, narratively speaking, because it houses the whole story in miniature: we see Pitts as this fragile character, hiding from a world in which he doesn't fit (the same fragility that will turn out to be his downfall); his genius, reading (and correcting!) this intensely arcane book of mathematical logic at age twelve; and the mathematical logic itself, which will form the basis for his model of information processing in the brain and, in turn, of modern computer architecture. I immediately knew that scene was going to appear somewhere close to the beginning of the story. Next, Pitts runs away from home to go to the University of Chicago and meet Bertrand Russell. That's a classic plot point: the hero leaving home. Then Lettvin introduces Pitts, who's now homeless, to McCulloch. They immediately recognize something in each other, and that's the spark of the whole story to come. McCulloch invites Pitts to live with him, becoming a kind of father figure. The scenes at the McCulloch house where they do their most important work represent the paradise that is soon to be lost, the home for which he will always be homesick. Next, there's the scene where Pitts meets Norbert Wiener and becomes his new righthand man. That's a turning point, because it draws him away from McCulloch, initiating the downfall. And of course, when Wiener disowns Pitts, that's the turning of the knife, the wound from which he'll never recover. Lastly, there's the double death of Pitts and McCulloch at the end. When I came across the letter that Pitts sent to McCulloch as they were both dying, which was incredibly touching (I actually cried in the library reading room!), I knew that's how the story would end.

Review questions

- Which hormones do stories trigger, and do they affect your brain?
- What is the unifying theory of two plus two?
- What do you need to immerse readers in a story?
- From which story structures does the number three emerge?
- What is Hegel's dialectic?
- Why do storytellers and scientists argue?
- Which four ingredients do you need to craft anecdotes?
- What is the "post hoc ergo propter hoc" fallacy?

Links

"Should Scientists Tell Stories?" (*Nature Methods*): https://www.nature.com/arti cles/nmeth.2726

"Hegel's Dialectics" (*Stanford Encyclopedia of Philosophy*): https://plato.stanford. edu/entries/hegel-dialectics/

"Is Storytelling Bad for Science?" Sydney Ideas (Podcast): https://soundcloud. com/sydney-ideas/is-storytelling-bad-for-science

"How to write the perfect abstract" (Anna Clemens) https://www.annaclem ens.com/blog/how-to-write-the-perfect-abstract

Science Matters: https://www.sciencematters.io

References

Angler, M.W. (2017) *Science Journalism: an introduction*. London: Routledge

Ball, J. (2013) "Michael Douglas says cunnilingus gives you cancer – but is he right?" *The Guardian* [Online]. Available at: https://www.theguardian.com/news/datablog/2013/ jun/02/michael-douglas-oral-sex-cancer-facts (date accessed 26 September 2019).

Barraza, J.A. & Zak, P.J. (2009) "Empathy toward strangers triggers oxytocin release and subsequent generosity." *Annals of the New York Academy of Sciences*, vol. 1167, no. 1, 182–189.

Blanton, H. & Ikizer, E.F. (2019) "Elegant Science Narratives and Unintended Influences: An Agenda for the Science of Science Communication ." *Social Issues and Policy Review*, vol. 13, no. 1, 154–181.

Brookshire, B. (2009) "Book Review: Don't be SUCH a Scientist," Scicurious Blog [Online]. Available at: https://scicurious.scientopia.org/2009/11/23/book-review-dont-be-such-a -scientist/ (date accessed 12 December 2019).

Clemens, A. (2018) "Writing a page-turner: how to tell a story in your scientific paper," LSE Impact Blog [Online]. Available at: http://blogs.lse.ac.uk/impactofsocialsciences/2018/ 05/21/writing-a-page-turner-how-to-tell-a-story-in-your-scientific-paper/ (date accessed 27 January 2019).

Cohen, J.D. (2005) "The vulcanization of the human brain: A neural perspective on interactions between cognition and emotion." *Journal of Economic Perspectives*, vol. 19, no. 4, 3–24.

Cohen, S.D. (2011) "The art of public narrative: Teaching students how to construct memorable anecdotes," *Communication Teacher*, vol. 25, no. 4, 197–204.

Cooper, P. (2019) "28 Twitter Statistics All Marketers Need to Know in 2019." Hootsuite Blog [Online] https://blog.hootsuite.com/twitter-statistics/ (date accessed 28 September 2019).

Cron, L. (2012) *Wired for story: The writer's guide to using brain science to hook readers from the very first sentence.* Berkeley: Ten Speed Press.

Dahlstrom, M.F. & Ho, S.S. (2018) "Exploring the Ethics of Using Narratives to Communicate in Science Policy Contexts," in: Hornig Priest, S., Goodwin, J. & Dahlstom, M.F. (eds) *Ethics and Practice in Science Communication.* Chicago: University of Chicago Press.

Dahlstrom, M.F. & Ho, S.S. (2012) "Ethical Considerations of Using Narrative to Communicate Science." *Science Communication*, vol. 34, no. 5, 592–617.

ElShafie, S.J. (2018) "Making science meaningful for broad audiences through stories." *Integrative and Comparative Biology*, vol. 58, no. 6, 1213–1223.

Egri, L. (1946) *The Art of Dramatic Writing.* New York: Simon and Schuster.

Enfield, N. (2018) "Our job as scientists is to find the truth. But we must also be storytellers," *The Guardian* [Online]. Available at: https://www.theguardian.com/commentis free/2018/jul/20/our-job-as-scientists-is-to-find-the-truth-but-we-must-also-be-stor ytellers (date accessed 20 January 2019).

Gefter, A. (2015) "The Man Who Tried To Redeem The World." *Nautilus*, vol. 21 [Online] Available at: http://nautil.us/issue/21/information/the-man-who-tried-to-r edeem-the-world-with-logic (date accessed 21 January 2019).

Gottschall, J. (2012) *The Storytelling Animal: How Stories Make Us Human.* New York: Houghton Mifflin Harcourt Publishing Company.

Hasson, U. (2016) "This is your brain on communication," TED.com [Online] Available at: https://www.ted.com/talks/uri_hasson_this_is_your_brain_on_communication (date accessed 26 September 2019).

Heider, F. & Simmel, M. (1944) "An experimental study of apparent behavior," *The American journal of psychology*, vol. 57, no. 2, 243–259.

Hillier, A., Kelly, R P. & Klinger, T. (2016) "Narrative style influences citation frequency in climate change science," *PloS one*, vol. 11, no. 12, e0167983

Hunter, M.L. (2011) "Story-Based Inquiry: A manual for investigative journalists." Unesco [Online]. Available at: https://unesdoc.unesco.org/ark:/48223/pf0000193078 (date accessed 8 December 2018).

Katz, Y. (2018) "Scientific storytelling as a marketing discourse (my response to Nick Enfield)," Medium [Online] Available at: https://medium.com/@yardenkatz/scientific-storytelling-a s-a-marketing-discourse-response-to-enfield-473a0bade146 (date accessed 27 January 2019).

Kolodziejski, L.R. (2014) "Harms of hedging in scientific discourse: Andrew Wakefield and the origins of the autism vaccine controversy," *Technical Communication Quarterly*, vol. 23, no. 3, 165–183.

Ladouceur, R., Paquet, C. & Dubé, D. (1996) "Erroneous Perceptions in Generating Sequences of Random Events 1," *Journal of Applied Social Psychology*, vol. 26, no. 24, 2157–2166.

Lawson, E.A. (2017) "The effects of oxytocin on eating behaviour and metabolism in humans," *Nature Reviews Endocrinology*, vol. 13, no. 12, 700.

McAlpine, L. (2016) "Why might you use narrative methodology? A story about narrative," *Eesti Haridusteaduste Ajakiri, Estonian Journal of Education*, vol. 4, no. 1, 32–57.

Muurlink, O. & McAllister, P. (2015) "Narrative risks in science writing for the lay public," *Journal of Science Communication*, vol. 14, no. 3, A01.

Nan, X., Dahlstrom, M.F., Richards, A. & Rangarajan, S. (2015). "Influence of evidence type and narrative type on HPV risk perception and intention to obtain the HPV vaccine," *Health communication*, vol. 30, no. 3, 301–308.

Olson, R. (2018) *Don't be such a scientist: Talking substance in an age of style.* 2nd edition. Washington: Island Press.

Olson, R. (2015) *Houston, we have a narrative: why science needs story.* London: The University of Chicago Press.

Panda, S. & Pandey, S.C. (2017) "Binge watching and college students: motivations and outcomes," *Young Consumers*, vol. 18, no. 4, 425–438.

Peters, B. (2018) "We Analyzed 43 Million Facebook Posts From the Top 20,000 Brands, Buffer, " [Online]. Available at: https://buffer.com/resources/facebook-marketing-strategy (date accessed 28 September 2019).

Pielke, R. (2015) "Five Modes of Science Engagement," Roger Pielke Jr.'s Blog [Online] Available at: http://rogerpielkejr.blogspot.com/2015/01/five-modes-of-science-engagement.html (date accessed 28 September 2019).

Shelby, A. & Ernst, K. (2013) "Story and science: how providers and parents can utilize storytelling to combat anti-vaccine misinformation," *Human vaccines & immunotherapeutics*, vol. 9, no. 8, 1795–1801.

Speer, N.K., Reynolds, J.R., Swallow, K.M. & Zacks, J.M. (2009) "Reading stories activates neural representations of visual and motor experiences," *Psychological Science*, vol. 20, no. 8, 989–999.

Switek, B. (2009) "Book Review: Don't Be SUCH A Scientist," WIRED [Online] https://www.wired.com/2009/10/book-review-dont-be-such-a-scientist/ (date accessed 26 January 2019).

Torres, D.H. & Pruim, D.E. (2019) "Scientific storytelling: A narrative strategy for scientific communicators," *Communication Teacher*, vol. 33, no. 2, 1–5.

Van Laer, T., De Ruyter, K., Visconti, L.M. & Wetzels, M. (2013) "The extended transportation-imagery model: A meta-analysis of the antecedents and consequences of consumers' narrative transportation," *Journal of Consumer Research*, vol. 40, no. 5, 797–817.

Weilenmann, A.K., & Rajendran, L. (2018) "Against Storytelling – The New Paradigm of Scientific Publishing," *Publications*, vol. 6, no. 4, 45.

Woodford, R. (2003) "Lemming Suicide Myth: Disney Film Faked Bogus Behavior," *Alaska Fish & Wildlife News* [Online]. Available at: http://www.adfg.alaska.gov/index.cfm?adfg=wildlifenews.view_article&articles_id=56 (date accessed 27 September 2019).

Yorke, J. (2013) *Into the Woods: A Five-Act Journey Into Story.* London: The Overlook Press

Zak, P.J. (2015) "Why inspiring stories make us react: The neuroscience of narrative," *Cerebrum: the Dana forum on brain science*, vol. 2015, Dana Foundation.

2   Story Elements

What you will learn in this chapter:

- What is a story?
- Fractals
- Theme
- Character
- Conflict
- Point Of View
- Scenes
- Narrative and plot

I'm pretty sure all of you know intuitively what a good story is. All of us are wired for it, we can tell by our attention span alone whether we like a story or not. But why do we like it? What is it that a story can't forgo in order to still be a good story? I'd like to start this chapter with an idea on what a story actually is. The term is being used in an inflationary way. In journalism, everything is a story. If you listen to people talking on the streets, ordinary situations are a story. While munching on a burger, I overheard a discussion between two preteens at the table next to me. They had just sat down with junk food-laden tablets. "Have you taken the picture?" she asked her friend. "No, not yet". "Come on, let's do a story". And they did. Posted a picture of them on Instagram as an Instagram story, showing how they were eating burgers and chips. That's all fine. It's just not a story. It's a slice of life, yes. It's a picture. But it's not a story. Stories have a few very specific properties.

Let's just have a look at two of those now. One is that stories are often symmetrical. Around the middle of the story, things turn around and mirror each other. At the very end of a story, the protagonist is often the exact opposite of herself compared to the beginning. From my last trip to St. Petersburg, I brought back two wooden Matryoshka dolls. If you've never seen them: you can pop open every Matryoshka doll. Inside it, you'll find another one, just smaller, and it looks exactly the same. Open the smaller doll, and again you'll find a smaller, identically looking one. It's the same with stories. Stories have structure, and each piece of that structure contains the same elements. For example, one big story is subdivided into acts, acts into sequences (at least in filmmaking), sequences into scenes and scenes into beats. All of these follow the same rules, containing a tripartite structure (beginning, middle and end), protagonists, conflict and the other elements we're going through in this chapter. Most importantly, they embody change. All scenes must turn, that is subvert characters' and/or the audience's expectations.

I've dedicated the largest section of this chapter to character. Believe me, I've thought long and hard about it, because that meant axing other sections. But ultimately, it was an easy decision, because character is what most other story elements depend on. So we'll have a look into what makes three-dimensional characters, what you should look out for when reporting for characters and also at some psychological foundations. Of course, we'll also have a look at lots of examples. Good characters always have a goal, and they actively pursue it. They never achieve those goals easily but have to overcome obstacles. A good protagonist has an antagonist. Both don't have to be human. In science writing, it's perfectly fine if you line up two chemical elements, if that's your story. But there have to be opposing forces of equal strength. Usually it's enough to have another character who would suffer from the protagonist achieving her goal and you have another story element: conflict. In fiction writing, you can make up conflict and just throw obstacles into a character's way. And in real life? You can't make up anything. But you don't have to: science is rife with conflict, and you'll see a number of examples of where you could unearth conflict in science.

We'll also have a look at point of view, that is, through whose eyes you tell the story. Depending on what story it is, this could mean telling it from your own perspective; for example, when you're a patient, or when your reporting requires you to actively participate in an experiment, you could perfectly use pronouns like "I" and "me". In most cases, you won't. Instead, you'll use one of the third-person point of views (POVs). The POV decides a lot about what a scene will look like to your audience. The same facts presented through another lens can completely change how your audience perceives a scene or the whole story.

So what's a scene? First of all, a scene is the essential building block of narrative. When I write longform narrative pieces, I start my initial reporting with scenes in mind. Once I've identified them, I put them to the test: do they reflect the story's theme, or are they at least connected to it? If not, either the scene goes to the bin, or I have to rethink my theme. Both concepts are really important. That's why I've dedicated a section to each. In its simplest form, a theme encapsulates the story by following a three-part format: *A leads to B*. Here are some examples: "love defies death" (*Romeo and Juliet*'s theme), or "ambition leads to destruction" (*Macbeth*'s theme), or "indecision and fear lead to total loss, including yourself" (*Eleonora*'s theme).

The final section of this chapter deals with ordering those scenes. You don't just randomly draw them out of a bag and throw them into your audience's faces. Instead, you order them either chronologically or logically, or perhaps both. We'll also see what distinguishes narrative from plot. A lot of information that awaits you. But if I had to boil it down in one word, that word would be *selection*. You can report as much as you want and gather heaps of research material, but at some point you will have to select what makes it into your story and what doesn't. You'll have to select the characters, scenes, lines of dialogue, quotes, their points of view, which moments of conflict to include and most importantly, the take-home message to your audience. The first section, which deals with the notion of what a story is, will hopefully be your first selection tool on this journey.

What is a story?

Story has become a bit of an inflationary term. Everything is a story. In the media, every news item is a news story. That doesn't mean it contains the full set of story elements. A news story is not the same as a dramatic story. You know inherently what a good story is. If you encounter one, you "just know". But often times you don't know why a story is great or why it sucks. To make things worse, there is no single definition of what a story is, so we'll go through a few definitions in this chapter and gradually add the elements that make up a story. Let's start with what a dramatic story looks like. In its most minimal version, the following line is often attributed to playwright David Mamet:

Someone wants something badly and has trouble getting it.

In what's more probably attributable to him, a memo floating around the web, allegedly addressed to the crew of the now discontinued *CBS* TV show "The Unit", you can find the following definition:

Drama, again, is the quest of the hero to overcome those things which prevent him from achieving a specific, acute goal.

(Movieline 2010)

This definition contains a number of story elements: a protagonist (hero), a goal, obstacles (or conflict, Mamet's "those things") and a quest. Freelance science writer Emily Sohn expands that list in her chapter on finding ideas in *The Science Writers' Handbook*.

The elements of a good story include: characters, a journey, conflict, linked events, a news hook, and a big-picture idea. These elements distinguish a story from a topic.

(Sohn 2013:22)

She includes three more important elements, a news peg (which in dramatic writing is not needed but definitely good to have in science stories), story structure (linked events), and theme (a big-picture idea). The distinction between story and topic is important. Most fledgling science writers' pitches fail because they pitch topics, not stories. I have never had a story commissioned based on a proposal that said: "I'd like to write a story about rhino horn poaching". Topics are value-free, and that makes topic-pitches dull. In a story, you have a complication. And that's what a story, if you really boil it down to its core, is: ***a problem, and its solution***. "Solution" doesn't entail a happy ending. If you're trying to deliver solutions without a problem, everybody is going to say: so what? The "problem" part includes a number of storytelling elements. It has conflict, a character (doesn't have to be human), so something the problem happens to. The moment the problem occurs, the character's status quo changes and forces her to action. That's the inciting incident. This simple formula is also works well on social media (we'll see a number of them in the later chapters of this book).

But let's hear more definitions with regard to science. Investigative environment journalist Liza Gross draws a clear distinction between topic and story, and she points out that only if a story has characters, it actually is a story:

> No matter how interesting the topic, if you don't explore it through characters who encounter some sort of problem that's eventually resolved (for good or bad), you don't have a story.
>
> (Gross 2018)

On a conceptual level, a good story is an instance of a larger truth or moral lesson. It makes a point. It illustrates that larger truth by presenting a graspable instance of the problem. It uses the example to implicitly make that its point, without preaching tautologies from the ivory tower. As sad as it sounds, this is what scientists and journalists can learn from fake news producers: finding a specific example that illustrates your story's message. Biologist-turned-filmmaker Randy Olson supports this point, drawing on a storytelling article by Nicholas Kristof. He states the optimal number of cases you should pursue in a story is one:

> The quantity of one is as specific as things get. Two is less specific. One is where the power is at a maximum.
>
> (Olson 2015:41)

In fact, fake news stories succeed in evoking readers' empathy but fail in conveying facts. Science often succeeds in communicating hard facts but fails to tap into readers' emotions. Why? Because in their endeavour to differentiate and be as truthful and correct as possible, scientists sometimes present too much information, which makes it hard for readers to relate to any specific case in particular. Hence, the audience cannot develop any emotions and eventually opts out. On the other hand, "truthers" completely lack any facts, so they focus on picking a singular, emotion-evoking case they present, hence leveraging the powerful mechanisms of storytelling, while fooling their audience into believing that there is a larger truth behind their case study (which usually isn't). The crux is: emotions are one of the most powerful mechanisms to memorise facts. If you can get your audience to feel something, anything, while they are reading or watching or listening to your contributions, they will most likely remember your pieces' facts for a long time.

[...] a story begins with a character who wants something,
struggles to overcome barriers that stand in the way of achieving it, and moves
through a series of actions – the actual story structure – to overcome them. That's a succinct expression of what's generally known as the
protagonist- complication- resolution model for story.

(Hart 2011:10)

According to the author of "Wired for Story", Lisa Cron, a story is defined as follows: "Story is how what happens affects someone who is trying to achieve what turns out to be a difficult goal, and how he or she changes as a result. Breaking it down in the soothingly familiar parlance of the writing world, this translates to:

"What happens" is the plot.
"Someone" is the protagonist.
The "goal" is what's known as the story question.
And "how he or she changes" is what the story itself is actually about.

(Cron 2012)

Cron is quick to state that it's not the plot itself, or what happens, that is the story – the story is about the (inner and outer) change of the protagonist.

Sara ElShafie puts it like this: "A 'story', which I treat here as the more encompassing term, follows a protagonist on a journey to overcome an obstacle with something of consequence at stake. This journey will have a meaningful broad theme for the protagonist and/or the audience" (ElShafie 2018).

Great definition. ElShafie adds another element, stakes. If nothing is at stake, the story has no right to exist. It's not a story then. You can usually sum up the stakes in one word, like wealth, life or respect. These values often tap into very basic human needs. These inner needs not only define stakes when a problem occurs, but they also define how characters react and why they react the way they do. Characters and their real-life dialogue is also what defines many good plays, David Mamet has written. They are both incredibly important story elements, especially character, as the success of a story hinges largely on its characters.

John Yorke, BBC script editor and TV producer, defines a story using the Hegelian antithesis. In its simplest form, a story can be a discussion between two people. Both of them bring different viewpoints to the table. One is the thesis, the other one the antithesis. In listening and talking to each other, viewpoints of one or both may shift, a new state of knowledge emerges, synthesis. Take this as an advice when conducting interviews: while you're talking, your state of knowledge doesn't change. You don't learn anything. The only way you can do that is by listening to your dialogue partner and then weaving that new knowledge into your existing one.

Let's come up with a final definition of story before ending this section: "An empathic but flawed protagonist is forced to embark on a journey into the unknown to actively achieve a goal but is confronted with antagonistic forces. She fails to defeat these forces, but learns and changes along the journey, until she conquers her flaw and, after a moment of insight, defeats the antagonistic forces and achieves her goal. She then returns, changed, to the known." In mythology, you'll find a lot of flawed protagonists. For example, Sigurd the dragon-slayer has a vulnerable spot on his back, which leads to his death. Achilles' flaw is his heel, which also leads to his death. Other mythological heroes have psychological flaws instead of physical ones. Oedipus' flaw is hubris, which leads to, well, a special kind of hero's journey:

"Oedipus is a story of a fellow who, on different occasions during his lifetime, journeys in both directions through the same birth canal" (Walter 2010).

Take a moment and think about whether this definition of story can work to encapsulate the scientific method. In certain cases, it can. You have protagonists (scientists), a "known" world (scientific status quo with a research gap), goals (disprove a null hypothesis, develop a cure, decipher a historic manuscript, gather funding), flaws (misconduct, bad communication skills), moments of insights (surprise findings, often reported in journal papers), antagonistic forces (envious colleagues, trouble during experiment design, unexpected results, competition in gathering funding, supervisors), the "unknown" (unclear study outcome at its beginning), a learning curve, a change in the status quo (the research gap has been filled, or at least it's known why it can't be filled) and a resolution: it either worked as expected or it didn't. Try to play this basic story through with other scenarios.

Fractals

What do Romanesco cauliflowers, nautili and stories have in common? They're fractals. Fractals are self-repeating shapes and patterns of a composite object, where smaller units mimic the shape of the bigger object. They can be described mathematically. In computer science, recursion is used to create fractal geometrical shapes or structures. It's essentially an operation that you apply to an object and then repeat again and again. Think of fractals as a near-infinite crowd of mini-mes that together form a bigger version of themselves. Every mini-me has another mini-me sitting on his shoulder. And that mini-me has another mini-me sitting on his shoulder. To infinity. Fractals occur a lot in nature. In Romanesco cauliflower, the entire big bud consists of mini-buds that all look just like their bigger version. The smaller buds branch into yet smaller buds, and so on. It's mesmerising to look at them. There are fractals within ourselves. The brain's neurons and synapses have fractal-like ramifications. The lung and its ramified vessels can be described using fractals (Lennon et al. 2015). Some human skin cells differentiate and naturally group together into fractal-like clusters (Leggett et al. 2019). In other words: fractals are everywhere.

Stories are no different. Elemental building blocks mimic the whole. If you break down a story into its smaller units, you will find the same buildings blocks and structural elements over and over again – on all levels. In his storytelling book *Into the Woods*, John Yorke breaks down the structure of films into acts, acts into sequences and scenes, and scenes into beats. He argues that the essential elements, like a protagonist, goal, antagonist and the structural elements like inciting incident, crisis, climax and resolution occur at all of those levels. Playwright David Mamet shares this opinion. Everything needs to follow dramatic structure in a story. You will find the same storytelling and structural elements to varying degrees in every story, act and scene. The same way a story protagonist achieves her goal (or not) at the story's crisis point, a scene's protagonist in any given scene of that same story achieves her goal at the scene's turning point. Shakespeare divided his stories into five acts. Each act has its own thesis, antithesis and synthesis (Yorke 2013). He also notes story's symmetry. The last act mirrors the first. If you have five acts, then the fourth will also mirror the second. The third act in a five-act story is then the middle act, divided by the midpoint into two equal halves.

Thinking in fractals is essentially no different than outlining your work beforehand and then fleshing it out, step by step. Work from rough towards fine, from large towards small. It's how sculptors work. It's how painters work. British comic book writer and novelist Mike Carey uses a fractal methodology to flesh out his stories. Fiction writer Randy Ingermanson teaches the "Snowflake Method", which takes that same approach. Also, thinking in fractals provides you with a checklist once you've written your first draft. Does every atomic unit in your story reflect and resemble the whole? If not, it might be superfluous. Another way to look at fractals is to think of theme. Theme is your guiding light, the golden thread that connects everything. It's one of stories' crucial elements, because it gives it meaning.

Figure 2.1 A Romanesco cauliflower
It's a perfect example of fractals in nature. Also, it tastes delicious, for example with pasta.
Source and License: Samuel John/Flickr. License: CC BY-SA 2.0.

Theme

Theme is what your story is about. It's often called premise, moral, lesson, takeaway or the logical conclusion. It's the audience's takeaway. A theme is what you, the writer, want to convey to your readers. If you're writing an essay, a column or a feature, the theme can be an insight you gained while reporting for an article, or an epiphany you suddenly had while writing the story. When writing a short science news item about a novel study, your story's theme often reflects the paper's authors' hypothesis and conclusion. When scientists formulate their hypothesis at the beginning of a paper, that hypothesis is the glue that holds the whole research piece together. They design experiments, select samples, run experiments and analyse the data all based on that hypothesis. The conclusions they draw at the end may or may not disprove the null hypothesis (that's just the opposite of the hypothesis; scientists try to disprove that opposite of their hypothesis instead of proving the hypothesis).

Telling science stories in a way works similar. Once you've found your story's theme, you can use it like a filter to sift through all the information you've gathered during the reporting. Events and other information that are too vaguely connected to the theme go to the bin. A word of caution: omission is a powerful tool. Whenever you exclude information, make sure it doesn't unfairly distort the audience's views. But selection and rejection is a necessary tool. For every article I write, the lion's share of reporting doesn't make it into the story. That doesn't mean the research I did was in vain. On the contrary: the more material you gather, the higher the odds that patterns will emerge and you'll find a theme in the story. Theme is what rings in your audience's heads long after they finished the story. It's a larger truth they can identify with. You could start with a theme in mind and keep it until the end. You could find the theme during the reporting. You could disprove your theme during the reporting, based on the facts you found. This actually happens quite often.

Themes are often formulated as cause and effect-relationships, like *A leads to B*. For example, *smoking leads to lung cancer*. This would be an already quite concrete theme. For other stories, it could become more abstract, as the examples in playwright Lajos Egri's 1946 book *The Art of Dramatic Writing*. For example, the case of Paolo Macchiarini, an Italian surgeon who worked at the Swedish Karolinska institute, where he transplanted experimental artificial tracheae to patients, most of which died from complications. It turned out the transplants hadn't been tested properly and that Macchiarini's work was a prime example of scientific misconduct. More than a dozen patients died, and Macchiarini's career and that of several team members was destroyed. So a way to formulate a theme for this story could be: *egomania leads to destruction*.

This form, while perfectly valid as a storytelling device in fiction writing, entails a number of problems when used for nonfiction stories, because it implies causality. Many scientific studies, however, do not suggest a causal relationship between two phenomena. Unfortunately, some journalists imply causation as the underlying principle, when in reality there is no such relationship. The previous example about smoking and lung cancer is one such example. To my knowledge, you couldn't claim there's a causal relationship between the two.

How easily you can identify the theme of a science story depends greatly on your story's format. Short science news items often present the findings of a single recent study, including the principal investigator's (PI) motivation for conducting the research in the first place. These stories' themes are easy to spot. Read the studies, and you will find them in the abstract, conclusion and discussion sections. In research dissertations, you will probably find much of the motivation at the end of the introduction section of the dissertation. While such stories' themes can be complex, their brevity won't allow you to expand on it. In that sense, columns are quite different, because you get to choose the theme based on your own reporting and experience. Columns often start with a news peg, like a recent scientific discovery. Columns' themes typically revolve around the implications of these developments, trying to answer questions like: what does this mean? As an opinion writer, you should then prove that point by underpinning it with facts and figures that make your point. Your audience should be able to sum up the evidence by themselves and arrive at the same conclusion. For example, at the end of her *New York Times* op-ed, law professor Erin Murphy (2017) clearly states the story's theme – forensic science will deteriorate if politicians exclude scientists' opinion:

> We know what happens when prosecutors and police officers control forensic science, instead of scientists. We have already lived through an embarrassing parade of wrongful conviction, tragic incompetence, laboratory scandal and absurdly unsupported forensic findings.
>
> (Murphy 2017)

Beginning from the story's title ("Sessions Is Wrong To Take The Science Out Of Forensic Science") every single point she presents supports her theme and underpins her opinion, like a well-formulated plea. This is good column writing in action. A third science story format, magazine features, also works best when you build it around a central theme that you, the writer, will support with facts. We'll look further into themes and how you can craft them in the chapter on literary techniques. For now, just remember that your story must have a theme, a moral, a takeaway message. As a reader, I should never have to ask myself: what's this writer trying to tell me?

Character

No character, no story. All other elements hinge on characters. Goal, need, conflict, stakes, the decision points (inciting incident, crisis, climax), theme. They can't exist without character. Characters don't have to be human, but they have to be sympathetic, so the audience can identify with them. This works in both fiction and nonfiction. There is a good reason why profiles are such a popular format in journalism. The *New Yorker* has almost 2,500 profiles in its online archives, dating from 1925 to 2019. The *New York Times* has a dedicated profiles section for scientists as does the *U.S. National Library of Science*. True stories and biopics dominate Hollywood and have become the most popular type of commissioned spec script (Hellerman 2019). So why the attraction to people's personal stories? It's the same reason most features start with a zoomed-in, human anecdote: we just love good characters. That's why in this chapter we'll look into what makes a good character on the page.

Walter Pitts in the previous chapter's case study was a great example of a character in science. We'll see in a minute why. The author Amanda Gefter focused strongly on the character, and the story grew out of that. It *is* Pitts' story. Narrative journalist Jack Hart, confirms that character is the pivotal point of good stories because it influences the other story elements:

> Great narrative rests on the three legs of character, action, and scene, and character comes first because it drives the other two. The personality, values, and desires of a protagonist produce action. And the POV character's wants put her in a particular place, creating scene.
>
> (Hart 2011:75)

Indeed, by definition, three of the four main techniques of New Journalists like Tom Wolfe revolve around character: dialogue, third-person point of view and status symbols all strongly depend on the character. If you take into account Jack Hart's statement that character also drives scene, then also the fourth New Journalism element, scene-by-scene construction, depends on it. You can explain scientific problems by picking a concrete example and illustrating the larger issue. In medicine, this can be doctors or, more frequently, patients' narratives. Science policy reporter Maia Szalavitz has used this technique in a *New York Times* op-ed on opioid treatment. She hooks her readers immediately by introducing her story's protagonist:

> Before Joe Thompson switched treatments for his opioid addiction, he was a devoted stay-at-home father, caring for his infant son after his wife returned to work.
>
> (Szalavitz 2018)

In just one sentence, Szalavitz introduces the protagonist Joe Thompson, telling readers that he's a married man with an infant son and an opioid addiction. Szalavitz forgoes scenic writing and vivid details. Next, she writes that Thompson had been taking medication for two years but had relapsed and decided to switch his treatment. This is how the paragraph ends, leaving the audience wondering what happened after Thompson experienced the switch. Also, it's part of a character arc: it's part of Thompson's journey, including an important plot point, that is, when he relapsed and did the switch.

Szalavitz' opening, as short as it is, also highlights another important trait of well-written characters: it's a round, or three-dimensional character, at least as far as that can go within one paragraph. This depends on two elements. First, the character has to have relatable traits. Thompson is married and has a son. People with families can viscerally related to that. Second, the character has to have a flaw. Not an unforgivable flaw like being a mass murderer, but again a relatable flaw that the audience understands. Thompson's flaw clearly was his heroin addiction. A balance between virtues and flaws is what makes a balanced character. Also, the two are often in opposition. It's clear from the outset that Thompson's addiction conflicts with his father's role. And what this evokes is fear or at least worry in the audience that his family might lose him. Which, alas, turns out to be true. In the second paragraph, Szalavitz describes his attempts to reach his goal (defeating his addiction), but he doesn't achieve it. Antagonistic forces come from counselors who don't allow him to take the one medication that worked. Although this is not explicitly described, Thompson must have made a decision at some point to go back to take heroin. He then died of an overdose. As sad as this tragic story is, Szalavitz conveys a full character arc in just 138 words. In doing so, she shows all the traits a good character (and hence, a good story) needs to have:

- **Sympathetic traits**: this is often conveyed as exposition, but best as action. Who is this character? How can the audience connect to it?
- **Flaws**: perfect people do not exist – not in fiction, and certainly not in real life. We all have weaknesses, penchants, flaws. Showing them openly lends authenticity to characters. Walter Pitts' flaw was his alcoholism. Thompson's flaw was his opioid addiction.
- **Goal**: every character has to have a goal (some call it "want"). Some goals seem superficial. Those outer goals often implicitly depend on inner, hidden needs. The goal is often stated when a character's journey starts, and it can change throughout the story. Sometimes an outer, superficial goal is discarded as the protagonist gains new insights, and it is replaced by an inner, deeper goal that rather addresses a character's need. The scale of the goal is important, too. If the goal is just to obtain a candy bar, then that's very different from finding a cure against Ebola. As narrative journalist Jack Hart writes: "The bigger the want, the bigger the story" (Hart 2011:78).
- **Stakes**: if nothing is at stake, the audience won't care. Imagine this: a rich person wants to buy a Ferrari, goes to the car dealer and pays cash. Not much of a story. Nothing is at stake here. But this: a girl needs to buy insulin for her diabetes-stricken mother but can't afford it, so she robs a bank… Everything is at stake here: the mother's life and the girl's freedom (probably her life, too, if you imagine the story unfolding in the US). In Thompson's case, his life and the family's security was at stake.
- **Action**: characters need to actively pursue their goal. They have to work for it, and work hard. Thompson did that. He actively tried to get the approved treatment, although he didn't achieve his goal in the end.
- **Journey**: said action leads to a journey, which is a series of events that unfold in a certain order. Some of them are particularly important. They're called plot points. The inciting incident is one of them. It starts that journey. The crisis is a decision point where the character decides whether to move on and face the antagonist, or return. The climax is the final big plot point. In Thompson's case, the initial relapse starts his journey.

- **Change**: the not-so-secret sauce of story. Stasis is death, as in when you're flatlining. Where a character starts cannot be where it ends. If so, the character is not three-dimensional. Take the early James Bond movies. Thompson's case was extreme. He was alive in the beginning and dead at the end of the story. That's the outer, perceivable change. Change also occurs inside characters, when they learn new things and gain insights.
- **Dialogue**: although this may sound trivial. In stories, characters talk to each other. It's dialogue, and that dialogue helps with stuffing your writing with information (if you do it subtly), and it's also the way we communicate in real life. So this is a device that strongly resonates with the audience. In contrast, most journalists use quotes, which, although a necessary and valid tool of the trade, are not nearly as effective.

These are some of the most important character concepts from fiction writing but are also used in narrative journalism. You will not always unearth all these traits, which is perfectly fine. Making up any of them is no option at all. Ever. Facts are sacred. That is why sometimes you won't be able to write complete stories from start to end but rather employ your real-life characters' factual traits and events to achieve a specific goal with your storytelling. This could be illustrating the ramifications of a novel medical treatment or to simply hook your readers and get them excited about an otherwise overlooked scientific achievement. So far, using characters sounds like a lot of fiction. Does it work with science? Absolutely. In empirical science, the inciting incident can happen when a scientist makes an observation that prompts her to start a journey to find out what causes a phenomenon. It can also happen when she has an epiphany while conducting the actual research. Like in any good story, every attempt to solve the riddle links back to the goal. Good characters have a clear goal and are actively pursuing it. Luckily, this applies to many scientists. Sometimes, their own personal background motivates and influences their research. For example, science journalist Helga Rietz has written a feature, in which a medical doctor researches the physiology of the singing voice, by creating live MRI scans of an opera singer at the institute for Musicians' Medicine in Freiburg, Germany. Incidentally, the doctor is also a trained opera singer, which explains his passion for pursuing this kind of research. Rietz has a background in singing herself. The story won her a Silver AAAS Kavli Science Journalism award in 2015. Research papers reveal scientists' goals, but they rarely reveal the inner need driving the scientists to carry out the research. In science storytelling, you can use this, provided you can find unearth it. In Rietz' case, the doctor's inner need is a rather positive force. In other cases, when people are trying to hide their inner needs, this might become more difficult.

What's important to find good characters is spending time with them during their daily routines. So if you're reporting an operating room story, make sure you get access to that operating room and look over the surgeon's shoulder. If you're reporting a story on an indigenous people, make sure you accompany the anthropologists on a field trip. But also observe them in different social situations, like at home. This reveals the many facets that we all have, depending on the role we're currently in. Italian playwright and novelist Luigi Pirandello was obsessed with people's identity, the masks they're wearing, and the faces they are trying to disguise behind that mask. Acting coach Susan Batson has come up with a similar concept that she teaches actors to develop fully rounded characters. It's tripartite. The "need" is what's really driving a person. You can derive many of people's needs from psychologist Abraham Maslow's hierarchy of needs (Figure 2.2). His theory was that the most basic, physiological needs like eating, sleeping and sex need to be satisfied (at least to some extent), before needs in the higher ranks can emerge. To make an example: if you're completely hungry (at the very bottom of the hierarchy), you're unlikely to feel the need to realise yourself through creativity (at the very top of the hierarchy).

But most people won't show their needs right away (some don't even know it) and try to hide it using their "public persona", that's the image they construct of themselves. That's the way they want to be perceived by others. For example, this could be someone who works late hours, tries to come across as an ultra-conscientious, robot-like scientist (public persona) when in reality she is not, but missed out on the love (need) of important people in her life, like her parents. When the public persona fails to still the need's hunger, the "tragic flaw" comes into play. That's often destructive behaviour that pushes them further away from

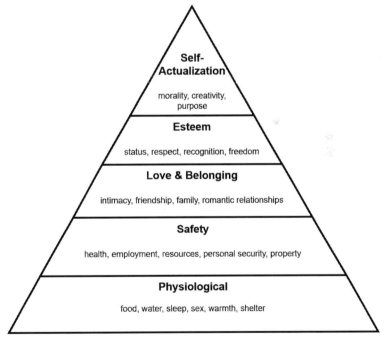

Figure 2.2 Illustration of Maslow's hierarchy of human needs
Note: The lower rungs cover essential needs, like eating and sex. The higher rungs, which can only be reached when the basic needs are satisfied, include esteem and creativity.

what they really want. In a video interview, Batson reveals her own need, public persona and tragic flaw. What she needed when she was little was a caring mother (hers was career-driven), so her public persona is being a rather mothering figure for others. If she can't do that, her tragic flaw becomes social withdrawal. It is often said that the more effort a character puts into hiding her true needs, the more compelling she is. If the tension between the true need and the public persona grows too high, inner conflict emerges. But there are other sources for conflict as you'll see in the next section.

Conflict

Without conflict, a story is not a story. Science is buzzing with conflict. In storytelling terms, that's good news. By definition, the character encounters obstacles along the road to her goal that she needs to overcome. It's the logical consequence of it (Hart 2011). There are six types of literary conflict:

1 Character vs. self
2 Character vs character
3 Character vs. nature
4 Character vs. supernatural
5 Character vs. technology
6 Character vs. society

Did you notice the duality in those conflict types? It's always protagonist vs. antagonist, with changing antagonists. Or, in Hegel's terms, thesis vs. antithesis. In stories, conflict often manifests in more than one of these types. For example, Walter Pitts' struggle was character vs. character (starting with the bullying in his childhood), character vs. society and character vs. self (depression and alcoholism). In science stories, you will find most of the above conflicts (with the exception of character vs. supernatural). Scientific quests and research projects are, technically speaking, often character vs. nature and/or technology. But not only. Take climate change science disciplines. Involved scientists often are also fighting against prominent deniers, and against parts of society.

Science is a business. A money-eating and -producing machinery. But most importantly, it's a human enterprise. Conflict may arise at anytime and anywhere. Unexpected results, conflicts of interest (Piller 2018), flawed scientific methods, misinterpretation of data, fabrication of data and misconduct in general (Stroebe, Postmes & Spears 2012), plagiarism (Stitzel, Hoover & Clark 2018), funding difficulties, internal power struggles, nepotism (Sandström & Hällsten 2007), sexual harassment (Tenbrunsel, Rees & Diekmann 2019) and of course strategic research espionage. Another conflict-spawning issue is the promotion in scientific institutions. Merited scientists get promoted into executive roles they sometimes can't do justice to because they lack leadership skills. But these are just a few examples. Even such an innocent activity as reaching out to the public can prove conflict-laden and put a scientist's career in jeopardy; just think of the Carl

Sagan-effect. So science is inherently conflict-prone, and conflict is at the heart of every story. That's why science is so well suited to storytelling. Conflicts start often with the characters and their needs. If you dig deep enough, you can trace misdemeanors back to a very human flaw, like the craving for recognition.

Academia is its own social construct with its very own rules of the game. It's organised in hierarchies, which means status counts. In nature, status determines who eats and mates first. In academia, it determines a scientist's power in terms of funding, getting and holding prestigious positions, publishing frequency, conference appearances, appointments to boards and expert panels and even media presence. All of the rewards are based on indicators that in turn are a broken mirror of what really counts in science (more on that in this book's appendix). Once a scientist has reached a certain celebrity status, she becomes more likely to get cited and enter important networks. This is called the "Matthew Effect" (Merton 1968).

But conflict is also in the very nature of science in a more positive way. It's at the heart of scientific discussions. Science is at its best when scientists present opposing views to each other, lay down and compare the evidence and finally achieve a synthesis that leads to a new state of knowledge, for the benefit of society. As a science storyteller, it's not your job to invent any kind of conflict that isn't there. But you need to be able to spot it. Conflict is always a clash between two opposing forces. That leads us to another quality of good conflict. The antagonist needs to be at least as powerful as the protagonist. If the antagonist is stronger (think of what's at stake), it's still a story. David and Goliath is an example of the latter case.

When he's looking for story ideas, narrative journalist Ted Conover specifically looks for people with conflict and problems that may or may not be resolved. Character, change and conflict are the three elements he needs to have in his stories (Boynton 2005). He's not alone. William Finnegan from the *New Yorker* also looks "for compelling characters who are in the midst of a morally complex conflict" (Boynton 2005). Apparently Gina Kolata from the *New York Times* has an eye for conflict in science, too. In one of her articles, she reports that a group of independent researchers overturned the long-held belief that red meat is harmful. The goal of this group of researchers naturally clashes with associations and physicians who tried to promote the opposite for years. It's the classic characters vs. characters-type conflict. The findings have caused an outcry among established associations:

> Some called for the journal's editors to delay publication altogether. In a statement, scientists at Harvard warned that the conclusions "harm the credibility of nutrition science and erode public trust in scientific research."
> (Kolata 2019)

This is active resistance, conflict in action. The conflict in this story is not limited to a single (group of) antagonists; the new findings also clash with advocates of reduced meat consumption to reduce human nutrition's carbon footprint. In

Figure 2.3 This is a picture from one of my storytelling workshops
Sophie Dussaussois (left) and Katharina Tschigg (right), who both work for the Institute of
Biomedicine at Eurac Research, reciting a play that illustrates static conflict. Background:
the four types of conflict, as found in Lajos Egri's "The Art of Dramatic Writing".
Source: Martin W. Angler.

terms of technique, Kolata doesn't write scenically (which for this news story
would have been inappropriate either). Kolata also shows that you don't have to
have a full story arc with all the story elements in journalism. It's often enough if
you have a few of these elements. Kolata's piece has protagonists, goals, conflict,
but it doesn't have a full character arc (nobody changes throughout her story), or
a climax. That is perfectly fine. Being a professional, Kolata maintains an objective third-person point of view, which for her story is sensible. Depending on what
story you write, you may want to assume a different perspective to narrate it. Let
us have a look at the various possibilities in the next section.

Point of view

"Drama is life with the dull bits cut out", Alfred Hitchcock said in a 1960 interview on the *BBC* programme "Picture Parade". His statement encapsulates what
is true of all writing: Writing well is all about choosing the right story compo-
nents. You'll have to choose the events that, if and when causally connected,
become your story's plot. You'll have to choose when you enter a scene and when
you exit it. And you'll have to choose not only your story's characters but also
from whose perspective you will tell it. Each scene or event will have a point of
view (POV) through which your audience perceives the story – just like all shots

in a documentary have a camera angle and perspective, that is nothing less than a window that allows your readers to peek into the story. Also, the POV you choose determines whose voice talks to the audience and whose thoughts they get access to, if that (Vogrin 2003).

There are four POV types, and we'll see them in more detail in the chapter on literary techniques. First-person frames the story through the eyes of the narrator and is indicated by the pronouns "I" or "we". One variant of the first-person POV is the unreliable narrator (depending on the character that's narrating). In his nonfiction book *The Electric Kool-Aid Acid Test*, literary journalist Tom Wolfe shifts his POV from a third-person to an unreliable first-person view (Weingarten 2010). In that mode, you can write monologues. Narrative journalist Jack Hart tells me on the phone what fascinates him about first-person POVs:

> When you write in the first person, you become a character yourself. So then you have to think about what you need to reveal in order for the reader to understand who you are and where you're going with this. And why you're motivated and all those sorts of character questions.
>
> (Hart 2019)

In science journalism, entire stories written in first-person POVs are not really common, but they do occur. Some science writers use it to tell personal anecdotes (for example, in feature leads), in opinion pieces, or when the narrator is directly affected by or illustrates a scientific concept or an issue. This happens when science writers are indeed the protagonists of the story they write, for example, when they are patients who try a novel treatment. Sometimes, they try to find explanations for medical or psychological phenomena that they observe in themselves. This is what science journalist Shayla Love did in her *Undark* feature "Science in Chinese Somatization":

> One day, a strange feeling washed over me, like the inside of my head was spinning. I returned to New York, and the dizziness worsened. When I started to feel numbness and tingling in my fingertips and toes, I saw a neurologist who ordered an MRI.
>
> (Love 2017)

Second-person narrates the story by addressing the reader directly. It's the narrator who talks to the reader. The pronoun of choice is hence "you". The second-person POV is not used very often in nonfiction writing. If it is used, it's either for thought experiments or to catapult readers right into the middle of a scene. Here's an example from *Science* correspondent Elizabeth Pennisi:

> Imagine you are a grazing animal, an antelope or an elk. The lush vegetation of a streambank or an open plain tempt you, but predators lurk there. You avoid this "landscape of fear," keeping to the safety of the forest and leaving the plants there to flourish.
>
> (Pennisi 2019)

Right after that, Pennisi switches back to third-person mode. In a book review for one of the *Science* blogs, scientist John Antonakis (2017) writes his full first paragraph using a second-person POV. It goes like this:

> Imagine you are part of an experiment. You and your coparticipants are shown photographs of two individuals and are asked to choose who is more leader-like. Unbeknownst to you, the individuals in the photographs are real-life candidates vying for a seat in the U.S. Congress.
>
> (Antonakis 2017)

He finally raises a question and then switches into first-person POV. Antonakis' blog post is a book review, so he obviously takes a stand. As you can see, in nonfiction science writing, POV can be used as a device, to go back and forth between perspectives for effect. First-person is visceral and close to the audience. Second-person directly addresses the audience, but you'll rarely find full science pieces written using that POV. Next, and quite importantly, you can use the third-person POV. There are multiple variants of it, depending on how much insight the narrator has into the characters' minds. It could be a single character, a number of characters (like Richard Preston's nonfiction book *The Hot Zone*), or the narrator could be omniscient and provide background that is unknown to the characters. The latter form is the most widely used in longform science journalism. The other forms are used, too, for example in profiles. But most often, the science writer takes an omniscient stand. In science writing, POVs frequently get mixed up. Ceridwen Dovey starts her New Yorker piece using a third-person POV:

> When Neil Armstrong stepped onto the moon, in 1969, the first images of his momentous leap were received and relayed by antennas at the Honeysuckle Creek Tracking Station, nestled in the foothills of a remote mountain valley in the Australian Alps, south of Canberra.
>
> (Dovey 2017)

However, on several occasions, Dovey switches into her own POV, like here:

> Instead, the guard directed me downstairs, to a stuffy room in the basement.
>
> (Dovey 2017)

This is not uncommon, and if you read successful science magazine journalism, you'll find that many pieces at some point incorporate the author's own point of view, personal experiences interspersed with background and even switching to other points of view. The power of POV lies in letting the audience participate in the story from various angles, which changes the rhythm and makes for more meaningful scenes. In the next section, let's have a look at what they are and why they're important in science storytelling.

Scenes

In the section about fractals, we've briefly touched upon scenes in that they mirror full stories. Indeed, like every story, a scene has a tripartite structure. It has a beginning, a middle and an end. More so, they incorporate change in that they have a turning point. If nothing in a scene changes, you should chuck it. If nothing actually happens in a scene, chuck it too. A good scene either propels the plot or reveals previously hidden information, either to a story's character or to the audience. In nonfiction writing, another word for them is "events". Just think of them at something that occurred at some point in time and that you could either observe first-hand or reconstruct from material you reported, like eye-witness accounts or documents. Events unfold over time and in a certain order. That's not necessarily the order in which you will present the story to the reader. But for each new scene you show in your story, like in a screenplay, you'll have to first show the audience where and when it happens. Narrative journalist Jack Hart recommends you start building scenes like a playwright:

> You must, after all, create a stage, a place where the story can unfold. Once you have a story space, you can people it with characters. Then, with a snap of your fingers, the characters can breathe, move, act.
>
> (Hart 2011:90)

Does this sound familiar? It's how many longform science stories start, catapulting you right into a lab or the field, alongside a discovery. Journalism professor Mark Kramer has some advice for when and how to do it. Most importantly, employ sensory language that appeals to all five senses. This will help you define the time and place the audience should immerse itself into. But there's a caveat: fledgling writers sometimes use too much detail in describing their scenes. Instead, you should just give the audience a sense of time and space and volume (Kramer 2007). Hart fully confirms this in his book *Storycraft*. In fiction writing, when a character is in a scene, she has to have a goal. She doesn't achieve that goal right away, because of conflict. It's an on-going duality, a forth and back. The character takes action to reach her goal, but an opposing force. That fiction writing notion can help you write your own scenes. Ask yourself: who's in my scene? What are they trying to achieve? Where do their interests clash? Does my scene at the very least show the audience more about the characters?

Scenes are also the incarnation of the storytelling principle "show don't tell" (Dibell 1988). In fact, scenes are the backbone and one of the distinctive techniques of New Journalism and often used by literary journalists like Tom Wolfe. Scenes have the power to put your readers right into narrative mode and feel they're right in the lab with the scientists or into the middle of the Sandy Como Bluff in the Montana wilderness as palaeontologists excavate fossilised dinosaur bones and brush the dust off them. In feature writing, you will often start your story with a scene, but you can also just use it as an anecdote that hooks the audience immediately.

A scene is one connected and sequential action, together with its embedded description and background material. It seems to happen just as if a reader were watching and listening to it happen. It's built on talk and action. It's dramatized, shown, rather than being summarized or talked about.

(Dibell 1988:8)

Every scene should fulfil a specific purpose, which ultimately boils down to either advancing the action line or exposing the character Dibell (1988). In other words: When reading an outline of your story, you should be able to tell why each specific scene is part of it, and what its actions and the consequences of these actions are.

The sensory details you want to show your readers are part of your reporting. Look out for them. How you do it really depends on your writing style. Some reporters have to draft scenes right after they've done the reporting (LeBlanc 2007). I do it very similarly but mine are more like rough sketches. After having done enough reporting, I take an empty index card and write down setting, action and characters. If you take such an approach, you'll have a full list of scenes after your initial reporting. After you've read studies, scoured additional documents and conducted some interviews, you'll have developed a good idea of what the audience needs to understand and what it doesn't. If done well, your stack of scene cards is already a rough outline. I also have index cards for background sections that aren't scenes. I highlight them differently, so I can distinguish them. When reporting for his award-winning *High Country News* story "Inside the Firestorm", science writer Douglas Fox had outlined an initial list of 20 scenes, half of which eventually made it into the story. That's perfectly normal. You'll always have to choose. That's the next part. You'll dig deeper into each scene and find out more. Sometimes, what you thought at the beginning will be overturned by what you discover. Some scenes may turn out to be obsolete. You will decide to merge certain scenes with others, and so on. If you're unsure whether to keep a scene or not, resort to your theme. If the scene isn't connected to the theme, it is usually not a loss to leave it out. And speaking of connections: you won't tell a story as a loose succession of scenes. They have to transition from one to another. Let's have a look at how conservationist Debal Deb starts his story on rice biodiversity in a scenic way:

One scorching summer day in 1991, having spent hours surveying the biodiversity of sacred groves in southern West Bengal, India, I approached Raghu Murmu's hut to rest. Raghu, a young man of the Santal tribe, sat me under the shade of a huge mango tree while his daughter fetched me cold water and sweets made from rice.

(Deb 2019)

The scene goes on and describes some action: Raghu's pregnant wife drinks red-hued starch that helps reduce postpartum anemia. That's an insight the author-narrator gains from that moment. It contains all the elements a good scene needs to have. It sets the stage using vivid description. It has characters, some action, a beginning and a moment of insight, a turning point. If his main idea is that bringing forgotten rice varieties are beneficial and hence should be brought back, then this scene follows definitely the theme. Although the story is not entirely written in a narrative way, Deb skilfully points out the turning points in it. For example, he mentions when he quit his job in 1996 and move to a West Bengal village. Those moments of change are important. That's why they are called turning points. They either change the course of the outer or the inner journey of a protagonist. You can flesh them out as scenes or reduce them to a single statement. When you're reporting for stories, look out for scenes and turning points. Sketch them, draft them and put them to the test: are they in line with your theme? If so, keep them.

Narrative and plot

All good stories have structure that embodies change. This can be chronological or logical change, but eventually, structure always leads from one story event to another. In some cases, these events are just ordered chronologically (Forster 1927). You could show them to readers just the way they unfolded. As we'll see later in this book (especially in the chapter on story formulas), this way of telling stories is often not attractive. Such narratives (Forster calls them "stories") just tell the audience what happened and when, but not why they happened. If you add causality, you have plot: that's a series of chronologically ordered events, connected by a cause and effect-relationship. One often cited example that highlights the distinction between story (that is chronological narrative without causality) and plot stems from his book *Aspects of the Novel*:

> We have defined a story as a narrative of events arranged in their time-sequence. A plot is also a narrative of events, the emphasis falling on causality. "The king died and then the queen died" is a story. "The king died, and then the queen died of grief" is a plot. The time-sequence is preserved, but the sense of causality overshadows it.
>
> (Forster 1927:86)

Unlike a story, a plot requires more intelligence and memory from the audience to be understood, Forster writes, which makes it impossible to tell plots "to a gaping audience of cave-men or to a tyrannical sultan or to their modern descendant the movie-public" (Forster 1927:86). In contrast, story only needs curiosity from the audience who repeatedly asks: "and then"? When you put scenes into a specific order, that's called a frame. A frame is the pattern in which the scene succession unfolds; it's an overarching story itself, and every story has a frame (Gutkind 2012).

Some scenes have special importance in storytelling. They are called plot points (screenwriter Syd Field coined the term) or turning points. A typical three-act dramatic story has at least two plot points: the inciting incident (which is sometimes called complication), which turns the protagonist's life upside down and sends her on a journey. It is a turning point because it changes the story's direction. That plot point raises the dramatic question of how the story will end and if the protagonist will achieve her goal. It also mirrors another plot point at the peak of the story's tension. That second big plot point is the climax. It's the payoff to what the inciting incident has set up. It's the moment when the protagonist either achieves the goal or fails to do so. But there are more plot points than those two. Every scene has its own turning point and *is* a turning point as well. Right before the climax comes the crisis, a reversal of fortune that throws the protagonist into immense danger. Also Jack Hart claims that most stories unfold chronologically, but he uses the crisis for an exception. The decision you, the writer, have to make is whether you start your story before the inciting incident, when nothing has happened yet, or right in the middle of the action, at the crisis point. If you choose the latter approach, you'll have to write a flashback scene and then catch up chronologically until you're at the crisis point again. After that, you'll pay off your story with the climax (Hart 2011).

Along the road, and among all the obstacles the protagonist faces, she will at some point gain a significant insight that will help her achieve the goal (if it's a comedy). Either that or it will, if it is a tragedy, at least help her or the audience understand why she failed. If you have all of these elements, congratulations, you have what Hart calls a story narrative. On the other hand, most news stories are written in summary narrative, which does not employ scenic writing, characters, goals and plot points. In comparison to story narratives, this mode is rather abstract and written from an omniscient third-person POV. Much of the best science feature writing in newspapers and magazines switches between the two modes. This works because science does need some explanations and background due to its complexity. Also, in real life, you simply don't always find all of the story elements. That's fine, you can just use those that your reporting yield. Especially, if those elements are turning points.

Let's take the example of Natalie Angier's *New York Times* news feature "Precious Gems Bear Messages From Earth's Molten Heart". In the lead, she describes how a miner and a mining engineer discovered the world-famous Patricia Emerald. I will include the following fragment:

> Let's move on, Mr. Klein said. This area is dead.
> No, no, no, Mr. Daza insisted. There's emerald here, I know it.
> Mr. Klein shrugged. O.K., one more shot – but that's it.
>
> (Angier 2017)

It's a piece of dialogue, and perfectly dialectic, although only three lines long. Klein is the thesis, he wants to give up. Daza is his antithesis, he wants to keep trying. The synthesis is one final try, that's the compromise. Angier's dialogue is also a scene. Two characters that oppose each other. Both have a scene goal. At the end, Klein gives in and Daza wins, and they blast another hole into the rocks. Because of this (note the causality), in the next scene, they find the Patricia Emerald. If the dialogue hadn't unfolded, or if Klein had won the argument, they would have never discovered it. Look out for these moments, and you're guaranteed to rivet your audience's attention.

Review questions

- What is the difference between narrative and story?
- How far can you reduce a story?
- How can you formulate a story in two sentences?
- How should you structure a theme?
- Which elements does a character need to become three-dimensional?
- How can you unveil the inner need of a character?
- What should you use the second-person POV for?
- What do you need to construct a scene?
- What is a plot point?

Links

Profiles in Science (U.S. National Library of Medicine): https://profiles.nlm.nih.gov/

Profiles in Science (New York Times): https://www.nytimes.com/column/profiles-in-science

Susan Batson on Needs, Public Personas and Tragic Flaws (16h Street Actors Studio): https://vimeo.com/95083377

References

Angier, N. (2017) "Precious Gems Bear Messages From Earth's Molten Heart," *New York Times* [Online]. Available at: https://www.nytimes.com/2017/12/11/science/gemstones-diamonds-sapphires-rubies.html (date accessed 12 December 2017).

Antonakis, J. (2017) "We know better, so why can't we stop making snap judgments based on appearance?" Books Et Al. Blog (Science) [Online]. Available at: https://blogs.sciencemag.org/books/2017/07/18/we-know-better-so-why-cant-we-stop-making-snap-judgments-based-on-appearance/ (date accessed 2 October 2019).

Boynton, R.S. (2005) *The New New Journalism: Conversations On Craft With America's Best Nonfiction Writers on Their Craft.* New York: Vintage Books.

Cron, L. (2012) *Wired for story: the writer's guide to using brain science to hook readers from the very first sentence,* New York: Ten Speed Press.

Deb, D. (2019) "Restoring Rice Biodiversity," *Scientific American,* October issue.

Dibell, A. (1988) *Elements of Fiction Writing – Plot.* Cincinnati: Writer's Digest Books.

Dovey, C. (2017) "Dr. Space Junk Unearths the Cultural Landscape of the Cosmos," *The New Yorker* [Online]. Available at: https://www.newyorker.com/culture/persons-of-interest/dr-space-junk-unearths-the-cultural-landscape-of-the-cosmos (date accessed 2 October 2019).

ElShafie, S.J. (2018) "Making science meaningful for broad audiences through stories," *Integrative and Comparative Biology,* vol. 58, no. 6, 1213–1223.

Forster, E.M. (1927) *Aspects of the Novel.* London: Edward Arnold.

Fox, D. (2017) "Inside the firestorm," *High Country News* [Online]. Available at: http://www.hcn.org/issues/49.6/inside-the-dangerous-and-unpredictable-behavior-of-wildfire (date accessed 11 December 2017).

Gefter, A. (2015) "The Man Who Tried to Redeem the World with Logic," *Nautilus* [Online] Available at: http://nautil.us/issue/21/information/the-man-who-tried-to-redeem-the-world-with-logic (date accessed 25 November 2017).

Gross, L. (2018) *The Science Writers' Investigative Reporting Handbook: A Beginner's Guide to Investigations*, Kensington: Watchdog Press.

Gutkind, L. (2012) *You can't make this stuff up: The complete guide to writing creative nonfiction – from memoir to literary journalism and everything in between*. Philadelphia: Da Capo Lifelong Books.

Hart, J. (2019) Personal phone conversation, 9 February 2019.

Hart, J. (2011) *Storycraft*. Chicago: University of Chicago Press.

Hellerman, J. (2019) "What is a Biopic & Why Are They Dominating Hollywood?" No Film School [Online]. Available at: https://nofilmschool.com/Biopic-films-In-Hollywood (date accessed 1 October 2019).

Ingermanson, R. (2009) *Writing Fiction for Dummies*. Indianapolis: Wiley.

Kramer, M. (2007) "Reporting for Narrative: Ten Tips, " in: Kramer, M. & Call, W., *Telling True Stories*. New York: Plume, 24–30.

Kolata, G. (2019) "Eat Less Red Meat, Scientists Said. Now Some Believe That Was Bad Advice," *The New York Times* [Online]. Available at: https://www.nytimes.com/2019/09/30/health/red-meat-heart-cancer.html (date accessed 1 October 2019).

LeBlanc, A.N. (2007) "(Narrative) J School for People Who Never Went, " in: Kramer, M. & Call, W., *Telling True Stories*. New York: Plume, 59–62.

Leggett, S.E., Neronha, Z.J., Bhaskar, D., Sim, J.Y., Perdikari, T.M. & Wong, I.Y. (2019) "Motility-limited aggregation of mammary epithelial cells into fractal-like clusters," *Proceedings of the National Academy of Sciences*, vol. 116, no. 35, 17298–17306.

Lennon, F.E., Cianci, G.C., Cipriani, N.A., Hensing, T.A., Zhang, H.J., Chen, C.T., Murgu, S.D., Vokes, E.E., Vannier, M.W. & Salgia, R. (2015) *Lung cancer – a fractal viewpoint, Nature reviews Clinical oncology*, vol. 12, no. 11, 664.

Love, S. (2017) "Science and Chinese Somatization," Undark [Online]. Available at: https://undark.org/article/science-chinese-somatization/ (date accessed 10 March 2018).

Merton, R.K. (1968) "The Matthew effect in science: The reward and communication systems of science are considered," *Science*, vol. 159, no. 3810, 56–63.

Movieline (2010) "David Mamet's Master Class Memo to the Writers of The Unit," Movieline [Online]. Available at: http://movieline.com/2010/03/23/david-mamets-memo-to-the-writers-of-the-unit/ (date accessed 29 September 2019).

Murphy, E.E. (2017) "Sessions Is Wrong To Take Science Out Of Forensic Science," *New York Times* [Online]. Available at: https://www.nytimes.com/2017/04/11/opinion/sessions-is-wrong-to-take-science-out-of-forensic-science.html (date accessed 13 January 2018).

Olson, R. (2015) *Houston, We Have A Narrative: Why Science Needs Story*. Chicago: University of Chicago Press

Pennisi, E. (2019). "Grazing animals shown to inhabit a 'landscape of fear'," *Science*, vol. 363, no. 6431, 1025.

Piller, C. (2018) "Hidden Conflicts?" *Science*, vol. 361, no. 6397, 16–20.

Rietz, H. (2014) "Arien für die Wissenschaft (Arias for Science)," *Neue Zürcher Zeitung* [Online]. Available at: https://www.nzz.ch/wissenschaft/medizin/arien-fuer-die-wissenschaft-1.18449716 (translation: https://www.aaas.org/sites/default/files/HelgaRietz_translation.pdf) (date accessed 17 January 2018).

Sandström, U. & Hällsten, M. (2007) "Persistent nepotism in peer-review," *Scientometrics*, vol. 74, no. 2, 175–189.

Sohn, E. (2013) *Finding Ideas*, in: Hayden, T. & Nijhuis, M. (2013) eds. *The Science Writers' Handbook*. Boston: Da Capo Lifelong Books, 9–23.

Stitzel, B., Hoover, G.A. & Clark, W. (2018) "More on plagiarism in the social sciences," *Social Science Quarterly*, vol. 99, no. 3, 1075–1088.

Stroebe, W., Postmes, T. & Spears, R. (2012) "Scientific misconduct and the myth of self-correction in science," *Perspectives on Psychological Science*, vol. 7, no. 6, 670–688.

Szalavitz, M. (2018) "The Wrong Way To Treat Opioid Addiction," *New York Times* [Online]. Available at: https://www.nytimes.com/2018/01/17/opinion/treating-opioid-addiction.html (date accessed 19 January 2018).

Tenbrunsel, A E., Rees, M.R. & Diekmann, K.A. (2019) "Sexual harassment in academia: Ethical climates and bounded ethicality," *Annual review of psychology*, vol. 70, 245–270.

Vogrin, V. (2003) "Point of View: The Complete Menu, " in Steele, A. (ed.) *Gotham Writers' Workshop: Writing Fiction, The Practical Guide From New York's Acclaimed Writing School*, New York: Bloomsbury, 77–103.

Walter, R. (2010) *Essentials of Screenwriting: The Art, Craft and Business of Film and Television Writing.* New York: Plume.

Weingarten, M. (2010) *The Gang That Wouldn't Write Straight.* New York: Three Rivers Press.

Yorke, J. (2013) *Into the Woods: How Stories Work and Why We Tell Them.* London: Penguin Random House UK.

3   Discovering Science Stories

What you will learn in this chapter:

- Science news values
- An interview with Jack Hart
- Finding stories in papers
- Anecdotes
- Interviewing I
- Interviewing II
- More story sources
- Case study: Genesis of two stories

Stories really are everywhere. They are about people, and people are where you will get them from. Science is a human endeavour. People conduct it, people participate in it (as patients, as citizen scientists), people who fund it and people evaluate it. Many scientific achievements come from very personal reasons. It's not for nothing that a physician didn't study philosophy, and it's not for nothing that a psychologist didn't study architecture. Behind every curriculum, behind every public persona is a very private, personal story. The same goes for the darker side of science. Behind sexist remarks, misogynism, harassment, there are people's stories. Victims' and perpetrators' stories. We need to find them and tell them.

Also, the decision about which story to run and how prominently, is a human decision. Which headline ultimately makes it into a newspaper is ultimately a (sometimes fiercely contested) human decision. But that decision is based on some proven mechanisms that have been around at least since 1965. They are called news values. Essentially, they're a checklist that helps you find out whether your story's topic fulfills all requirements to be run, and whether it's a cover story. The list stems from Norwegian sociologists and has unfortunately been misinterpreted. They meant it as a warning, but here we are. Almost all the news media employ it, consciously or not, to take news decisions. The strongest is negativity, most prominently expressed in the old saying "if it bleeds, it leads". These are the traditional news values. Science has some extra news values like anniversaries, and we'll have a look at them too. Once you start looking at magazine covers, newspaper stories and documentaries with news values in mind, you'll never stop doing so again. And it'll make your life so much easier when you're pitching stories.

Next, I've called up narrative journalist and former Pulitzer Prize jury member Jack Hart, and he talked me through his story-crafting process when he was an editor at *The Oregonian*. He had valuable advice on finding stories, assessing their quality and planning them, so I want to share that with you. I keep citing him in this book, which alone should be proof of how highly I value him. In that section, we'll also have a look at one of his stories and the importance of theme in finding out what the actual story is.

Then we'll have a look at how you can unearth story elements in scientific papers. I found some interesting comparisons between. Here's one thing I guarantee: you will never run out of science stories, because of the sheer amount of journal papers that appear. A whopping 2.5 million papers are published annually (Ware & Mabe 2015). That is why I have dedicated one section of this chapter to the storytelling elements you can distil from papers. That and well, it's a book about science storytelling. If you're lucky, some of the papers even contain anecdotes, those little stories that make every otherwise dry and dull concept come alive. Anecdotes are always personal, either yours or somebody else's stories. With the right techniques, you can dig them up. Anecdotes lend your story a sense of immediacy and transport the audience right into your story. They're also a vehicle that helps them to better remember factual information. That's one of the biggest benefits in science storytelling.

If you don't write your own anecdotes, you have to tap into other people's minds. Interviewing to the rescue! It's a huge and complex topic, but much boils down to actually be a human and not follow textbook rules. So I've tried to put together two sections of no-nonsense advice that you can readily apply. If you don't find the time to read through all of them: just be a good listener and don't talk all the time, because the interview is not about you. It's about curiosity and being able to learn from your interviewee if you just let them think long enough. Sometimes, that means enduring awkward pauses. The interviewing sections are two of my favourite ones in this book.

To round out this chapter, I've also included a section on story sources other than scientific papers and interviews. Essentially, you can find stories everywhere, if you look close enough. To make it more practical, the final section provides a look at two science stories and how their authors conceived them. You can do a lot of planning (and you should outline and plan for scenes if you're wired that way), but ultimately, you won't be able to control all the factors. That means you have to improvise and be ready to rethink your story as you report it.

Science news values

Part 1: Traditional news values

This is one of the few double-length sections in this book (sorry, but it'll be worth it, promise). Once you have the hang of it, your life as a journalist will become a lot easier. These are the factors journalists and editors use to decide which stories to pitch and run and where to place them. In the first half of this section, we'll have a look at the traditional news factors, news story selection and the resulting bias. In the second half, we'll look into science-specific news values.

Let's start with selection. Every day, we take lots of decisions, 35,000 some claim, 227 of which are on food alone (Hoomans 2015). Some of these decisions are conscious ones, such as: what should you buy for dinner? Others are happening unconsciously as you move through the world. They're quick and intuitive decisions, impossible to pass through our conscious, thinking circuitry. There's just no time to consciously think through all the choices that life confronts you with. Imagine thinking: oh, I slipped. Which foot should I put my weight on next so I don't fall and break my neck? *Oh, snap.*

Story selection is a bit of both: part conscious decision and part what so many seasoned journalists like to call intuition. "Intuition" simply means they have absorbed news values to a degree where they don't have to consciously decide if the story will fly. It will, because they know. And you will know, too. News values drive the news, news values determine which story will run and news values decide which story will become a magazine's next cover story. The stories you select have to be relevant to your audience. So the more you know about how old they are, which jobs they work and what level of education they have, the easier it gets to select stories. Publishers put a lot of effort and money into finding out who their audience is. The stories then get hand picked for that audience. But there are a number of universal factors that determine the newsworthiness of a jour-nalistic story, and they are mostly based on a 1965 landmark paper by Norwegian sociologists Johan Galtung and Mari Holmboe Ruge. The paper contains twelve common general-journalism news factors. I've adapted the following list from Galtung and Ruge (1965):

- **Frequency**: is there a noticeable trend that matches the media's frequency?
- **Strength/Superlative**: is the event something of a big magnitude?
- **Clarity/Unambiguity**: does the event have clearly defined implications?
- **Meaningfulness/Cultural Proximity**: Is the event related to the audience's culture?
- **Consonance**: does the event meet the audience's expectations?
- **Unexpectedness**: could the event surprise the audience? Is it "unexpected within the meaningful and consonant" (Galtung & Ruge, 1965:67)?
- **Continuity**: has the event been on the news before?
- **Composition**: has the publication run a lot of stories of the same kind? Then an outlier, a story related to a different topic, has better odds of being run
- **Reference to Elite Nations**: are so-called elite nations, like the US or Russia, involved in the event?
- **Reference to Elite People**: are important individuals, such as heads of states, involved in the event?
- **Personalisation**: is the event a result (seemingly) of humans' actions?
- **Negativity**: has the event negative implications?

The final element of the list is one of the strongest in terms of precedence: negativity. If something bad happens, it will lead, regardless of the medium. If a terror attack or major disease outbreak happens, it will end up on newspapers' front pages. It will dominate the television programmes and it'll go viral on the social media. Everybody in journalism uses Galtung and Ruge's (1965) list, consciously or not, as a reference for which stories to run, when and where. Their paper has almost 5,000 citations on Google Scholar. That's just how journalism's news selection process currently works. But (and that's a big but), Galtung now says in an interview that their paper wasn't meant as a guideline. On the contrary, it was meant as a warning. Indeed, in their paper, Galtung and Ruge write that if the news continues to portray the world in such a negative way, populism and general negativity would emerge among the audience (Haagerup 2019). *Reuters* confirmed this tendency in its 2017 Digital News Report, stating that people turn their backs on the news because they make them feel miserable (Newman *et al.* 2017). Galtung and Ruge argued that negative stories enter the news more easily because they often satisfy more than just one news value (for example, frequency). Negativity is very connectable. No other news value forms so many combinations with other news values. The more news values a story contains, the stronger it gets (Galtung & Ruge 1965). That means negative stories are by definition the strongest and most successful in the news industry. This is a vicious circle. The way the media select real world events is not unbiased, which clearly involves the outlets' political views. Once the news is out, it affects readers' perceptions. Then again, the media responds to what readers are used to and demand:

> If [a newspaper] wants a mass circulation, all steps in the news chain will probably anticipate the reaction of the next step in the chain and accentuate the selection and distortion effects in order to make the material more compatible with their image of what the readers want.
>
> (Galtung & Ruge 1965:68)

So yes, selection is a must, but it also tends to introduce bias. Science tackles selection bias by drawing random samples that are representative for entire populations. There are different types of selection bias, like sampling bias, where the sample drawn is a non-random sample that excludes certain parts of a population. Studies performed using such samples can hardly infer conclusions that are valid for the entire population. Similarly, also the media suffer from selection bias. Like science, media bias can take various shapes. For example, gatekeeping bias happens during the selection process, whenever staff journalists decide which stories to run and which ones to kill. Bias happens during editorial meetings, before and during pitches and when deciding on the angle of a story, while structuring and writing it. Gatekeeping bias is the decision to prefer running one story instead of another one that perhaps doesn't fit into an outlet's agenda or editorial strategy. Gatekeeping, selection bias and news value-based selection of stories obviously shape the audience's perception of the world, as Galtung and Ruge write. If the audience constantly reads negative stories on newspapers' front pages, this may cause them to think there are mostly bad things happening in the world. The news is too sensationalist and negative. In the same *Guardian* interview, psychologist Hans Henrik Knoop not only confirms the findings of *Reuters'* Digital News Report but also adds that policy and public debate suffer from this negative worldview. It doesn't stop there. The continuous flow of negative news could cause apathy and fear among the audience, Knoop says (Haagerup 2019). It seems there is some evidence to it: while it is known that extremely negative events like terror attacks worsen mental health issues like anxiety and depression, this also seems to happen with the daily, subtle negativity readers encounter in the media (Wormwood *et al.* 2018). Ironically, this picture of news values is rather negative. But a positive counter-movement is underway. It's called "constructive journalism". Constructive journalism not only points out the negativity of events unfolding but also applies positive psychology techniques. Sometimes this may mean providing a solution, prospection (depicting possible futures). This doesn't mean constructive journalism ignores negative events. It just approaches them differently. This may even reflect in the way questions are asked. For example, after an attack, a journalist could ask government officials what could be offered or done to stop the attack (McIntyre & Gyldensted 2017). They all are making a solid point: just pointing out problems does not solve them. In terms of the Hegelian dialectic, current journalism misses its synthesis, the cathartic relief for the readers. It's conflict-laden (thesis and synthesis) but doesn't provide any solutions. In the long run, we'll probably need an updated list of news values that is a bit more constructive (constructive journalism so far hasn't defined its own), but for now the current news values are nonetheless the de facto standard to help you find out whether your story is relevant to the world.

Part 2: Science news values

News values in science are based on the traditional news values, but have been formulated a bit more specifically by scholars. As you will see, there are additional news values that we can add to the traditional ones. For example, in a 2015 interview, former *BBC Science Focus* editor-in-chief Graham Southorn told me what science editors look for are also science anniversaries, an additional news value. This includes the anniversary of an influential scientist's birth or death date, or the anniversary of a discovery. The full interview with Graham Southorn is in my previous book, *Science Journalism: an introduction* (Angler 2017). But let's start at the beginning.

It's always important that you distinguish between topic and story. A topic is a general and rather vague term, like "gene editing". It has no clear angle, and it does not contain any sort of story. On the other hand, a clear idea like "This doctor clones babies" has an angle, an opinion that shines through and a protagonist. You can implicitly find that there is conflict, too. So lots of news values, and a strong topic. Incidentally, it is also one of the most popular topics in science coverage. Badenschier & Wormer (2012) write in their paper that the most popular science topics worldwide are medicine, health and biology. They also write that health, medicine and behavioural sciences dominate the coverage of the *New York Times*.

Medicine, environment, technology and biology were the most covered topics in German newspapers (at least in 2003/2004 and 2006/2007). In both periods, coverage of medicine was unrivalled. If you cover any of these fields or their sub-disciplines (say, neuroscience), then that's good news for you. Traditionally, the natural sciences get more coverage than the social sciences (perhaps with psychology being the most prominent exception).

Some factors that determine science coverage are time-dependent. Almost always, politics trumps science. While general news easily make the front page, science news is often only regarded as a nice-to-have section. However, while the sports and politics beat depend on topicality, science news have a somewhat longer lifespan, sometimes with readers not realising that they have outlived their topicality, hence editors running them also if a study, say, has appeared some time ago (Badenschier & Wormer 2012). On the other hand, some science news can make the transition from science news values to general news values, triggered by time-dependent factors. Apart from that, three time-independent factors exist that determine how science news are selected (from Badenschier & Wormer 2012:66):

- **Importance**: political, economic, social, cultural, ethical and/or scientific importance
- **Surprise (astonishment)**: new/different than thought before; exotic ("cocktail-party-suitable")
- **Usability**: Life advice (medical, technical)

For longform stories, they add, another factor of high importance comes into play, namely the "narrative factor" or fairy tale approach. To which extent one of these three (four with narrative) factors outweighs the others is hard to estimate. Although science news values do depend on general news values, Badenschier and Wormer (2012) came up with a set of additional news values, tested them and interviewed seasoned science journalists about their selection process. They eventually boiled down their tentative list to 14 news values. Here's the list:

- **Astonishment**: extent to which an event causes amazed reactions ("Aah!")
- **Political relevance**: importance of an event for politics or legislation
- **Composition**: mix of topics within a distinct science page and the whole issue of a newspaper/broadcast etc.
- ***Range (number of affected people)***: number of people participating in an event or affected by the event
- **Controversy**: contrasting of differences in opinions
- **Reference to elite persons**: political, economic, cultural or scientific power of a person, group, or institution ranked by its position in the hierarchy
- **Economic relevance**: importance of an event for the economy
- **Relevance to recipients/society**: importance of an event for the recipient of the article or even the society in total

- **Graphical material**: extent to which an event becomes news just because pictures or figures are available
- **Scientific relevance**: importance of an event for the scientific progress
- **Intention**: type of science communication
- **Actuality (Trigger)**: reason for the selection of an event at the present moment (coming from the general news situation, the research operation or both)
- **Personalisation**: inclusion of persons and importance for the reported circumstances
- **Unexpectedness**: extent to which an event was not expected

I will add to the above list a few more selection factors that I did not investigate scientifically, but because they are obvious. They are important because they introduce bias. For example, universities in countries that have less of a VIP status in the world have less chances of getting covered than the more notable ones. The same is true of individual researchers. So here are the three additional science news values that I'd point out.

- Study published in high-profile journal with a high impact factor (IF)
- Study published by a research institution with a high reputation (Badenschier and Wormer initially included this value in their catalogue as "prominence" but then discarded it)
- Awards and prizes won by scientists (again, this would in part be covered by "prominence")

The more news values your story fulfills, the better its chances to run in an outlet. Selection is often intuitive and complex. In this context, "intuitive" is a dangerous word, because it means people take decisions based on their gut feelings, which may be biased. If science itself is not objective in the first place, how can science reporting be? News values are really important in terms of figuring out what the editors want and what the public wants. But always catering to that does not fairly and objectively reflect the scientific reality. For example, take my added news value that assumes winning a science award increases your chance of being covered by the media. Sounds legit, right? The only problem is that you most likely profit from this if you're a male scientist. A 2011 study from the Southern Methodist University points out that women receive fewer science awards than men due to gender bias. Part of the problem is predominantly male award committees. Women are also underrepresented as Nobel laureates (Modgil *et al.* 2018) so again they would not just receive less credit from their scientific peers but vanish altogether. Lise Meitner and Mileva Maric are just two examples of brilliant female scientists "hidden" behind their husbands' fame. Bear that in mind whenever you select your news stories. And dare to cross boundaries and propose pieces that are constructive and that highlight non-prominent research. The current news values have been here for more than 50 years. But that doesn't mean they're immutable or can't be complemented or even replaced.

An interview with Jack Hart

For narrative journalist and former Pulitzer Prize jury member Jack Hart, good stories can come from everywhere. But once a journalist has conceived an idea, a discussion with the commissioning editor is what makes the idea round. Hart works on structure with his writers early in the process. I called Hart to discuss how some of the award-winning stories he worked on with journalists came into being. One of the journalists Hart frequently worked with is Tom Hallman. At the time he came up with the idea for the 2001 Pulitzer Prize-winning story "The Boy Behind the Mask", Hallman was already established. That's why he got tipped off: one day, he received a call and got wind of the story of Sam Lightner, a teenager with a facial deformity who was about to enter high school – a time when appearance is everything. Sam Lightner was also about to undergo recon-structive surgery in order to fit better in. This is what happened after Hallman received the call:

> When [Hallman] came to me and told me about this kid with this terrible deformity who was headed off to Boston Children's Hospital for a life threatening surgery to connect it. I said, "Well, isn't that interesting? He's perfectly functional but just to look more normal and to fit in he's willing to risk his life."
>
> (Hart 2019)

This piece from Hart and Hallman is also a prime example of how the theme can change over time, as the reporting goes on. Hallman had already finished his reporting, but both he and Hart weren't sure what the ending could be, because they hadn't quite established the theme yet. Eventually, Hallman came up with an insight from his reporting that synopsised the story's take-home message.

> Hallman came back one day from reporting, and we had no ending at this point. We were months into this project. But then he said, "I got it. I really got it, and it's the kicker for the story." This kid, Sam Lightner was his name, was standing in line after the surgery registering for high school, which was a seminal event in terms of him coming of age. And a high school counselor came up to him and said, "You don't have to stand in this line. Come here. I'll take you up here and we'll step in behind here and get you registered right away." And Sam looked up at him. Hallman is there seeing all this because he wanted to be there for his high school registration. And Sam said, "No, I'll stay here. This is where I belong." That encapsulated the whole point that we were trying to make.
>
> (Hart 2019)

Hart keeps mentioning the importance of choosing (for example, a POV when you write a scene), and he tells me too, that, without a theme, you can't know what to report. Theme is also an important selection tool:

If you don't have a theme how do you know what to report? He got excited because he saw that happen. And there it was.

(Hart 2019)

It seems there is a lot of intuition that goes into finding the initial theme and where to start with your reporting. So I asked him: how much is intuition, and how much is craft?

Well, I think that both things happen. But the most successful narrative writers make a study of it. When Hallman attempted his first narrative and we realized this was something we wanted to pursue, he discovered that Jonn Franklin was teaching at Oregon State University, which is just down the highway from Portland where he and I were working at the Oregonian newspaper. Hallman started going down there once a week for a private lesson. Franklin had written the very first book on narrative journalism to appear in the American market. It's called "Writing for Story".

(Hart 2019)

Because Hart had a budget at the Oregonian, he organised writing workshops, in which journalists were taught where to get ideas from, how to structure narratives and how to style their texts. Some ideas come from inspiring setting, as that's one of narrative's essential ingredients, Hart tells me. For example, when he watched the Netflix documentary "The Most Unknown", he was amazed by the film's concept: nine scientists from different disciplines visit another in different places of the world. The documentary not only changes disciplines but also setting. Hart had himself been in one of those settings, the Haleakalā on Maui. "That alone helps engage interest," he says. Exotic places entice the audience's interest, so travelling is definitely a good way to conceive new ideas. Apart from meeting interesting people with stories to tell, sometimes the exotic places alone justify running a story on them.

Other stories start from the idea how ordinary items in our lives are consumed and where they actually come from. It's tracing their journeys, from production to consumption. Hart tells me that the idea for such stories can be that the small tracked item highlights a larger issue. One such story he worked on with writer Rich Read was "The French Fry Connection". The story wasn't what Hart calls a "story narrative" but rather an explanatory narrative, where the action elements serve as narrative thread to glue together pieces of explanation:

The point was to follow a product from the Pacific Northwest to the Pacific Rim to explain the Asian economic crisis that took place in early 2000s. So, he just followed the load of potatoes as they were turned into French fries, and shipped to Indonesia, and then diverted because of the riots when Surakarta was being overthrown. And then they were diverted to Singapore and it concluded with him watching a Eurasian families kids consume these French fries in a McDonald's restaurant on Orchard Road in Singapore. So there's nothing dramatic about that whole story. But it did provide a continuous action line in which he could do diversions and expository explanatory sections, and talk about globalization. And the interrelationships between the countries, and the import, export web, and how this economic crisis developed and took place. And why it mattered to people in the Pacific Northwest.

(Hart 2019)

Finding stories in papers

The most frequent objection to using storytelling techniques both in scientific manuscripts and in conveying science to a lay audience is that science simply doesn't unfold like a story. It's true that you won't find all story elements in journal papers. You'll have to interview the scientists and ask for those that aren't there. An interview is also what helped me understand which storytelling elements I can gather from papers and which not. Early in 2019, I called narrative journalism guru Jack Hart at his home in Portland, on the day a historic snow storm had struck the city. One of my questions was just about that. Does applying storytelling techniques water down science? And does science even contain the necessary story elements?

> Bullshit, what subject could be better? You have a protagonist, you have a built-in story structure to every scientific project. You have a protagonist and a complication and, with any luck, a resolution. It's just like sports. There's a built-in structure. It's highly appropriate to narrative.

(Hart 2019)

Read the journals, as each paper contains a story within it. The catch is that the story material is not written in story form. So what you need to do next is call the scientists who worked on the paper and try to reconstruct the story together with them. You can find certain elements in the paper, but you'll have to ask the scientists for others. For example, setting. You could ask the scientists where they were and what they were doing when a particular idea cross their mind. Ask them about what was at stake during the research process. What would have happened if they hadn't discovered the answer to their problem? Also, ask them about their emotions (Hart 2019).

Apart from the questions, how much story is in a research paper? A lot. Theme, for example. If a scientist hadn't included a take-home message, they wouldn't have produced the paper in the first place (Buenz 2019). The first place I look for theme in a research paper is the conclusions (or results, or discussion) section, followed by the introduction (especially the latter part of that section often touches upon researchers' motivation, which in turn is a strong indicator for the theme). Biologist Sara ElShafie works with Pixar storytellers and runs workshops on science storytelling. In one of her papers, she likens the structure of scientific manuscripts to the narrative arcs:

Scientific manuscripts and presentations commonly follow a structure that actually reflects a dramatic arc, in a sense. A typical manuscript starts with an Introduction (Exposition), followed by Methods (Rising Action), Results (Climax), Analysis (Falling Action), and ends with Discussion and Conclusions (Denouement).

(ElShafie 2018)

But the way those story structure elements are presented in papers is not in the natural order the research events unfolded. This is called the "IMRAD" format (an acronym for Introduction, Methods, Results and Discussion), and it is, narratively speaking, enough for most scientists among the audience. But if you communicate with the general public, it's best to start with the "so what" question, that is, theme.

In a way, all of research is story (Buenz 2019). Independently from the discipline, you will always have one or more researchers trying to solve a problem. This can be writing about a theoretical physicist trying to solve a problem at her desk. True, there may be not much physical action, but the "action" can place in her mind, and those thought experiments will eventually reflect in the physicist's publication. So the scientist becomes the story's protagonist, and the problem that prompted her to embark on the research journey eventually becomes the story's inciting incident. Even though it's not a physical quest, it's still a quest (Hart 2019). If you can unearth the scientist's motivation for undertaking the research, you'll often have your story's theme. In PhD proposals, this is often the research gap, or a section titled "significance". In scientific papers, you will find much information in the "introduction" section, which usually starts with the status quo (which in storytelling terms definitely does not get to the point quickly enough), establishing the limitations in a scientific field. The introduction then usually points out (towards the end of it) the actual research gap. That's your theme and answers the "why". The "methods" section will show you the "how" of the story. This is often the most complex part of a study, and you'll probably have to ask scientists from the field for advice on how to interpret the methods, and if they're valid at all. Sometimes, the methodology is flawed and doesn't allow for reproducing the study at hand. As a science writer, you should definitely point out such limitations. The "who" (protagonist) and the "what" emerges from the abstract and introduction. If you ask additional questions (for example, those that Jack Hart suggests), you'll be able to round out your characters.

Nonetheless, it's true that some studies make it easier for you to unearth storytelling elements than others. Scientific writing is starting to take into account the conscious use of storytelling elements. In climate change science, including elements like sensory language (vivid descriptions using active language), connectivity (linking ideas logically together, that's the equivalent of cause and effect-event connections from the previous chapter) and appeal to the reader (the "why" of the story) are significantly linked to an increase in the citation frequency (Hillier, Kelly & Klinger 2016). It makes sense: after all, scientific peers too are human readers who'd like to be entertained. Also, the conscious use of story elements in scientific papers lowers the odds of being misinterpreted, for example, by journalists. That means that more correct information reaches the general public, so story elements in science make for a real win-win-win situation.

Scientific writing coach Anna Clemens has a slightly different approach to story elements in scientific papers but still covers all the elements. She advises scientists to include the six elements of plot in their papers, and she links them to the following specific journal paper sections (Clemens 2018):

- *Main character*: the object of the study
- *Setting*: background, introduction
- *Tension*: literature gap to be filled

  - (Clemens' advice: use adversative conjunctions like "but")

- *Action*: findings, interpretations
- *Climax*: conclusions drawn from the research
- *Resolution*: what do the findings mean? Implications and future research

She argues studies should also contain three more essential story elements: first, theme. The story's moral should be summarised in one sentence. Chronology is the natural sequence of events, and even Hollywood films don't usually jump forth and back in time. Purpose is the third of the elements: everything that's in the scientific manuscript should feed into the theme and be there for good reason. If it isn't, chuck it (Clemens 2018). That is to say, as more and more studies are being written this way, it should become easier. Obviously, this is highly dependent on the discipline you're covering. In medicine and psychology and other social science disciplines, chances are you will encounter case studies, which might shift your focus from choosing the study authors as protagonists to choosing the characters from the case study instead.

Roberta Ness, an epidemiologist from Pittsburgh University with more than 200 publications under her belt, likens scientific publications to mystery stories. While she points out that there is no direct mapping between a mystery story's elements and a scientific paper's elements, she does draw some parallels. The "methods" section is detective work, where you can find meticulous descriptions of how the case was solved, as well as details about the study subjects. You can find the story climax in the "results" section of a paper (here, Ness deviates from Clemens' notion, who links the "findings" to her storytelling element "action"). The findings should be part of every story based on a study. Negative control results (in the findings) in mystery terms would correspond to those suspects who did not commit the crime in question. Third, Ness likens the story's resolution to the "discussion" section of a paper. Her advice for scientists is to provide a feeling of resolution, pointing out whether the study's goals have been achieved and point out the study's limitations with respect to the main results.

Anecdotes

In science writing, you can use anecdotes to illustrate a larger issue and introduce your readers to an otherwise abstract topic. But it doesn't stop there. *Vice* editor Ankita Rao says in an interview with *New York Times* reporter Knvul Sheikh that you can use personal first-person anecdotes to illustrate a situation or lend authority to an argument. Rao has written a 2017 *Motherboard* article on eating disorders in pop culture, in which she includes her personal account of anorexia. "It's much harder for readers to discount arguments based on science or statistics if they are bolstered by personal experience" (Sheikh 2019). Other reporters like Steven Leckart actively undergo stressful situations in order to recount them as first-person anecdotes to their readers. It's their goal to immerse the audience in situations that they couldn't otherwise undergo themselves. "First-person anecdotes can also help lighten the tone of a serious piece or demystify complicated or arcane concepts, such as a convoluted scientific process" (Sheikh 2019).

You can use anecdotes to enliven your leads, but only if they reflect your story's theme. This works especially when you have features' delayed leads. Some outlets do this systematically. The *Wall Street Journal* story formula starts with an anecdote that illustrates the theme. Then comes the actual lead and the nut graph. The theme is stated explicitly, and this should occur no later than in the sixth paragraph. Next, you should point out to the audience why they should be reading is. This part is all about relevance. Then follow the details. You have to provide proof (facts, studies, expert opinions) to underpin your point and convince readers. Finally, answer readers' questions why this happened in the first place (history) and what can be done about it (future) (adapted from Mencher 2011). If you want to add a bit of tension, don't finish the anecdote in the lead, but pay it off only at the very end, as a kicker (Clark 2008). This is how science journalist Patricia Luna kicked off her *Undark* story about air pollution in Chile:

> On a midwinter Saturday just before dusk, Angelica Calderón, a 22-year-old mother of two, sat in the waiting room of the public hospital in Coyhaique. Her youngest child, just two months old, was suffering from an aggressive respiratory infection that kept him in intensive care for more than a week […].
>
> (Luna 2018)

It's a snapshot, a moment when Luna either was present herself at the hospital, or the mother (or hospital staff) recounted it to her. So the reporter either witnessed the scene herself (probable) or reconstructed it (possible) from eyewitness accounts (in this case, less probable but still possible). The anecdote isn't complete. It ends with the mother's complaint that her son's condition is down to air pollution. The anecdote hints at the theme. It even raises a dramatic question: what is going to happen to the child? Luna then deviates and addresses the larger issue connected to the location. Coyhaique's bad air is caused by household air pollution, through burning wood. She expands on the various causes, including the location between the mountains and meteorological phenomena. Luna doesn't return to the hospital anecdote until the very end of her story:

> Back in the public hospital, Angelica Calderón stared blankly as she waited for news on her son. "All of this must be due to the same thing: pollution," she said, "because the air is really bad."
>
> (Luna 2018)

Calderón sounds resigned when she adds that no matter what efforts she'll make, she can't avoid the polluted air from outside. The anecdote's dramatic question isn't really resolved, which left me, as a reader, a bit dangling. Although first-person anecdotes are the most effective because of their immediacy, third-person narratives like Luna's are very graspable too. They require a different type of reporting, since you can't just recall them like your own memories. It takes more effort to get them. If you're lucky, you'll witness moments yourself, record them and then recount them as anecdotes. Sometimes, like science writer Douglas Fox, you plan on witnessing a specific event, but things don't work out as planned. For his award-winning piece (which we'll have a closer look at in the final section of this chapter), Fox had to resort to interviewing a crew member of a flight through a blaze and ask him for the sensory details, feelings and all the details that he would have otherwise recorded himself. The answers helped him reconstruct the scene and start his piece with a gripping anecdote. So digging up good anecdotes depends on which questions you ask. First of all, you need to ask open questions. Master storytellers and interviewers put their interviewees into a reflective state of mind without being too blunt. This can include questions that make them browse their memories and choose. A possible question is: what's the best moment you had this week / during the project / while in the field? Was there a situation when you cried? In his book *Storycraft*, writing coach Jack Hart cites his colleague Ken Metzler in saying that in order to get to those stories, you have to tell them first. Put in your story, and then ask for another one. That's how you connect with interviewees. "Because it shows a human being actually expressing personality in the world, nothing reveals character like an anecdote" (Hart 2011:160).

Science writer Angela Saini writes in a *Guardian* piece how she unearths anecdotes. Scientists often start talking about stories when the interviewer has already turned off the recorder and the actual, factual interview is over. She says that she often doesn't write down questions at all but does her homework and then engages in actual conversations with the scientists, unearthing many more gossipy stories that involve money, power and passion: "the key is to find out what really makes scientists and engineers tick: their fears, their hopes and what drives them" (Saini 2011). Many US editors support that same idea that the best stories emerge at the end of an interview. Some of them ask at the end of the interviews whether their interlocutors would like to add anything that they didn't discuss during the interview (Reimold 2013). This strongly resonates with my own experiences. When I started out, I would always show up with a list of questions, and I wanted answers to those questions. Over time, I developed an uneasy feeling that by mechanically going through interview lists a natural conversation could not unfold. Of course, if the science is complex, you'll need some specific answers in order to be able to explain. But this should be a discussion on eye-level, a dialogue between the both of you, not some sort of police interrogation. Would your friends be happy if you constantly interrogated them? My point is: anecdotes and good stories emerge naturally when all participants in a discussion feel at ease. Nowadays, I'll jot down a few questions. They help when the discussion gets stuck. But what I really try is to get an emotional, natural discussion. And yes, I got the best answers, including anecdotes, way after I had turned my recorders off. You can still jot them down as memory minutes afterwards, and then follow up with your sources and ask for confirmation and additional details. Subtle cues help, too. Just turn off your recorder, or set your notepad and pen aside. I always ask interviewees three ***emotion-evoking closing questions***:

1   **Did we address everything that our readers need to know on the subject? What would you like to add?** That's their chance to debunk myths and tidy up misconceptions. Usually a matter close to their heart.
2   **If you could change anything in your discipline (or the study's subject), what would that be?** That is their chance to express what they're unhappy about. If all was well, they wouldn't want to change anything. This question is usually emotion-evoking.
3   **Is there something that the media portrays wrongly about this subject? How would you change that?** This is their chance to correct common misrepresentations. Also this question frequently evokes (predominantly negative) emotions.

Where else can you get anecdotes? Some disciplines work with anecdotes and narratives, like psychology and certain branches of medicine. Their press releases sometimes contain clinical anecdotes, so look out for them. Read the studies, their appendices and extract the original anecdotes. Then go the extra mile and call the scientists. In some cases, they might be able to put you in contact with patients or study participants. Be aware that the anecdotal case studies presented in press releases are not always correct (Goldacre 2011). In historical stories, you might not be able to do that, so you'll have to get your anecdotes from historical documents. Libraries (like the *Library of Congress*), the web archive and other digitalised document sources are extremely helpful with that. Some institutions and foundations like the National *Foundation for Infectional Diseases* put anecdotes onto their website (*Real Stories, Real People* contains a number of real-world stories on what happens to people if they don't vaccinate). In times of asinine conspiracy theories like the anti-vaccine conspiracy, initiatives like this are not only doing a great service to the public, they're prime story material, too.

Anecdotes are memorable moments in the lives of your story protagonists. They often are plot points, so you don't want to miss out on them. They are also inextricably tied to people. If you don't weave in your own anecdotes, you'll have to talk to people to get them. That's what we're going to look at in the next two sections.

Interviewing I

Let's make this first part as practical as we can. I want you to walk away from the interviewing sections with tips that you can readily apply. First, curiosity is everything. Don't conduct an interview just because you have to. Chances are you're not an expert in the same field as the scientist you interview. Remember what we've established about the Hegelian dialectic? Every good dialogue, every conversation is a chance to walk away with a changed state of knowledge. Try to see every interview like that: your chance to grow and get smarter. You will learn and grow from interviews you conduct, even from those you think are not relevant to your life. Which leads us to the first tip I've learned over the years. Be quiet. If you talk all the time, you'll just spill out what you already know, but you won't get any new information. The interview is not about your ego, and it's not for showing off how much you know about a topic. With some scientists, you can indeed earn their respect by showing off how much you know about what they're working on. You can use that by preparing well and making sure you ask confirmatory questions that contain the right jargon and buzzwords. But there's a big drawback to this approach. Your interviewees will relapse into using jargon, too.

So, most of the times it's better to keep it simple, like in actual writing. Ask simple questions. If you do that, many scientists see a chance to educate you (and the public) and start explaining. Before you can ask any kind of question, you will need to prepare, before the interview happens. Some interviewees have written and produce a lot, books, articles, podcasts, television shows and much more. Time is limited, and often you can't make the time to consume all of this and reflect on it before you interview them, because of deadlines. So again, you'll have to select and reject. Focus on a few seminal pieces. If you can't even read one book, read articles they have written in order to promote or announce them, and read interviews they've given about them. Also, read the book reviews. Some newspapers and magazines publish excerpts of books and provide commentary on them (Rosling 2018 is an example). All of these are fair game in preparing your interview.

When you conduct the interview, come with a set of prepared questions, answers that you would need to get. But don't fixate on them. Keep them as a backup. You can always get the factual questions answered in a focused follow-up interview where you just ask clarification questions. What you want to have is a conversation, and you'll see that most of your questions get answered automatically. Ask open-ended questions that your interviewee can't answer with a yes or a no. Then, most importantly, give them space to answer. People make pauses during their answers, some take a long time to think. Do not cut them off. It's a mistake I made in the beginning, because I felt uncomfortable with too long a pause. Practice this. Over time, you'll become really good at winning the pause game. Another mistake I frequently made in the beginning is rush them from question to question. Yes, it's true that not everybody thinks in a structured way. Most scientists do, I figure. So if you let them talk, their thoughts will flow logically and connect the arguments.

When you ask open-ended questions, make sure you let them do the brain work. For complex issues, ask them to break them down. Don't be afraid to ask questions like: "How can our readers understand this?" Ask them to compare very complex mechanisms to very simple pictures. Encourage them to use simple but sensory, active language. Let them come up with an analogy in nature or everyday life for something as complex as quantum mechanics. I do this frequently during my workshops. Some really found good metaphors this way. They continue using them to explain to lay audiences. You and your interviewee have to be on the same page for this to work. You have to work together. So that's what you tell them before the interview: "I know this is a really complex topic, so let's try and find a way to break this down together for our audience and make sure they can't misinterpret things – but walk away with this sense of 'Aha, I got it!'" When they answer, listen. Do nothing else. Just take in what they feed you. Then, follow up on what they said. Your next question ideally is connected to that, because like in every piece of writing, interviews need to have logical transitions. Otherwise, they don't flow. Imagine you're on a first date. She tells you about her awesome six-months trip to Macau. You nod it off, smile and then move on to your next question: "So, do you want children anytime soon?" Woah. No. That's a hard cut. The logical way to keep the conversation running would have been to ask her what she did in Macau, what the coolest place to go was, how the people are there, to tell you about the new friends she made on the trip, how the food is and whatnot. Even asking her *if* she liked it there would be a pretty bad question, because it's a closed-ended question. If she's not talkative, the conversation stops. You have to show genuine interest in your interviewee's life if you want them to open up. Wouldn't you want the same? I interviewed Jack Hart for this book, and at some point he casually mentioned his newly published novel. Don't overhear these gems. Be empathic: if you had just released a novel, wouldn't that be exciting? So I hooked into that, because I'm an avid reader and love good stories. I just had to, because I'm curious about these things. But it also led the conversation into a new, interesting direction. My point is: no matter the circumstances, an interview should never sound like an interview. You always want to have conversations. Find out what moves your interviewees and what's important in their lives.

So logically follow up and hook into whatever kind of information your interviewee gives you and use that as a springboard to ask more detailed questions. Dig deeper. When interviewing, listen attentively. Do nothing else. Use an audio recorder or your smartphone if you need things on the record (not recommended for dates, though). This makes sure you're not distracted by anything else but focus on one thing only: your interviewee. Also, it's a sign of respect. People do notice that. That's why I never take notes during presentations, because otherwise I won't be able to follow the speaker's train of thought. Instead, I record. If it was a bad talk, I delete it. If it was a good one, I listen to it and show up with follow-up questions. One mistake I often made, and it's a pretty bad one, is preparing the next question in my mind while they're talking. That's fear of not having a question ready when they're done, because you can't know how long their answer is going to be. Don't do that. Don't fear the pause. Embrace it. I'm getting better at it, too. But it takes practice. After talking with people at parties, they frequently tell me: "This is so private, and nobody else knows about this. I don't even know why I just told you this." Neither do I. And I don't target questions or something. But I guess it's just because I'm genuinely interested in them and their stories. And of course, because I listen empathically. When you listen, just listen. You have a brain, and it records enough information so you can formulate your next question after your interviewee finished talking. I'm finished talking for this section, and in the next one, we'll establish a few ground rules of good interviewing before going into some narrative journalists' and even an FBI negotiator's interviewing practices.

Interviewing II

Here are some more fundamentals for interviewing. When you interview some-body, you want to be there in person. The best interviews are face-to-face con-versations. They'll get you the most non-verbal cues. You can observe somebody's posture, demeanor, all the sensory details. You get to see the interviewee's work or private surroundings. Perhaps you get a glance of what people she surrounds her-self with. This information complements the actual interview and is at least as valuable as the spoken words. Second best are video calls, using Skype or Zoom. You still get some of the details, but you're strictly limited to the frame of the camera. With all the technical advances and broadband access that we have, technology still often gets in the way of making these good experiences. I had many interviewees turn off their cameras (and I had to turn off mine) because the band-width wouldn't allow for a proper connection. Third best are phone calls, so audio-only conversations. That's a bit of a step backwards compared to video calls. You have no visual cues but still get some acoustic signals of what happens around your interviewee – provided they're at home. I've held phone interviews with people that sat behind their car's wheel while they were stuck in an LA traffic jam, and I've held interviews with people who sat cozily in their living rooms (who still does that?). Fourth best, email interviews. I wouldn't really consider those interviews, because you can't have a conversation. It's very unidirectional. You send them questions. They send you the answers. That's it. Resort to email interviews only when there's absolutely no other option to get a statement from your interviewee. Email answers aren't candid, they're canned. The interviewee can (and will) think about her answers before writing them down. Before sending them to you, she can still edit them. This way you get safe answers, but not good ones.

It's important to establish ground rules with your interviewees before you get going. Tell them what the interview will be about, and what you need. If you interview them for narrative, if you need anecdotes and boiled-down metaphors and analogies for your readers, let them know. Be transparent and turn them from being sceptical into your accomplices. Tell them what's on the record and what's not. If they don't want to talk on record, you can still ask them whether you can use their statements (without explicit attribution) as background information. Also, and quite importantly, let them know if you intend to record the interview. It's not mandatory in all countries, but stay on the safe side. If you need to, prepare release forms and let your interviewees sign them as soon as the interview ends.

In science reporting, you'll rarely just interview one scientist and then write your story. The very minimum for a study-based news story is the principal investigator (or at least somebody who was actively involved in the research), and a second, independent scientist from the same field who is able to comment on the findings, their significance, the methods and much more. Also, think about balance. For controversial topics, the notion prevails that if you interview one person from camp pro and another from camp con, your duty is done. Wrong. Think about climate change. Writing a piece that features one scientist who acknowledges it and another ones who denies it, gives the audience a false impression that both sides have equal weight. In reality, they don't, because there are far more scientists who can show that climate change is human-made, whereas only a few deniers believe that's not the case. So giving them equal weight, without providing commentary or the journalist's point of view, just for the sake of "balanced reporting", is dangerous. In the US, this has happened in the largest newspapers like *The New York Times, The Washington Post,* and *The Wall Street Journal,* introducing bias to the audience's perception of whether climate change is human-made or not (Boykoff & Boykoff 2004). If you're writing a profile on a scientist, talk with her, but also make sure to interview people who are close to them. Business partners, mentors, supervisors, family members, friends can all provide different perspectives on a person's life. My take-home message here: time permitting, hold as many interviews as you can.

When the topic is easy, that is just the promotion of new research results, most will talk. Most people have good reason to talk to you. It's pretty well known today that if you promote your research well in the media, both funding and citations increase, which in turn raises the social status of the scientist. As a journalist/science writer, it's your duty to smell agendas, because "no one ever talks to the press without some ulterior motive: a celebrity promoting a movie, a candidate running for office, or someone seeking catharsis" (Wilkerson 2007:33). Wilkerson, a Pulitzer Prize-winning journalist, too, recommends being a good listener instead of trying to lead your interviewee somewhere. Over the years, she has developed a strategy, "accelerated intimacy", designed to get to your interviewee's core:

Like an onion, the first things being talked about are the most useless in an interview (in terms of narration, at least), so she proposes a seven-phase arc that encompasses the different stages of an interview:

1 **Introduction**: interviewee is still opposed to you.
2 **Adjustment**: interviewee is unsure if she wants to put in the time, and you're in a hurry.
3 **Moment of connection**: when interviewee signals that she's at ease.
4 **Settling in**: interviewee starts enjoying the interview, and so do you.
5 **Revelation**: when interviewee is comfortable enough, she might disclose candid information. Even if irrelevant to you, she might reveal something important to her, which in turn signals an increased level of trust.
6 **Deceleration**: you think you have enough material, but interviewee wants to go on. Let her.
7 **Reinvigoration**: interviewee feels free to share almost anything with you. You close your notebook and she actively cooperates. This is the center of the onion.

Narrative journalist Jon Franklin writes that psychological journalistic interviews can be similar to the process psychiatrists apply to get to know their patients. It's about understanding why your interviewee has become the person she is today. Franklin asks his interviewees what the first memories are they can recall. This puts them into a narrative state of mind and encourages them to come up with details on places, subjects, characters and moods. This allows you to answer more detailed follow-up questions that expand on the story provided by your interviewee. Don't ask them about specific feelings and emotions but about their experiences and thoughts. Ask them about different life episodes, and do ask things like whether they were raised by both parents, how they experienced high school years and how many relationships they had. Franklin argues that people are most interested in themselves, so they will most likely answer these questions (Franklin in Kramer & Call 2007:34). Speaking of psychological interviews. Have a look at those who do it best, like former FBI negotiator Chris Voss. I just want to point you to a few key techniques he uses. The first is mirroring. Just repeat the last few words of a your interviewee's statement as a question. That's it. It will prompt them to expand on the topic, without them noticing. Next, ask open-ended questions that start with "how" and "what". Make sure they are about the other person. For example, you could ask your interviewee "how can you make sure readers understand X about your study?" That'll let them do the brain work. Labelling, his other technique, goes in the same direction. It's simply assigning labels to their emotions without being judgmental about them. It usually goes like this: "It seems you are worried about X".

Can you apply Wilkerson's, Franklin's and Voss' techniques to scientists? Absolutely. In fact, it's probably even more important to dig deeper with scientists than with many other types of persons. Many are cut from a different cloth than most other people, that is they hide behind a mask of unrealistic objectivity. This, on the other hand, can cause them to refuse answering childhood questions. But you can still pose those "first-memory" questions but direct them more towards their scientific endeavours: what was their first memory as a scientist? How would they describe their careers' evolutions? How was their relationship to their supervisors? Did they frequently change topic or have difficult discussions with their supervisors? Did they struggle while being students? Why did it take them longer to complete their degrees (*if* that was the case – the answer will definitely reveal a personal story). Are there moments that made them lose "faith" in academia or that encouraged them? Did they ever feel abandoned or embarrassed as PhD students? What was their most difficult presentation in their academic career? These are still personal questions, some perhaps a bit private. But they'll give you a deeper understanding of who the person behind the scientist is.

More story sources

Journal papers and interviews are not the only sources you can find science stories in. Science news aggregators and news services like ScienceDaily, EurekAlert! and Phys.org provided the standard fodder, a range of editorially pre-selected stories, boiled down into a digestible format. The upside: you'll easily find good story material on these sites. That material already contains enough news values to become legit science stories. Writing about these topics works if you're working on staff. If you're a freelancer, chances are a staff writer will have already covered the more prominent stories. Another downside: the aggregators create filter bubbles, pushing research that gets amplified across all major outlets, but alas at the expense of less prominent research that might just be as interesting. Do consider the blog networks as story sources as well. This can be popular science blog networks, like *Discover magazine*'s or *Scientific American*'s blog network. Many of the stories on those websites are written by scientists and touch upon recent findings. Quite importantly, blog stories have an extremely quick turnaround and hence often have the edge on print publications. Most importantly, science blog posts often offer a fresh angle on otherwise stale topics. When you consider blog posts as sources, make sure to have a look at journals' and scientific institutions' blog networks. For example, *PLOS ONE* and *Nature* run extensive blog networks, covering a wide range of disciplines. Also check out museums' and other scientific institutions' blogs and subscribe to them via services like RSS in order to get notified whenever they publish new blog posts. If all of that seems a bit over-whelming, online aggregation services like *ScienceSeeker* provide a curated list of fresh science blog posts. Online preprint archives are a fantastic story source to find fresh research that hasn't been peer-reviewed yet. That's of course a caveat, but on the other hand, peer review with all its shortcomings is not an absolute guarantor of scientific quality (Thacker & Tennant 2019). Many disciplines have online preprint archives, like ArXiv, BiorXiv, SocArXiv and PaleoArXiv. You can and should of course also scour the social media like Facebook and Twitter. Stories that have run there usually have been significantly amplified, and you perhaps don't want to repeat them. But you can watch topical discussions on current topics unfold on some social media channels. Scientists take especially to Twitter for scientific discussions (Van Noorden 2014). Sometimes, these short conversations are conflict-laden, sometimes, scientists weigh in on science policy, and sometimes perpetrators of misconduct get called out. All of that is fantastic science story material, because it starts with science characters. Also, if you find a scientist who tweets about a scientific issue, it's likely you can win her over for an interview. A survey has shown that the most common reason why scientists take to Twitter (28 per cent) is because they want to reach a large, diverse audience, the general public. And: it's hugely popular. A whopping 93 per cent of the 587 participants had a Twitter account (Collins, Shiffman & Rock 2016). If you want to go the extra mile, create topic-based lists on Twitter to follow specific beats.

Don't forget to look for stories offline! Newspapers and regional magazines contain rich characters and anecdotes you can use, as freelance science journalist Emily Sohn writes. Also, go and visit institutions that are close by. Short news pieces in local outlets can often spark story ideas, and following up with the por-trayed scientists can yield great stories. Even ads can lead to stories. "Everything in the paper is fair game" (Sohn 2013). It doesn't stop here. Sohn has more bril-liant advice: Talking to people and spending some time with them is usually the freshest way to gather story material. Go to small science meetings and big con-ferences, talk with friends, strangers, at home and at weddings. Vacation time is vacation time, but you'll often meet lots of interesting people on your trips. Some writers develop "story scouting" processes, scouring papers and abstracts until they find stories that are worth reporting. That's one way to finance travelling.

But the approach also works locally, even when cold-calling researchers and getting introduced to other researchers. Also, don't forget that stories you're working on can spin off other story branches that you couldn't expand on in the original one (Sohn 2013).

Tampa Bay Times journalist Lane DeGregory confirms many of these story sources: talking to strangers, neighbors and spending some time at bars, where people are quite likely to share stories. She also recommends reading bulletin boards (DeGregory 2007). I had good experiences with the latter. That's a particularly good source at universities and museums, as you'll often find talk, workshop and summer school announcements that focus on very specific issues. The speakers and trainers are usually only in town for a short time, so make sure you don't miss these opportunities and scan them regularly. DeGregory has more sources she recommends scanning. Most importantly, try ignoring VIPs and instead focus on "losers" that didn't achieve what they wanted, or generally on people for whom a lot is at stake (DeGregory 2007). That's a bit of an issue in science. Positive results, that is, that positive results have better chances of getting published than negative ones. "When negative results aren't published in high-impact journals, other scientists can't learn from them and end up repeating failed experiments, leading to a waste of public funds and a delay in genuine progress" (Mehta 2019). Mehta is on to something: the pressure to publish positive results, to succeed, can cajole scientists into misrepresenting their research, and in extreme cases, this can lead to misconduct and fraud. You can trace the problem back to funding agencies who fund only research projects that yield positive results. But negative results are just as valuable as positive ones, as they show other researchers which solutions they needn't target anymore (Mehta 2019). Look out for these stories, for "failed" research projects, and tell those stories. Right now, a lot is at stake for researchers who can't deliver positive results, in terms of publishing volume, funding and reputation.

Case study: Genesis of two stories

Let's have a look at how two science writers found their stories and how they approached them. Science writer Douglas Fox' 2017 story about new technology to monitor wildfires for *High Country News* won him an AAAS Kavli Science Journalism Magazine Gold award. Fox' story starts with a vivid description from the inside of a propeller plane that is packed with atmospheric research equipment. He ends the first paragraph using foreshadowing, technique that hints at conflict and keeps the audience reading. We'll see it in more detail later in this book. In the second paragraph, Fox zooms out and describes the scenery and the problem (wildfires). That paragraph is also full of measurable facts that show the sheer scale of the fire and the environment it threatens. The next paragraph catapults readers back into the plane and introduces one of the story's characters, researcher David Kingsmill. Over the next few paragraphs, Fox builds up tension, showing how the plane gets tossed around by up- and downdrafts in the middle of a plume, right above the wildfire (Fox 2017). Kingsmill is not the story's protagonist. Fire meteorologist Craig Clements is.

But Fox wasn't there. As he writes in a behind-the-scenes article (Fox 2018), he had imagined the reporting for the story quite differently. When he started reporting it in 2016, he had put together a list of scenes. He had counted on following Clements and looking over his shoulder while he was in the field. But that didn't happen, so Fox asked his editor to kill the story. Thankfully, they didn't. Fox recalls that especially the above lead scene was challenging. But he was not aboard the plane himself. So he had to reconstruct the scene by interviewing Kingsmill, the scientist who sat beside the pilot. Fox describes how he reported the rest of the scene:

> I viewed his photos and listened to his detailed sensory recollections - the sound of pens and notebooks clattering against the windows – and the deceptively innocuous "cool blue" of the plume as it first appeared on standard cockpit radar, during the plane's initial approach. I interviewed another scientist who often flies on the plane, to better understand its instruments. I viewed photos of the plane's interior. And I studied aviation weather radar, to confirm Kingsmill's recollections.
>
> (Fox 2018)

On top of that, Fox did a lot of legwork and consulted many sources to reconstruct the story. He had outlined around 20 scenes initially, half of which made it into the finished story. He obtained GPS flights lines and satellite imagery of the wildfires that he then laid over existing maps of the area. He used material from Google and the US Geological Survey (US). He used radar images of the wildfires, checked fire reports and talked with firefighters. Without pre-planning it, Fox writes he had hoped to find another vivid, dramatic scene while reporting, but at first didn't. Then he researched Project Flambeau, a 1967 experiment with controlled fires that simulated nuclear attacks on American cities. He managed to backtrack USGS descriptions and pinpoint today's location. To his surprise, he noticed that the place is still scarred after 50 years, which even the scientists hadn't known (Fox 2018). It's a story within a story. You can't plan these, but if you're on the lookout for such story gems, as Fox calls them, you can find them. The story wasn't planned like this but emerged from it during the reporting. As you'll read later on, this is often true of a story's theme, too.

As Fox' examples shows, reporting for narrative is effortful. You'll usually have a hunch or a starting point that arouses your interest. Perhaps it's a short news report that prompts you to dig deeper. From there, you'll have to read documents and talk to people in order to get them. Along that road, you'll discover new facts and have some insights that might change the course of what you initially thought your story would be. It also happened to science writer Amanda Gefter, whose story on Walter Pitts we've seen in the first chapter. I asked her how her story came to be, and this is her answer:

> I had become really interested in the rise of modern neuroscience in the 1950s, when scientists first got the idea that the mind could be reduced to the mechanistic workings of the brain, and that the brain was in some sense processing information. Those things sound so obvious today, but required a

huge conceptual leap at the time. I've always been fascinated by how people are able to make such out-of-the-box, counterintuitive conceptual leaps. So I was tracing the history and all roads lead back to a 1943 paper called "A Logical Calculus of the Ideas Immanent in Nervous Activity" by Warren McCulloch and Walter Pitts. I was curious who those guys were, so I started digging around. I was amazed by how little was known about Pitts, though the few tidbits I found were intriguing – hints that he had been a homeless runaway, a child prodigy, a true genius. McCulloch was a wild character, too, as was Jerry Lettvin, who introduced them. I was struck by the fact that all three of them wrote poetry and had a very literary sensibility. That was fascinating to me, because what was so striking about cybernetics (the field they helped found, from which the sub-fields of cognitive science, computer science, information theory and artificial intelligence as we know them were born) was so radically interdisciplinary. I mean, it's not often that a whole new scientific field comes into existence. Physics, biology, chemistry, astronomy…the basic divisions have been around a long time! But cybernetics was really a brand new species of science. And I found myself wondering whether the artistic, literary sensibility that McCulloch, Pitts and Lettvin shared played a role in that. They were scientist-poets; they didn't compartmentalize their intellectual interests. I found that extremely inspiring. So that's the story I initially wanted to write – how three "poets of the mind" revolutionized science. I wanted to read some of their poetry, and found that McCulloch's papers, including an unpublished collection of his poetry, were at the American Philosophical Society library in Philadelphia, so I went there to read them. That's where I found all the letters between McCulloch, Lettvin and Pitts, and as I got to know more about Pitts and about his almost father-son relationship with McCulloch, it became increasingly clear that he was the beating heart of the story. So mid-research, I shifted gears, dropped the poetry angle, and started working on a profile of Walter Pitts, centered around his relationship with McCulloch.

(Gefter 2019)

Gefter's answer is a gem in and of itself. Not only does it show her fascination with her story. It also shows the central role of compelling characters in good stories. This is true of both Fox' and Gefter's stories. The other remark I want to make is about those moments of insight that these writers experienced. It's that moment when you say, "oh, now I see where this is going" that your story changes, your focus shifts and you're on to writing a truly great piece. It's the moment your story becomes "your" story. It's a perfect match that moments of insight inside the story (that is, the characters' epiphanies) are what make stories special, and the writers' epiphanies are just as valuable when reporting them.

Review questions

- Which are the strongest news values?
- What is wrong with news values?

- Which story elements can you find in journal papers, and where?
- Which questions can you use to evoke emotions?
- What is the number one interviewing rule?
- What is a common mistake you should avoid while listening?
- What do interviews and onions have in common?
- Where do you get your material from if you cannot observe an event in person?

Links

"Making The News – Top Tips" (Wiley Author Service): https://authorservices. wiley.com/asset/editor-documents/Making%20the%20news%20final.pdf

"Real Stories, Real People" (National Foundation for Infectional Diseases): http://www.nfid.org/real-stories-real-people

"Interview questions that work for newbie science reporters" (International Journalists' Network): https://ijnet.org/en/story/interview-questions-work-newbie-science-rep orters

"The Boy Behind the Mask" (Chicago University Press): https://www.press. uchicago.edu/books/hart/Hallman1.html

"The French Fry Connection" (Chicago University Press): https://www.press. uchicago.edu/books/hart/Read1.html

"Meetings of Minds, or, How to Talk to a Scientist" (The Open Notebook): http s://www.theopennotebook.com/2015/03/17/meetings-of-minds-how-to-ta lk-to-a-scientist/

"Interviewing for Career-Spanning Profiles" (The Open Notebook): https://www. theopennotebook.com/2018/03/27/interviewing-for-career-spanning-profiles/

References

Angler, M.W. (2017) *Science Journalism: an introduction.* London: Routledge.

Buenz, E.J. (2019) "Essential elements for high-impact scientific writing," Nature Career Column [Online]. Available at: https://www.nature.com/articles/d41586-019-00546-7 (date accessed 4 October 2019).

Boykoff, M.T. & Boykoff, J.M. (2004) "Balance as bias: global warming and the US prestige press," *Global environmental change*, vol. 14, no. 2, 125–136.

Clark, R.P. (2008) *Writing Tools: 55 Essential For Every Writer, 10th anniversary ed.* New York: Hachette Book Group.

Clemens, A. (2018) "Writing a page-turner: how to tell a story in your scientific paper," LSE Impact Blog [Online]. Available at: http://blogs.lse.ac.uk/impactofsocialsciences/2018/ 05/21/writing-a-page-turner-how-to-tell-a-story-in-your-scientific-paper/ (date accessed: 2 February 2019).

Collins, K., Shiffman, D. & Rock, J. (2016) "How are scientists using social media in the workplace?" *PloS one*, vol. 11, no. 10, e0162680.

Connelly, F.M. & Clandinin, D.J. (1990) "Stories of experience and narrative inquiry," *Educational researcher*, vol. 19, no. 5, 2–14.

DeGregory, L. (2007) "Narrative as a Daily Habit," in: Kramer, M. & Call, W. *Telling True Stories*. New York: Plume, 239–243.

ElShafie, S.J. (2018) "Making science meaningful for broad audiences through stories," *Integrative and Comparative Biology*, vol. 58, no. 6, 1213–1223.

Fox, D. (2018) "Firestorm: Douglas Fox on the Reporting Behind His Award-Winning Story," AAAS News [Online]. Available at: https://sjawards.aaas.org/news/firestorm-dougla s-fox-reporting-behind-his-award-winning-story (date accessed: 7 February 2019).

Fox, D. (2017) "Inside the firestorm," High Country News [Online]. Available at: https:// www.hcn.org/issues/49.6/inside-the-dangerous-and-unpredictable-behavior-of-wildfire (date accessed: 7 February 2019).

Galtung, J. & Ruge, M.H. (1965) "The structure of foreign news: The presentation of the Congo, Cuba and Cyprus crises in four Norwegian newspapers," *Journal of peace research*, vol. 2, no. 1, 64–90.

Gefter, A. (2019) Personal correspondence.

Goldacre, B. (2011) "Anecdotes are great – if they convey data accurately," *The Guardian* [Online]. Available at: https://www.theguardian.com/science/2011/jul/29/duchennes-m uscular-dystrophy-surrogate-outcomes (date accessed: 4 February 2019).

Haagerup, U. (2019) "Academic who defined news principles says journalists are too negative," *The Guardian* [Online]. Available at: https://www.theguardian.com/world/2019/jan/18/ johan-galtung-news-principles-journalists-too-negative (date accessed: 1 February 2019).

Hart, J. (2019) Personal phone conversation on 9 February 2019.

Hart, J. (2011) *Storycraft: The Complete Guide to Writing Narrative Nonfiction*. Chicago: The University of Chicago Press.

Hillier, A., Kelly, R.P. & Klinger, T. (2016) "Narrative style influences citation frequency in climate change science," *PloS one*, vol. 11, no. 12, e0167983.

Hoomans, J. (2015) "35,000 Decisions: The Great Choices of Strategic Leaders," *Leading Edge Journal* (Roberts Wesleyan College) [Online]. Available at: https://go.roberts.edu/ leadingedge/the-great-choices-of-strategic-leaders (date accessed: 1 February 2019).

Kramer, M.W. & Call, W.L. (eds.) (2007) *Telling True Stories: A Nonfiction Writers' Guide from the Nieman Foundation at Harvard University*. New York: Plume.

Luna, P. (2018) "In Chile, Bounded by Mountains and Smothered by Wood Smoke," Undark [Online]. Available at: https://undark.org/article/air-pollution-chile/ (date accessed 5 October 2019).

McIntyre, K. & Gyldensted, C. (2017) *"Constructive journalism: An introduction and practical guide for applying positive psychology techniques to news production,"* The journal of media innovations, vol. 4, no. 2, 20–34.

Mehta, D. (2019) "Highlight negative results to improve science," Nature Career Column [Online]. Available at: https://www.nature.com/articles/d41586-019-02960-3 (date accessed 4 October 2019).

Mencher, M. (2011) *News Reporting and Writing*. New York: McGraw Hill.

Modgil, S., Gill, R., Sharma, V. L., Velassery, S. & Anand, A. (2018) "Nobel Nominations in Science: Constraints of the Fairer Sex," *Annals of Neurosciences*, vol. 25 no. 2, 63–79.

Ness, R. (2007) "Writing Science: The Story's the Thing," Science Careers [Online]. Available at: https://www.sciencemag.org/careers/2007/04/writing-science-storys-thing (date accessed: 2 February 2019).

Newman, N., Fletcher, R., Kalogeropoulos, A., Levy, D. & Nielsen, R K. (2017) "Reuters Institute Digital News Report 2017," Reuters Institute [Online]. Available at: https://reu tersinstitute.politics.ox.ac.uk/sites/default/files/Digital%20News%20Report%202017% 20web_0.pdf (date accessed 3 October 2019).

Reimold, D. (2013) *Journalism of ideas: brainstorming, developing, and selling stories in the digital age.* London: Routledge.

Rosling, H. (2018) "Good news at last: the world isn't as horrific as you think," *The Guardian* [Online]. Available at: https://www.theguardian.com/world/commentisfree/2018/apr/11/good-news-at-last-the-world-isnt-as-horrific-as-you-think (date accessed 6 October 2019).

Saini, A. (2011) "Listen out for jokes, anecdotes and secrets – they're science writing gold," *The Guardian* [Online]. Available at: https://www.theguardian.com/science/2011/may/12/science-writing-gold-scientists-secrets (date accessed: 3 February 2019).

Sheikh, K. (2019) "Journalists as Characters: Using First-Person Narration to Drive Stories," The Open Notebook [Online]. Available at: https://www.theopennotebook.com/2019/04/30/journalists-as-characters-using-first-person-narration-to-drive-stories/ (date accessed 5 October 2019).

Sohn, E. (2013) "Finding Ideas," in: Hayden, T. & Niyjhuis, M. (eds.) *The science writers' handbook: everything you need to know to pitch, publish, and prosper in the digital age.* Boston: Da Capo Press, 9–22.

Thacker, P.D. & Tennant, J. (2019) "Why we shouldn't take peer review as the 'gold standard'," *The Washington Post* [Online]. Available at: https://www.washingtonpost.com/outlook/why-we-shouldnt-take-peer-review-as-the-gold-standard/2019/08/01/fd90749a-b229-11e9-8949-5f36ff92706c_story.html (date accessed 4 October 2019).

Van Noorden, R. (2014) "Online collaboration: Scientists and the social network," *Nature news*, vol. 512, No. 7513, 126.

Ware, M. & Mabe, M. (2015) "The STM Report: an overview of scientific and scholarly journal publishing," STM Association [Online]. Available at: https://www.stm-assoc.org/2015_02_20_STM_Report_2015.pdf (date accessed 6 October 2019).

Wilkerson, A. (2007) "Interviewing: Accelerated Intimacy," in: Kramer, M. & Call, W. (eds.) *Telling True Stories.* New York: Plume, 30–35.

Wormwood, J.B., Devlin, M., Lin, Y.R., Barrett, L.F. & Quigley, K.S. (2018) "When words hurt: Affective word use in daily news coverage impacts mental health." *Frontiers in psychology* [Online]. Available at: https://www.frontiersin.org/articles/10.3389/fpsyg.2018.01333/full (date accessed: 1 February 2019).

4 Narrative Structure

What you will learn in this chapter:

- What is a story arc?
- Common structures in science writing
- Narratives in science
- Story shapes
- Creating tension
- Cause and effect
- Narrative structure in scientific writing
- Case study: A science detective story

Good stories have a very important trait. They grip the readers from the beginning and never let them go until they've read the last word of the last paragraph on the final page. They make the audience wonder what happens next. But thinking a simple sequential "this happens, and then that happens" approach would be good enough to keep them wondering is a fallacy. If you write a story that just enumerates facts, paragraphs and scenes one after another, you're readers will eventually ask themselves: "so what?" "Why do you tell me this, writer?" Good stories are glued together by a cause and effect mechanism. Scenes, paragraphs, ideas must be interconnected by cause and effect, too. Soon after the beginning, your character is thrown into the story by an inciting incident that uproots her life or at least her state of knowledge. By the time the story reaches its climax, it must be crystal clear to the audience that climax had to happen this way. This is where the narrative power of persuasion lies. Causality. And that's also where its dangers lie. If you write a story that is very rich in style, and if your command of English is so good that you can write beautiful descriptions using sensory language, and if on top of that you're a master of evoking graspable pictures in your readers' minds, that still doesn't mean you're able to tell a story. That's what lots of beginning writers (fiction writers and nonfiction writers alike) struggle with: crossing the "so what" border (theme!) and glue together a string of events that readers just have to read to the end. Some writers have done the opposite: Dan Brown, best-selling American novelist, writes one page-turner after another. People just can't stop buying his books. But it's not because of his style. Much rather, it is how he writes scene after scene, how he ends them, how he creates tension that leaves the reader hinged after each chapter, longing for more. He has a system. He has a structural system that works (the same goes for James Patterson). He's a master of plotting and constructing gripping narratives. What Brown apparently isn't is a master of is style. For instance, have a look at how he overuses adverbs in his dialogue. Well-written dialogue doesn't need to tell the audience that Karen told Robert "sadly" that she's afraid (I just made this one up). That's a violation of the style rule "show don't tell". Rather, describe that she's crying, or sobbing or whatever. In fact, Brown has drawn a lot of criticism for his style. Linguistics professor George K. Pullum doesn't seem impressed by Brown's prose at all:

> Brown's writing is not just bad; it is staggeringly, clumsily, thoughtlessly, almost ingeniously bad. In some passages scarcely a word or phrase seems to have been carefully selected or compared with alternatives. I slogged through 454 pages of this syntactic swill, and it never gets much better.
>
> (Pullum 2004)

He's not a fan of his plots either, but let's cut Dan Brown some slack here. In all honesty, his structure works. Jesus does it work. And structure is one of the most important tools you have in writing. Without it, all the other elements are useless. That's why in this chapter, we're going to have a look at some proven principles of narrative structure (both in nonfiction and fiction contexts) that you can apply to your science stories. We'll have a look at what narrative arcs are and which sort of structures are commonly used in science writing. I've also included a digression on narratives as part of the scientific process. Why? Because I want to show you that narrative and science can be married. Obviously, you should never forcefully superimpose a narrative structure on scientific facts just because you think it'd make for a pretty story. But if the scientific facts contain narrative elements, then this chapter will help you figure out what to look for, track them down and select and order them.

Putting events in the right order is another important aspect I'll cover in this chapter. You can do so in different ways, and we're going to have a look at how established writers do this. You can order events in a way that creates tension for your readers, and we'll have a look at a number of techniques to further make them wonder what's going to happen next. In doing so, I'll also show you the principle of cause and effect, which says nothing other than that events should be the logical consequence of one another. Don't confuse it with scientific causality, because that's what bad science writing in the media does. Finally, we'll dissect a detective story together to find out how the author sneaked in the explanatory parts (the science-y stuff where readers quickly wander off if you don't get them back on the story line). It's a continuous swerving forth and back, and it requires some practice to pull that off. Some researchers have tried to draw and visualise stories as graphs. We'll have a look at a few of them. In fact, you'll see how astonishing it is that only a few graph types are responsible for the majority of stories out there. This can help you outline your stories before you start writing, and it can also help you track down problems in case something in your story doesn't sound right. I'm outlining a lot. I write scenes on index cards and shuffle them around until I figure out what works best. If the plot gets too complicated, I draw graphs too, in order to find out where the tension is highest. I outlined this book (although it doesn't have a narrative structure, so I didn't draw a plot graph for it). But I do that for all magazine features I write. It's really, really helpful to know how narratives work and then use that knowledge to plan, write and then rewrite them. So let's first have a look at what a narrative arc is.

What is a story arc?

All stories follow a two-dimensional structural shape that you can visualise using a graph in a coordinate system. Stories consist of events that are logically and chronologically connected. Each event is like a point on a narrative line. The slope of this line tells you how high the tension is (that's your tension-axis) as the story progresses (that's your time-axis). So essentially, the story arc is a curve with the story's plot points on it. The arc simply connects them. You can draw a story arc in order to analyse an existing story (which I would recommend), and you can draw a story arc to place the events from your reporting on it and later on outline and ultimately flesh out your story. It's a tool that, together with the theme, helps you keep on track when writing a story. Narrative journalist Jack Hart uses story arcs to outline all of his stories before he writes them. He also uses them to discuss stories and assess the quality of journalists' story ideas when working with them as their editor. Narrative arcs can take many shapes, depending on which approach you take in terms of act structure. You can perfectly subdivide a narrative arc into the three acts beginning, middle and end (to which Hart assigns protagonist, complication and resolution, respectively). However, the most common depictions of story arcs subdivide the story into five parts. This goes back to German novelist Gustav Freytag, who analysed Shakespeare's plays and eventually came up with a five-act structure, Freytag's pyramid (which you can see in Figure 4.1):

1 **Exposition**: introduce the protagonist and other characters. Hint at the imminent complications. The complications arise from the protagonist's flaws.
2 **Rising Action**: recount a series of events that increase tension (they're usually obstacles the protagonist faces), building up to the climax
3 **Climax**: a reversal of fortune (Greek: "peripeteia"). If things went well for the protagonist, they'll go downwards from here on (and vice versa). The protagonist must make a choice. Do note the "mirror" aspect again.
4 **Falling Action**: after the climax, tension diminishes. The consequences of the protagonist's choice become apparent.
5 **Denouement**: either a catastrophe, or catharsis happens. The protagonist comes to terms with her situation, and so do the other characters. All conflicts are resolved.

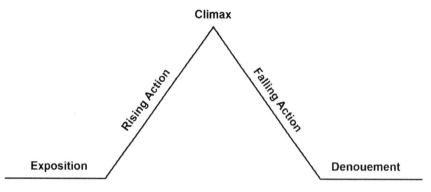

Figure 4.1 Freytag's pyramid illustrates the dramatic story arc
Source: Martin W. Angler.

Right in the centre, you'll find the "midpoint" occurs, where tension is highest. In a tragedy like "Macbeth", the five-act structure looks like this (Yorke 2013, BBC no date):

1   **Exposition**: main characters introduced, witches prophecies, decision to murder Duncan is taken.
2   **Rising Action**: Macbeth murders Duncan and becomes king (key moment).
3   **Climax**: Macduff defects and joins Malcolm.
4   **Falling Action**: Macbeth gets abandoned (worst point). He returns to the witches. Macduff's family gets killed. He and Malcolm plan the invasion.
5   **Denouement**: final battle. Lady Macbeth and Macbeth die.

Also television writer John Yorke mentions Freytag's structure as the base of the five-act structure and slightly renames it as follows: Exposition, Complications, Climax, Falling Action and Catastrophe (Yorke 2013). Yorke's book, while aimed at TV and screenwriters, takes a valid approach to explaining how stories work. Indeed, Yorke himself uses a five-act structure to show how stories work. He also goes a step further and uses the five-act structure to show how characters change over the course of an unfolding drama. In act one, the protagonist is unwitting, grows her knowledge and experiences some sort of awakening at the threshold to act two. In act two, she experiences doubt, overcomes reluctance to face the complications and accepts the challenge. In act three, she experiments with the newly gained knowledge and gains key knowledge (sort of an epiphany) at the midpoint, right at the center of act three, then continues experimenting with that knowledge. In act four, the protagonist is again full of doubts, and her reluctance grows anew. It is not until act five that she truly reawakens, becomes accepting and once and for all conquers the initial challenge (in fiction, this is often the moment she faces and defeats the archenemy for good). Here, she experiences sort of a rebirth. Hence, Yorke uses the same structure not only as a narrative arc but also as a character arc. Can you build a scientist's story using this structure? Absolutely.

When he worked at *The Oregonian,* Jack Hart designed his own five-act story arc based on Freytag's pyramid. Instead of a triangular shape, Hart draws his plot points onto a mound-shaped curve, renames Freytag's "Climax" into "Crisis", the "Resolution" into "Climax" and the "Denouement" into "Falling Action". During the outlining process, Hart and his collaborating writers add important story events as plot points to the arc. The most important two plot points that must be present on his story arc is the inciting incident right after the exposition and the climax at the height of the story's tension. Hart's curve is not perfectly mound-shaped but slightly curved to the right. This indicates that longest part of the story is dedicated to complications. Right after the climax, the story takes a steep fall-off. Indeed, this is good practice. The denouement shouldn't last for too long. Hart adds another twist. The sequence in which you see the events unfold on the arc is not necessarily the same sequence in which you present the events to the audience. You can start telling the story either right before the inciting incident or at the crisis point of the story, when things go wrong for the protagonist. Hart calls this an "in medias res" opening. The award-winning stories he edited are often longform features. But you don't have to write a long story to come up with a complete narrative arc. It's possible to write an essay that runs 800 or even just 600 words long. The arc just has to contain a protagonist, a complication and a resolution:

> Literacy educators sometimes use a framework called "Somebody Wanted But So" to talk about narratives – that is, all stories have a "somebody" (a character) who "wants" something (which animates the plot), "but" something happens (the conflict), "so" (more action results, which leads to a resolution).
>
> (Schulten 2019)

Try and come up with your own examples. One starting point could just be writing down the aforementioned story elements that make a narrative arc for an essay. *The New York Times Learning* editor Katherine Schulten also comes up with an example of an essay (not a science essay though) that almost opens like a classic fairy tale. "It was an ordinary day, until" (Schulten 2019). She also recommends weaving structural and linguistic elements into the story, like transitions and adding details to raise the tension. There are many similarities between essays and features, especially in their purpose to entertain, educate, inform and inspire, and both forms can include the author's personal experiences. But it's structure where they differ. While a feature's structure is often based on its subject, "an essay can have just as much factual information, but it's based around this unique, personal, internal logic", science essay teacher Janet Hopson says (Walker 2013). As you can see, almost regardless of the form, story arcs are centred around characters. What does that do with science? It adds a human face to a seemingly objective enterprise. Not all writing structures do that. In the next section, let's have a look at the most common science writing structures.

Common structures in science writing

In this section, I'd love to give you an overview of some of the most relevant science writing structures in the field. Let's start with the least exciting but highly effective and widespread structure: the inverted pyramid. It orders information in descending order of importance. It's typically employed for breaking news. In science writing, you would use it to write a news report about a new study. The lead is the most important part of the inverted pyramid. It tries to answer as many of the relevant journalistic questions, the "who", "what", "when", "why" and "where" (the five Ws) and the "how". You can accomplish this in one or two paragraphs. Here's an example:

> Archeologists recently discovered an ancient lost city north of Tel Aviv. This large, 5,000-year-old city, bustling with around 6,000 people, was the "early Bronze Age New York," of the region and likely one of the first complex cities in what is now Israel […]
>
> (Saplakoglu 2019)

This paragraph contains the who (archaeologists), where (near Tel Aviv), when (the discovery was made recently, the city existed 5,000 years ago), what (an ancient lost and complex city). The why and how don't shine through yet, but the author expands on that later on. It's rather typical that the how (the answer to which you'll find in scientific manuscripts' "Methods" sections) follows in a later paragraph. In the inverted pyramid, the paragraphs following the lead dig into more detail. In Saplakoglu's example, they detail which university the researchers work for, where exactly the site is located and whether the find was an accidental discovery or not. Connected back-ground information complements such news reports and usually is one of the last parts of the texts. Sometimes, an outlook is included at the very tail of the text. Nothing that follows the lead is necessary to understand the gist of the news. Readers could walk away and still have grasped the most important aspects. The inverted pyramid was designed so that newspaper editors could easily trim away the tail in case there was not enough space in the newspaper. This structure retains absolutely no tension but gives the audience all information upfront. It sounds like a drawback, but this structure makes it an effective form for online science writing, like blog posts. Think of Sapla-koglu's lead in terms of keywords. Online search engines could perfectly index it.

When you write longer and more complex articles, it gets trickier. First, nobody likes explanations. Inverted pyramids' leads are called direct leads. In features, you will rather find indirect leads that tell the audience an anecdote. They often open scenically and introduce a character facing a problem. Such leads are called indirect or delayed leads. Sometimes, the writers don't give away the initial anecdote's resolution immediately. Instead, they use the anecdote to lead over to a paragraph called the "nut graph". The nut graph provides context, the theme, the larger issue and answers the "so what?" question. "Like a nut, it contains the "kernel", or essential theme, of the story. At *The Philadelphia Inquirer*, reporters and editors called it the "'You may have wondered why we invited you to this party?' section" (Scanlan 2003). Nut graphs can be as short as one paragraph, but some span several paragraphs. Here's an example. This is the lead of a

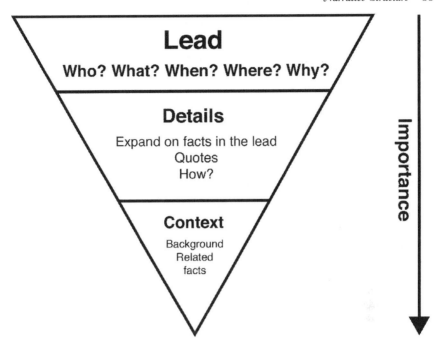

Figure 4.2 The inverted pyramid
Source: Martin W. Angler.
Note: The inverted pyramid is one of the most common structures in journalism and especially suited for news reports. It works just as well online.

story about measuring trees' biomass, written by Christine Swanson and published in *New Scientist*:

> Excitement in the room was palpable on the morning of 5 December last year. The day before, the launch of SpaceX's Falcon 9 to supply the International Space Station had been delayed for 24 hours. That followed the discovery on board of mouldy food [...]
>
> (Swanson 2019)

It's graspable, it's scenic and it makes you imagine engineers clapping their hands and hugging each other without the author telling you explicitly. Right after the lead, Swanson sweeps into the nut graph. The transition is obvious, as she uses the SpaceX launch as an explicit connector and then moves on to the larger issue.

> The SpaceX launch was just the beginning. GEDI is in the vanguard of a new wave of innovative sensors that will assess the world's plant life and how it is changing – how much carbon, for instance, is lost to the atmosphere [...].
>
> (Swanson 2019)

Swanson then goes on to describe why it is important that we holistically understand how trees function. In the paragraph preceding the aforementioned, she explicitly states her theme that despite our advances in space, we still haven't fully understood how such a large biomass as forests work. She expands a bit more on the "why should I care" factor of her story. But this is not only a switch from lead to nut graph, it's also a switch from a very concrete and scenic example to the story's gist, which looks at it from an elevated vantage point. It takes a different rung on the ladder of abstraction (which you'll see in a minute). Also, it's what Jack Hart calls a summary narrative as opposed to a fully developed story narrative. Summary narratives switch between story paragraphs and explanatory passages. If you use good transitions (like Swanson in the above example), you'll get away with a lot of explanation, despite readers disliking it. Different authors have given these summary narratives different names. The first German science journalism professor Winfried Göpfert calls it the "AB-structure", and Michelle Nijhuis calls it the "layer cake" structure (that's my preferred term, probably because of my sweet tooth). This is by far the most common structure for science features, because in most cases, you don't have all the story elements. When you do, it's usually a profile you're writing, with all the necessary plot points like inciting incident and point of insight, climax and resolution.

Summary narratives work differently from full story narratives: you start a story with a graspable, scenic example that highlights your theme. Then you transition to the nut graph. Between the explanatory passages, you advance the story arc. You end your article with the final piece of the story arc and pay off the dramatic question that you set up in the beginning (Pitzer 2011). Even if you don't have a full narrative, you can use the storytelling elements that you gathered through your reporting. Sometimes, that's not much. If all you got is an anecdote, tell half of it (protagonist and complication) in your lead. Write all of the explanatory passages, and then, at the end, you finish the anecdote (resolution). That's a bookend narrative. You will get away with all that explanation, because right at the start, you've pushed your audience into narrative mode.

The *Wall Street Journal formula* is very similar to this approach, and it's easy to remember (Figure 4.2). First, it starts with an anecdote that illustrates the theme. Second, it states the theme explicitly (that's in the nut graph). Third, it answers questions of relevance and topicality. After this, no reader should think: "so what?" The next sections then add details and prove the theme. This part is a bit like an essay, where you present proof for the single ideas. The final section then answers why this is happening and provides an outlook or proposes a solution (adapted from Mencher 2011).

Narratives in science

Bringing science and story together is not exactly a new thing. Although anecdotal evidence is frowned upon in science (when it becomes a fallacy: for good reason), and despite some scientists discounting storytelling, certain disciplines acknowledge the power of stories and utilise narratives as part of qualitative research methodologies. In this section, we're going to have a look at which disciplines employ narratives and why. Narratives are not only used as a qualitative

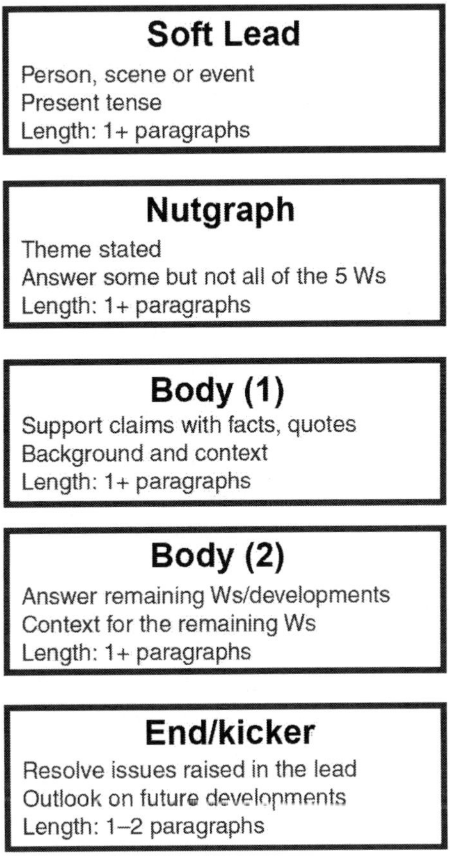

Soft Lead

Person, scene or event
Present tense
Length: 1+ paragraphs

Nutgraph

Theme stated
Answer some but not all of the 5 Ws
Length: 1+ paragraphs

Body (1)

Support claims with facts, quotes
Background and context
Length: 1+ paragraphs

Body (2)

Answer remaining Ws/developments
Context for the remaining Ws
Length: 1+ paragraphs

End/kicker

Resolve issues raised in the lead
Outlook on future developments
Length: 1–2 paragraphs

Figure 4.3 The *Wall Street Journal* story formula
This formula incorporates many more story elements than the inverted pyramid. The most important elements are the anecdotal lead, and the nut graph.
Source: Martin W. Angler.

research tool but also as a means to evaluate research. This is where it's getting interesting if you think about research's societal impact (the appendix will show more on that). Two environmental researchers have conducted a study into how narratives can help evaluate citizen science projects. You can see citizen science itself as a unique form of science communication. The goal of such evaluations is to assess how well a science communication initiative has fared and then improve it where necessary. Current practices of science communication evaluation haven't addressed properly how participants' education and attitude changes during and after participating in a citizen science project. If you collect participants' narratives, you may be able to understand their experience in context and then feed that back into future project designs. Using narratives, you could understand "context-based evaluations through time-oriented structures (event-focused, causal, temporal) revealing how changes occur and evolve from a personal perspective" (Constant &

Roberts 2017:4). For me, all the necessary story elements are there, especially protagonists and change. The authors go on and define a number of narrative criteria. Not only does storytelling increase information uptake, it also weaves the newly acquired knowledge into one's personal beliefs and identity. They propose the following ways to collect participants' narratives:

- **Narrative interviews**: in narrative interviews in the social sciences, ask questions using a narrative and semi-structured style. Avoid "how" and "why" questions (they yield generalised responses) and instead ask "what" and "when" questions (they yield more details). Multiple-choice questions are sort of discouraged. Instead, ask participants for examples and allow them to reflect.
- **Photo-essays**: discuss photographs taken during the citizen science project with participants. Participants employ the "photo-voice" method in taking pictures of scenes they associate with the research topic.
- **Research diaries**: these are written daily accounts of how the project unfolded. Let both researchers and participants reflect on their recorded experiences. The diaries could be used in conjunction with photo-essays. Birders already use this method.
- **Storyboarding**: in citizen science, storyboards could be used to let participants answer (using text and/or pictures) open-ended questions during or after a project. This could help determine what they perceive as being scientific.
- **Digital storytelling**: short videos of two or three minutes' length serve as digital stories. Their content: audio recordings of a personal narrative, accompanied by a selection of pictures that are shown one after another. Together with the narrator's voice, this is a powerful mechanism to share their experiences and reflections.

So, taken together, these narrative methods can allow science communication researchers to determine the impact of their research projects, one example being citizen science. But there are other fields outside science communication that employ narratives.

Narrative medicine is one of them, and it deals with improving medical practice by taking patients' stories into account. Rita Charon, physician and director of the "Narrative Medicine" programme at Columbia University has written a book about it (Charon 2004). The idea is that if physicians know the stories of their patients' ailings, then the stories help them better understand the people. Added value: the patients feel understood. In one of her articles, Charon gives an example of a 33-year-old mother who suffers from a disabling illness. Her physician asks her about her son, and she tells him that at seven years of age he has just developed the telltale symptoms. They grieve together, the physician is clearly emotionally involved. Charon argues that medical treatment alone can't get patients to find meaning in their sufferings and grievances. She therefore proposes to minimise the gap between health professionals and their patients by letting them develop narrative competence. By definition, narrative competence "enables the physician to practice medicine with empathy, reflection, professionalism, and trustworthiness" (Charon 2001). She goes further, claiming that narrative knowledge has become increasingly important in nursing, law, history, philosophy, anthropology, sociology and religious studies. In all the fields where it is applied, it helps researchers understand a person's situation over time by finding the meaning in their stories. She also points out that medicine has never really been without narrative, because it's an enterprise where humans help other humans. Listening to the stories of patients with empathy paves the way for physicians to answer the patients' narrative questions like the following (Charon 2001):

- What is wrong with me?
- Why did this happen to me?
- What will become of me?

Charon has more proposals. She adds that the quality of medical research could be improved using narrative practices. While bioethics practice and educational programmes already let their practitioners and students write hone their narrative skills and improve their adoption of patients' perspectives (for example, by writing narratives of their own experiences), other theses still need to be confirmed. For example, do physicians with natural storytelling abilities have an advantage over their "classic" colleagues? Also, and quite importantly, "more and more patients have insisted on achieving a narrative mastery over the events of illness, not only to unburden themselves of painful thoughts and feelings but, more fundamentally, to claim such events as parts, however unwelcome, of their lives" (Charon 2001).

The take-home message here is: science employs narratives at various (if not all) levels. If you want to write about science, you can use narrative techniques. It's legit. Within science itself, narrative techniques are used to conduct and then evaluate science. Some disciplines lend themselves better to it than others. Climate change, for example, employs narrative methods, as Moezzi, Janda and Rotmann (2017) show in their study. As examples of how storytelling can be used in (climate change) research, they present as possible data sources participant observation, "workshops, interviews, conversations, written documents, newspapers, images and internet sources" (Moezzi, Janda & Rotmann 2017:Table 1).

Story shapes

Let's continue with more story structure. I can't emphasise this enough, so once again: it's pretty clear that you can't just lump your raw material into any given story structure. It's the facts, the data you have been reporting and researching that will determine which story structure will be the most apt to figure out how your story works. Some writers draw up their plots to plan and outline their stories. This way, they come up with a skeleton they can later flesh out. Other writers are organised enough thinkers to immediately start writing with the structure implicitly in their minds, right off the bat. Some scholars use story shapes to analyse stories. There are even algorithms that perform such analyses (you'll see one in a minute), which means there must be a programmable, logic system behind them. Indeed, most representations of story structures manifest as two-dimensional line graphs of sorts, where one axis is time and the other one is tension or action (like Freytag's and Hart's). The planner then distributes plot points on that axis. That's it. Plotting and outlining is all about selection and ordering. And rejection.

Investigations practically never result in short pieces. In his book *Story-based Inquiry* (freely available, just Google it), investigative journalist Mark Lee Hunter details how to come up with an appropriate narrative at the end of an extensive investigative journalism project. You can structure your narrative in two ways. First, use a picaresque structure to order events by place, with the characters moving across those places over time. Homer's Odyssey is an example of this structure. On a more contemporary note, Michael Moore tends to use that sort of structure in his documentaries (Hunter 2011). I can't help but think of James Bond movies when I read about this structure. Hunter doesn't really draw his structures as story shapes. If he did, he'd have probably a third axis: tension, time (the regulars) and place. Hunter's second type of narrative sounds familiar: it's the chronological structure, which you should use when ordering your events by time. Ultimately, it's the material you gathered during the reporting that will determine which structure is the best for your story, but "one of these forms is right for your story" (Hunter 2011:66). Here is a short recipe on how to structure narratives. Begin with a moment that hooks the audience. Start in the present, go back in time to show how we got there (past), then bring it all the way back to the present moment (this will allow the readers to absorb the story), and then say where the story is headed to next (the future). As for chronological stories, Hunter advises to not continuously hop back and forward in time, as this confuses the readers. Instead, his "present-past-future" structure reflects and answers the following three questions (Hart 2011):

- Why should I care about the story?
- How did this terrible or wonderful event come about?
- Will it ever be over? How?

While Hunter doesn't draw his story shapes, you've read about somebody who does in the section about story arcs: Jack Hart.

Hart's structure is very close to Freytag's dramatic structure. Hart makes a few specific claims as for the chronology. First, nonfiction narratives follow chronological structures most of the time. Second, the order of the events as you depict them, corresponds largely to the order the events actually unfolded. In narratology terms: the "fabula" (how the events unfolded in real life) overlaps with the "sujet" (how you order the events). What you can do is start at the crisis point (cajoling the reader into the middle of the action of a struggling character), then work your way chronologically from the beginning back to the present (i.e. the scene you started with) and then finish the story chronologically from there until the end (Hart 2011). It is reminiscent of

Hunter's description of the chronological structure. Here's a short breakdown of Hart's (2011) five phases:

1 **Exposition**: character and protagonist definition. Who are they? Just give readers enough information to understand who the characters are and what the complications in their lives are. Address some of the basic physical traits of your characters, some personality aspects (show don't tell). Do not expose everything about your protagonist, as exposition is the enemy of narrative. Instead, blend: "You launch action immediately and then blend the exposition into it, submerging it in modifiers, subordinate clauses, appositives, and the like" (Hart 2011:27). You can use techniques like foreshadowing to hint at bad things going down later on. You can also afford to weave in one or two paragraphs of unblended backstory. The inciting incident is the first plot point and a clear line of action that stops the exposition and starts the rising action. This is where the protagonist has to engage with the complication.

2 **Rising action**: most of the plot points are contained in this segment of the story. Each plot point has one job: spin the story into a new direction. They complicate the protagonist's life and raise the stakes. You keep throwing into the story a variation of smaller and bigger questions to be resolved, and you'll resolve them one by one, oscillating between the rising and falling interest of your readers. At the end, you will reveal the answer to the big dramatic question or mystery. End section, paragraphs and chapters using cliff-hangers, that is leave the reader dangling at the exact moment the protagonist is in danger, facing an unresolved problem.

3 **Crisis**: Greek: peripeteia, the reversal of fortune. That's a twist that in the traditional three-act structure throws the protagonist into a huge problem. Her life or the fulfilment of her goal or both is seriously at stake. The protagonist is in the greatest danger now, and things don't look good for her. When you outline your story, you can start it either before the inciting incident or here, at the crisis point. Beware of too many flashbacks or flash-forwards, especially because the audience needs to live through the story. If you disrupt that experience too often, it reminds them that the structure has been orchestrated by you, the writer.

4 **Climax (resolution)**: that's the moment the dramatic question is resolved. It's usually a single event. The protagonist either fails to achieve her goal (tragedy), or she succeeds (comedy). Doesn't matter. It's always a story.

5 **Falling action (denouement)**: answer the remaining open questions, and then finish the story. Tension is lowest at this point, and you don't want to drag it. That's why Hart's curve is skewed to the right.

If you want to have a look at fiction story shapes, Kurt Vonnegut is your man. In 1947, he submitted his master's thesis titled "The Fluctuation between Good and Evil in Simple Tales" to the University of Chicago. It got rejected, and Vonnegut left his alma mater without a degree (he later obtained it in 1971). In his thesis, Vonnegut allegedly had identified six types of story shapes that he would often bring up during later story seminars.

The story types essentially depend on how a character's fortune develops over time. Vonnegut shows the basic coordinate system in which they reside as a two-dimensional graph, with the y-axis ranging from ill fortune (bottom) to good fortune (top) and the x-axis ranging from the beginning (left) to the end (right) of the story. He then draws a curve for each type of story. You should watch one of the videos, notably the 1995 version, which is really fun to watch (Vonnegut 1995). In the video, Vonnegut shows three of the shapes, "man in a hole" (fall-rise), "boy meets girl" (rise-fall-rise) and "Cinderella (rise-fall-rise, but from a lower starting point)". He also states that his shapes could be fed into computers. Aha!

That is exactly what a team of US-Australian data scientists did: they ran 1,327 stories obtained from Project Gutenberg through an algorithm and checked tens of thousands of words in those stories for their emotional semantics in order to determine whether they would fit into the following six categories, which are based on Vonnegut's (and other) story shapes (Reagan *et al.* 2016):

1   Rags to riches (rise)
2   Tragedy, or riches to rags (fall)
3   Man in a hole (fall-rise)
4   Icarus (rise-fall)
5   Cinderella (rise-fall-rise)
6   Oedipus (fall-rise-fall)

Reagan and his colleagues used a (digital) hedonometer to gauge the happiness factor of these words and find noticeable clusters and spikes of where they occurred. The algorithm draws graphs (which you can find in the study and on the hedonometer website, fully link provided in the Links section of this chapter). For example, "The Wind in the Willows" follows the "Oedipus" structure. "The Magic of Oz" follows a "Man in a Hole" (fall-rise) structure. The researchers went a step further and tried to measure the success of a story based on how many times readers had downloaded it. The first four story shapes (including "Icarus") were the most prominent ones among all stories they had tested. But those were not the most successful (in terms of downloads). Instead, "Icarus", "Oedipus" and "Man in a hole" style stories were most often downloaded (Reagan *et al.* 2016). Although Vonnegut had no possibility to test as extensively, he's right in the video when he says about "Man in a hole", while he draws the graph: "Somebody gets into trouble, gets out of it again. People love that story! They never get sick of it!"

Back to science. Reagan and his colleagues were inspired by Vonnegut, alright. A team of researchers in Canada was in turn inspired by Reagan and Vonnegut and came up with three story shapes that are particularly apt for science (Figure 4.4). Almost all scientists they talked to confirm that the road to discoveries involves a lot of problems they had to solve. The challenge is to find these and include them in the story as plot points. So of course, it's again down to selection and rejection.

But without further ado, here are the story types that Green, Grorud-Colvert and Mannix (2018) identified:

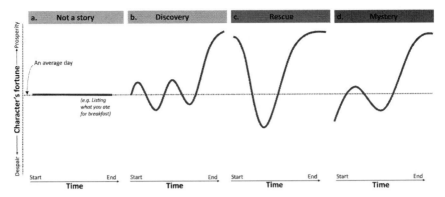

Figure 4.4 The relative shapes of select paradigms for science stories
Solid black lines show the relationship between the main character's fortune and the progression of a story from start to finish, relative to an average day (dotted line). A good story needs a character that experiences both highs and lows, moving from despair to prosperity.
Source: Green, Grorud-Colvert & Mannix (2018). License: CC BY 4.0.

- **Discovery**: the reader is taken on a journey through successes and failures of experiments, analyses. The story then slowly moves towards the big discovery (not unlike the variations), which should be sort of an epiphany, potentially exceeding researchers' and readers' expectations.
- **Rescue**: science in service to society. Science solves a problem that affects society, so they call it also "hero to the rescue". Such stories present a problem and then show how science has a solution for them. Here the key is that the audience enters the story when the character's fortunes are high. Then they experience a loss, and then science comes to help and solve the issue, potentially inspiring hope and action.
- **Mystery**: unexplained phenomena have always instilled the curiosity in scientists. But also the scientific process itself can be a mystery story, as testing hypotheses and following leads can yield unexpected findings. In terms of character fortune, the story starts where a sort of an inciting incident has happened that throws the protagonist into misery. What unfolds then are a series of complications the character has to solve in order to get back to normal life. These are science detective stories. The story we'll analyse in the last section of this chapter is a true detective story, so have a look at it!

Creating tension

Imagine you're sitting in a movie theatre. Lights dimmed down, the buttery smell of popcorn lingers in the air. The opening sequence starts with a bit of backstory. This appears on the silver screen:

Camp Crystal Lake. 1958. Local mom Mrs. Vorhees kills all but one camp counselors to avenge her son Jason, who drowned the year before because the then counselors were having sex. So whoever has sex, dies. The sole survivor of the killing spree, Annie, eventually chops off Vorhees' head.

That's it. End of story. Sorry for the spoiler, but you had since 1980 to watch this movie. If you are not familiar with it: It's "Friday the 13th", Sean Cunningham's infamous slasher film. What have I just done? I've ruined the movie for you (if you haven't seen it yet) because I removed all the tension from it and gave away all plot twists right at the beginning. This is information that the actual movie withholds and reveals little by little. In fact, especially horror movies are really good at this. "Friday the 13th" doesn't reveal who the murderer is right away. It makes you wonder. It makes you ask yourself: who could it be? It makes you dread the monster by not knowing. Good horror movies are really good at this. You are scared of the monster, because you don't know what or who it is. You don't really see it. You just feel that something is off. The moment it is revealed, the terror actually decreases.

My attempt at summing up the movie removes all tension and terror from it. It's a matter-of-fact description that answers the basic journalistic questions: What (murder), when (1958), where (Camp Crystal Lake), why (revenge) and who (Mrs. Vorhees). I'll spare you the how, in case you haven't seen it. Hence, my description is like a hard news lead. Straight "facts", right away, without any sort of embellishment.

At this point, all spectators would walk out of the theatre, asking for their money to be reimbursed. And rightfully so. Movies frequently last for 120 or more minutes, but you have taken away already all of the tension during the opening. The spectators have nothing more to expect in that movie, they know it all. What would they wait for, now? The same is true of longform journalistic writing. You need to make the reader wonder what happens next. If they don't, you've lost them. You can't give away all the crucial information right at the beginning, like in an inverted pyramid-story. Good stories withhold pivotal moments that cajole the story into a new direction (plot points), which keeps readers turning pages, but that alone is not tension.

So how do you do that? For starters, something needs to be at stake. If a life's at stake, that's a lot, but the risk of not achieving a noble goal is just as good. Tension emerges at the sentence level. Tension-evoking sentences spark a question. You do this by showing or telling readers there is something more that they need to know but not revealing right away what it is. Filmmakers use symbols for that. Do you remember the 1999 horror flick "Blair Witch Project"? It used wooden stick figures to hint at and foreshadow the presence of a lurking evil. Or the 2017 survival horror film "The Ritual". Whenever the party of friends encounters pagan symbols carved into tree barks, that means trouble. Yes, these are horror movies. But you can apply the same techniques to writing non-fiction narratives. Do that once or twice – show a symbol and then let something happen, that is – and you've conditioned your readers like Pavlov's dogs. The moment of tension is created when readers start anticipating. Whenever they see the symbol, they'll ask themselves: "I know something's about to happen – but what?"

Foreshadowing is pretty similar. It's a literary technique. It's hinting at something that readers then might suspect will happen. You can again use symbols, or you can let your characters do the work, like Shakespeare's Romeo, when he's reluctant to attend the Capulets' party, fearing this might lead to his premature death (which does happen in the end anyway). It's the difference between being pretty sure something is going to happen and actually knowing it for sure.

Another way to create tension is the pacing of a story. You control how fast your story progresses. Good stories vary their rhythm and hence become dynamic. Gradually shortening your sentences increases the tension, readers will expect your story to move toward either a plot point or the climax. Your audience is used to anticipating that. A fast pace signals action to follow, a slow pace calmness. Once you've figured out your story structure, think about the pacing and where you want to build tension into it. You want to raise the tension before and not right at the plot points. Increasing the pace through rhythm is a good device to do so. Have a look at the following example. Science writer Christopher Solomon writes about a veterinarian who finds an otter. He skillfully creates tension by using a number of literary techniques:

> Two weeks earlier, salmon set-netters had found the otter on the beach on the far side of Barbara Point. The dying creature was too weak to remove a stone lodged in her jaws.
>
> (Solomon 2017)

Solomon starts off with a flashback to set the scene. The description alone of what happened ("had found the otter") sparks a question. You don't just find an otter. So something must have happened. What? Then, the second sentence amplifies that itch to know what happened. Two words alone ("dying creature") are enough to raise the dramatic question: what becomes of the otter? Is it going to live or die? The following paragraphs in the story (I've put a link in the "References" section) further tighten the tension by increasing the story's pace. Solomon shortens the sentences. Anticipation, withholding information, pacing. It's all there, although Solomon doesn't use any symbols. It keeps you reading.

Like Solomon, you're the author who knows what happened in real life, and you know the exact chronological order the events unfolded. But that doesn't mean you're going to tell the story that way (that's the difference between fabula and syuzhet). Start at a point on the narrative arc that makes the readers wonder what happens next. The main device to make the audience wonder what happens next is a cliffhanger. When you write a layer-cake feature, where you alternate between story and explanatory paragraphs, every time you transition from the story to the explanation, you risk losing your readers. Television writers know this best, because every time a commercial break interrupts the story, they risk losing their audience. That's where cliffhangers come into play. You can pull this off in a number of ways. Stop the action when your character seems to almost reach her goal. Stop it when she is in great danger, when something is severely at stake. Stop the action when there is a major revelation (soap operas do this a lot).

Patricia Luna's story on air pollution in Chile accomplishes something like that in the first paragraph. The protagonist's son is in danger, and the audience doesn't know how his story ends.

Cause and effect

We already discussed in the chapter on story elements how important events and their order are. Here, I'll make a case on what story events are and how you can order them for effect. If one event causes another, they are easily connectable. Also, readers are able to follow those event sequences easily. Better still, cause and effect relationships lend meaning to events. Why would you include them in the story if they have no effect on it? Or if they aren't the result of another event? In that sense, performing a simple test, namely asking yourself whether a particular event you want to include in your story is causing another event, or being caused by one, is a valuable countermeasure to waffling and unnecessary digressions. It keeps you on track and your story running. This is valid also for non-story passages, like explanatory writing. Consider the following example from Bill Schutt's highly praised non-fiction book *Cannibalism: A Perfectly Natural History*. In chapter four of his book, he describes the natural behaviour of golden hamsters and their stressors. The passage runs two paragraphs long and increases in tension as it moves on. The first paragraph merely describes the basic facts about golden hamsters. The second paragraph then moves on to showing readers the hamsters' stressors based on the previous description. Tension increases as readers get a clue as for where he's going. And then he delivers: "As a result of this laundry list of captivity-related stresses, female golden hamsters, especially younger ones, frequently cannibalize their pups" (Schutt 2018). Cause and effect. Right there.

Cause and effect glues together events. It is one of the driving factors that keeps the audience reading, listening and watching your piece. It is one of the factors that makes storytelling so persuasive. Everything seems logical, everything seems connected. But if writers misuse the technique, if they only imply cause and effect without real-life causality to back it, then they're misleading the audience. You can frequently find this false cause and effect used in fake news stories, like in anti-vaxxers' stories. They narrate a series of events, for example a child getting a flu shot. The child then unlearns how to speak and move overnight. The parents' conclusion: it must have been the flu shot that caused it. As "evidence" to back the claim, they produce facts like flu shots containing minimal amounts of theoretically harmful substances like mercury. I am writing "theoretically", because it depends on the dose whether they actually do cause damage or not. Once established, such an interlinked series of events is so powerful in evoking the audience's emotions that it is very difficult to debunk a new myth. This is also known as the "post hoc ergo propter hoc" or simply "post hoc" fallacy. In other words: implying causality where in reality only correlation exists. You wouldn't believe how many times I've heard the story of Grand Aunt Lina who chain-smoked and drank schnapps every single day and lived to almost 105. Heck, she even danced a waltz at her 100th birthday. So chain-smoking and drinking must have no effect on staying healthy, right? Wrong. That's why anecdotal evidence is largely frowned upon in science.

But let's not forget we are wired for story. Most storytelling books point this out, and there is a humongous amount of scientific evidence to support this. Two Australian researchers Muurlink (a psychologist) and McAllister (an anthropologist) state that we have a tendency to interpret causality into actually random events that happen in proximity to each other (for example, when they happen one after another). They also refer to a study claiming that we're essentially unable to consider events as independent (Muurlink & McAllister 2015). While this is a huge pitfall and can lead us to draw all the wrong conclusions, it is also where the persuasive power of story lies:

> That aspect of the story that sees events that are not just linked in a random series, but linked in a sequence that implies cause and effect, is also likely to partially explain the power of the story.
>
> (Muurlink and McAllister 2015:4)

Think of story events this way: you have a string with green beads. They're all beaded onto the string one after the other. Every bead is a story event, plot point or not. What you're holding in your hands is a story, perhaps it's the actual sequence of events as they have unfolded. As a storyteller, what you would do is take all the beads off the string, bead them up again but alter their sequence in a way that is most effective for story. The problem with the actual sequence of events is that it often deflates all the tension already at the outset. Narrative journalist and former *Oregonian* editor Jack Hart illustrates this in his book *Storycraft*, where he advises his readers to start with an "in medias res" opening, right at the crisis point of the narrative structure of the story. Muurlink and McAllister (2015) call the different strings by their names in narratology, "fabula" (the actual chronological sequence of events as they occurred) and "sujet" (often: "syuzhet", that's the plot); and they add that in the latter the events "are given meaning and told" (Muurlink and McAllister 2015: 2). While that is a perfectly acceptable definition, the ordering of events alone does not lend a story its meaning. Theme does. That's the golden thread that runs through a story and helps you select the events. All of that doesn't mean that the two authors are story advocates. Muurlink and McAllister are critical in their analysis of whether narrative and science can be married, and one of their criticisms is whether a cause and effect chain can actually explain all of science.

Nor am I saying that you should find cause and effect when there is none. Of course this is not a formula for every type of scientific research. But in some cases, it is obvious that one event caused another. For example, the *New Yorker* story about the demon core, a plutonium experiment gone terribly wrong in 1946 in a Los Alamos lab, where physicist Louis Slotin had accidentally dropped a tamper on a plutonium core, causing a nuclear reaction that turned out to be much larger than intended. Slotin and one of his co-workers died, which is described as a different event in the story. Both are clearly dependent events, and they also occur one after another, temporally speaking. It's obvious you wouldn't present the accident without (at least at some point) showing the audience also event that caused it. It would appear to have happened out of the blue and let readers wonder why it occurred in the first place.

A final note on cause and effect. It is good practice to depict the cause first and then the effect, not vice versa. If you describe a piece of research action, don't explain why the researcher did it after describing the action. Instead, describe the researcher's need, and then describe the action that follows that need. Unless, of course, you want to spare the "why" in order to increase tension. As always, the exception proves the rule.

Narrative structure in scientific writing

There are many differences between scientific, scholarly and science writing for lay audiences. Language, style and structure are three of the most important differences. That's a pity, because the research process in and of itself already contains the most important storytelling elements. And most of all: it hasn't always been like this. Scientific journals have been around for a mere 350 years. Compulsory peer review involving external reviewers gained a foothold only in the middle of the previous century. Nowadays, the most common way to structure a scientific manuscript is called IMRAD, an acronym for the sections in a manuscript an author should cover. They are:

- Introduction
- Methods
- Results
- (And)
- Discussion

Since "And" is not a section, this list boils down to a mere four sections. IMRAD isn't an old structure, either. It's a mere 100 years old. In medicine papers, it's been around since the 1940s and dominates most manuscripts since the 1980s (Sollaci & Pereira 2004). Major publishers release their own guidelines about what the IMRAD structure is and how authors are expected to follow it. *Springer Nature* is one of them (Nature and other publishers have their own guidelines, sometimes ordered slightly differently), claiming in their guidelines that this structure (Springer 2019):

- Gives a logical flow to the content
- Makes journal manuscripts predictable and easy to read
- Provides a "map" so that readers can quickly find content of interest in any manuscript
- Reminds authors what content should be included

Now, if you've ever read a study, you may be inclined to agree with some points, like the last: the structure "reminds authors of what content should be included". But does it add a logical flow to the content? Hardly. Does it make journal manuscripts predictable? Yes, absolutely. You know what to find where, at least in most cases. Does it make them easy to read? No, here I will make a case for just superimposing "some" sort of structure on a piece of writing doesn't automatically make it an easy read. Blabbering on right at the beginning about what needs to be done in a given scientific field, what research has been done and where the research gap is that this study tries to fill is clearly an important part of the scientific method. But it doesn't make for an easy read. At all.

And yet, it's all there, if you believe scientist-turned-storyteller Randy Olson: "It is the structure of a story, which has a beginning (I), middle (M&R), and end (D)" (Olson 2015:6). He also points out that early scientific manuscripts in 1665 (that's when scientific publishing started) were much more descriptive and read like literature. They then moved on to a tripartite structure in the 1800s until finally ending up with the IMRAD structure in the 1900s (Olson 2015). He then goes on to explain how you can use the IMRAD elements, which I'll cover in the next chapter in more detail.

Biologist and science storytelling teacher Sara ElShafie goes a step further. She draws a clear parallel between the IMRAD structure and Freytag's pyramid. Specifically, she writes that a scientific manuscript's introduction corresponds to Freytag's exposition, the methods to the rising action, the results to the climax, the analysis to the falling action and the discussion and conclusion to the denouement of the story. So, Olson and ElShafie agree that there are similarities in story structure. They also point out that the classic hero's journey is the way most stories are written and consumed, which in turn obviously means that we're all used to that kind of structure. Fairy tales, movies and novels are written this way. Kevin Padian, professor of integrative biology at the University of California, Berkeley, draws on Propp's sequence of events of stories. Propp (who is also one of the narratologists who defined "fabula" and "syuzhet") had analysed 100 classic Russian folk tales and tried to identify a common pattern, the morphology of folk tales – not unlike what Joseph Campbell did (just with more stories). Propp found 31 common structural elements, and Padian outlines a nine-step, adapted version of it. Scientific endeavours can be seen from that perspective, following that pattern, Padian argues, and he comes up with an example:

When scientists do research, it can be thought of as a quest, and the 'gift' of funding (NSF, NIH, etc.) to develop our research data "transforms" our question into a "triumph" of an answer. That follows classic narrative structure.

(Padian 2018:1226)

While this reads legit, Padian continues by saying that the way scientists actually present their research is far from telling a real story but rather a perversion of traditional story structures. The shape of story can differ depending on the scientific discipline, and he also investigates what makes a good science story: it can be based on beliefs, but it has to be both testable and tested in order to be a science story. Otherwise it's just a story (Padian 2018). The way scientists translate their research into journal papers are anti-narratives. Explaining why you undertake your research, giving readers a sense of discovery and hence also an understanding of the importance of your work and improves the story part (Padian 2018). If you're a scientist, you can and should incorporate such aspects into your scientific manuscripts. If you're a science writer, you can and should look out for such elements, starting from the abstract.

So, can scientific writing structures be married with classic storytelling techniques? Yes and no. It really does depend on the topic and the elements you already have in your study. If you're having second thoughts about the selection process, think of this: whatever you put in a (non-narrative) scientific paper has already undergone a selection process. There is no way you could possibly fit years' worth of research into 30 or 40 pages. Remember when had a look at the two ways our cognition works (Bruner 1986)? We have a rational mode of thinking for logic, and we have a narrative mode for making sense of the world and giving meaning to events. What makes the difference is cause and effect. This even reflects in how science is conveyed. We either have logical science communication that does not imply cause and effect-relationships between events, or we have storytelling that does indeed that (Dahlstrom 2014). We are wired to like the narrative mode. If we misuse it or don't pay attention, we might run into falsely attributing cause and effect between events when no such relationship exists. But carefully applied, cause and effect is one of the most powerful devices to structure our stories, regardless of whether it is a scientific manuscript or a popular science story, or even a fictional one that you're handling. So what's in for scientists when they use storytelling elements? The obvious advantage is that more people will understand and remember them. In scholarly writing, there is growing evidence that utilising story elements increases the citation count of journal papers, at least for some scientific disciplines. Let me point you to one particularly interesting study in that field. In writing papers on climate change, Hillier, Kelly and Klinger (2016) found that the following six narrative elements can be linked to the citation count:

1   **Setting**: specifically mentioning time and space helps readers create a mental image.
2   **Narrative perspective**: the presence of the narrator. This can be first-, second- or third-person narrators. First-person point of views are usually most effective in immersing readers into a piece of text. In scientific writing, you would express this by using pronouns like I, me, my, we, our etc.
3   **Sensory language**: sensory and emotional words help establish a personal identity and are appealing to readers.
4   **Conjunctions**: temporal or causal ordering of events are crucial for narratives. Conjunctions are the way to express this, so they looked at the presence of conjunctions that signify cause and effect, contrast or temporal ordering.

5 **Connectivity**: essentially, logical links between ideas. Here, they had a look at how often scientific paper authors used words from previous sentences in the following ones to connect the two?

6 **Appeal to reader**: the moral of the story (we previously called this theme). The take-home message, a call for action and an idea of why the authors tell the story.

These are the six factors they tested for, but not all turned out to be influential. If you look carefully at them, you'll easily recognise the elements we've discussed before as the essential story elements. Pay attention: two out of six list elements explicitly deal with narrative structure, namely conjunctions and connectivity. That's a third, so quite a significant role for narrative structure in my book. So what's the researchers' final verdict? "Articles featuring more narrative writing styles are more often cited. This effect is independent of year of publication, number of authors, or abstract length" (Hillier, Kelly & Klinger 2016). The four actually influential factors are: sensory language, conjunctions, connectivity and appeal to readers. So half of the factors go to narrative structure! Also, and I'll definitely close this section with that, they report they are surprised that professional science communication utilises rather expository writing styles instead of narrative ones and that it assumes citation frequency depends on the strength of the science alone. Are you surprised? Just look at how fake news spreads. It's almost always (unsubstantiated) stories. How does science counter this? With facts and figures. When I run my science storytelling workshops, I often start with three or four fake stories, mostly from anti-vaxxers. I also show Ian Gromowski's narrative, a baby who died in 2007. His parents attributed his death to a Hepatitis B shot, but that was never proved (Shelby & Ernst 2013). Then I come up with how renowned newspapers counter these stories. They come up with fancy graphs and numbers. These may stoke the audience's cognitive brain regions, but not their emotional ones. That's what fake stories achieve by drawing on story techniques. They have protagonists, complications, stakes, resolutions. Also, do you think we make cognitive, rational decisions? Think again. What neuroscientists found out in their landmark 2000 study is that emotions have a huge impact and in fact are a crucial factor when we make decisions. If the part of our prefrontal cortex is damaged, where emotions arise and where we make decisions, we're seriously impaired in making decisions (Bechara, Damasio & Damasio 2000).

Case study: A science detective story

In this section, let's have a look at story structure in action. It's a piece published in *WIRED* about toxicologist James Scott, written by editor Adam Rogers in 2011. The 3,500-word long story is written like a traditional detective story. I'd strongly recommend that you open the piece in your browser now (I've put the link in the "Links" section) and read it as we go along here. I've numbered the paragraphs sequentially (P1, P2, etc.) and distinguish between story and expository paragraphs as well as commenting in abbreviated form on his style. So let's see how Rogers pulls off his masterpiece.

P1, P2: Setting. This is exposition, written using a lot of sensory language.

P2: Protagonist introduced and connected with the setting: the detective and his first job.

P3: Story. Problem statement. The client. Introducing another character through conflict with neighbors, which is elegant. Rogers outright states the character "had a problem".

Hypothesis stated ("black mold comes from distillery").

P4: Story. Detective arrives at "crime scene" and collects evidence. Again, very sensory.

P5: A bit of science explanation, then Rogers swivels back to story. The antagonist now has a name, it's a fungus.

P6: Greatly written, short paragraph: Conflict, plot point, new revelation and dialogue at the same time. Very condensed.

P7: Explanation. How does fermentation work?

P8: More explanation. How does distillation work? Note the transition.

P9: Background on distillation. This is essentially a digression (relevant). History of distillation. Elegantly done by nesting a story as background into the higher story. Nice!

P10: More explanation. Note how the three explanatory paragraphs vary in style and rhythm (mainly in length, that is), in order to not put off the reader.

P11: More background. This explains how additives flow into distillates.

P12: Again, background. He's showing conflict (evaporation and connected loss).

P13: Again, explanation. By now it should be clear that the explanatory paragraphs follow a cause and effect chain. This paragraph shows why the premium buyers emerged.

P14: Explanation.

P15: Story. What sparked the protagonist's interest in the subject?

P16: Scott's story. A bit more insight on how his dorm looked like. The goal clearly is to underpin his commitment to fungus research.

P17: Explanation, more exposition on the field of mycology. It's not very attractive.

P18: Explanation. How does naming fungi work in mycology?

P19: Explanation and story, smartly blended into each other. Rogers lets another interviewee add the background. This is a strong way to provide insight into a character.

P20: Point of insight, this is an important plot point!

P21: Now we're really back on the story track. Note the sensory language and the similes. Also, this paragraph is crucial, because it ties in Scott's knowledge with how he can apply it to solve "the case". Now some of the previous explanatory information makes sense. Note the logic and cause and effect structure.

P22: Story. Scott's attempt at solving the issue. This contains action. He actually does something and tries his own approach.

P23: Story. This is a setback. The solution didn't work.

P24: Story. Scott doesn't give up but feeds the lazy-growing fungi with Whiskey (this ties in with **P20**).

P25: Story. There still is an open question. The detective/protagonist needs to find a connection as for where the fungi get their food from (ethanol). He finds it through consulting another character, a sommelier.

P26: Story, mixed with exposition. Scott continues his research and finds another candidate for the culprit. He orders a sample to verify or dispel his hunch. Sort of a crisis point here. Tension building up as readers wonder: Will he solve it now?

P27: Story. Action happening, as Scott performs another experiment.

P28: Story. Another setback. Pivotal moment again. Logical connection between the false culprit and why it couldn't work is drawn.

P29: Scott seeks more advice. Do note how this paragraph ends on a cliffhanger. You don't get an idea if this new (third) hunch will work or his travel to the Canadian expert is going to be in vain. It ends on "packed his bags". So it's another crisis point.

P30: Story (character and scene-setting in action). Another character is introduced with very sensory language and careful scene-setting. The comparison with Gandalf is no accident, as is the detailed description. This must mean something.

P31: Story. Protagonist and mentor dig into the archive. They find a potential candidate. But no confirmation yet (cliffhanger. "it seemed like a match" leaves it open).

P32: Story. A reversal of fortune. The finding doesn't give them clarity, yet. Identifying the fungus is difficult, as it has been named using a catch-all term. But now the digression on naming fungi becomes clear.

P33: Story. Scott does more research and finds: The fungus has been misidentified, misnamed and mistranscribed several times. This seems to be the lowest point in the story. Is this the real crisis?

P34: Story. The wrongly named "fungus" from previous research matches with the sample from the distillery. But Scott and Hughes have to rename it – it's a new species. This is the point of insight. The climax! But before they can name it, they need to grow a culture to confirm it. This, too, is part of the nomenclature process. Again, they succeed.

P35: Story. The two researchers name the new fungus genus after its initial discoverer: Baudoinia.

P36: Story. Now, after the climax, it's time to tie up loose ends. How does the story end for the neighbors? The company who bought the distillery pays for washing the affected houses once a year. Not satisfying in terms of actually solving the issue.

P37: Story. Scott doesn't give up. He wants to go deeper (like a true detective). Other researchers pick up interest and study and explain how it possibly survives wide temperature ranges.

P38: Explanation. Evolution might explain how the fungus strives in urban environments. Although a bit lengthy, still effective.

P39: Story. In perfect movie mode, although tension is low at this point. What became of Scott? He is tenured and still researchers the black fungus - but in another location.

P40: Story. So he collects a sample to research the black fungus.

P41: Story. Another plot twist (perfect!) This opens a new story – because the fungus is not Baudoinia – new challenge!

Note how Rogers introduces more and more "story" style paragraphs the closer we get to the real crisis and story climax. This is perfectly in line with, for example, action movies that introduce more action the closer you get to the grand finale. It makes sense, because readers are prone to lose attention during explanatory sections, not during well-crafted action (in our case: "story") sequences.

Review questions

- What are the five stages of a story arc?
- How do news reports and magazine features differ in structure?
- What is the Wall Street Formula?
- How are narratives used in medicine?
- Which story shapes did Kurt Vonnegut define?
- How do tension and stakes work together?
- What is foreshadowing?
- What is the difference between "fabula" and "syuzhet"?
- What is the IMRAD structure?

Links

"Hegel's Dialectics" (Stanford Encyclopedia of Philosophy): https://plato.sta nford.edu/entries/hegel-dialectics/

"The Hedonometer Rating" (Hedonometer.org): http://hedonometer.org/ books/v2/v3/

"The Dan Brown Plot Generator" (Slate) https://slate.com/news-and-politics/ 2009/09/the-dan-brown-sequel-generator.html

"Unraveling the Mystery of the Canadian Whiskey Fungus" (*WIRED*): https:// www.wired.com/2011/05/ff-angelsshare/

References

BBC (no date) "Form, structure and language," BBC Bitesize GCSE [Online]. Available at: http s://www.bbc.co.uk/bitesize/guides/zpdq2hv/revision/2 (date accessed 7 October 2019).

Bechara, A., Damasio, H. & Damasio, A.R. (2000) "Emotion, decision making and the orbitofrontal cortex," *Cerebral cortex*, vol. 10, no. 3, 295–307.

Blake, M. & Bailey, S. (2013) *Writing the horror movie*. New York: Bloomsbury.

Bruner, E. (1986) " Ethnography as narrative," in: Turner, V.W. & Bruner, E. (eds.) *The anthropology of experience*. Urbana: University of Illinois Press, 139–155.

Charon, R. (2004) *Narrative Medicine: Honoring the Stories of Illness*. Oxford: Oxford University Press.

Charon, R. (2001) "Narrative Medicine A Model for Empathy, Reflection, Profession, and Trust," *JAMA: The Journal of the American Medical Association*, vol. 286, no. 15, 1897–1902.

Cohn, N. (2013) "Visual Narrative Structure," *Cognitive Science*, vol. 34, 413–452.

Constant, N. & Roberts, L. (2017) "Narratives as a mode of research evaluation in citizen science: understanding broader science communication impacts," *JCOM Journal of Science Communication*, vol. 16, no. 04, A03 [Online]. Available at: https://jcom.sissa.it/archive/16/04/JCOM_1604_2017_A03 (date accessed 3 August 2019).

Dahlstrom, M.F. (2014) "Using narratives and storytelling to communicate science with nonexpert audiences," *Proceedings of the National Academy of Sciences*, vol. 111, supplement 4, 13614–13620.

ElShafie, S. (2018) "Making science meaningful for broad audiences through stories," *Integrative and Comparative Biology*, vol. 58, no. 6, 1213–1223.

Gefter, A. (2015) "The Man Who Tried To Redeem The World With Logic," *Nautilus* [Online]. Available at: http://nautil.us/issue/21/information/the-man-who-tried-to-redeem-the-world-with-logic (date accessed 5 August 2019).

Green, S.J., Grorud-Colvert, K., & Mannix, H. (2018) "Uniting science and stories: perspectives on the value of storytelling for communicating science," *Facets Journal* [Online]. Available at: https://www.facetsjournal.com/doi/full/10.1139/facets-2016-0079 (date accessed 4 August 2019).

Hart, J. (2011) *Storycraft*. Chicago: Chicago University Press.

Hillier, A., Kelly, R.P. & Klinger, T. (2016) "Narrative style influences citation frequency in climate change science," *PloS one*, vol. 11, no. 12, e0167983.

Hunter, M.L. (2011) "Story-Based Inquiry: A manual for investigative journalists," Unesco [Online]. Available at: https://unesdoc.unesco.org/ark:/48223/pf0000193078 (date accessed 4 August 2019).

Jones, M.D. & Crow, D.A. (2017) "How can we use the 'science of stories' to produce persuasive scientific stories?" *Palgrave Communications*, vol. 3, no. 1, 53.

Mencher, M. (2011) *News Reporting and Writing*. New York:McGraw Hill.

Moezzi, M., Janda, K B. & Rotmann, S. (2017) "Using stories, narratives, and storytelling in energy and climate change research," *Energy Research & Social Science*, vol. 31, 2017, 1–10.

Muurlink, O. & McAllister, P. (2015) "Narrative risks in science writing for the lay public," *Journal of Science Communication*, vol. 14, no. 3, A01.

Olson, R. (2015) *Houston, We Have a Narrative: Why Science Needs Story*. Chicago: Chicago University Press.

Padian, K. (2018). "Narrative and 'anti-narrative' in science: how scientists tell stories, and don't," *Integrative and Comparative Biology*, vol. 58, no. 6, 1224–1234.

Pitzer, A. (2011) "Jack Hart on 'Storycraft' and narrative nonfiction as an American literary form," Nieman Storyboard [Online]. Available at: https://niemanstoryboard.org/stories/jack-hart-storycraft-narrative-nonfiction-interview/ (date accessed 8 October 2019).

Pullum, G.K. (2004) "The Dan Brown Code," Language Log [Online]. Available at: http://itre.cis.upenn.edu/~myl/languagelog/archives/000844.html (date accessed 5 August 2019).

Reagan, A.J., Mitchell, L., Kiley, D., Danforth, C.M. & Dodds, P.S. (2016) "The emotional arcs of stories are dominated by six basic shapes," *EPJ Data Science*, vol. 5, no. 1, 31.

Rogers, A. (2011) "Unraveling the Mystery of the Canadian Whiskey Fungus," *WIRED* [Online]. Available at: https://www.wired.com/2011/05/ff-angelsshare/ (date accessed: 30 May 2019).

Saplakoglu, Y. (2019) "Ancient Megalopolis Uncovered in Israel Was the 'New York City' of Its Time Period," Live Science [Online]. Available at: https://www.livescience.com/ancient-city-discovered-israel.html (date accessed 8 October 2019).

Scanlan, C. (2003) "The nut graft tells the reader what the writer is up to," Poynter [Online]. Available at: https://www.poynter.org/archive/2003/the-nut-graf-part-i/ (date accessed 8 October 2019).

Schulten, K. (2019) "Narrative Arc: 'The Ballad of Tribute Steve'," The New York Times Learning Network [Online]. Available at: https://www.nytimes.com/2019/09/04/learning/mentor-text-narrative-arc.html (date accessed 8 October 2019).

Schutt, Bill (2018) *Cannibalism: A perfectly natural history.* New York: Algonquin Books.

Shelby, A. & Ernst, K. (2013) "Science and story: How providers and parents can utilize storytelling to combat anti-vaccine misinformation," *Human Vaccines & Immunotherapeutics*, vol. 9, no. 8, 1795–1801.

Sollaci, L B. & Pereira, M.G. (2004) "The introduction, methods, results, and discussion (IMRAD) structure: a fifty-year survey," *Journal of the Medical Library Association*, vol. 92, no. 3, 364.

Solomon, C. (2017) "The Detective of Northern Oddities," Outside [Online]. Available at: https://www.outsideonline.com/2143191/detective-northern-oddities (date accessed: 11 June 2019).

Springer (2019) "Overview of IMRaD structure," Springer.com [Online]. Available at: https://www.springer.com/gp/authors-editors/journal-author/overview-of-imrad-structure/1408 (date accessed 2 August 2019).

Swanson, C. (2019) "Seeing the woods," *New Scientist*, vol. 243, no. 3250, 34–37.

Tyng, C.M., Amin, H.U., Saad, M.N. & Malik, A.S. (2017) "The influences of emotion on learning and memory," *Frontiers in psychology*, vol. 8, no. 1454.

Vanoost, M. (2013) "Defining narrative journalism through the concept of plot," *Diegesis*, vol. 2, no. 2.

Vonnegut, K. (1995) "Kurt Vonnegut, Shape of Stories (subtitulos castellano)," Youtube [Online Video]. Available at: https://www.youtube.com/watch?v=oP3c1h8v2ZQ (date accessed 4 August 2019).

Walker, C. (2013) "The Art of the Essay," The Open Notebook [Online]. Available at: https://www.theopennotebook.com/2013/06/25/the-art-of-the-essay/ (date accessed 8 October 2019).

Wellenstein, A. (2016) "The Demon Core and the Strange Death of Louis Slotin," The New Yorker [Online]. Available at: https://www.newyorker.com/tech/annals-of-technology/demon-core-the-strange-death-of-louis-slotin (date accessed 2 August 2019).

Yorke, J. (2013) *Into the Woods: How stories work and why we tell them.* London: Penguin Random House UK.

5 Story Formulas

What you will learn in this chapter:

- The hero's journey
- Science documentary formulas
- The story spine
- Theme construction
- Ultra-short stories
- Headlines
- Case study: Stories on climate change

Writing and formulas. That actually sounds like the death of creativity. I know. Many people frown upon the idea of just filling in the blanks. I get it. Feels a bit like painting by numbers. If you can just fill in a prefabricated template with text, then all of a sudden everybody can do it, right? Wrong. If everybody could do it, they would. It's just not that easy. First, you can approach stories in two ways: An analytical way, where you run a story through a formula and find the elements that match that formula. You might say: ah, I get what the writer did. It's what we did at the end of the previous chapter. If you're a good analyst who can dissect a story, that still doesn't mean you're able to write one. A good film critic understands what a director is doing in a movie, and why. But that doesn't turn the critic into a director. A food critic may understand all the ingredients a master chef has used, and she may have the finest taste buds on Earth, able to sense every little nuance. But that doesn't turn the food critic into a master chef herself. You build stories. Like a building. Brick by brick you put them together. The story formulas and patterns I'll show you in this chapter are tools for finding and constructing your story. Nothing more, and nothing less. They help you figure out the blueprint of your story, but it's not going to write itself. You will have to flesh it out yourself if you want to write a real story, or otherwise you'll just end up with a blueprint. Fiction writers use these story formulas, and non-fiction writers use them too.

I didn't invent them. Most of the people I cite here didn't invent them. But they were smart enough to see patterns emerge from sometimes large bodies of written work. And they have extracted them. Although "story formula" may sound mechanical, I would always find a lot of beauty in finding the patterns in science stories and then spend hours and days in trying to apply these patterns to my own stories. It's like Mark Forsyth writes in his brilliant book on rhetoric, *The Elements of Eloquence*:

> Ancient Greeks were going around collecting their formulas, they weren't plucking them out of thin air or growing them in a test tube. All that the Greeks were doing was noting down the best and most memorable phrases they heard, and working out what the structures were, in much the same way that when you or I eat a particularly delicious meal, we might ask for the recipe.
>
> (Forsyth 2013)

Once you start noticing patterns in writing, there is no way back. You can't unsee them. You'll find logical structures everywhere, from Forsyth's book's rhetoric tropes to poems to science stories. There are formulas for writing premises, for writing pitches and for writing movies. In this chapter, we'll have a look at some of them, both in and out of a science context. Story is a universal language that everybody can connect with. You can use these formulas to improve the abstracts of your papers, to write popular science stories, you can use them at cocktail parties to explain your research to lay people, you can use them to boil down your hard work to its very essence.

Storytelling has a huge appeal to many people, including marketing folks, social media editors and many more that try to sell you something. Whenever a certain technique has been established to "help" others sell their services and products, lots of consultants will mushroom, offering advice. That's why you'll see a lot of superficial advice in blog posts and self-published online articles. A lot of it is utter rubbish. I mean, it's not necessarily wrong (some of it is), but it's just hollow. It's text that shouldn't have been written. Take Michael Schilf's advice in the form of the following story equation: $S = (C + W) \times O$. Story equals character with a want who faces a number of obstacles. What he writes is certainly right, and I do appreciate his professional qualifications. But his 600-word piece is not exactly helpful. This equation doesn't get your started writing. You can't practically apply it, and I don't really see how it would help you progress as a writer. So, in this chapter I've tried to give you tried and tested story formulas that you can use right after or even while reading this chapter, separating it from the myriad of guff advice pieces out there on the web. By the way, this short digression was just one of the techniques you're going to see in action. We're going to see a number of them in this chapter, and yes, they have to do with filmmaking. They're like templates, where you can fill in the blanks and construct a basic structure that will help you as guidance while writing the actual story. Pixar, no less, uses them, but also scientific agencies and universities.

Experiment with them. You can apply these story spines also to write short social media teasers. They're no guarantee to make your science posts go viral. But they improve the odds you're story will be perceived as worthwhile. It's just astounding how short a good story can get. Would you say one sentence is enough to tell a story? Or merely six words? This chapter will deliver some answers. Obviously, when we talk about short stories, we need to have a brief discussion about headlines as well. Is there such a thing as headline storytelling? Yes, and they even follow the cause and effect principle. But there are also some caveats, so let's have a look at those as well. I'll end this chapter with a look at how the National Park Service uses a specific storytelling technique and further refines it to craft effective climate change stories. So let's get this chapter started with one of the most universal and oldest concepts in storytelling: the hero's journey.

The hero's journey

Nothing in the rest of this chapter makes sense except in the light of understanding the common patterns underlying all stories. That's why I'll digress a little here and come up with the basics of the hero's journey. Perhaps you haven't heard about it, but you have definitely seen practical implementations of this universal story blueprint. We'll first have a look at what it actually is, the steps it entails and then see how scientists employ that template for a number of purposes in order to get their research across. It's a form, not a formula (ElShafie 2018).

In 1949, US literature professor Joseph Campbell wrote a book that would change the world of storytelling and influence Hollywood to this very day. The book is titled *The Hero with a Thousand Faces*. In it, Campbell expresses his theory that traditional myths are based on a single pattern: the hero's journey, or monomyth. In his book he compares and studies classical stories and myths like "Prometheus", extracts the elements that make up this pattern and eventually distills the hero's journey into the following process:

> A hero ventures forth from the world of common day into a region of supernatural wonder: fabulous forces are there encountered and a decisive victory is won: the hero comes back from this mysterious adventure with the power to bestow boons on his fellow man.
>
> (Campbell 1949)

Campbell's monomyth is heavily influenced by psychologists Freud and Jung, especially through his Jungian psychoanalytic archetypes. Campbell provided a form for the plot of the hero's journey, consisting of 17 steps. This structure has been adapted multiple times, perhaps most notably by screenwriter and movie executive Christopher Vogler in his 2007 book *The Writer's Journey*, which itself is based on a seven-page memo that he wrote to teach screenwriters how to best use Campbell's hero's journey. It is (surprise, surprise) subdivided into three parts or acts – separation (or departure), initiation and return. A rite of passage (Campbell 1949), that is often depicted, along with the following elements, as a circle divided into two halves (see Figure 5.1): The ordinary, known world, and the unknown, special world the protagonist is plunged into. So here are Campbell's (1949) 17 elements. For this, I will stick

Figure 5.1 The hero's journey

to the male pronoun (sorry not sorry) unlike I usually do, in order to represent accurately what Campbell meant.

I DEPARTURE

1 **The call to adventure**: the hero experiences a loss or is confronted with a task.
2 **Refusal of the call**: he is reluctant to accept the mission – it's a risk.
3 **Supernatural aid**: a mentor appears and encourages/convinces her.
4 **Crossing the threshold**: he accepts the challenge and crosses over from the ordinary known world into the unknown.
5 **Belly of the whale**: he is overwhelmed by the tasks he's confronted with in the special world. It's only now that he starts to realise what he's gotten into.

II. INITIATION

1   **The road of trials**: the hero must pass trial after trial. He will fail multiple times (trials show up in threes) but at the same time also feels he is able to manage it.

2   **The meeting with the goddess**: the hero meets the queen goddess, and the woman which, in mythological terms, "represents the totality of what can be known" (Campbell 1949:106).

3   **Woman as temptress**: the hero is tempted to stray from his actual goal. He will eventually have a moment of insight and regret it (in that case, that's a pivotal plot point). Oedipus is a good example.

4   **Atonement with the father**: a confrontation (initiation) with the greatest powers in the hero's life (in classical tales often a father figure, hence the name of this element). The hero must abandon his own ego, then the "god" ("the superego"), then sin ("the repressed id"), only then can he start to trust the father figure.

5   **Apotheosis**: the hero realises that godlike powers lie dormant in him. Campbell: "The wise realize, even within this womb, that they have come from and are returning to the father; while the very wise know that she and he are in substance one" (Campbell 1949:157).

6   **The ultimate boon**: the hero gets what he wants, either as a gift, or he steals it. The quest as such is fulfilled. But he's still in the unknown world.

III. RETURN

1   **Refusal of the return**: the hero may be reluctant to return. But in order to complete his journey, he has to return and utilise the elixir to the benefit of his community or tribe.

2   **The magic flight**: if indeed the elixir was stolen by the hero, then it's time to flee now. It could also be that whatever goddess or supernatural power has handed the gift to the hero might want him to stay. The way back starts.

3   **Rescue from without**: the hero needs help on his way back. This often occurs in the form of some good deed the hero has done on his way towards obtaining the elixir that now pays off.

4   **The crossing of the return threshold**: the hero enters back into the known world (in Figure 5.1, that's the upper half of the story circle). He must now blend his insights and the elixir together.

5   **Master of two worlds**: inner and outer world are united. Whatever the hero has learnt and brought back from the unknown, he can now use it here, in the known world. This, by the way, is beautifully visualised in the 1999 movie "The Matrix", when Neo flies away in the real world, just after hanging up the phone. It's the movie's final scene.

6   **Freedom to live**: the elixir is in place, living freely is established.

One of the most prominent movies that was made based on this structure is the first film of the original "Star Wars" franchise. Screenwriter and director George

Lucas confirmed that he used Campbell's monomyth as a blueprint to conceive and write the space opera. But if you pay attention, you will find it as the skeleton of many, many, many successful movies, like "The Matrix", the "Indiana Jones" (also Lucas) series or "John Carter". This approach has its pros and cons, as writer Peter Suderman prominently pointed out that in 2013 many Hollywood films had become formulaic (Suderman 2013). Yes, that's true. And yet, this narrative structure, Campbell's narrative cross-section of so many folk tales and myths, rings familiar when you watch, read or listen to them. Campbell's structure has been adapted and simplified many times. You should definitely get a copy of Christopher Vogler's "The Writer's Journey", which we will revisit in the chapter on screenwriting techniques.

But why does it still work after thousands of years? In chapter one, we already had a look at the general brain science of story. Sociologist Olivia Efthimiou and psychologist Zeno E. Franco (2017) had a closer look at heroism, which "describes behaviours manifested in the risk-laden moral, mental and/or physical challenge, calling the individual to rise to it, which culminates in some form of psychological, spiritual, physical and/or social transformation" (Efthimiou & Franco 2017:34). They put it clearly: "From an evolutionary standpoint, the first stories are hero stories - therefore storytelling cannot be separated from the heroic" (Efthimiou & Franco 2017:34). What they suggest is, drawing on Campbell, that the evolution of story is linked to biological evolution. Campbell's hero's journey mirrors the different stages of human development, so we might be developmentally equipped to pursue a hero's journey of our own throughout our lives. They also add that these theses and this perspective called "biopsychological view of the human" are still speculative in nature. From a negatively framed epigenetic point of view, this might mean that we inherit traumatic experiences of our ancestors, coded right into our DNA. On the other side, this could also be true for any strengths we could inherit. To substantiate the link between heroism and biology, Efthimiou and Franco (2017) cite research showing that the heroic have reproductive advantages. The two researchers end their study with the following statement:

> If the hero's journey truly is universal and primordial in its origin, as the world's vast vault of hero mythologies (verbal, written, pictorial) suggests, the bold question arises: Is this evolution a form of heroic design? To answer the question 'what does it mean to be a hero', therefore, would be to answer the question what it fundamentally means to be human.
>
> (Efthimiou & Franco 2017:40)

So, all of that is really nice in fiction, you might say. Right. But what about science? Can you apply this to science stories? Yes and no: science does not always correspond to ideal story structures. But, as with all of the storytelling structures and formulas presented in this book and in the world, you don't have to apply the full set, every step of a story paradigm to your science story. If you can find some story elements and string the elements together to even just a loose narrative, then it will be often good enough to craft an enticing science story. You can also use the hero's journey to describe certain processes in science. In higher education, it is used in freshman orientation, teacher education, music therapy, forestry, management, instructor self-reflection, even in psychotherapy (Georgas, Regalado & Burgess 2017). At Brooklyn College at the City University of New York, Professor Matthew Burgess runs an undergraduate course on English composition, part of which is to get students used to academic writing and eventually produce a research paper. In said course, Burgess teaches the hero's journey as a way to let students come up with stories on how they got into research. The students become the heroes in their own research stories. This starts even before the actual research is prompted: for example, they might see their admission or accepted visa application as Campbell's call to adventure. When they move to the campus and start their first semester, they have crossed the threshold and entered the new, hitherto unknown world. Burgess then issues another call of adventure, an assignment to write an academic paper. The students then have to embark on their research journey, go into libraries and conduct interviews to find the answers to their research questions. The librarians at Brooklyn College then show the students the research tools, again using the hero's journey. Assignments like essays can be seen as the obstacles on the road of trials. Combined with the variety of research methodologies they have to apply on the road, the hero's journey's road of trials reflects the non-linearity of the research process. What they find is issues that Campbell calls the "transformation of consciousness", and on their way back, students have to integrate that with their existing body of knowledge, by presenting and discussing them (Georgas, Regalado & Burgess 2017). Looking at this perspective, it all makes sense from a storytelling perspective. Too much research stops a paper getting published in a scientific journal. But that approach doesn't bring the research journey to a full conclusion. Public outreach should be part of the scientific method, but that is hardly recognised by most researchers. They have to take their "gift", the knowledge they have gained and bring it back to society, thereby improving it. We're all part of society. That includes scientists.

Science documentary formulas

In 1984, Randy Olson graduated with a PhD in evolutionary biology from Harvard University. In 1988, he became a professor of zoology at the University of New Hampshire. In 1992, he received tenure as a marine biology professor at that same university. He published scientific articles, some of which to this day are highly acclaimed. A stellar academic career. Yet, his last scientific publication (check it on Scopus) dates back to the mid-nineties. That's when Olson, then in his late thirties, quit his job and moved to California to attend film school. He became a documentary filmmaker, writer and producer. Most of his documentaries (some of which are also highly acclaimed, a few others received mixed reviews) revolve around conservation and science. Olson has written a number of books on storytelling in science. Some of his work has drawn criticism from scientists, because they perceived it as offensive. Essentially, Olson kept saying that scientists are bad storytellers. Although you should never generalise, to some extent there might be some truth in it. I have attended terrible presentations from physicists, computer scientists, biologists and also from the social sciences. Those presentations were geared towards journalists and lay people, so they should have conveyed their research in a digestible way. Because their goal clearly was that journalists would pick up their stories. Except, what they told us weren't stories at all. This is what Olson criticises, but he also offers a remedy: story. In *Houston, We Have a Narrative* (Olson 2015), he comes up with three intuitive story formulas that help scientists and science storytellers write science stories in a conceivable way. This section deals with those three "templates", as Olson calls them.

The first template he introduces is the Dobzhansky template and works on the word level. It is named after the eponymous geneticist. Olson felt inspired to name it after him, because of Dobzhansky's following statement that was sort of an epiphany for him:

> Nothing in biology makes sense except in the light of evolution.
>
> (Olson 2015:82)

So, in order to understand the whole field, you need to understand a story of change, the narrative, which in this example is "evolution". Evolution is the narrative of biology. That's the statement. Olson argues that it helps you finding the narrative. He turned Dobzhansky's statement into the following template by replacing "biology" and "evolution" with blanks:

> Nothing in _____ makes sense except in the light of _____.
>
> (Olson 2015:83)

Olson tested it with colleagues and friends. What this word template does, he argues, is distill apparently heterogeneous pieces of information into a single word that helps then explain a phenomenon at a glance. He makes another case for this single-word narrative by pointing out that for companies, it can overlap with their brand (he draws on Apple Inc.). A final example: "Nothing in *California climate change* makes sense except in the light of *loss*" (Olson 2015:85), an example an environmental lawyer came up with. Try to apply it to your life story, and try to apply it to sum up your favourite movies. That's what Olson recommends. I've tried to apply it to the "Godfather" series. Here's my attempt: "Nothing in the life of the Corleone family makes sense except in the light of honour". Works for me. This is the unifying element. From this perspective, it's the question "What is this story about?" that you can answer with the Dobzhansky template. But if you apply it more specifically, you could probably also use it to find a character's need. For example, "Nothing in the life of Michael Corleone makes sense except in the light of his desire to distinguish himself from his father." Works again. Olson comes up with another example, when he was trying to figure out the one word that summed up what his documentary "Flock of the Dodos" was about. It wasn't "creationism", "controversy" or "evolution". It was "truth". That word, he argues, sort of implies a narrative, a struggle to achieve it, and was hence the best choice. In my view, the Dobzhansky template is strongly connected with a story's theme, summed up in one word (and missing the two other elements from Egri's template, which you'll read about later). So try and keep his message and try to answer for every story you plan, for every speech you give: what is this story/ speech at the core about? Without that narrative, information just becomes loosely arranged, without really having a golden thread. Further digging into the second part of the Dobzhansky template, Olson cites the geneticist again:

> Without that light, it becomes a pile of sundry facts – some of them interesting or curious but making no meaningful picture as a whole.
>
> (Olson 2015:87)

He points out that this is where the weakness of many scientific presentations (see Figure 5.1) is. Just piling up information and unleashing it, without that glue that story provides, onto the audience. "This was okay in a world short on information", Olson argues. Today, that doesn't work anymore. If you can answer the Dobzhansky template, you essentially have your story's narrative and can also answer frequent questions like: "Why should we care about your story/proposal?"

Olson has got a second template up his sleeve. It's his most popular one, and it actually shows more of a structural element than the Dobzhansky template. He calls it the ABT (and, but, therefore) template. It allows you to summarise your story in one sentence. It's a tripartite structure. The origins of this structure go way back to Hegel and Aristotle. This does make sense, after all Hegel's dialectics (thesis-antithesis-synthesis) is also a tripartite construct. It's the beginning-middle-end structure, or protagonist-complication-resolution, as Hart (2011) puts it. When scientists just list a pile of facts instead of a story, they use a different structure, the AAA ("and, and and"), which is not a narrative and hence not effective (Olson 2015). The reason for that is simple, and you've seen it in the previous chapter. The AAA is just a sequence of events without any logical connection (by the way, sort of what you will also encounter in anecdotal evidence). Event B is not a logical consequence of event A, and so on. There is no complication, no inciting incident, and no resolution. So it's not a story. The ABT, however, follows a different structure that incorporates story elements. "But" is an adversative conjunction. That means, within the ABT, it throws the sentence, the whole situation into a new direction. That's what all good plot points do: they make the story change direction. The ABT is a tripartite structure, and while the first part lists one or more facts (connected by "ands"), the story doesn't start until part two ("but"), which is the story's inciting incident. In Campbell's hero's journey terms, this is where the protagonist leaves the ordinary world and enters the special world (Olson 2015). This may implicitly point to a dramatic question that readers want to get answered. For example, when the "but" is somebody who gets murdered and the protagonist is wrongly blamed, the "therefore" would rather be about the protagonist finding herself in a situation where she needs to prove herself innocent. The third clause, triggered by "therefore", indicates that the following action is a logical consequence. That's where Olson introduces cause and effect into the ABT, which is essential for story structure and to keep readers enticed. You can use the ABT to describe a story setup (like the wrongly accused murderer in the previous example). In that case, only when you flesh out the story, she will resolve her problem (fingers crossed). Or you can use the ABT to describe a fully resolved story. Olson (2015) mentions both possibilities. In the workshops he runs, he tested the ABT and let participants describe a picture's contents before they knew about the ABT, and after. The time to describe them dropped from initially 30 seconds to a mere 13 seconds. Using the ABT, the participants were eager for the story to progress. Olson calls this "advancing the narrative". The problem, he writes, is that some people never get to the "but". He also applies it to Hasson's (2008) aforementioned neurocinematics study (in which Hasson compared the brain activity while watching a suspenseful Hitchcock movie against watching mere footage of people walking their dogs in a park). Olson finds that the boring park footage follows an AAA structure, while the Hitchcock flick follows the ABT. Although Olson's ABT was inspired by "South Park" (its creators use it by replacing the "ands" with "buts"), he traced it back to Frank Daniel, former Sundance creative director. Also, and most prominently, Olson cites Abraham Lincoln's Gettyburg Address and Watson and Crick's groundbreaking 1953 paper on the DNA double helix structure. They both used the formula, although it wasn't known as such back then. Olson also introduces the DHY structure ("despite", "however", "yet") structure, which lies at the other end of the narrative spectrum. If the AAA is boring and non-narrative, the DHY contains too many complications, confusing the readers. According to Olson, the ABT lies in the middle and is the optimal solution in terms of narrativity. You can use it for about everything: presentations, scientific papers' abstracts and all sorts of other stories. It's an elevator pitch, a story in a nutshell. There are three types of the ABT (Olson 2015):

1   **iABT**: this is the informational ABT. Its goal is to include all the information on a need-to-know basis; you don't have to be concise. It's narratively structured, but a relatively long sentence that you shouldn't use in public speeches.

2   **cABT**: this is the conversational ABT, stripped of all that information. The goal is to make non-expert audiences relate to what you have to say. So you'll use the following structure: "We were looking at one way but realized there's another way therefore we're looking at that way" (Olson 2015:121, see also Figure 5.2). Olson recommends you use this when somebody asks you what exactly it is you're trying to say. Because of the relatable narrative structure, even non-specialists will think you have something in common. This is narrative relatability. You can also use character relatability, that is figuring out who your audience is (for example, from a specific city or working in certain professions) and then relate to their fields.

3   **kABT**: the middle version between the iABT and the cABT. Take the cABT and add back some of the information that you took out of the iABT in step two (Olson 2015). This is also where language and style comes into play

Figure 5.2 Randy Olson's ABT, applied to scientific presentations

Tullio Rossi's comic compares standard "and-and-and" presentations to "and-but-there-fore" presentations.

Source: Tullio Rossi. Animate Your Science (www.animateyour.science). License: CC BY-ND 4.0.

(more on that in the next chapter): The iABT tends to be highly jargon-laden, and the cABT is too simplistic. The kABT is supposed to contain plain, simple English terms, and not too many of them.

Olson has a third template up his sleeve, the paragraph template. It is centered around Joseph Campbell's hero's journey, the original 17-step story structure which Hollywood executive and writer Christoph Vogler in 2007 boiled down to a 12-step process. Feature writer Peter Suderman pointed out in 2013 that story formulas can also become too formulaic, so movies start "feeling" the same, especially if you know what that formula is (he referred to a Blake Snyder's screenwriting book *Save the Cat* that defined the very minute a storytelling element should be invoked in a screenplay). Loglines are Hollywood's way of constructing one-liners that sell. You can find a separate section in a later chapter of this book, but here is how Olson's coauthor Dorie Barton defines it (Olson 2015:132–133):

1   In an ordinary world
2   A flawed protagonist
3   Has a catalytic event that upends his/her world
4   After taking stock
5   The protagonist commits to action
6   But when the stakes get raised
7   The protagonist must learn the lesson
8   In order to stop the antagonist
9   To achieve his/her goal

It's another fill-in-the-blanks template, and it can yield awkward results if not approached seriously. A slightly longer version of it is the "story circle" (Olson offers workshops on that), which has twelve elements:

1   Call to adventure
2   Assistance
3   Departure
4   Trials
5   Approach
6   Crisis
7   Treasure
8   Result
9   Return
10 New life
11 Resolution
12 Status quo (but changed)

Now, Olson (2015) doesn't necessarily recommend you use and complete all of them in their entirety. Much rather, he offers three ways you can find problem-solution approaches based on the Logline Maker that will help you formulate specific science problems. First, when a problem comes up (step three), the protagonist performs an action (step five). It's only initial action and not the definite solution to the problem. Second, a new problem pops up in step six (stakes raised), and the hero (scientist) needs to overcome the obstacle by gaining some insight (steps seven and eight). Third, the flawed protagonist. In step two, the protagonist's flaw is shown, in step seven she has to confront and overcome it. The irony is that many scientists see themselves as flawless, which Olson (2015) clearly criticises. He writes:

> And yet ... if you're a scientist, you kind of want people to trust you by having them think your work is flawless. And yet ... there are these things called error bars and error measurements and confidence intervals and all kinds of other signals that suggest the scientist is not a flawless character after all.
>
> (Olson 2015:136)

I couldn't agree more. Science is not objective. It's a human enterprise. It's fueled by politics and money. It's a business machinery that is packed with conflicts of interests. Scientists are ordinary people with ordinary needs like love, status and respect. They will fight, deceive, kill to get their needs satisfied. Can you see it? Science is the perfect raw material for story.

The story spine

A couple of years ago, a research institution I am also working for decided to redesign their website. A team of US consultants was brought in, and they came up with an exercise: we should write the company's story to develop common ground. We received a template with blanks to fill in. I immediately recognised the structure, since I had seen it before.

Fast forward a few years. Pixar is the number one animation studio in the world. Pixar's story artists have conceived stories in the form of feature and short films that are easy sells at the box office. Nowadays, their global box-office gross frequently exceeds a billion US dollars, and production costs for feature films like the recent "Incredibles 2", with production costs reach up to US$200 million per film (Lynch 2018). It's quite obvious that Pixar's team of storytellers, writers and animators is not a bunch of amateurs. They have developed their own storytelling approach, and most of their films follow that structure. When I write "developed", I actually mean taken a proven approach, experimented with it and then adapted it to their needs. This is why using established, existing storytelling forms (and patterns, and formulas) are not a bad thing. On the contrary. It's actually part of the process. Every highly prolific writer has established structures that work for her. They reuse existing structures. It's what George Lucas did. It's what the Greeks did with rhetoric figures (Forsyth 2013). It's what you should do to tell good stories, regardless of whether they are fiction or nonfiction stories. Good stories follow good structure. So, Pixar discovered a storytelling formula they have become famous for using: the "story spine". It's again a fill-in template that helps you figure out the main plot points of your story. Playwright Kenn Adams invented it in 1991 as a tool to improvise on and learn story structure. Back then he didn't call it "story spine" but just "once upon a time". You'll see in a minute why. In his 2007 book *How to Improvise a Full-Length Play*, Adams proposes students fill in the blanks alternatingly, one blank per student. And this is what the story spine looks like:

- Once upon a time…
- Every day…
- But one day…
- Because of that…
- Because of that…
- Because of that…
- Until finally…
- And ever since then…

I haven't numbered the steps in order to make it read more like a story. Structure-wise, it's all there. But Adams doesn't just give you a naked spine. He also introduces a structure (have a look at Jack Hart's story structure in the previous chapter) that is very reminiscent of other established story structures. He divides a two-hour length entire play into the following structural elements, which in essence provides you with a more elaborate, detailed and granular version of Aristotle's beginning-middle-end structure (Adams 2007):

- **Beginning**: the beginning is an expository part that not only introduces the characters and the story's setting but also how they live their lives. The average length is about 25 per cent. What does the characters' routine look like? Story spine elements:

  - Once upon a time…
  - Every day…

- **First Significant Event**: this is a single event that breaks the routine. It ends the beginning and starts the middle section. The character is thrown into the unknown world. In other terms, this is the inciting incident and transitions the story. This is where in Campbell's terms the hero crosses the threshold. Story spine element:

  - But one day…

- **Middle**: obstacles, obstacles, obstacles. Characters struggle to overcome them as they make progress towards the climax (road of trials in Campbell's terms). The average length is about 50 per cent. What is really interesting is that Campbell (1949) asserted that the conflicts come in threes. Adams (2007) includes exactly three in his structure. Also, note how strongly they introduce cause and effect into the story. Story spine elements:

- Because of that...
- Because of that...
- Because of that...

- **Climax**: again a single action that paves the way for the protagonist's success or failure in terms of achieving her goal. Story spine element:

  - Until finally...

- **End**: the protagonist either succeeds or fails to achieve the goal, based on the climactic moment. A new status quo is established (Adams calls this the "foundation"). The average length is about 25 per cent, like the beginning. Story spine element:

  - And ever since then...

Now, this structure has been altered and passed on lots of times (as it goes). In his article for *Aerogramme Writer's Studio*, Adams (2013) appreciates the addition of a ninth element, "And, the moral of the story is..." which clearly is the story's theme. Yet, all the modifications prompted him to write said article, reminding readers of what the original story spine looks like. He reminds his readers that the spine is nothing but an outline, and that having established that structure, you still have a lot to do to actually write the story. But the basic foundation is laid.

Back to Pixar. Pixar uses the story spine, too. Khan Academy hosts an online course called "Pixar in a box", in which story artists, editors and directors share their techniques. You should definitely watch the videos and complete the exercises of the module "the art of storytelling". It's free, and I've included a link to it in the "Links" section at the end of this chapter. One of their videos is actually titled "Story Spine". In it, the interviewed story artists explain that they outline stories using so-called story beats (despite the varying terminology, these are plot points) and put them on index cards on the wall. As with every good outlining technique, not getting lost in details is key. What they do look out for is whether a character is making a decision and whether there is cause and effect. A moment of insight? That's a beat. The Pixar people's advice: Focus on the "what" is happening in a story (when outlining), not so much on the "how". They also show that they're using Adams' eight-step story spine to plan their stories, including the "moral" element at the end of it.

So can you use this story structuring technique in science? Yes, you can. Cell molecular biologist and postdoc Rayna M. Harris has written a Medium post, in which she uses Adams' eight-step story spine to describe how she broke into her research field, starting from her wish to become a marine biologist, to the inciting incident (the end of her gap year in Costa Rica), and how she crosses the threshold into research, all the way through to obtaining her PhD. What she has written is some sort of narrative CV, using Adams' template. It's short and concise, so make sure you have a look at it – the link is in this chapter's "References" section. Interestingly, Harris isn't the only marine biologist who employs the story spine. Sea Rotmann from New Zealand has written a paper on using the story spine for a very specific purpose. Over the course of five years, she had 160 energy experts recount behaviour change stories using the story spine. In her paper (Rotmann 2017), she describes the process of using Adams' story spine to bring a multi-stakeholder audience together, by using the common language of storytelling in an attempt to overcome all sorts of barriers, like interdisciplinary and language barriers (Harris 2017). The story spine has many fields it can be applied by business and economics consultants, by salespeople and managers and by NGOs to attract funding (Rotmann 2017). This is the template she gave her participants (Rotmann 2017:305):

- **Once upon a time**… [the background, where you outline the setting and who you are – including your mandate, your main stakeholder/s and your main restrictions]
- **Every day**… [where you outline the problem and the end users' behaviours you/ we are trying to change. It may include some of the end users' technological, social, environmental, etc. context/ s – the ones that are most important to this issue]
- **But one day**… [where you outline the idea/solution and how it is meant to change the end users' behaviours – concentrate on your specific tools you will bring to the table]
- **Because of that**… [where you outline the implementation of the intervention and the opportunities for success]
- **But then!** [where you outline what can/will/has gone wrong and why]
- **Because of that**… [where you outline how you have reiterated the intervention because of what you have learned]
- **Until, finally**… [where you outline how you have measured the multiple benefits that accrued to you/r organisation/sector and what the main results are]
- **And, ever since then**… [where you outline the wider (e.g. national) change that has occurred because of this intervention and any possible lessons going forward or future research that needs to follow]

Rotmann has slightly adapted the template and used it to collect a total of 160 stories between 2013 and 2016, subdivided into the categories "Personal Stories", "Behaviour Changer Stories", "Case Study Stories" and "Country Energy Stories". The best-liked story was about a maintenance person who changed more energy-efficient lights in a hospital and led the executives to the insight that with the money saved they could buy more intensive care basinets in the neonatal unit. While Rotmann (2017) appreciates the effectiveness of cause and effect that this form introduces, she also cautions that causality can often not be proved.

Theme construction

We briefly touched upon theme (often called premise, you'll see in a minute why I'm bringing this up here) in the first chapter of this book. The Dobzhansky template is one tool to find your theme. "Nothing in X makes sense except in light of Y", Y being the narrative or the one-word theme (Olson 2015). In this section, I'll try and dissect themes a bit further and help you construct them using a number of approaches apart from the Dobzhansky template. First, let's have a look at how research identifies themes before we proceed to the more artsy-crafty part.

Behavioural scientist Gery W. Ryan and anthropologist H. Russell Bernard from the US have found a dozen techniques that social scientists use to identify themes in texts. These are analytical tools, so they help you find themes in already existing texts. That means they are not going to help you to find a theme before you start writing. But if you have a text that feels somehow off after writing, if it fails to meet the "so what?" test, or if you're unsure whether it has a theme at all, then you might as well try out one of the following ways to test it for theme. The word-based techniques are the fastest but shallowest, while the other techniques are slower but more profound. Let's have a look at a selection of the dozen techniques they found (adapted from Ryan & Bernard 2000):

1 **Word repetitions (word-based)**: this means finding those keywords (in context) that are semantically similar, so have the same meaning, and counting their frequencies. Essentially, this is pattern recognition.

2 **Indigenous categories (word-based)**: look for terms that sound unfamiliar and keep appearing in the text. "The basic idea in this area of research is that experience and expertise are often marked by specialized vocabulary". In other words: look out for jargon.

3 **Compare and contrast (block-based)**: this is like interviewing a chunk of text, line by line and asking yourself: what is this about? You then compare the chunks in terms of meaning and find out what connects them.

4 **Searching for missing information (block-based)**: here, you don't look for themes in the text, but you look for themes that are missing. This sounds awkward, right? But it may indicate that the author of a piece of text assumed you would not know what she didn't explicitly mention. Or that she deliberately didn't address an aspect or a theme because it was too difficult.

5 **Metaphors (linguistics-based)**: search for metaphors, similes and analogies. People often demonstrate their thoughts, behaviours and experiences through analogies. Find the patterns in the metaphors' meaning. "Nailed in cement" or "Rock of Gibraltar" are both metaphors used by surprised divorcees (the partners on the receiving end), but they have the same meaning.

6 **Transitions (linguistics-based)**: pauses in speech, and new paragraphs in text hint at thematic transitions. Native American language analysis has yielded that "now", "now then" and "then" indicate thematic shifts. By implication, if these transitions are missing, it shows that the texts are rather uniform in terms of theme.

7 **Connectors (linguistics-based)**: look for relationships between ideas in a text by looking at the connectors and conjunctions. "Because", "since", and

"as a result" indicate causal relationships. "If", "then", "rather than" indicate conditional relationships. You have more than that: Hierarchical relationships ("is a"), and temporal relationships ("before", "after", "then"). Negative characteristics occur far less often, so looking for "non", "no", "not" is a quick way to identify themes.

Ryan and Bernard (2000) come up with more techniques, but they also state they don't know which one technique is best for identifying themes in a text. So it's probably fun to experiment with all of them a bit.

As for the actual construction of a theme, I have already established in the first chapter of this book that a story without a theme isn't a story. Sometimes you'll start with a theme in your mind, and sometimes you'll have to discover it while you're writing a piece. Screenwriters John Yorke and Richard Walter write in their storytelling books that it's rather likely that you don't start with a predefined theme in mind (bear in mind: they are referring to fictional texts). Playwright Arthur Miller stated he'd write two thirds of a play, then discover the theme, print it out and then write using the theme as a guideline (Yorke 2013). Sometimes you'll nail it from the beginning, and sometimes you'll find the theme that has emerged while writing and editing your text is different from the one you had imagined at first. All of that is fine. When television writer Shonda Rhimes, creator of "Grey's Anatomy", talks about theme in her Masterclass video series, she distinguishes between "idea" and "premise". An idea, Rhimes says, is just a vague way to express that you want to write a story about something, without actually knowing its specifics. A premise, on the other hand, is way more specific, creates tension and has structure. What helps finding the premise is thinking like a journalist and trying to answer the journalistic questions: who, what, when, where, why, and how? What she hints at is that by using this technique, you introduce a protagonist, her goal and the obstacles she is going to face (Rhimes 2018). What are the protagonist's needs, wants and flaws? She describes the premise for her famous television series "Grey's Anatomy": "I wanna do a show about surgical competitive interns, at the center of which is Meredith Grey, a woman who is hiding the fact that her mother has Alzheimer's" (Rhimes 2018). She also discloses that in the early stages, she tries to figure out who the story is about and what journey the protagonist is on. I've included a link to an excerpt of her Masterclass video in the "Links" section, make sure to read through it. Rhimes' approach is more specific than what Lajos Egri did in his stage play premises (we'll get there in a minute) and also makes for a good elevator pitch. That's concrete enough to tell it to your friends as a "pub pitch" and ask them whether they have any questions. Rhimes says that their questions will tell you whether you're on to a good story or not. For example, if they wonder what happens next and how the story ends, that's a good sign. If they seem confused, if what you tell them doesn't make any sense or causes raised eyebrows: not so good. The Egri-style theme then, that greater, universal truth is actually the abstraction of your protagonist's struggles. Or, by implication, the protagonist's story is an instance of a greater truth. The story shows that truth instead of telling it. You need both: story and theme. Screenwriting teacher Richard Walter confirms this in his book *Essentials of Screenwriting*. He also comes up with a number of examples of movies and their themes. They are (Walter 2010):

- **Star Wars**: love is stronger than hate.
- **Citizen Kane**: you can't buy love.
- **E.T.**: love thy neighbour.
- **The Terminator**: to feel pain is to be human.

The theme tells you what your story is about. If you follow Shonda Rhimes' approach, you'll end up with a well-crafted specific premise. In the chapter on screenwriting techniques, I'll show you another tool that is very popular with screenwriters, because it helps you not only with your elevator pitch but also with constructing a micro-story: the logline.

BBC storytelling master John Yorke defines a premise as follows: "A theory is posited, an argument explored and a conclusion reached" (Yorke 2013:192). He distinguishes between subject matter and theme. For example, in "Die Hard", the subject matter is terrorist taking over a skyscraper, while the theme is: "can we only become strong by facing our weakness?" (Yorke 2013). That difference is very similar to topic and story idea in journalism. If you try to get a commission for a topic (say, genetics), you'll fail. If you have a good story (with a theme), you'll get that commission. Yorke often formulates his themes as questions, and so can you. Essentially, all the story elements are there. A protagonist, an obstacle and a potential solution, or at least a journey is hinted at that one might hope will lead to a resolution of the conflict. For Yorke, themes follow the dialectic structure formula thesis-synthesis-antithesis. His point is: if you write dialectically, themes will emerge naturally. Although Yorke disagrees with Egri as for when the premise should be formulated, their elements are similar. Egri, too favours a tripartite structure that is a very boiled-down version of the actual story: protagonist-conflict-conclusion. In his premises, the construct is often a declarative sentence, that is: subject-verb-object (with the verb often being "leads to", so it's "A leads to B"). Note the causality in all of the approaches to premise. And Egri makes another important point: the writer's conviction needs to shine through. Which side do you champion? Let's make it value-laden: Is the outcome of your premise a good or a bad thing? This, by the way, is also a good way to write some types of headlines.

Ultra-short stories

If you think that premises are as short as it gets, you're wrong. As long as you can incorporate the essential elements, a protagonist, a complication and (hinting at) a resolution, you're alright. That's a story. Quite famously, there is a six-word story making the rounds on the internet. That's right. Six words. It is often attributed to Ernest Hemingway but nobody has ever proven that. It goes like this:

FOR SALE: BABY SHOES. NEVER WORN.

Take a closer look. It's a sad story. Although being implicit and leaving readers in the dark, it does contain story elements. Here's one way to interpret it. It could be the story of a stillbirth. The parents had equipped themselves but never got round to actually take care of the baby. Because the baby died, they are selling its shoes. Note the causality. Protagonist-conflict-resolution. It's all there. In fact, six-word stories have become immensely popular. You can find a dedicated subreddit /r/sixwordstories that showcases hundreds of six-word stories, and they get ranked by Reddit users there. While that is a highly non-scientific way to assess their effectiveness, it does tell us something about which constructs are popular. It's funny that the most popular in 2018 was a science-related story: "You were in the control group". Here's another one that encapsulates the first John Wick film in six words: "Grieving husband's puppy murdered. Kills everyone." Brilliant. I've included a link to the ranked list in this chapter's "Links" section. Note how the control group story contains an epiphany, a singular moment of insight. The John Wick story, on the other hand, is a proper journey. Every month, *WIRED* magazine asks its readers to deliver six-word stories via the #wiredbackpage hashtag. It then chooses the best story and illustrates and publishes it in the magazine. I'm not saying write your science stories like that. But I'm saying write six-word stories because they are fun and hone your storytelling skills. They're just an excellent exercise in boiling down an idea.

If you can boil down your science story to a one- or two-liner, you're essentially there. These stories are perfectly shareable online and work on social media.

You can use all the formulas, the ABT, also to tell social media stories, even the story spine, because you can boil it down to only a few sentences. What you can often observe on the social media are teasers and titles that really are their authors' comments. Many don't contain the full story in order to lure in the reader and get that valuable click. This is not exactly the same as clickbaiting, but it has the same goal. And in essence, it works like one of the narrative delayed leads in magazine features (Angler 2017, really sorry about the self-citation, but I'm not pursuing an academic career anyway, so I guess the damage is somewhat limited). Either way, in the "social media for scientists" workshop I run at a research institution, I keep pointing out the different styles in which texts are written for Twitter and Face-book. But apart from the styles, the question is whether or not you should incorporate storytelling elements. Of course you should. The medium-long answer is, yes, but only if the underlying story lends itself to it.

On its business blog, Twitter clearly recommends integrating storytelling elements (with a nod to marketing). These include setting (recommendation: be specific about place and time), character (see product as a character), plot (starts at realising there is a problem and ends with using a product to solve said problem), conflict and a complete story arc (including rising tension, climax and whatnot) (Reese 2018). Can you transport these recommendations to science instead of marketing? Absolutely. It's the shortest story structure you could possibly come up with: problem – solution. That's it. That essentially mirrors science: what it often does is tackle problems and try to solve them. Insofar, your research project, or the outcome of it, could substitute the "product". The character doesn't have to be a "product" either, but it can be a scientist having solved a particular problem or even a non-human element, like a chemical element or a new medication. What Reese (2018) points out is that you should tell those stories as visually as you can: Twitter videos reel in ten times more user interactions, and running a series of photographs to tell a story visually is a good idea, too.

Because Twitter has a character limit of 280, you need to be able to tell a story in very few words. The most effective length on Twitter, however, is between 70 and 100 characters. Facebook allows for many more characters, a whopping 63,206, to be precise. But make no mistake: the most effective length (that is, with the best odds of users engaging with your post) is a mere 80 characters. If you're posting video stories on Twitter, they shouldn't exceed 30 to 60 seconds. As always, the exception proves the rule. There are far longer videos you can find. For example, *National Geographic* does it frequently. Why does it work? Because a) of the storytelling elements like stunning setting (places readers normally don't have access to), protagonist, complication etc. and b) the dramatic structure. You just have to know how the story ends.

That is also why fake news and viral stories work. True, linguists and computer scientists and lots of other researchers have made important discoveries to automatically detect them, and they have laid bare the linguistics of fake news texts. But what actually makes them persuasive is the storytelling. For example, what makes anti-vaccine social media stories believable is the deliberate use of anecdotal evidence. Anti-vaxxers frequently come up with the same type of narrative: they take their child to the GP because they have to, it receives a flu shot, and then it stops talking overnight (Shelby & Ernst 2013). The child becomes autistic. A sequence of events, but with implied meaning. Can you see the themes emerge? Flu makes your child ill. Parents should be the ones to decide which shots their child gets. Powerful, isn't it? It also contains all-important elements: protagonist (child), complication (autism) and resolution (formulated as the theme). On top of that, it contains one of the most powerful news values: negativity. Negativity and topicality supersede all other news values. So, if you craft a short social media story that is positive in nature, I'm afraid it won't be able to compete with the actual fake news story. In other words: if you tell a happy story of how well that flu shot worked for your child – that just won't cut it. Instead, what Shelby and Ernst (2013) found is that if you tell a story of what happens if you don't vaccinate your child, and if you make clear that it could have prevented with a vaccine, that can be powerful. They draw on a real-life example of a father who hadn't vaccinated his child against Tetanus and nearly watched him die. The father experiences a real moment of insight, and showing how the child suffered from getting infected with Tetanus evokes a lot of empathy in the readers. It works. And yes, it also taps into negativity. Alas, that's how the news works. Essentially, that counter-story uses also anecdotal evidence, the same mechanism as the fake stories. That is to say: if you want to craft social media stories, make sure you use storytelling elements, and do tap into your readers' emotions. In doing so, don't make anything up, and you're all set.

Headlines

Can a title tell a full story? Absolutely, although it doesn't have to. For example, have a look at this headline, written by Hannah Frishberg for her *New York Post* article (Frishberg 2019):

"Diabetic groom-to-be dies after taking cheaper insulin to pay for wedding" (Frishberg 2019)

The headline contains a full story arc, including a protagonist, part of his journey (groom-to-be), his flaw (diabetic), a complication (taking cheaper insulin) and a resolution (dies). It also shows a perfect chain of cause and effect. The story ends tragically, alas, because the protagonist dies. He doesn't get what he wants (to live and to marry his girlfriend). But it's a whole story wrapped up in 11 words. Now, while the *New York Post* is sensationalist, the *Washington Post's* version isn't. Here's how they framed the headline for the same story: "He lost his insurance and turned to a cheaper form of insulin. It was a fatal decision" (Olivo 2019).

Again, the headline hints at a protagonist (with less details about his life, i.e. the forthcoming wedding), while only hinting at his flaw by mentioning the insulin. There is also a clear cause and effect chain (the headline author implies that because of losing his insurance, the protagonist turned to cheaper insulin). The story is resolved, because "fatal decision" tells the reader that the protagonist died. For a second time, cause and effect is invoked.

Can you work with storytelling elements in less grim science news' headlines? Yes. Take the following example about how staring down seagulls deters them from snatching your food at the beach.

How to stop a gull from stealing your food.

(Camero 2019)

It's a headline Camero wrote about the findings of a group of biologists who study seagull behaviour at the University of Exeter. Her piece is a short news item, so the headline is supposed to be non-metaphorical and to the point, telling the quintessence of the story. Apart from the headline type (which doesn't give away the whole story but merely promises that the article will deliver the answer), all the storytelling elements are there. We have a protagonist (you, the reader), an antagonist (the seagull). Both have a clear goal (a pack of chips, "your food" in the headline). "Stealing" implies the fact that both you and the gull aim for the same goal, which is bound for conflict. The headline doesn't give away the resolution of the conflict, but it implies that if you will read on, the article is going to deliver the answer (which it does).

Not all titles will try to convey a full story arc or give you a sense of a character's journey. The title can also express a story's theme, or it can stem from an entirely different storytelling pillar. For example, dialogue. In 1965, John McPhee wrote his nonfiction book *A Sense Of Where You Are*, a profile of Princeton basketballer Bill Bradley. In a conversation at the University of Colorado-Boulder, McPhee reveals that the title is actually a piece of dialogue that he had jotted down while spending time with his protagonist on the Basketball court. McPhee had submitted the manuscript without a title, and his editor extracted the title from the dialogue. According to McPhee, it was his editor's best title ever (Nijhuis 2011). It's also a point of insight the protagonist lets readers participate in. So you actually have two story elements here: dialogue and a point of insight.

If you look at what works best online, you might be inclined to think that story doesn't really count in headlines on the web. The rules of online headline writing seem to be backed by marketing wisdom, like using questions to increase share-ability and hence the odds of going viral online, at least if you believe popular articles like Sheri Jacob's (2017) piece for *The Daily Egg*. In it, she also quotes SEO specialist *MOZ* in saying that headlines using numbers ("30 ways to…"), addressing readers directly ("What you should…"), how-to ("How to lose weight"…), normal ("Ways to make ABC more pleasant") and questions, those are the most preferred ones (Jacob 2017, drawing on *MOZ*' findings). That said, nobody has found a surefire, guaranteed formula for headlines to go viral. But these rules are mechanic, quantified and dangerous. Why dangerous?

Think about science writing. Storytelling often implies causality, but that's not always the case. Many types of studies merely find associations but no causal relationships. In a piece for *Health News Review*, science journalists Kathlyn Stone and Joy Victory (2016) caution against writing headlines that promise too clear-cut messages, and she points out the differences in headlines' narratives. This advice obviously opposes the usual advice to be as specific and as clear as possible. But getting the headline factually right doesn't mean you have to be vague. On the contrary, being more precise can actually solve the problem. Stone and Victory point out that "may" and "might" headlines have their own short-comings, especially when they are being followed by constructs that promise again cause and effect, such as "the answer". Here's an example: "Meditation may be the answer to relieving chronic back pain." Conditional forms often simply obfuscate a lack of knowledge and are a perfect means for authors to escape responsibility. Also, they add little value for the readers. Does it work or not? Such headlines tell very little about that. Stone and Victory suggest rewriting such headlines in multiple steps to get more specific:

1   "Study participants who added meditation to treatment plan report more relief than control group". This version is much more precise, without making any false promises. It contains protagonist, complication and a possible resolution. But it's too long to be a headline. So, Stone and Victory (2017) suggest further reducing it and show how it's done:
2   "Meditation: Study shows it helped some back pain sufferers". This version has a kicker in the beginning that defines the domain, i.e. the topic of this piece. It still contains all the elements without losing any of its precision.

Can you go shorter still? Again, yes! Randy Olson pointed out on Twitter a headline he had found in the *Malibu Times*. It was for a piece on RVs leaking their sewage into the Pacific, and the residents complaining about it. The title? "Affluent oppose effluent". Three words, and it's all there. Protagonists, antagonist and conflict. No resolution, obviously, but that's the goal of the headline: lure readers into reading the full article. I would add that despite how perfectly condensed the title is, I'm not too big a champion of wordplays in headlines. Besides, it only works if you read it. On air, it'd be way less clear.

What I would recommend for writing headlines: as long as you are being factually correct, experiment with the form. Extract headlines as full stories (for news pieces), or partial story arcs (features), metaphors (only in print, please), use parts of dialogue (hat tip to John McPhee), use the ABT, use a condensed story spine. When you do, be clear in your statements and avoid ambiguities. Writing a good headline is like poetry, and very much like cooking a great dish. It takes time to condense and boil it down. As for what ingredients you use: everything is fair game, as long as your ingredients are high quality. And make sure your headlines are correct, word for word.

Case study: Stories on climate change

Scientific organisations, agencies and academia start recognising the potential of telling stories. Stories are especially popular because they allow scientists to implement the gathered knowledge right away. So it's no wonder that the National Park Service (NPS) has appointed Olson as a story consultant and now uses the ABT structure. In 2014, they tried it out during a session at the World Parks Congress. Under the premise that every place has its own climate story, the organisers asked participants to put together stories using Olson's ABT format. Rockman (2015) sums up the method up like this: "*And* introduces facts; *But* includes facts with present tension; and *Therefore* introduces a solution." She adds that the ABT is a way to help speakers think and organise a set of facts enticingly. It makes sense, because, as she states, climate stories are not just sets of facts but actually ask for narrative. The resulting stories helped the NPS see climate stories not as complex scientific problems but to understand change and challenge themselves (Rockman 2015).

In its "Cultural Resources Climate Change (CRCC) Strategy" report (Rockman *et al.* 2016), the National Park Service gets even more specific and puts quite a bit of weight on the ABT to develop climate change stories. The report authors recommend using Olson's ABT template to write climate change stories, focusing on narrative and not characters. They found four categories of climate change stories that lend themselves to applying narrative storytelling, and trying to answer the attached questions (adapted from Rockman *et al.* 2016):

1 **Change in the material world**: how does climate change manifest in the world? (mountains, landscapes, houses)
2 **Change in experience and lifeways**: how does climate change influence the daily life of the traditional and indigenous population?
3 **Insights on change from past societies**: how have past societies responded to climate variations and faced challenges?
4 **Origins of modern climate change situation**: how has the modern climate change situation come to be?

So, the NPS has come up with four frames that better help narrow down the type of story so it can be told narratively. I found a number of beautiful statements in their report that really reflect this book's theme. For one, they state that "climate stories are not fiction, but research organized as narrative" (Rockman *et al.* 2016:17). This encapsulates perfectly why scientists don't have to be afraid of using storytelling techniques (and nor do non-scientists who tell science stories). The report includes a story example, built on the ABT, that falls into the "insights" category. I've highlighted the keywords that pinpoint the ABT:

> Circa AD 1064, Sunset Crater in northern Arizona erupted. The area now known as Wupatki National Monument (WUPA), 15 miles north of Sunset Crater, received 2–4 inches of ash and corn cobs encased in lava are evidence of the damage from the eruption. **AND** tree rings show that weather patterns in the area that had been wet turned dry at about this time and continued predominantly dry for several decades.
>
> **BUT** despite the stresses of the eruption and change in climate, the local Sinagua people remained nearby. They moved to the plains below the crater, and began to farm again, with the addition of cinder mulch. Stones and lithic material have been used to improve soil conditions in many places around the world in prehistory, but had not previously been used in northern Arizona. The cinders helped the dry soils retain moisture and may have improved farm yields beyond pre-eruption levels. Protection of the cinders may have waned after several decades, possibly alongside the continuing drought, but this innovation helped the Sinagua reestablish their lives after the volcanic disaster.
>
> **THEREFORE**, the history and archeology of this area provide an example of traditional agriculture and innovation using local materials that may be useful in some places in the future as the climate becomes hotter and drier.
>
> (Rockman et al. 2016:17)

The National Park Service also came up with a shorter example for the first category ("material change") that describes the "why" of their research and hence serves as an efficient outreach tool.

> The Catoctin cabins were built as the first recreational camp for disabled children in the 1930s **AND** are still in use today as nature retreats, **BUT** projections indicate increasing temperatures will lead to structural damage from more intense rainfall events, **THEREFORE** NPS is researching ways to preserve historic mortar.
>
> (Rockman et al. 2016:31)

They also applied the word ("Dobzhansky") template and figured out that this story's theme is "stewardship". The ABT they've come up with follows a problem-solution approach, which frequently works in social media stories also. It's perfectly imaginable how they could further boil down this one-sentence ABT into a social media or even blog title. On Facebook, it could run as it is, and probably also on Twitter. To further boil it down, though, would mean to choose the right words, play with them and ruthlessly select and reject. That's what I'm going to dive into in the next chapter, which is all about language and style.

Review questions

- What is the hero's journey?
- How can you apply the hero's journey to research projects?
- How does the Dobzhansky template work, and which story elements does it contain?
- Which version of the ABT would you use to explain your research at a party?
- What can you use the story spine for?
- Which elements does a theme consist of, and should you order them?
- Which story formula would you use to write a science tweet?
- How can you tell a story in a headline?

Links

"Pixar in a box: The art of storytelling" (Khan Academy): https://www.khanaca demy.org/partner-content/pixar/storytelling

"Top 500 six-word stories" (Reddit): https://www.reddit.com/r/sixwordstories/ comments/9erwj1/top_500_sixword_stories_2018/

"Very short stories" (*WIRED* magazine): https://www.wired.com/2006/11/ very-short-stories/

"Using Stories to Learn From the Past" (NPS): https://www.nps.gov/subjects/ climatechange/upload/CCRP-Newsletter-Q1-2015.pdf

References

Adams, K. (2013) "Back to the Story Spine," Aerogramme Writers' Studio [Online]. Available at: https://www.aerogrammestudio.com/2013/06/05/back-to-the-story-sp ine/ (date accessed 9 August 2019).

Adams, K. (2007) *How to Improvise a Full-Length Play*. New York: Allworth Press.

Angler, M.W. (2017) *Science Journalism: an introduction*. London: Routledge.

Camero, K. (2019) "How to stop a gull from stealing your food," *Science* [Online]. Available at: https://www.sciencemag.org/news/2019/08/how-stop-gull-stealing-your-food (date accessed 11 August 2019).

Campbell, J. (1949) *The Hero with a Thousand Faces*. 1st edition. New York: Pantheon.

Efthimiou, O. & Franco, Z.E. (2017) "Heroic Intelligence: The Hero's Journey as an Evolutionary Blueprint," *Journal of Genius and Eminence*, vol. 2, no. 2, 33–44.

Egri, L. (1946) *The Art of Dramatic Writing*. New York: Simon and Schuster.

ElShafie, S. (2018) "Making science meaningful for broad audiences through stories," *Integrative and Comparative Biology*, vol. 58, no. 6, 1213–1223.

Forsyth, M. (2013) *The Elements of Eloquence: How to turn the perfect English phrase*. London: Icon Books.

Frishberg, H. (2019) "Diabetic groom-to-be dies after taking cheaper insulin to pay for wedding," *New York Post* [Online]. Available at: https://nypost.com/2019/08/06/dia betic-groom-to-be-dies-after-taking-cheaper-insulin-to-pay-for-wedding/ (date accessed 10 August 2019).

Georgas, H., Regalado, M. & Burgess, M. (2017) "Choose Your Own Adventure: The Hero's Journey and the Research Process," Association of College & Research Libraries Conference 2017 Proceedings [Online]. Available at: http://www.ala.org/acrl/sites/ala. org.acrl/files/content/conferences/confsandpreconfs/2017/ChooseYour OwnAdventure.pdf (date accessed 8 August 2019).

Harris, R.M. (2017) "My first STEMprov Story Spine," Medium [Online]. Available at: https://medium.com/@raynamharris/my-first-stemprove-story-spine-62ffa6259ec (date accessed 9 August 2019).

Hasson, U., Landesman, O., Knappmeyer, B., Vallines, I., Rubin, N., & Heeger, D.J. (2008) "Neurocinematics: The neuroscience of film," *Projections*, vol. 2, no. 1, 1–26.

Jacob, S. (2017) "The Science Behind High-Performing Headlines," *The Daily Egg* [Online]. Available at: https://www.crazyegg.com/blog/high-performing-headlines/ (date accessed 11 August 2019).

Lynch, J. (2018) "Pixar's most successful movies at the box office, including record-break-ing 'Incredibles 2'," *Business Insider* [Online]. Available at: https://www.businessinsider. com/pixar-most-successful-film-2016-6?IR=T (date accessed 9 August 2019).

Nijhuis, M. (2011) "John McPhee on Characters, Structure, Titles, and Facing the 'Low Dread' of Writing," The Open Notebook [Online]. Available at: https://www.theop ennotebook.com/2011/11/08/john-mcphee/ (date accessed 11 August 2019).

Olivo, A. (2019) "He lost his insurance and turned to a cheaper form of insulin. It was a fatal decision," *Washington Post* [Online]. Available at: https://www.washingtonpost.com/local/ he-lost-his-insurance-and-turned-to-cheaper-form-of-insulin-it-was-a-fatal-decision/2019/08/ 02/106ec79a-b24d-11e9-8f6c-7828e68cb15f_story.html (date accessed 10 August 2019).

Olson, R. (2015) *Houston, We Have a Narrative: Why Science Needs Story.* Chicago: Chicago University Press.

Reese, N. (2018) "How to use storytelling to craft better Tweets," Twitter Business Blog [Online]. Available at: https://business.twitter.com/en/blog/how-to-use-storytelling-to-cra ft-better-tweets.html (date accessed 10 August 2019).

Rhimes, S. (2018) "Developing the Concept," Masterclass [Online]. Available at: https:// www.masterclass.com/classes/shonda-rhimes-teaches-writing-for-television/chapters/ developing-the-concept# (date accessed 10 August 2019).

Rockman, M., Morgan, M., Ziaja, S., Hambrecht, G. & Meadow, A. (2016) *Cultural Resources Climate Change Strategy.* Washington, DC: Cultural Resources, Partnerships, and Science and Climate Change Response Program, National Park Service.

Rockman, M. (2015) "Using Stories to Learn From the Past," CCRP Newsletter Q1–2015, NPS.gov [Online]. Available at: https://www.nps.gov/subjects/climatechange/upload/ CCRP-Newsletter-Q1-2015.pdf (date accessed 11 August 2019).

Rotmann, S. (2017) "'Once upon a time…' Eliciting energy and behaviour change stories using a fairy tale story spine," *Energy Research & Social Science*, vol. 31, September, 303–310.

Ryan, G.W. & Bernard, H.R. (2000) *Techniques to identify themes in qualitative data. Handbook of Qualitative Research.* 2nd edition. Thousand Oaks, CA: Sage Publications

Schilf, M. (2015) "The Story Equation: S = (C + W) x O," The Script Lab [Online]. Available at: https://thescriptlab.com/features/screenwriting-101/3353-the-story-equa tion-s-c-w-x-o/ (date accessed 6 August 2019).

Shelby, A. & Ernst, K. (2013) "Story and science: how providers and parents can utilize storytelling to combat anti-vaccine misinformation," *Human vaccines & immunotherapeutics*, vol. 9, no. 8, 1795–1801.

Stone, K. & Victory, J. (2016) "5 tips for writing better health news headlines," *Health-NewsReview* [Online]. Available at: https://www.healthnewsreview.org/2016/04/5-tip s-for-writing-better-health-headlines/ (date accessed 11 August 2019).

Suderman, P. (2013) "Save the Movie! The 2005 screenwriting book that's taken over Hollywood – and made every movie feel the same," Slate [Online]. Available at: http s://slate.com/culture/2013/07/hollywood-and-blake-snyders-screenwriting-book-sa ve-the-cat.html (date accessed 7 August 2019).

Walter, R. (2010) *Essentials of Screenwriting: The Art, Craft and Business of Film and Television Writing*. New York: Plume.

Yorke, J. (2013) *Into the Woods: How Stories Work and Why We Tell Them*. UK: Penguin Books.

6 Language and Style

What you will learn in this chapter:

- The language of fake news
- The ABCs of journalism
- A word on jargon
- Good writing practices
- Transitions
- Clichés
- Sensory language
- Case study: Return of the wild

The best structure is in vain if you're using shitty language to flesh it out. If you're telling a story you need to create mental images in your readers' heads. There are words that work better for that purpose and words that don't work so well. But there is more to it than just beautifully describing places, moments and characters. Style is a lot more than just creating graspable images in your readers' heads. You can reveal a lot about style if you read your texts out loud. Does it sound right? This should always be the final test before submitting or publishing it. If it sounds monotonous, you might want to have a look at your sentence and paragraph length. Ask yourself: is there enough rhythm in it, or do all sentences sound equally long? The same is true of paragraphs: If you vary their rhythm (that is, their length), the piece becomes more interesting. Imagine this: when are you more likely to fall asleep behind the wheel? When you're driving on a long, straight, monotonous highway, or on a road that winds its way up a mountain? Like a good mountain road, you have to keep your readers awake. In this chapter, you'll find some techniques to do that.

If your copy sounds boring or even trite, chances are you are using words that aren't yours. They've been used before. They're standard or bureaucracy speak. In that case, look out for clichés and dead metaphors. "They're shortcuts to comprehension that we use when we are creatively lazy or mentally bankrupt" (Helitzer 2005:64). Most of them are non-recyclable, so it's best if you come up with your own mental images. Then let your readers in on them. If you still want to use clichés, we can't be friends. Of course, it sometimes happens to all of us.

That's why it's really important that you dedicate some time to spot them, and then cut and slash them. This is one of the reasons why editing and revising is so important. They have an incredible power to turn a well-structured text into a lousy read. So I've dedicated an entire section of this chapter to them, along with some techniques to avoid and rewrite them.

Although this is not strictly a journalism book, I'd love to show you the ABCs of journalism. They are just three little keywords. Every well-written piece respects them, and you can apply them in spoken language, too. We'll have to have a word on jargon, too. If you're not going to read beyond this introduction, here's the main takeaway. Avoid. The slightly longer version of this piece of advice is: if you can't avoid jargon, explain it. Use metaphors and similes to do that. Original ones, please. We'll also talk about word choice. That's why I've included a section on writing practice. Especially in science, it's easy to fall into the narcissistic trap and try to sound super smart. It happens to the best of us at some point. Whenever you can, replace loanwords with English words. Replace complicated with simple ones. Replace long words with short ones. That said, if you occasionally sprinkle unusual words into your text, you'll catch your readers' attention. I'm talking about English words that aren't frequently used and seen in writing, not acronyms, jargon or loanwords.

We'll also have a look at transitions. It's something that keeps exciting me, even after more than a decade of professional writing. It's the glue that keeps together the different ideas of your text. It connects them logically. So that's where style and structure intermingle to finally form a compelling read your audience will love to read. The best writers do it in a way that their readers don't even notice. Another method to immerse your readers into a story is to use present tense. A subtle way to signal a switch from story to expository writing is changing the tense from present to past. In most cases, the simple present and past will do.

Of course, a section on sensory language can't be missing in a chapter like this. It is indeed one of the means to immerse your readers right into a scene. It's fantastic if you describe places, characters and situations. As you'll see, you don't need much description to create images in your readers' heads. In fact, reducing it to single adjectives instead of over-elaborate adjective caravans is much more effective and way less confusing for your readers. The takeaway here: be subtle in your descriptions. Your readers are smart.

What bookends this chapter? First, let's look at the masters of storytelling language. I'm talking about fake newsers. Although they have no substance at all, they're good at delivering stories that arouse readers' emotions, and that is no accident. Maybe knowing how they write will help you catch a liar in the future, who knows?

In the final section of this chapter, we're going to analyse how Emma Marris' story of wolves in California employs style. How does she pull it off? She applies many of the stylistic principles shown in this chapter. I would recommend you read her piece right before reading the section. It'll help you get a feeling for good style. You can find a link to it at the end of this chapter. I read her piece in one shot, and for good reason, as it turns out. So let's get started with fake news. What language do fake newsers use?

The language of fake news

Yes, I added a section on fake news to this chapter. Boom. I mean, it's fascinating to observe and analyse. It works. It's viral content that spreads without any factual substance. But why does it work? Here, I'd like to take a look at the linguistic clock-work that makes fake news tick. It's pretty obvious that they also follow a narrative structure, employ anecdotal evidence and whatnot, yes. But apart from that, you will also find language elements that help them make what they are: highly persuasive. Computer scientists are working hard on algorithms that can detect fake news. I appreciate those efforts, and I'm quite damn sure they will improve how the giant online platforms work. At some point. BUT (and that's a capital but), fake news is primarily a human problem. They tap into our emotions, manipulate us into falling for false cause and effect conclusions and then cajole us to sharing them further.

In 2018, a team of MIT media and management researchers found a few worrying things in their often-cited study. Lies reach up to a 100 times more people than true stories. The scientists had investigated 126,000 tweets from 2006 to 2017, spread by 3 million people. Also, and most notably, they found that robots don't have as much influence as many had assumed until then. Instead, humans are responsible for the majority of fake news spread. In fact, rumours and fake news are 70 per cent more likely to be retweeted than true statements. The MIT researchers have a few theories as for why that's the case. First, they think the novelty of a statement could push people to propagate the findings, as it would raise their social status to be the first ones in the loop. But, it turns out that was not really easy to prove. So they had a look at emotion-laden words. They took a lexicon of the National Research Council, consisting of 140,000 words that are associated with eight emotions that are based on psychologist Robert Plutchik's wheel of emotions (Plutchik & Kellerman 1980). They are: anger, fear, anticipation, trust, surprise, sadness, joy, and disgust. The MIT scientists compared the list against 32,000 Twitter hashtags and found that fake news prompt (human) users to reply with surprise (which confirms the "novelty" theory) and disgust. Truthful news, however, inspired users to reply with words that indicated sadness, anticipation, joy and trust (Vosoughi, Roy & Aral 2018).

Fake news is often carefully crafted. And despite all the effort, it's possible to spot a lie. Because that's essentially what fake news is. A big fat lie. But humans are pretty bad at detecting it (Conroy, Rubin & Chen 2015). So computer scientists try to employ artificial intelligence to detect fake news before, or instead of, humans. In other words: even if you're a very careful fake newser, it shows in your texts. The frequencies of certain pronouns, conjunctions and negative-emotion words are one approach to test texts automatically for being fake news (Conroy, Rubin & Chen 2015), although they admit that approach is limited. So, where should we look to find lying people online? Where could we find clues as for which language is used to deceive other people? That's right: online dating. Psychologist Jeffrey T. Hancock and communication professor Catalina L. Toma took a closer look and found a few cues. First, they establish that anytime you deceive somebody, it affects you emotionally and cognitively, this was known before. Lying produces anxiety, which, when you're talking to somebody, can manifest as hesitance and delayed answers. Toma and Hancock (2012) then identified the linguistic cues that indicate the emotional and cognitive states of lying. They specifically looked at pronouns, prepositions, articles, conjunctions and auxiliary verbs. These are non-content words and quite difficult to control when you're lying. Content words are easier to control, at least in theory. Many people can't control them, either. Essentially, when you lie online, it puts your brain into a state of anxiety, shame and guilt. This reflects in the words you use, and the amount of negative-emotion words surges. Examples are: "hate", "sorry", "worthless". If you try to control these words, a mechanism called "psychological distancing" kicks in. You'll reduce the amount of personal pronouns like "I", "me", "we" to distance yourself from the lie. At the same time, negations like "no", "not" and "never" will increase, because your commitment to the false statement is low (Toma & Hancock 2012).

They found more than that: when you're consciously trying to conceal a lie, you'll have to increase the amount of brain power, or cognitive complexity, to do so. Again, this shows in your choice of words. Exclusive words like "but", "without" and "except" are less likely to appear, because they differentiate between categories, which requires cognitive brain power - which you don't have when you're writing up lies. I guess that's good news for the ABT we've seen in the previous chapter. At least it's not intrinsically lie-prone. The second conscious indicator is the use of motion verbs. Concrete, short verbs like "walk", "move" and "go" seem to increase when people lie online. The reason: they're easier to string together and demand less complexity from your already-busy lying brain. Toma and Hancock (2012) also write that liars are actually more prone to writer shorter texts, because it's easier to avoid getting caught lying when the fake message is short.

Other researchers confirm these findings to a large extent, and they add a few more. Interestingly, Hauch et al. (2015) could not confirm all of their research questions. For example, they had assumed that liars would use more uncertain terms than truth-tellers, but the opposite happened. In their study, liars expressed anger as the most frequent emotion, and they denied accusations. Generally, liars used more emotion-laden words. In terms of passive voice or verb tenses, they found no differences between liars and truth-tellers.

I'm not saying let's do it exactly like they do it. After all, that would be lying to the readers. But what if truthful science writing utilised some of those storytelling and linguistic techniques to write truthful stories? You can certainly apply a few of those techniques, like the use of motion words, or writing shorter and more concise texts. These methods play into some of the most fundamental principle of journalism: Accuracy, brevity and clarity, and that's what we'll look at in the next section.

The ABCs of journalism

True, there is both an art and a craft part when it comes to writing. This goes for both fiction and nonfiction writing. The art is often developing the right intuition of applying the most effective technique to achieve a specific goal. For example, letting a character speak when it doesn't really fit into the story structure or the theme adds no value. Have you ever had the feeling that something doesn't "fit" into a story at a particular moment? That's already one important writing principle: whatever you write should be on the page for good reason. Everything that doesn't belong in the story goes to the bin. That is why I throw away more than 90 per cent of my reporting, especially for longer pieces. That's not to say that the information in it hasn't added any value. In fact, it has shaped my understanding of the topic, the characters and the story, up to the point that a theme emerges. Sometimes, I don't start writing real copy until that hasn't happened. Or, to view the problem from a different perspective: if a queasy sensation in my gut hinders me from grabbing the keyboard to start writing, if the words don't flow, then I usually haven't anything to say, yet (either that, or it's one of my bleeding ulcers popping up again). When writers don't have anything to say, they haven't developed the theme yet. Usually.

And when they have something to say, there are a few very good writing principles that apply universally, no matter whether they're writing hard news or narrative pieces. Since this book is about science writing, it makes sense that we look at some journalistic principles first, starting with the famous ABCs of journalism. "A" is for accuracy. Above all, what they write should be correct, regardless of whether you quote, paraphrase, attribute, state. In the 2018 edition of their stylebook, the *Associated Press* states the following:

> We abhor inaccuracies, carelessness, bias or distortions. We will not knowingly introduce rumor or false information into material intended for publication or broadcast; nor will we distort visual content. Quotations must be accurate and precise.
>
> (Associated Press 2018)

Writing accurately means also that you verify all information before you put it into a piece (Mencher 2011). I keep citing Mencher's advice (also in my previous book), because he looks at these principles from various angles. One of these angles is language: "Words are chosen carefully to match the situation, event or individual. The writer who settles for the imprecise rather than the exact word lives dangerously, teetering on the brink of being misunderstood or misleading readers and listeners" (Mencher 2011:32). He makes an example: "We don't say she was 'unusually tall.' We write she was 'an inch over six feet tall.'" (Mencher 2011:32). See the difference? The first statement is subject to interpretation. How tall is unusually tall? There's no measure. The second statement, however, you can measure that. Accuracy means choosing the right words. They must not be ambiguous. As you'll see in a minute, the principles actually are all somehow related. And it doesn't matter if you're writing longform narrative pieces for a magazine or a short news item, as literary journalist Gay Talese confirms in a panel discussion (Giles 2002): "There is no excuse for any inaccuracy that is the result of someone wishing to make the story a little bit more readable."

"B" is for brevity. The accuracy bit can be overdone in terms of length. If you're a scientist, you're used to getting away with rambling on for pages. As long as it's factually correct, you can waffle as much as you want. This can easily become too nitpicking an attitude. If you want to point out all the caveats, all the catches and limitations, that's rather a sign of fear of getting nailed down on your statements. That's not what good writing is. If you're a news journalist, you have less leeway. Space is limited in newspapers and magazines (less so online, but still), so editors will ruthlessly cut your text, force you to rewrite it, or straight out reject it. You have to get to the point and boil down a story to its quintessence while finding the right words to get your audience enticed about it. The true masters at brevity? Poets. Mencher claims that creative work is based on omission. I would weigh in and add that it's all about selection and rejection. You can apply this principle to all levels of abstraction of a story: words, sentences, paragraphs, story structure, characters. Include what is relevant for the story, and don't digress too much. At the very least, don't stray from the theme. And I'm saying this as someone with a natural inclination to digress. The supreme exercise in brevity then must be headline writing, as Mencher (2011) confirms. Ironically, if you overdo it, you can introduce ambiguity in titles, which then become sometimes unintentionally, sometimes intentionally, hilarious. Here are a few I found:

- Students Cook & Serve Grandparents (unknown source)
- Come inside: The World's Biggest Sperm Bank (*The Guardian*, 2012)
- Chick Accuses Some of Her Male Colleagues of Sexism (*LA Times*, 1995, "Chick" is the surname of the victim)

While the topics mentioned in the headlines are newsworthy and/or serious, the ambiguity of a single word sometimes can introduce uncertainty or a laugh. That's one of the reasons why word plays are frowned upon in headline writing.

Also, and quite intuitively, how well your readers understand your message depends on how clearly you deliver it. So here's my favourite of the ABCs: "C" is for clarity. I hate writing, editing and reading vague copy. It's just a waste of time. For the author, who produces it, because it has no content. For the readers, because they don't get any take-home messages from artificially blown-up texts. To make things worse, writers who don't select the most succinct words to express their thoughts may have not yet fully grasped what they want you to know about it. They probably haven't understood it themselves. Vague speech and writing is just a sign of fear. Fear of getting pinned down. That is why politicians are often so vague in selecting their words. They want to appeal to as many people as possible, and at the same time, they don't want to provide anyone with a target (Gruber 1993), while keeping the freedom to fully deny their statements later on. Here's an example: if you walk into a butcher's and ask for half a pound of pork loin, you'll probably get it without much discussion. But if you go in and ask for "just meat", you're being unclear for no apparent reason. The butcher will have to ask you what sort of meat you want, what cut and how much of it. It just takes longer to communicate. In terms of writing style, Mencher has clear advice for you: "Delete adjectives and adverbs, irrelevant quotations. The guide: Make it brief but clear and complete [...] Clarity is enhanced by simplicity of expression, which generally means short sentences, everyday language, coherence and logical story structure" (Mencher 2011:49). In terms of clarity, I had a long and insightful phone call with *The Guardian*'s now retired science editor Tim Radford in 2015. His advice: if you can use a short word instead of a long one, use it. If an English word exists that expresses what you're trying to say, use that instead of loanwords. This I can fully advocate. Many scientists I have seen write, write for their own sake without caring about the audience, and for what Mencher calls the "enchantment with the sound or look of your writing" (Mencher 2011:48). They just want to sound smart, and that's never a good idea. This attitude causes the opposite of what Radford recommends. It introduces a penchant for choosing long, overcomplicated loanwords, and, worse, jargon. And jargon equals death.

A word on jargon

Avoid. Essentially, that's it. That's my advice. But hang on. Of course, this is too simple and too strict a claim. At the other extreme end of the spectrum of understanding, scientists use too much jargon in their publications, presentations and talks. Here's why I think they do: first, they want to sound smart in front of their audience, which is part of their professional social system. I'm not saying they are not, but wouldn't it be actually clever to consider whom they are talking to and then adapt the level of abstraction to the audience? I would certainly explain the Manhattan Project differently to my children than to a bunch of scientists (that is, if I had any children and if I was in the position of actually being able to explain the Manhattan Project to any physicist). Connected to that is fear. Fear of "dumbing down" science, fear of losing face, fear of damaging their reputation. Maybe it's also fear of opposition. It's not just that idea that an increasing count of loanwords and Greek- and Latin-based jargon makes you sound smart that seems to be etched forever into science education and scientists' brains. It's also practical. You can't be criticised for claims that people don't understand. You will have the support of academia if you continue writing in cipher. It's just fashionable (I could have written "in vogue" here, had I wanted to sound cool) to use lots of loanwords. David Shariatmadari, a *Guardian* editor, has just written a book on language. In a piece for said outlet, he has pointed out jargon as a gut issue, citing politician (and former journalist) Michael Gove:

> Since becoming a member of parliament I've been learning a new language ... No one ever uses a simple Anglo-Saxon word, or a concrete example, where a Latinate construction or a next-to-meaningless abstraction can be found.
>
> (Gove in Shariatmadari 2019)

If, in academia, you dare to care about whom you are talking to and what you want them to know, you risk being disrespected by your academic peers. That is why I mentioned "fear" as one of the roots of jargon-laden writing. Carl Sagan is probably the best-known case of a scientist who is a natural in communicating science to the public. To be clear, Sagan was also an established astronomer. To date, his h-index on Google Scholar clocks in at 74, and his most-cited paper from 1992 has been cited almost 1,200 times. Alas, Sagan also faced a lot of backlash from his academic colleagues for doing public outreach. This perception is known as the Sagan effect: the more visible you are, the lower your academic qualities. Indeed, some scientists may be renowned just for being VIPs, but most of the times, you will not have to fear backlash for outreach. Most importantly, communicating discoveries is part and parcel of science (Martinez-Conde 2016).

Now, in science writing (as opposed to scientific writing), you can avoid much jargon, but not all of it. In one of his *National Geographic* articles, Ed Yong points out the pitfalls that hamper the general public from understanding science writing. His list includes "passive voice, laboured construction and roundabout sentences" (Yong 2010). But what Yong really focuses on are overly technical and scientific terms, in other words: jargon. Jargon comes into play when you as the author are so familiar with the terms you bandy about that you simply assume everybody else in the world is familiar with them, too. Wrong. And that's not only true if you're trying to reach the general public but also fellow scientists that may not be exactly specialised in the same niche field as you are:

> Writers should always remember that the more technical you get, the more restrictive you get, even if people are writing for a scientific audience. Eventually, other scientists who aren't from the same narrow speciality become part of the amorphous "general public".
>
> (Yong 2010)

Do use some jargon. Explain the terms that are crucial, the ones your audience needs to know. In said phone call to *The Guardian*'s former science editor Tim Radford, he told me that it took him decades to familiarise the general public with the term DNA. Decades. His secret? He kept repeating and explaining it. Over and over again. Just don't assume your readers will know what it means without any explanation. You can do so in an accessory clause. If the term is too complicated, you might want to digress for a moment and dedicate a paragraph or two to it. Your tools? Use metaphors and similes to make people relate to it. If you know and care whom you are writing for, you will know what your readers are interested in. Make it graspable and relatable, paint pictures in their minds. If you can, use an anecdote. Most often, when terms or concepts are boring or raise eyebrows, then the audience cannot attribute any kind of meaning to it. That's also what good storytelling does: it lends meaning to abstract concepts. I once started doing extreme value exercises with engineering students. They couldn't have given less of a shit about the topic, even if they tried. Once I noticed, I told them how it's an actual problem that engineers need to calculate the smallest can surface for packaging tomatoes. This sort of exercise helps the companies keep the material costs at a minimum. Once I had made it graspable, the students were game for some calculations. In written form, I could have weaved this in as an extra clause in the sentence containing the extreme values. As a side note, did you notice how many storytelling elements there were in? Problem (material costs are too high), solution (extreme value exercise), and protagonists the students could identify with because of their own education (engineers). How else can you reduce your jargon when writing for a lay audience? Use an English dictionary. Every writer must have one. Then just test the word by asking yourself a few questions:

- Is this a loanword?
- If so: why did I use it? (be honest with yourself)
- If so: can I find a synonym in plain English?
- If so: can I find a shorter word in plain English?
- Is this a word with three or more syllables?
- If so: can I find a shorter one?

In all cases: If the answer is yes, replace. If you want to write "superfluous", I'm not going to say you shouldn't. But it's rooted in Latin. And it's four syllables long. Chances are that, depending on your audience, not everybody will know what it means. A look at the Oxford English Dictionary shows alternatives: "redundant" (not much of an improvement), "worthless", "pointless", "obsolete" (shorter but still borrowed from Latin), "unnecessary", "uncalled for". Lots of alternatives, some shorter, some not. Which one fits best depends on the context of your writing. I argue that everybody knows what "worthless" and "pointless" mean. "Obsolete"? Not as many. And if you want to really go short, just turn it into "extra". Reducing jargon to a minimum ensures that more people can understand it than just your closest peers, and it also makes it much more readable and enjoyable. And shorter. Extra note: have you noticed how perfectly this jargon-macheteing falls in line with the ABCs of journalism?

Here's an extra tip: Yong (2010) recommends that you signal jargon explanations by using words like "basically" or "effectively". I see Yong's point, I really do, although I'm not a big supporter of such expletives, and adverbs have done no good in the world. He also mentions that it's the goal of some scientists to educate the world (I think that's a horrible goal as it sounds patronising, a bit like force-feeding geese before Thanksgiving). He brilliantly points out the difference between how it's done and how it should be done: "You educate people by explaining complex ideas in a simple way, not by explaining simple ideas in a complex way" (Yong 2010).

Good writing practices

Writing is like sculpting. You take a marble block and chisel away until you shape a rough draft of the sculpture. It's highly imperfect and lacks all the details, but in essence you have outlined where you will apply the chisels and rasps and files next to bring out the fine details. Then you start improving the rough shape, and iteration after iteration, it will start looking better and more detailed, until your desired level of details emerges. At the end, you will hone and polish it before you declare it finished.

In writing, like in sculpting, you have a number of tools you can apply to improve the clarity, to hone and polish it and to chisel out the fine details. This section deals with those tools. Every guild of writers falls victim to bad writing practices, and that's part of the learning process. Try. Fail. Learn. Repeat. That is my life's mantra. And it perfectly reflects storytelling: without failure, you won't learn. Without risk-taking ("try"), you won't create anything. In fact, in writing, the risk you'll have to take as a writer is being criticised as a bad writer (Litt 2016). In his *Guardian* piece, writer Toby Litt refers to fiction writers. But bad writing can happen to everybody. Not just novelists. Not just scientists. Not just journalists. That means the following techniques work in all domains. Let's start with words. Ideally, the action should always be crystal clear and make readers never guess: who does what? At the verb level, this means writing active verbs and using the simple present or past. The present's added benefit is that it immerses readers right into the action. So whenever you can, and at the latest when you're revising, substitute actives for passives and use the simple present and past as tenses. Also, try to avoid attachments like "sort of", "tend to", "kind of", "must have", "seemed to", "could have" and "use to" (Clark 2008). Writing coach Roy Peter Clark (2008) calls them barnacles. Brilliant.

Journalism commits its very own word crimes that are known as "journalese", which is "the death of freshness in anybody's style" (Zinsser 2001:33). What you shouldn't do is use adjectives as nouns ("the greats", "the notables") and nouns as verbs ("to host", "emote", "beef up"). The only way to become a good words-craftsman and build a good vocabulary is to read a lot, learn the fine nuances between synonyms and consult your dictionary. A good writer, in a way, is like a poet who cares deeply about words (Zinsser 2001).

And like a poet, you should play with words – even in nonfiction, serious stories. If this means breaking the rules occasionally, so be it. This principle also includes finding apt rhetoric figures and choosing words that readers normally wouldn't expect, for example in headlines. "Jubilant mob mauls four dead Americans" (Clark 2008) is a headline that uses familiar words ("jubilant", rather in upbeat stories, and "mauls" rather in dog-bites-man-stories) in an unfamiliar context. Again, this requires that you cultivate an extensive vocabulary, so you can choose the most concise word. Once you've written them down, pay attention to their sound and rhythm. Read them out loud. Use the words that sound well to your ear and don't go for fancy words (Strunk & White 2000).

Adverbs are unnecessary most of the time. If you choose strong nouns and verbs, you won't need them, and your sentences will be way shorter. All the good style guides and writing coaches (including Clark, also Strunk and White) recommend avoiding them, and for good reason. Adverbs further describe what has already been described, and they often add no new information to writing. Remove adverbs whenever you can, for example "when it carries the same meaning as the verb (smile happily)" (Zinsser 2001:16). They tell readers what to think. But that would violate the cardinal storytelling rule "show, don't tell." Why would you write: "He stood sadly in the rain" instead of "He stood in the rain and cried"? Readers have brains to think. They can make their own conclusions.

Always respect clarity, that goes also for sentences. Try to write declarative sentences whenever you can (this also works well in news headlines). Subject-verb-object. SVO. That simple. Who does what, and to/with/for whom/what (Clark 2008). In high school, we had a very strict maths and physics teacher, let's call him Mr. G. (I'm being euphemistic here. Everybody shat their pants when it came to examination time). Mr. G. had a penchant for order and structure. If you had written a blackboard full of formulas, and if he spotted an unreadable character somewhere along the lines, he would make you erase your entire calculations from scratch (yes, this has happened to me, and yes, we got in an argument, and yes, I received a fail grade for arguing and being belligerent). But apparently he was on to something that I would apply to this day in my writing: if you have written too complicated a sentence, and if it's not clear, then you are better up rewriting it from scratch. Better still, try and split it into two or three sentences. Because most likely, your sentence encapsulates more than one idea. And that's another style rule. Express one idea per sentence, not more. That's an easy way to spot if the current sentence you're writing expresses that same idea than the previous, just using different words. Declutter your text by putting such sentences between brackets, reading it again and then trying to read the text without those sentences. Is there information missing? If not, cut. This technique also works with single words and entire paragraphs (Zinsser 2001). If there was one piece of advice that I keep finding everywhere, it is this: keep it simple. Write as simply as you can. That means choose the most concise word. Cut out all unnecessary words from your sentences. Cut out all unnecessary sentences from your paragraphs.

But don't overdo it: sentences that belong together should go together, separated by a comma. Don't write a full stop until you finished the idea the first sentence contains. The full stop will not only make readers pause, but it also focuses their attention (just like the colon) on the word that follows the punctuation mark. Of course, you can use that for effect (Clark 2008). At some point, if you write sequences of too many very concise sentences, reading them can become monotonous. That's also because they tend to be short rather than long. Varying rhythm in terms of sentence length can be helpful. But here's a caveat: if you write loose sentences that start with a main clause and then add extra clauses using conjunctions like "and" and "but", then the latter clause just details the idea in the first one. Use them sparingly in your sentences, so your paragraph's rhythm can benefit from them. But if you have long successions of them, replace a few of them and vary your style: separate clauses with semicolons, write periodic sentences with two clauses instead. Periodic sentences are the opposite of loose sentences. In them, the main clause (or predicate) is at the end. As long as they are not too long, periodic sentences create suspense. And there is an easy way to convert "but"-based loose sentences into periodic sentences: switch the clauses, with the main clause going to the front. Eliminate the "but" and start the new sentence with "although" (Strunk & White 2000).

Transitions

In 2011, I attended a writing workshop led by German science journalism professor Winfried Göpfert. He was quite pleased with one of the sample texts I gave him. He asked me why I thought that was the case. I didn't have an answer. Göpfert said: "Bad texts are like a thick drink, hard to swallow. But good texts will make you want to guzzle them."

It's a nice analogy, but how do you write guzzle-texts? The ideas need to be logically interconnected, like a mesh. Readers have to be able to recognise a logical flow from one sentence to the other. It's the logical spine of your story, so in a way we're back at structure again. I've claimed before that every sentence should express just one idea. The same is true of paragraphs: express one idea, and let the sentences be your thesis and substantiating evidence, just like a mini-essay. That's the logical part. But there is also a craft part. If you want to glue your sentences and paragraphs and story together, you'll have to use transition words, phrases or even entire paragraphs. Here's a list of transition words you can use to connect sentences and paragraphs, subdivided into categories (adapted from Perelman & Barrett 1997):

- **Cause and effect**: so, that's why, hence, thus, therefore, that's why, as, since, because, which proves
- **Sequence**: and, next, first, last, too, in the first place
- **Comparison/contrast**: like, also, although, but, however, nevertheless, still, yet, that said, though, albeit, as if
- **Example**: that is, for example, for instance, in particular, like, which shows, in fact
- **Purpose**: for this purpose, for this reason, to this end, to, in order to
- **Time and location**: after, now, later, afterwards, then, above, below, beyond, here, there

Most writing recommendations state that 15 to 20 words is the ideal sentence length. But long sentences break up monotony and introduce rhythm. So use them, and transition words are a way to glue them either clauses within a sentence or single sentences. Let's have a look at how Esther Landhuis uses transition words to connect her sentences in an *Undark* article.

> OIT could soon go mainstream. [Paragraph ends here]
> **But at the moment**, allergists remain deeply divided over the treatment, **which** doesn't work for everyone and carries uncertain risks. **In contrast**, the traditional approach – avoidance of the trigger food – achieves safety for the vast majority of individuals. **In fact**, someone with a food allergy has a greater chance of being murdered than dying from an allergic reaction. **And yet** that fact belies the hidden stress and fear that grips many of the estimated 32 million Americans with food allergies. **For them**, the possibility of

a life-ending reaction looms large, and many are eager to see the FDA approve a drug that advocates say could put those fears to rest.

(Landhuis 2019)

I've made Landhuis' transitions bold, so you can spot them at a glance. "But at the moment" links the previous paragraph (where "OIT" is mentioned) to the following one. It's not referring to an object but rather signals contrast. Even "the treatment" is a logical connection to the previous sentence, because now it's clear that "OIT" is a treatment, even if you just read this excerpt. Note how Landhuis uses a transition word or phrase at the beginning of almost every sentence to glue them together. You don't get a chance to stop reading. "In fact" is another transition. "And yet" signals another turning point, contrast, conflict. "For them" is a clear reference to the 32 million American in the previous sentence. And that shows what transitions are: grappling hooks, that you, the writer, throw back into the previous sentence or paragraph. There, the hook latches onto an idea (substantiating or rebuffing it: "OIT could soon go mainstream" → "But at the moment") or to a concrete linguistic object ("32 million Americans" → "For them").

Transitioning from paragraph to paragraph takes a bit of preparation. Every paragraph has some sort of structure. The first sentence has to grip the readers, just like the lead of a story. In order to do that, you have to find a transition from the last sentence of the previous sentence and then go on and develop the story from there. So when you write a paragraph, think about how you'll transition into and out of it. You can also use the last sentence of a paragraph to add a twist of humor or surprise to excite the reader. "Make the reader smile and you've got him for at least one more paragraph" (Zinsser 2001:56).

To glue a new paragraph to the previous one, you can refer to the subject or an object in the previous' paragraph's last sentence. It's perfectly fine to repeat the noun (or a variation of it). It just makes it clear to the reader why the new paragraph exists: because you have to add something. In that sense, well-crafted paragraphs connect existing knowledge with new knowledge, which changes readers' state of knowledge. It's storytellling at work, at the paragraph level. Here's another example:

> [...] But sand represents defeat. A city with streets of sand is a city at the **edge**. [Paragraph ends here]
>   **That, of course, is why I was there**: Timbuktu is the ultimate desti-nation for **edge**-seekers.
>
> (Zinsser 2001:266–7)

Zinsser's transition is effective because he connects one of the objects of the final sentence in the previous paragraph and repeats that word in the new paragraph's first sentence. It is even more effective because he taps into cause and effect with the kicker at the beginning of the new paragraph. "That, of course, is why I was there." Eight words that turn this transition into a logical succession. And that's what's key: making it logical that two sentences or paragraphs follow each other. Transitioning is actually a creative process and allows you to come up with all sorts of relatable nexuses. That's your only criterion. Here's an example of how environmental journalist Sarah Gilman connects two paragraphs:

> 'For me, it's a story of hope.' [Paragraph ends here]
>   It's also a story of last resort.
>
> (Gilman 2019)

She ends the previous paragraph with a quote from a scientist. Then she starts the next paragraph by mirroring that quote and tweaking it so it becomes a contrasting statement of her own. Brilliantly done and a clear connection between both paragraphs.

Clichés

Much of this chapter is actually easy to sum up in a word or two. The secret to writing concise copy? Omit. Or select and reject, my favourite. Jargon? Avoid. Clichés? Ditch. In 2015, I talked with Natalie Angier, *New York Times* science journalist and Pulitzer Prize-winner. She made it pretty clear how much she hates clichés like "to have a hawk's eyes", as well as truisms. Award-winning science journalist Deborah Blum suggests using analogies and original metaphors instead (see the interview in Angler 2017). If you cut and slash all meaningless words from your text, clichés won't survive, either. But what's the problem with clichés? They're empty. Dead. They're cheap and show little effort and love for language. Clichés are vague. They are often exaggerations of what you are trying to describe with them. Some clichés are just overused, tired, dead metaphors. Clichés also disguise as idioms and phrases. They stem from different fields than they are being applied to. Because they're so sneaky, and because they are such a huge indicator of bad style, I will dedicate this section of the chapter to them. You'll find lots of clichés in everyday language. Think of the following clichés:

- **At the end of the day**
- **Every cloud has a silver lining**
- **At long last**
- **To burn the midnight oil**
- **Too little too late**
- **To go a long way**

There is a simple test whether you're using a cliché: ask yourself, has this been used before? If so, forget it. If you have read it anywhere else, it's a cliché. Good metaphors are original. That means you have to create them. I didn't invent this test. George Orwell did. It's the first of his six writing rules in his essay "Politics and the English Language": "Never use a metaphor, simile, or other figure of speech which you are used to seeing in print" (Orwell 1946). You'll find the "regular" clichés in science writing, and you'll find even more of them in scientific writing. Apart from the "normal" ones, some clichés are specific to science writing. Geologist and science journalist Betsy Mason has compiled a list of five science clichés that she regularly encounters in science writing. I've added a few more (adapted from Mason 2009):

1 **Holy Grail**
2 **Silver bullet**
3 **Shedding light**
4 **Missing link**
5 **Paradigm shift**
6 **Rosetta Stone**
7 **Baffled**

What I find remarkable is that these science-y clichés are for the most part overly positive. Former Council for the Advancement of Science Writing (CASW) president Cristine Russell adds another one: "breakthrough" (Graber 2014). In fact, many clichés are just blatant exaggerations. Strunk and White (2000) state that overstatements weaken your statements. Eventually, your readers will stop trusting your claims.

So let's not let that happen. The first step is finding the clichés in your writing. That's easy, as a quick Google search reveals often quickly, if somebody else has used a phrase or idiom before. For scientific writing, you can do the same with Google Scholar (or any other scholarly literature search engine). Once you find one, what can you do to get rid of it? Try to come up with original images. Write down the original phrase, and then start playing with it. Write down alternatives. For example, the cliché "snow white" could become "white as snow white" or "gray as city snow". If there is not enough time, forget about the metaphor and just write it straight (Clark 2008). Also, watch out for clichés of vision, like "it's lonely at the top" or "suburbs are boring". They are just prejudiced frames.

There is no scientific proof to it, but I have a hunch that lighthearted, positive, gee-whiz articles have a higher cliché frequency. In other words: when you're trying to be funny and employ, say, puns, you risk drawing on a cliché. I haven't really come across many clichés in investigative science writing. Also, think about how lots of science news gets into the news circuit: via press releases. It's quite obvious that press officers tend to whitewash (sorry, haha!) their stories and overstate their importance. They have an agenda. They try to "sell" their institutions' science, and they tend to overstate the importance of their institutions' work. Journalists writing to deadline often transfer that PR-speak into rather shallow reports. Clichés are the result of lazy writing and a lack of time to come up with original images. That is why some writers in the news industry are particularly efficient at introducing clichés in the process. The title of an *Independent* article is: "The trillion dollar question: Have scientists found the holy grail of plastic?" (Weston 2019). Kudos for placing two clichés in one headline. We have

Figure 6.1 Clichés: a 19th century comic poking fun at then common clichés
Source: Heidelberger historische Bestände digital, Universität Heidelberg.

the "X dollar question" and a "holy grail". Now, this is just anecdotal evidence, so that's my personal, totally non-scientific insight, but: I found a fun game to play. Chances are, if you find one cliché in a text, then that author has probably a knack for using them regularly. When I googled "at the end of the day" on Google Scholar, I found an interview with Mike Davis on his book "Planet of Slums". Here are a few stylistic bloomers from the interview:

• At the end of the day
• See the glass as half-full or half-empty

- It is only a matter of time
- A silver lining
- Make a difference

Clichés happen to all of us. You'll occasionally find them in the better outlets as well, although that's much rarer. It really does pay off if you throw in an extra round of editing to spot and kill them. Just ask yourself when writing: is it you who came up with the metaphor? If not, ditch it. I've added a link to a list of clichés to the "Links" section of this chapter. If you want a summary, have a look at the University of North Carolina's Writing Center's guide to clichés and how to avoid them. You guessed it: I've included a link to that, too.

Before you leave this section with the impression that clichés are always bad, here's some advice from writer and poet Emily Hiestand. She cites poet Starbuck, who wanted his students to take precisely the words and clichés that are frowned upon and reanimate them. "Just so, prose stylists are free to roam the whole continuum and speech, exploring formal, colloquial and date words as well as the specialized lingo of engineers, neurologists and teenagers" (Hiestand 2007:200). Hiestand adds that yes, you should generally prefer simple words to fancy ones, but also take in consideration that uncommon words do sound well.

Sensory language

Good science writing has two big pillars. I'm not going to say "first" and "second", because they're both equally important. They need to exist in parallel, or else you won't get a fully functioning text. One of the pillars is correct facts. The other is sensory experience. How do you recognise a really good story? As a reader, you don't. You just go along with it. You live it. You experience it. It's a visceral ride, on which you identify with the story's protagonist. Lots of narrative bricks help you get the readers to feel that. Gripping structure is one such brick. The other one is adding sensory details. Jack Hart's brilliant book *Storycraft* shows S.I. Hayakawa's ladder of abstraction, a writer's tool that allows you to "zoom in" and "zoom out" (a technique we'll have a closer look at in the chapter on literary techniques). Whatever you write, you're on a stave of the ladder. If you're on a higher stave, you're talking about abstract concepts. That's the non-graspable stuff you can't describe in detail; but it's needed to understand the story's theme and to see the big picture (sorry for the cliché). The lower you go on said ladder, the more graspable your story gets. The lower you go, the more sensory details are involved, and the more you get more into descriptive writing.

When you set a scene, you give readers orientation. Use all senses, sight, sound, smell, touch and taste, and describe how you experienced it. If you're just starting out, make sure to not go too much into detail: "Give the reader a feeling of volume, space and dimension, but don't build a diorama" (Kramer 2007:27). This means, as a reporter, as a writer, you'll have to observe and note the sensory details always. Sometimes, that's not possible. When you're reporting about events in the past, you can ask contemporary witnesses, or, if they're all dead, you can read historical

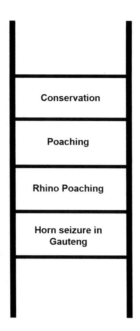

Figure 6.2 The ladder of abstraction
The ladder of abstraction was first defined by English professor S.I. Hayakawa. It's a tool that helps you understand whether your text is zoomed in (lowest rung) or out (highest rung). For longer pieces, going up and down the ladder is advisable.
Source: Martin W. Angler.

documents and then take the sensory details from there. When you describe some-body else's recollections don't state it like "George recalls trudging through the snow"; but rather ask that person to help you build the scene (Kramer 2007). So, unless you are writing from a first-person point of view, you'll want to describe this as value-free as possible. Take notes of how you feel in a certain moment, and take them into consideration (Kramer describes with how he felt in an operating room), but reproduce what your characters said and felt.

You can equally do this in a lab you work in, in a professor's office and in any other setting. The rule is "show don't tell". Does a lab supervisor have lots of saints' images on her desk? If so, describing her desk tells readers more than actually telling: "that's a religious person." Your readers aren't simpletons. They'll get it. So record sensory details, write them down, record them, everything is fair game (as long as your activities stay legal). "The good writer uses telling details, not only to inform but to persuade" (Clark 2008). Have a look at this passage, taken from Lucas Joel's "Undark" article, in which he follows plant ecologist Daniel Katz:

> Katz and his team are now trying to answer that question. Donning a neon orange vest – a tack designed both for safety while working next to roads and to

help avoid being mugged, Katz says – and driving a beat-up rental minivan he uses for his fieldwork [...]

(Joel 2019)

Notice two telling visual details in the passage: the orange vest tells you that he's a pragmatic worker, not afraid to get his hands dirty. The beat-up rental minivan evokes another picture in my mind, without including too much detail. What does it say about Katz? This man doesn't give a shit about status symbols, which in turn evokes empathy in readers. With both details, Joel just used one adjective to make the scene imaginable and give his readers details about his protagonist.

So, sensory details can drag readers into a scene and reveal character. Adjectives are a fine tool to do so, but you need to be careful not to use abstract ones. Consider this sentence from *USA Today*: "Bethany Hamilton has always been a compassionate child". Writers use adjectives like "compassionate", "enthusiastic" and "popular" to describe characters. But they're abstract, you can't picture them (Clark 2008). If you write this way, you're trying to spoon-feed readers your opinion, without showing them what is actually happening. Replace abstract adjectives with action. Who did what? Simple, declarative sentences are effective in describing action.

Adjectives are clearly not the only way of adding sensory details. If we're talking about auditory details, you can use actual dialogue (a literary technique introduced to journalism by the New Journalists) instead of just saying "the professor and his student argued". What does argue mean? Show your readers what they actually said to each other, let them know if the characters yelled at each other. Let them partake in the fight. The principle is always the same: show don't tell. Choose onomatopoeic verbs and nouns that sound like the words they're describing when pronounced. Examples are: to hiss, to snap or to whoosh. They're instantly imaginable. Tom Wolfe used onomatopoeic words to write about car races: "Wolfe wrote 'Ggghhzzzzzzzzhhhhhhggggggzzzzzzzeeeeee-gawdam!' to simulate the sound of Johnson's car peeling out" (Weingarten 2010).

When you collect sensory input, make sure you acknowledge that those details can deceive you either. In Tom Wolfe's New Journalism techniques, recording man's status symbols was one of the main pillars of literary journalism. In his view, the symbols expressed the individuals' social status. If you just observe and record them, you might be mistaken. Instead, "the meaning of such details isn't always inherent in the objects themselves but in the importance to our subjects" (Harrington in Kramer 2007:129). Journalist and professor Walt Harrington adds weight to his statement by telling the story of him initially misjudging a household's decor items and only discovering their true meaning when asking the house owners.

I'll make a final point about the types of verbs you can use to write about sensory input. Linking verbs, like "to be", but also (and this might be the misleading thing about describing sensory input) sense verbs like "smell", "taste", "feel" and "look" describe no action but stasis, something that just... is. According to Hart (2011), they're the weakest of verbs, while strong verbs need to convey action. Exposition is necessary, though, so the linking verbs have a right to exist.

But use motion verbs to signal transitions from expository to story passages. The strongest verbs are transitive verbs that demand an object (Hart 2011).

Case study: Return of the wild

Let's have a look at some of these techniques in action! Emma Marris has written a piece about wolves returning to California, and it's a great read. You'll find a link to it in the next section. It'd be asking too much to analyse every single style element of her piece (it's about 3,000 words long), so I have to do what? Select and reject. Read it before proceeding with this section, or read it as we go along. Marris starts her piece with some scene setting. It's short, succinct and effective:

> It is a frosty spring morning, and I'm tracking celebrity wolves in Southern Oregon.

The first clause contains exposition and sets the scene. She doesn't use a lot of words for that. One adjective conveys the mood. The second clause is action. It sets the point of view of the story. It's Marris' journey, and we're going to see it through her lens.

> Scientists call him OR7, the seventh wolf in Oregon to be captured and fitted with a tracking collar.

Marris uses a jargon-y abbreviation and then elegantly branches out into a subclause to explain what OR7 stands for. Note how she doesn't explicitly say "OR stands for", and "7 stands for". This tells us a lot about the author: she doesn't think the audience is dumb. It's a straight technique to get jargon, acronyms and abbreviations out of the way.

The next paragraph is very sensory. Marris describes how she looks at the wolf's feces. The informal language she uses, "poop", is to the point and tells us what kind of writer she is. Pragmatic, she wants to be understood, and she's not afraid to call poop poop. Marris appeals to all senses like sight ("The sun is raising steam off the graveled timber roads"), and sound ("So far, all we've heard from the receiver is static – none of the pings that would indicate that OR7's collar is in range").

Her text is constantly in motion, they're on a journey. The name of the wolf they're chasing, "Journey", reflects that, too. What Marris does particularly well is blend motion with description. For example, the third paragraph starts like this: "We drive to the site of this very brief interspecies encounter and find a few monstrous piles of poop, bristling with elk hair". The first clause is action that drives their journey forward. The second part, after "and" is a description, using sensory language. It goes on like this: "Stephenson bags them". Brilliant. A simple declarative sentence that contains a strong verb and on top of that is transitive.

Marris' transitions are smooth. Consider the following excerpt, where she connects "pups" to "OR7's children" and "pups" in the previous' paragraph's final sentence. The connecting word "indeed" in the new paragraph signals that she will now substantiate her idea (although a sentence later Marris will relativise it a little). Here is the connecting bit between the two paragraphs:

> [...] but as he prepares to document the second round of pups for this family that lives within one or two long day's walk of the California border, he says some of OR7's children could "easily" settle down in the Golden State. [Paragraph ends here]
> Indeed, on 20 August 2015 the California Department of Fish and Wildlife announced that camera traps had caught snaps of fuzzy wolf pups playing in Northern California.

Marris uses metaphors sparingly, her writing is to the point and her images are original. She doesn't unnecessarily embellish her sentences and insofar respects the ABCs of journalism. No wonder that you won't find any clichés in her text. The rhythm in her writing is remarkable. In the but last paragraph, a 12-word-long sentence is followed by a 77-word-long sentence. The shortest overall? One word. Her median sentence length is about 18 words – perfect! It's equally hard to find passives: Marris' writing is active for the most part. The following is a rare exception:

> Indeed, until recently, it was often repeated [...]

She does use adverbs several times per paragraph, but I couldn't spot a single instance where they were unnecessary.

Marris varies the rhythm of her paragraphs: the shortest is just a single sentence:

> Coyote caught up with Wolf, and they went on.

The longest paragraph runs 288 words long. It contains background information on previous wolf occurrences in California. Marris chooses to tell a story within the story. Instead of just stating that there were only two specimens (the paragraph starts this way), Marris then lets another character, geneticist Sarah Hendricks, tell her own quest to find out. It's a full quest with a protagonist (Hendricks), a complication (very small samples), a climax (do they contain DNA?), an intermediary success (yes, they do!) and a resolution (alas, the sample size is too small to draw proper conclusions). "Story within a story" is a known literary technique, and it's also used in screenwriting.

I found one more stylistic technique I'd like to point out: her variation of tense. Readers need orientation within the text, and changing the tense is one way to signal change in the timeline. Whenever you use the present tense, you'll immerse your readers right into the story. Marris does this whenever the action unfolds in the present of her story, like in the following passages:

> We drive to the site of this very brief interspecies [...]
> Now I think I might be looking at his poop.

But when she jumps out of the present narrative, also her tense changes. Whenever she gives readers background, she uses the simple past like here:

> California eradicated the wolf from its landscapes so quickly and thoroughly that the animals barely appear in the historical record.
> Back in 1991, ecologist Robert Schmidt, then at Berkeley, combed through more than fifty European historical accounts [...]

What Marris' writing does here is show a lot of thought that went into writing this article. If you don't carefully analyse all the stylistic elements (and I've just taken a small selection), you won't even notice what it is that turns it into such a great read. And that's what good story does: it makes you forget that you are reading a story; instead, you're part of it. This is just masterful craft at work. It's not only nicely structured, it's also written in a way that grips you from the beginning and doesn't let loose until you're through. As Winfried Göpfert would say: this text invites you to guzzle it.

Review questions

- How does fake news employ language to persuade readers?
- Which one of the ABCs of journalism can be exaggerated?
- How can you spot and eliminate (or replace) jargon?
- What do transitions have to do with the Hegelian dialectic?
- How can you use adverbs and adjectives to create images in your readers' minds?
- Which linguistic elements connect sentences, which ones paragraphs?
- What clichés are common in science writing?
- What types of verbs exist, and how can you employ them for telling stories?

Links

List of Clichés: http://www.clichelist.net/

"Clichés" (University of North Carolina Chapel Hill): https://writingcenter.unc. edu/cliches/

"Return of the Wild" (Boom California): https://boomcalifornia.com/2015/11/ 23/return-of-the-wild/

References

Angler, M.W. (2017) *Science Journalism: an introduction*. London: Routledge.

Associated Press (2018) *The Associated Press Stylebook 2018 and Briefing on Media Law*. New York: Basic Books.

Clark, R.P. (2008) *Writing Tools: 55 Essential Strategies for Every Writer*. London: Little, Brown.

Conroy, N.J., Rubin, V. L. & Chen, Y. (2015) "Automatic deception detection: Methods for finding fake news," *Proceedings of the Association for Information Science and Technology*, vol. 52, no. 1, 1–4.

Davis, M. (2006) "Planet of slums," *New Perspectives Quarterly*, vol. 23, no. 2, 6–11.

Gilman, S. (2019) "The Rat Spill," *Hakai magazine* [Online]. Available at: https://www.hakaimagazine.com/features/the-rat-spill/ (date accessed 20 August 2019).

Graber, C. (2014) "Single Best: Cristine Russell," *The Open Notebook* [Online]. Available at: https://www.theopennotebook.com/2014/07/22/single-best-cristine-russell/ (date accessed 20 August 2019).

Gruber, H. (1993) "Political language and textual vagueness," *Pragmatics. Quarterly Publication of the International Pragmatics Association (IPrA)*, vol. 3, no. 1, 1–28.

Hart, J. (2011) *Storycraft: The Complete Guide to Writing Narrative Nonfiction*. Chicago: The University of Chicago Press.

Hauch, V., Blandón-Gitlin, I., Masip, J. & Sporer, S.L. (2015) "Are computers effective lie detectors? A meta-analysis of linguistic cues to deception," *Personality and Social Psychology Review*, vol. 19, no. 4, 307–342.

Helitzer, M. & Shatz, M. (2005) *Comedy Writing Secrets, 2nd ed.* Cincinnati: Writer's Digest Books.

Hiestand, E. (2007) "On Style," in: Kramer, M. & Call, W. *Telling True Stories*. New York: Plume, 198–202.

Giles, B. (2002) "Sharing the secrets of fine narrative journalism," *Nieman Reports*, vol. 56, no. 1, 7.

Joel, L. (2019) "As the Forest Moves Back in, Pollen Is on the Rise in Detroit," Undark [Online] Available at: https://undark.org/article/detroit-public-health-problem-pollen/ (date accessed 21 August 2019).

Kramer, M. (2007) "Reporting for Narrative: Ten Tips," in: Kramer, M. & Call, W. *Telling True Stories*. New York: Plume, 24–28.

Landhuis, E. (2019) "Why Parents Are Turning to a Controversial Treatment for Food Allergies," Undark [Online]. Available at: https://undark.org/article/oral-immuno therapy-food-allergies/ (date accessed 20 August 2019).

Litt, T. (2016) "What makes bad writing bad?" *The Guardian* [Online]. Available at: https://www.theguardian.com/books/2016/may/20/what-makes-bad-writing-bad-toby-litt (date accessed 16 August 2019).

Marris, E. (2015) "Return of the Wild," Boom California [Online]. Available at: https://boomcalifornia.com/2015/11/23/return-of-the-wild/ (date accessed 21 August 2019).

Martinez-Conde, S. (2016) "Has contemporary academia outgrown the Carl Sagan effect?" *Journal of Neuroscience*, vol. 36, no. 7, 2077–2082.

Mason, B. (2009) "5 Atrocious Science Clichés to Throw Down a Black Hole," *WIRED* [Online]. Available at: https://www.wired.com/2009/07/blackholescience/ (date accessed 20 August 2019).

Mencher, M. (2011) *Melvin Mencher's News Reporting and Writing, 12th ed.* New York: McGraw Hill.

Orwell, G. (1946) "Politics and the English language," *Horizon*, vol. 13, no. 76, 252–265

Perelman, L. & Barrett, E. (1997) *The Mayfield handbook of technical and scientific writing*. Mountain View: Mayfield Publication Co.

Plutchik, R. & Kellerman, H. (1980) *Theories of emotion, 1st ed.* New York: Academic Press.

Shariatmadari, D. (2019) "Language wars: the 19 greatest linguistic spats of all time," *The Guardian* [Online]. Available at: https://www.theguardian.com/science/2019/jun/17/language-wars-18-greatest-linguistic-spats (date accessed 15 August 2019).

Strunk, W. & White, E.B. (2000) *The Elements of Style*, 4th edition. New York: Longman.

Toma, C.L. & Hancock, J.T. (2012) "What lies beneath: The linguistic traces of deception in online dating profiles," *Journal of Communication*, vol. 62, no. 1, 78–97.

Vosoughi, S.Roy, D. & Aral, S. (2018) "The spread of true and false news online," *Science*, vol. 359, no. 6380, 1146–1151.

Weingarten, M. (2010). *The Gang That Wouldn't Write Straight: Wolfe, Thompson, Didion, Capote, and the New Journalism Revolution*. New York: Crown.

Weston, P. (2019) "The trillion dollar question: Have scientists found the holy grail of plastic?" *The Independent* [Online]. Available at: https://www.independent.co.uk/news/science/plastic-waste-holy-grail-science-a8906676.html (date accessed 20 August 2019).

Yong, E. (2010) "On Jargon, and Why It Matters in Science Writing," *National Geographic* [Online]. Available at: https://www.nationalgeographic.com/science/phenomena/2010/11/24/on-jargon-and-why-it-matters-in-science-writing/ (date accessed 15 August 2019).

Zinsser, W. (2001) *On Writing Well: The Classic Guide To Writing Nonfiction*. New York: HarperCollins Quill.

7   Screenwriting Techniques

What you will learn in this chapter:

- Screenplay structure
- Scenes
- Writing dialogue
- Film grammar and cinematic writing
- Setting scenes
- Elegant exposition
- Loglines
- Case study: Story Collider

The whole world seems to complain about diminishing attention spans. Marketers and online businesses vie for online readers' attention. "There's too much noise! We need to stand out! Tech is going to solve the problem!" Not quite. Much of it is marketing guff published by people who want to sell you a product that "solves the problem". In fact, some of the studies that showed how our attention span decreases have been refuted. If you can put your readers into narrative mode and employ the not-so-secret secrets of storytelling, their attention span won't suffer. The only way to stand out is a good story. Have you ever seen somebody closing a good novel after eight seconds? Walking out of a movie theatre after twelve? I have. One bloke once ran out and you could hear him throw up in the toilet next door (not because of the movie, I hope). Yes, I left a movie once because it sucked (I'm not going say which one, but I was 18 and Richard Gere and Winona Ryder starred in it). Of course not all movies are good. But Hollywood knows its business. It manages to glue your butt to the seat, endure your sweaty seat neighbor's evaporations and the kid behind you who kicks your seat, and your girlfriend rustling in her goddamn sweet popcorn bag. Despite all odds. Not only do you endure it. Not only do you pay money for the experience. You hardly even notice all these nuisances. That's because you're deep in narrative mode. You're in the story.

That is why in this chapter we'll have a look at some specific screenwriting concepts and techniques that you can employ to tell every kind of story. Scenic writing is key to vivid stories. New Journalists like Tom Wolfe adopted the technique beginning in the 1960s, although the New Journalism techniques existed long before. Scenes catapult your readers right into the story, so we'll have a look at the structure of scenes, how to set a scene and how to use descriptive language to do so. And we'll talk about camera shots and how you can transform the concept into written text. Filmmakers and screenwriting teachers have established a number of universal scene-writing rules that apply to nonfiction storytelling as well. One is to enter your scenes as late as possible, leave out most of the exposition and get the hell out before the scene becomes boring. Again, this mirrors the overall structure: you can apply that same rule to entire stories. Exposition is inevitable, but there are ways to just tell your audience straight what you think they should know. Or, if you prefer the more elegant way, you can feed them expository information through action and dialogue, without them even noticing.

Dialogue is of course key to story. Look at stage plays. They are mostly dialogue. Most of the text you encounter in a screenplay? Dialogue. You'll find good reasons why film dialogue is unlike everyday street dialogue. Crafting good dialogue requires a lot of writing and rewriting. So we are going to look at what makes good dialogue memorable and what you can leave out. Speaking of leaving stuff out: in this chapter, we'll also play around with loglines, which are a screenwriter's tool to craft one-sentence synopses they can pitch to an executive in 30 seconds. With that exercise, you'll learn how to nail your story without giving away how it ends. Like most good writing, even these one- or two-liners follow structural guidelines. If you include the right elements, your logline can't fail.

Does all of this sound too artsy to be applied to nonfiction writing? It isn't. Screenwriter Nora Ephron ("Silkwood") started out as a journalist. Like so many others, Ephron emphasises how important structure is and that journalists and nonfiction writers often underestimate its importance and simply try to report, like herself at a young age, what happened. I will make a short note to say that every single screenwriting book that I have ever read points out the importance of structure in narratives. Ephron (2007) tells the story of how she struggled to identify the beginning, middle and end of "Silkwood". Does that sound familiar? It's again a selection and rejection-pickle. Which moments do you include in your story? Where do you start it? That is why I included in the first section of this chapter a very brief introduction to plot points and moments to look out for when reporting about science. Ephron (2007) ends her piece by advising writers to do enough reporting (something journalists are used to), and eventually, the story's structure will emerge. It's valid advice, and it has resonated a lot with me since the first time I read it. When I can't get started on a story's structure (I always outline longer stories), I just haven't done enough reporting. Writer's block is a myth. So let's get reading and writing! Oh, and before leaving the chapter, have a look at the case study at the end of it, where the artistic director of Story Collider tells you how scientists get professional training to form emotional connections with their audience – instead of lecturing them.

Screenplay structure

Yech, another section on structure? Afraid so. But once you're through, you'll have a much better understanding of how screenwriters think in stories. If you want to tell science stories, you don't have to write a full screenplay. Also, this is once again to emphasise how important structure is. If there is only one story element you have time to learn, make sure it's structure. Don't worry, this section will be lightweight enough for you to just extract whatever elements you need to piece together a nonfiction story.

When he talks about story structure, BBC storytelling master John Yorke starts with Hegel's dialectic. It's a three-part structure, as we've seen in the chapter on narrative structure. Thesis, antithesis and synthesis. In story, thesis becomes protagonist, antithesis becomes antagonist and the synthesis ranges from the point of insight (epiphany) to the climax of the story and its resolution. The protagonist has to learn something she didn't know at the beginning of the story in order to be able to beat the antagonist (if there's a happy ending). In a "BBC Writers Room" interview on story structure, Yorke points out that the simplest story is a dialogue between two people with opposing views. One might learn something from the other that she didn't know before, and based on that change her opinion (BBC Writers 2018). That's a story. It's thesis (first view), antithesis (second, opposing view), and synthesis (insight and new status quo). In Hollywood screenplays, Hegel's dialectic translates frequently into the three-act structure (Yorke 2013):

- **ACT ONE**: establish a flawed character
- **ACT TWO**: confront them with their opposite
- **ACT THREE**. synthesise the two to achieve balance

Yorke explains the three-act structure drawing on how students learn. "Students encounter something of which they're unaware, explore and assimilate it, and by merging it with their pre-existing knowledge, grow" (Yorke 2013:27). He makes a point writing that we order the world dialectically. It's the way we learn. It's the way we perceive the world.

You can observe this also in horror movies. The confrontation in Yorke's structure is the antagonist. You can see that embodiment of protagonist and antagonist nowhere clearer than in horror films. In fact, the antagonist (often "the monster") is an externalised projection of the protagonist's fears (Blake & Bailey 2013). In terms of technique, knowing this is quite important. By describing the antagonist, you often expose more about the protagonist (and in a more elegant way) than actually telling the audience what the protagonist's flaws are. I've talked about transitions in terms of language in the previous chapter. They are important because they keep the audience reading. If done well the audience doesn't have a chance to stop reading, watching or listening. If you transport that concept from language to structure, the same rules apply. Instead of words, you have major plot points that end acts and start new ones. In three-act screenplays, the two most important transitions are the inciting incident (act one transitions to

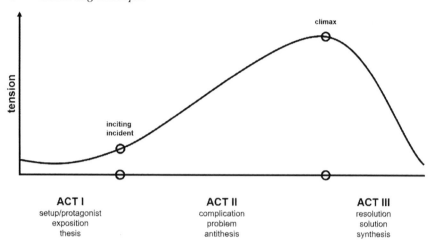

Figure 7.1 The three-act story structure
The second act of a screenplay is typically twice as long as each of the other two acts. There is also a simplified tension curve superimposed. Note the two turning points (inciting incident and climax) that are also the transitions from one act into another. Tension heightens over time.
Source: Martin W. Angler.

act two) and the crisis (act two transitions to act three). They are called plot points, or turning points. Whatever story you write, watch out for these plot points. Plot points are short events that change the direction of the story. When I write nonfiction stories, for example for history magazines, what I particularly look out for in the raw material are such plot points. What started the protagonist's journey (inciting incident)? What particular insight or epiphany did she gain along the way (point of insight)? What's the make-or-break point where she had to make a decision of whether to return to her old life or confront the dramatic problem of her story (crisis)? You can be sure that I assign separate index cards to each of these points. These plot points are characterised by conflict and opposition. When you're writing nonfiction scenes, you can't make anything up. But you decide where your scenes start and where they end. If you end a scene on such a moment of opposition, you have a cliffhanger. It's a moment of conflict that the audience craves to know how it ends. This, too, is part of selecting the right moments when crafting a story.

Particular plot points are plot twists, unexpected reversals of fortune that the audience didn't expect. In order to pull that off, you need to withhold information, so having an identical syuzhet and fabula (how the story is told versus how the story events actually unfolded) is not advisable. Turning points change with what McKee (1997) calls the value charge: something is at stake for the character when entering a scene (or an act, in this context). When she discovers new information, the value at stake changes from positive to negative or vice versa. All right, before all of this gets too Hollywood-ish, let's have a look an epiphany moment that actually changes how a value looks in science writing:

He had always assumed that the sequoia and foxtail pine stands surrounding him would last far longer than he would, but when he considered the possible effects of rising temperatures and extended drought, he wasn't so sure – he could see the "vignette of primitive America" dissolving into an inaccessible past. The realization threw him into a funk that lasted years.

(Nijhuis 2016)

It's a perfect turning point (I've put a link to the story in the "Links" section). Michelle Nijhuis describes the realisation of ecologist Nate Stephenson, whose turning point happened in the quoted passage. Right then, his attitude changed. Stephenson understood that the mission of the Parks Service had to be to protect the future, not just to care about the status quo. So he started campaigning. When you write science stories, scour the papers for moments that overturned researchers' hypotheses, delivered data that didn't match the expected experiment design (if they did run experiments). Look for keywords like "surprise", "expect" and "disappoint". You'll find these in the results or discussion sections of the papers. Regardless of whether they mentioned it in a paper or not, call the scientists and specifically ask them for moments that overturned their expectations, whether they had situations when they wanted to give up or when all seemed lost. Also ask them about the best thing that happened to them in the process of doing research. It makes them reflect. If the science you're writing about is your own, just ask yourself those same questions. Think in turning points and plot twists that changed your state of knowledge.

The greatest thing about turning points? They are strongly cause and effect-based. Their "magic" lies in being unpredictable by the audience and emerging as the logical consequence of some prior action. Such unpredictable surprises are also often called plot twists. We'll have a deeper look at them in the next chapter. But now, let's dig deeper into scenes!

Scenes

Up until now, I have referred to story units mostly as "events". In screenwriting (and in fiction writing, but also in narrative journalism), they're known as scenes. I've briefly touched upon scenes in the second chapter of this book. In screenwriting, they are the smaller units of acts and sequences. They have their own structure, too. Every scene has a beginning, a middle and an end, and contains strong story elements like desire, action, conflict and change. That makes it "a story in miniature", as screenwriting teacher Robert McKee puts it in his brilliant book *Story* (McKee 1997). If the scene causes no change, if nothing really happens that either reveals something about a character or moves the story forward, then it probably shouldn't be in your story. In a scene, a character pursues a scene objective, and that scene objective must be connected to his greater story objective. The character performs an action to achieve his goal. But she can't anticipate the world's reaction to it. "The effect is to crack open the gap between expectation and result, turning [the character's] outer fortunes, inner life, or both from the positive to the negative or the negative to the positive in terms of values the audience understands are at risk" (McKee 1997:233–4). So scenes have a turning point, and they are turning points in and of themselves. Because they fail to meet characters' expectations, they spark questions – which in turn sparks the audience's questions. What happens next? This technique is perfect for creating suspense.

The actions and reactions within a scene are called beats. One character says or does something, the other one (or the world) reacts. That's a beat. A single-word value is at stake, like truth, wealth or health. The turning point within the scene mirrors the crisis in an act or story. Like in a story's crisis, the character must decide what to do next about her value. This is also the set-up for the next scene. The audience doesn't know what's going to happen, so again, that's perfect to make them wonder what will happen next. Because the set-up for the next scene is contained in the previous one, you can omit it and enter the scene late. "Come in late, get out early" is a well-known maxim among screenwriters. Getting out early means: you can skip the climax and resolution. Again, this makes the audience wonder what'll happen next. Also, they won't be able to discover the scene's structure. You can tighten the scene to the point of confrontation (Yorke 2013).

Let's have a look at a real-life, nonfiction science example of a turning point within a scene. Sebastian Junger's *Vanity Fair* piece on PTSD has all the elements of a good scene. This one caught my eye, because it impressively illustrates how the gap McKee mentions opens:

> I mentally buried all of it until one day, a few months later, when I went into the subway at rush hour to catch the C train downtown. Suddenly I found myself backed up against a metal support column, absolutely convinced I was going to die.
>
> (Junger 2015)

It contains all the elements of a good scene. Junger is the protagonist. He has a simple goal: catch the train. "Suddenly" signals the turning point of the scene. A huge gap opens, from a simple everyday goal like catching the train to thinking you're going to die. The value at stake is sanity. It turns from positive to negative. Junger went into the scene as a "normal" (if that condition exists in the world), functioning person. When the panic attack strikes, his plan is foiled. As we learn later on in the story, he didn't manage to catch the train but had to go home on foot after the incident. He didn't achieve his goal. It's a moment of internal conflict that manifests in external conflict: because of the panic attack, Junger can't take the train. It's a story in miniature, as McKee writes. Apart from the action, a scene also requires some description of where you are, the atmosphere. By convention, screenplay scenes typically start with the slugline, which tells a screenplay reader at a glance where the action unfolds. The slugline contains three elements: is it an internal (INT) or external (EXT) scene? Second, location. Third, time of day. It could look something like this for Junger's story:

INT. NYC DOWNTOWN SUBWAY STATION – DAY

In a screenplay, what follows after the slugline is a description of the action that happens, followed by the scene's dialogue. In real life, when writing about science or nonfiction in general, you can't fix scenes that don't work somehow. You have to work with the material that you either observed first-hand or that you've reported. It has to be on the record. In journalism, that's what's called reconstructing scenes. Adam Hochschild, nonfiction book author and journalist, comes up with a number of elements that nonfiction scenes should have (adapted from Hochschild 2007):

- **Accuracy**: that's probably the main difference to fiction writing. You need to have proven facts before putting them into a scene.
- **Atmosphere**: describe all the sensory details.
- **Dialogue**: people need to talk to each other, as opposed to mere quotes.
- **Emotion**: convey how people felt. If you interview people, record how they felt. Ask them, but also observe their body language and actions.

Emotion is a connecting factor. Empathy is often evoked when the audience went through similar hardships as the portrayed character. Shared experiences are a huge connector. It's how people fall in love with each other. It's the genesis of friendships. It's how the audience vicariously experiences what the character experiences. In the above example, I instantly knew what a panic attack feels like, because I have experienced them myself. You think you're going to die, and your body reacts accordingly. I also remember that the first one for me was the hardest, because you have no clue that you are not actually going to die, if you've never heard about them.

Junger doesn't use dialogue in his passage, but that is one of the distinguishing elements between daily news journalism and stories. Use dialogue instead of quotes. It's one of the four techniques literary journalists started using in the 1970s, when Tom Wolfe wrote his New Journalism manifest. Wolfe also formulated the other paradigms of narrative journalism: scene-by-scene construction, status symbols, dialogue and point of view. Note how both scene-by-scene construction and point of view are connected to scenes. You'll have to tell a scene through somebody's viewpoint. One of Wolfe's novelties was to write from a first-person point of view. Up until then, mostly third-person views were used (Kaplan 1987).

So once you've gathered them, what do you do with all these elements, before you write them up as scenes? You outline. Whenever I write a narrative piece, for example, for a history magazine, I plan my story using index cards. I started out with post-its and even found some of them attached in books, stemming from the time I started writing magazine pieces. I could still flesh them out and write the story. Nowadays, I use index for everything, even newspapers pieces, even for presentations I give. The golden rule? One idea per index card. It's always the same pattern, and we've had this before. One idea per sentence. One idea per paragraph. One idea per scene. And they all have to be connected by the story

Figure 7.2 My (atypically tidied up) story desk
I've organised this book initially into one index card per chapter. Each main index card
then grew into a stack of cards, containing one card per section. Every card highlights the
main points, and I use their backside for writing down the sources.
Source: Martin W. Angler.

spine and its theme. Screenwriters like Dustin Lance Black or John August outline
their scenes using index cards. August has a rule of not putting more than seven
words on an index card. They write the sluglines on the index cards' headers. Heck, I
even planned this book using index cards: for every chapter, I take an index card and
write the title on its header. Just below the title, I list the contents. For every section, I
then take another index card and label it and put whatever I have to say about it on
the card. On the flipside, I write down the book titles, papers and other sources.
Each chapter becomes a stack with a title card on top. Gay Talese wrote down scenic
details using a pencil and paper and would later pin them onto a corkboard, one
piece of paper per scene, to outline the story (Weingarten 2010).

Writing dialogue

When I first got in touch with dialogue in nonfiction writing, it seemed at odds
with journalism's objectivity. I expect dialogue on stage, in films and in novels.
But in nonfiction writing? I told myself, think again. Whenever I had held an
interview, it had been a dialogue. All conversations are. It's a back-and-forth. So

what leads to quotes is dialogue between interviewer and interviewee. When such pieces are published as interviews, they get some polishing, but they do remain edited conversations. Dialogue. This is the reason interviews are very popular: When well done, when the interviewer engages with her subject and does not just follow a strict set of prepared questions, they become like real-life dialogue.

Dialogue is how people communicate in real life, so why shouldn't this be used in journalism? But writing dialogue is more than just recording and then vomiting out all that people say. It is another instance of my beloved principle "select and reject". Alfred Hitchcock put it this way: "Drama is life with the dull bits cut out." The same is true of dialogue. In fact, what you should look for in dialogue is change, conflict and character development. Just like scenes, good dialogue fulfills one of these purposes. So when you select which parts of dialogue you want to include in your story, choose it according to these criteria. Some fiction series take a mixed approach, like the Netflix series "The people vs. O.J. Simpson". Its creators base the dialogue on police records, but they also made some of it up to make it more dramatic (Morell 2018).

You can't do that. In nonfiction writing, dialogue must be accurate. Here is one approach how to use quotes and dialogue from journalism professor and *Tampa Bay Times* reporter Kelley Benham French: do it sparingly. Single-word quotes can be very effective. And dialogue trumps quotes. It's easier to read than actual narrative, because dialogue is how we listen to the world and communicate (Benham 2007). That is why she uses short bits of dialogue to intersperse her narrative with, as it "gives the story some breathing room" (Benham 2007:105). You can extract such bits of dialogue from meeting protocols, recordings, conferences, court documents and much more. If you don't hear and record the actual dialogue, you find sources that have recorded it. This could be as well be an email exchange. In her *BuzzFeed* piece about how an astronomy professor sexually harassed one of his students, investigative reporter Azeen Ghorayshi comes up with these lines of reconstructed dialogue:

> "It's not good if a person in power is out of their fucking mind," Ott wrote to her in December 2014, referring to an issue with another student.
> "Well we are all out of our minds," Gossan replied.
> "Yeah, but your insanity does not affect other people's lifes [sic]," he said.
> (Ghorayshi 2016)

Obviously, Ghorayshi wasn't present when the online conversation between the professor and his student happened. But she got access to it and could hence reconstruct it. Like Benham suggests, Ghorayshi uses dialogue sparingly in her piece. It's a particular point, a brief moment of Ott's self-doubt, you can feel his inner conflict. But he doesn't explicitly *say* he has an inner conflict. That's what is called subtext, and that is another important element that screenwriters look for when writing dialogue. Subtext is the "show don't tell" principle applied to dialogue. What the character says makes it clear to the audience what she means, but she doesn't have to explicitly say "I feel like this". If you're being too explicit, that's what's called "on-the-nose" dialogue. You can see that difference often in television series and movies where characters explicitly tell other characters what the writer thinks the audience should know. Just no.

Recognising the difference between subtext and text is also what screenwriting professor Richard Walter emphasises aspiring screenwriters should focus on. He comes up with the example of the 1992 film "Terminator 2". The Terminator walks into a bar and demands a biker hands over his motorcycle, his boots and his clothes. The biker responds: "You forgot to say please". If you take that answer literally (text), the biker just wanted to hear the magic word "please" and would have given the Terminator all of his belongings. No. What he meant (subtext) was that the Terminator was about to get the battering of his lifetime (Walter 2010). The difference between the subtext and text in this case is irony. The biker meant the opposite of what he said.

Screenwriting guru Walter has more advice for writing dialogue, and I'll intersperse the following section with my own take on applying them to nonfiction. One principle is to economise. Be as short as possible (note how well that fits into the previous chapter's ABCs). Even if a piece of dialogue has purpose, ask yourself if the way you said it can be made more memorable by shortening it. When Clint Eastwood in "Escape from Alcatraz" is asked what his childhood was like, his answer is: "short". In nonfiction, you can't make up dialogue. But you can spot elements like succinct answers and select them instead of long ramblings. This works for both quotes and dialogue. Next, Walter advises to get to the point: cut out all expletives like "I think", "well" and "you know". They add nothing to the story and, with all respect to accuracy in citing in nonfiction, removing them doesn't change the meaning of what your interviewee said. It's also important to aim for rhythm. If you read your dialogue out loud, what does it sound like? Unlike real speech on the streets, it needs to be rhythmic. That's what makes quotes memorable. "The way people really talk, however, is available in the streets for free. The way people really talk is boring" (Walter 2010:106).

So what you do in nonfiction dialogue writing is watch out for memorable elements. If you can find them, they're real nuggets. And there are also benefits to selecting dialogue pieces from recorded speech: unlike screenwriters, you don't have to worry that they sound made up by you, the writer. Because you didn't make them up. You can edit such speech lightly, removing expletives ("well", "you know"), you should turn dialect and slang into standard language and remove vocalised pauses ("uh", "er"). Contract where possible, and don't feel obliged to turn a "we're gonna" into a more formal "we are going to". Most of all, pick the quotes and dialogue that show conflict, an exchange or a fight.

Film grammar and cinematic writing

Like written language, film has its own language. "Composed of fundamental units, called shots, films rely upon edits to join shots together into larger strings called sequences (a series of shots united in time and space), just as words become sentences" (Villarejo 2007:24). This includes film grammar. The way shots in a film are connected, the way meaning is conveyed via film techniques, that is the language of film. Those conventions are known as film grammar. For example, the masses in Leni Riefenstahl's "Triumph des Willens" always move in the same on-screen direction, or flashbacks are often signalled by dissolves (Villarejo 2007). Understanding it will not only help you write more cinematically, it will also improve your outlining skills. You've seen the story spine in the chapter on storytelling formulas, and we'll start from there in this section. Pixar's story artist Louis Gonzales breaks down the story spine. Every completed line of the eight-part story spine is what Gonzales calls a major beat. It's a logical unit, a plot point. Break these major beats down into scenes. Every major plot point transforms either into one or more scenes that belong together. A scene, in turn, is the logical unit at a specific time and/or location where a character learns something new and carries the story forward. Next, what the pro story artists do is break down the scenes into minor beats (Gonzales in Pixar in a box 2015). For example, one of Pixar's storytelling course participants came up with the following example from the film "Star Wars: The Force Awakens":

> Major beat (scene): Rey Meets Finn
> Minor beats: Rey interrogates Finn about his jacket and discovers he helped Poe escape; Finn lies to Rey; Finn tells Rey BB-8 is carrying a map to Luke Skywalker.
>
> (Diogo Fouto in Pixar in a box 2015)

So minor beats are self-contained units that are connected by a golden thread that runs through a major beat. As you see, it's all hierarchical. That makes it easier to start outlining your story once you've pieced a rough outline together (for example, using the story spine). You just go from general to specific. Once they have all major and minor beats, story artists think about the visual shots. One or more shots per minor beat is the rule. And like you order a story's events, the shots need to be arranged and ordered in editing, too. What the Pixar story artists then do is they put up all their shots as a sequence, called a storyboard. Others don't, like documentary filmmaker Jon Else. Still, he keeps in mind how each shot and sequence fits into the documentary film's narrative (Curran Bernard 2004). You have a number of different types of shots, the most important of which are the wide (or establishing) shot, the medium shot (character in her environment), and the close-up shot. Filmmakers use the different shot types to achieve different effects. The wide shot contains a lot of information in the frame. It shows the audience where they are in the story (time *and* location, actually). It essentially describes the environment and doesn't show much action. It's "show don't tell" par excellence if well done. And you can use subtext in it. Documentary filmmaker Curran Bernard says you can use these shots for weaving in expository information. Here are a couple of examples:

> Exposition can also be handled through visuals: an establishing shot of a place or sign; footage of a sheriff nailing an eviction notice on a door ("Roger & Me"); the opening moments of an auction ("Troublesome Creek"). Toys

littered on a suburban lawn say "Children live here." Black bunting and a homemade shrine of flowers and cards outside a fire station say "Tragedy has occurred."

(Curran Bernard 2004:16)

Changing shots within a scene is crucial if you want to write scenically. You can't tell a whole story from a wide-angle perspective. Changing the shot types in writing, that is zooming in and out of details, or moving up and down the ladder of abstraction in terms, adds rhythm to the story and prevents it from becoming monotonous. You can do that in writing. After all, every kind of film (fiction and documentary alike) starts as a script before filming begins. Here's an example of a story that ran in *National Geographic* on the Virunga national park:

Standing where the Semliki River flows out of Lake Edward with the Rwenzori Mountains glowering in the distance, serenaded by a moaning Greek chorus of water-besotted hippos, and gazing down at a thoroughly uncontaminated tableau of swimming elephants and strutting saddle-billed storks backlit by a low morning sun [...]

(Draper 2016)

This is clearly an establishing shot put on paper. It's expository, it sets the scene (which is just as important as character, plot, dialogue and theme). You can't find a character in Draper's passage. What would correspond to a medium shot in his piece looks like this:

"It was a beautiful place," Kambale said one afternoon as he stepped carefully through the weed-choked ruins of the Rwindi Hotel in the central sector.

(Draper 2016)

It shows one of the story characters in their environments. Although in the story this paragraph doesn't immediately follow the previous I mentioned, you would usually move from wide to medium to close-up shot. It's both expository (showing the character's environment) and moving forward the story, as the characters either talk or act. Draper goes into close-ups, too, to describe an ambush on an accountant:

[...] only to be waylaid by three men who jumped into his path and pointed Kalashnikovs at his chest. They tied his hands and dragged him off into the bush.

(Draper 2016)

In terms of language, the only way he could have made this more immediate is using the present simple for this scene. But you can't get any closer than pointing a Kalashnikov at somebody's chest. As a writer, you get to choose your framing (what you show the audience, and what you omit), and the staging (where the camera points to). Those two are important elements of film grammar and have a profound effect on not only what you perceive but also how you perceive it. For example, shooting from a low angle will let a character appear authoritative or even threatening. When you're writing, you're not operating a camera. But you can describe what is in the viewers' frame. Shot length also drives the audience's sense of how fast the narrative progresses towards the story climax. A rapid succession of shots drives up adrenalin and adds a sense of action and immediacy. Action movies frequently lower the shot length (while increasing the number of shots) in action-filled sequences. The closer you get to the climax, the faster the pacing. "Scenes tend to get shorter, action tighter, stakes higher" (Curran Bernard 2004:28–29). In writing, you can achieve the same effect. Write a number of short "shots" using short and direct sentences. Change the perspective (for example, view scenes through different characters' eyes) from shot to shot, and you'll have your audience gripped. This technique heightens attention. But like in a good movie, at some point you will have to give them a break and slow down. Sentences get longer, and so do the paragraphs. This is the time to sneak in expository paragraphs. Think rhythm. And with all this in mind, let's have another look at how to write scenes.

Setting scenes

Good scenes are no accident. Before shooting starts, the scene is prepared. It is set. Whatever is in the frame is there for good reason. Someone put it there on purpose. In writing, this should be no different. Like in Hollywood, as the writer, you set the scene. A number of scene-setting features that go beyond action, dialogue and theme. Here they are (Kramer 2007):

- **Camera and microphone control**: move the camera within a scene, just like filmmakers, but if you do, make sure you do it on purpose. Move it carefully, for example, from inside a house to the outside. What you shouldn't do is change perspectives in the same shot.
- **Sense of volume**: position events and details within the location, so the audience gets a feeling of all dimensions of that location. For example, you can let the characters speak from another room, or you can describe what happens outside a building while a character is talking.
- **Austere timing**: start scenes at the latest possible moment before the main action begins, and end them as soon as that action ends. In doing so, Kramer is referring to the "late in, early out" rule. This is often the finishing touch.
- **Emotional weight**: if you want to convey emotions, write them as scenes, not explanatory passages.

Details are key to writing good scenes, especially when they are close-ups. Use metaphors and similes for that purpose. When interviewing people for nonfiction story details, Kramer turns his interviewees openly into accomplices, asking them to help him reconstruct what happened. He first interviews positive sources first and then moves on to adversarial ones. Another important aspect (we've had a look at this in the chapter on idea-finding) is securing access. When reporting a story on a California farm for his book, Kramer made sure he would fit in visually, dressing like a farm executive. Once he had pieced together a series of scenes, he read that part of his book to the farm executives, who corrected inaccuracies and provided more details to deepen his scenes. The scenes he had written were both reconstructed and observed, which is why they were so rich: "Re-created and recollected scenes, done with honor and craftsmanship, work wonders. But the strongest, fullest, and most delicately built scenes follow field reporting that is attentive to sensory data, idiosyncratic quotes, pacing, personality, mood and odd but telling detail" (Kramer 2007:138–9).

So you should have recorded details before you establish the camera shot. This includes collective details that characterise social groups and thematic details that help convey the story's theme (Hart 2011). The observation part Kramer mentions is something that you should always do first-hand, whenever time and money permits. Sure, you can collect some of the details digitally, especially visual details like pictures. But nothing beats being there and experiencing sensory details first-hand. Let's have a look at all of this in a real-life science writing example. This is how reporter Tom Kizzia constructs a scene in his piece about whale hunting and global warming for the *New Yorker*:

> On a trip to the ice edge, Tariek Oviuk, a hunter from Point Hope, felt a strange sensation: the lift of ocean waves beneath his feet. The older men, nervous about rising wind, hurried back toward shore, but the younger hunters remained, stripping blubber from a few small beluga whales.
>
> (Kizzia 2016)

Before this excerpt, Kizzia describes how the hunters harpoon whales and drag them onto ice sheets, but the sheets are too thin to carry the weight of the whales. Note how many storytelling elements there are. Kizzia writes about Oviuk's and the older men's feelings, not his own (although he experienced the same, he was there, after all). The scene goes on like this:

> Then the crack of three warning shots came rolling across the ice, and the hunters scrambled for their snowmobiles. "As soon as we heard those shots, my heart started pounding," Oviuk recalled.
>
> (Kizzia 2016)

The senses he conveys through his writing are sight, sound and touch. Also, the first scene of his piece starts in the middle of the action – "late in". And right after writing how Oviuk's heart started racing, the author pulls you out of the scene – "early out". It is impossible not to want to read on. It's a cliffhanger. Also, Kizzia positions his camera purposefully. He starts with a very short establishing shot that he wraps up as the very first sentence, merely mentioning where you are: Point Hope in Northern Alaska. That's it. He then zooms into a medium shot (which is indeed the first scene), giving you both a sense of what you're looking at and introducing the characters on a whale hunt. The medium shot helps you both grasp the surroundings and what the characters are doing in it. Also, it is rife with conflict from the outset. The hunters have one goal: hunt whales. But the ice sheet is too thin. Zooming in further, Kizzia follows Tariek Oviuk's perspective. He changes the camera angle again in the following scene that starts like this:

> Oviuk told me the story, a few months later, we were sitting in the kitchen of his friend Steve Oomittuk, a former village mayor, eating strips of maktaaq – chewy beluga blubber [...]
>
> (Kizzia 2016)

He's now taken a first-person point of view. Also, note again how he draws you in with sensory details like the chewy beluga blubber. This is cinematic nonfiction storytelling at its best. Scene-setting such as Kizzia's throws the audience right into the story. It is the writer who provides the details, but the audience's emotions are their own. The vicarious emotions are as real as real-life emotions. Brain scans have proved that in several studies. "The writer's mission, I realized, is not to describe what's out in the world in all its detailed complexity. The mission is to tap what's already in the reader's head by carefully selecting a few details that stimulate existing memories" (Hart 2011:91). That is why you don't need to over-describe when setting a scene. This ties in perfectly with everything that we know about the brain on story. The "give them two plus two" principle, the Gestalt law of reification (we automatically complete shapes) and the Kuleshov effect that states we ascribe different meanings to different picture sequences, depending on the context. In order to understand the context, some exposition is necessary. So let's see how you can sneak that in.

Elegant exposition

In the section on dialogue, I briefly addressed on-the-nose dialogue, which is just a character bluntly stating her intentions. Fiction or nonfiction, you have to give the readers information. When you introduce a character, how much do you tell your readers about her? What do you tell them? And how do you deliver that? That is exposition. When you set and describe a scene, that is also exposition. It usually doesn't propel the story forward, but it shows your audience more about characters and locations. As Sheila Curran Bernard writes in her book on documentary storytelling, exposition is the five Ws, the journalistic questions: what, who, when, where and why. I would also add how. This is where journalism and fiction intersect, at least in terms of methodology. But in a story, you can't afford to give away all your factual information right at the start, like a news piece written using the inverted pyramid. Also, it's boring to read. When you write exposition or explanatory passages, what happens in readers' brains is that you drag them out of narrative mode right into cognitive mode (have a look at chapter one for a brief digression on how the brain functions on story). Cognitive mode is nice and all, but it's boring. When in cognitive mode, the audience becomes conscious of the fact that they're just reading a story. This means they realise they are not *in* the story anymore. It's those passages where you lose them. Exposition is part of storytelling (think of the set-up part of comedy writing, and Freytag's pyramid). But it doesn't have to be boring. So screenwriters have come up with a number of ways to sneak in exposition without the audience noticing.

It's tricky. Exposition is telling, drama is showing. One way is to let characters handle exposition and tell others characters what they (and the audience) need to know. There are two types of character-delivered exposition (adapted from Yorke 2013):

1   **Audience and characters don't know the information**: questions characters ask fill in both the audience and other characters on which facts they need to know. That is why many new series include an ingénue. Yorke mentions cops and doctors as interrogators – they have a real need to know. That's why this part is easier than the next.

2   **Audience needs the information and doesn't know – but the characters all know**: if the characters don't have a need to know, create one. Give them a reason. Inexperienced writers would let their characters repeat expository information using phrases like this: "you know you've got..." or "you heard what so and so said". How can you make this less dull? Add character desire. When a few characters know the information you're giving, you can give it to the audience explicitly. But when all know it, it is underlying – it's showing. Inject conflict. These are the dramatic rules: desire, when confronted with an opposite desire, creates conflict. For example, instead of letting one character deliver a whole piece of information to another, let them argue over that information.

Another way is using reluctancy. If one character does not want to give away that piece of information (for example, a withdrawn character), the curiosity of the audience is immediately stoked. When you use any of these techniques, ensure the characters sound like themselves. If the audience gets wind that these are your words and not the character's, you lose them. They're out of narrative mode, and out of the illusion you created: your story is kaput.

Screenwriting teacher Robert McKee calls these techniques "dramatized exposition". He has a simple rule for turning dull exposition into dramatised exposition: convert exposition into ammunition. If all characters know the expository details, let them use it as ammunition to achieve what they want or need. Also, don't cheat and just shoot (or, when writing, describe) a moment where photographs tell (as opposed to show) the audience what you want to know them (McKee 1997).

While this is a fiction writing technique, you can use it to select better quotes and dialogue for your nonfiction pieces, and you can ask questions that get your nonfiction story's characters to disclose expository information. This clearly taps into investigative question-asking techniques, especially when you feel they are getting reluctant.

Let's take a step towards nonfiction exposition. Some documentary films pack all the information the audience needs right into the beginning, as on-screen narration. The downside of this: the audience doesn't know why it needs to know this information right at the outset; when it does need to know it later on, it won't remember it (Curran Bernard 2004). How else can you weave documentary narration into the story? You can let your characters argue (Curran Bernard follows pretty much Yorke's advice). Her example "Yeah? Well, we wouldn't even be in this mess if you hadn't decided to take your paycheck to Vegas!" (Curran Bernard 2004:16) hints at conflict. You can also reveal expository details through newspaper headlines and other printed material. Just describe it. Auditory exposition through voice-overs is also common practice in documentary film-making. Visuals will also reveal a lot, if carefully chosen. You can use establishing shots of places and signs, but your possibilities don't stop there:

> Toys littered on a suburban lawn say "Children live here." Black bunting and a homemade shrine of flowers and cards outside a fire station say "Tragedy has occurred."
>
> (Curran Bernard 2004)

Newspapers, signs and landmarks give the audience a sense of location. So, while these are filmmaking techniques, how can you transport them onto a page? Sheila Curran Bernard just did. What she describes are shots. And shots make scenes. Write shots. Write scenes. Don't forget that all films are texts before they become films. Be descriptive in writing such scenes, and make sure that give your audience only the expository details they need to know. Here's a final tip: when expository writing is done badly, it often becomes the main clause of a sentence. When it's done well, it slips into subordinate clauses, while the main clause is action. The exposition then gets mentioned only casually.

Loglines

We had a look at some templates in the chapter on narrative structure, like the Dobzhansky and the ABT template. All these tools help you boil down a full story, or at least parts of it (depending on which ABT template you take). Most professional screenwriters don't just sit down at the desk and start typing out a full screenplay. Rather, they develop scene ideas, outline them in one way or another, boil their ideas down, chuck them and then come up with more research. Over the course of this process, they develop several summaries like synopsis, step outline, a treatment and the actual screenplay, which in turn undergoes a number of revisions until it becomes final. But that's not all. After a screenwriter has written an uncommissioned, speculative screenplay ("spec script"), she needs to sell that script. Since Hollywood executives are impatient people (sorry for stereotyping), she has very little time to pitch them her script and tell them what it is about. Screenwriting has a tool for that, and Shonda Rhimes says in her MasterClass lesson on television writing, every pitch should start with a logline. The logline sums up the story's narrative without giving away the resolution. It whets the appetite. Loglines are one (two, at the very most!) sentence(s) long. And that does not mean an infinitely long sentence with many clauses. Cap it at 30 words. As so many constructs in writing, loglines follow a structure. Here is one way to structure a logline (Sorkin 2019):

1   **Protagonist**
2   **Inciting incident**
3   **Goal**
4   **Central conflict**

The order is not important. You can start with the inciting incident. That's indeed what many writers do. What's nice is that you're already familiar with loglines if you've ever watched television and if you've been at the movies. Just look into your TV guide or the film guide at the movie theatre, and you'll find these one- or two-liners that make you want to watch the film without telling you too much about it. Look up movies on the Internet Movie Database (IMDB), and you'll find a logline for each of it.

The inciting incident often starts with "when this or that happens" to mark the moment in time when things go south for the protagonist. For the protagonist, don't come up with names. At this point, the audience doesn't know the characters by name and doesn't care about them, either. Instead, write the protagonist's profession or something that describes action, like "beekeeper", "nuclear physicist". Add one adjective that describes conflict or the character's flaw. In the case of the physicist "a dyscalculic physicist" would imply conflict, right? At the same time, it reveals a character's flaw, which makes your audience empathise with it. Next, the goal. What are the hero's actions? This part includes a strong verb that shows what the protagonist needs to do to fulfill his quest. Last, the conflict, or rather, antagonist. Who or what stands in the protagonist's way of reaching her goal? This is often combined with the stakes (we'll see another logline structure in a minute). Use strong visual words like "fights" and "struggles", rather than "wonders" or "learns" (Sorkin 2019). As you can see, the words Sorkin chooses imply conflict in the action, or resistance. All these elements of conflict make the audience wonder how the conflict is going to end.

Here's my attempt at churning out a logline for a movie: "When his puppy is murdered, a widowed hitman returns from retirement to kill its murderers." Takes less than a minute. Afterwards, I looked up the original IMDB 20-words-logline, which reads like this: "An ex-hit-man comes out of retirement to track down the gangsters that killed his dog and took everything from him." There are plenty of other versions of loglines floating in the web. Filmmaking software producer *StudioBinder* has released two slightly modified versions. The first goes is practically identical to Sorkin's. The second goes like this (Unitas 2019):

1   **Protagonist**
2   **Action**
3   **Antagonist**
4   **Goal**
5   **Stake**

It's essentially a reordered version of the previous logline, plus the added stakes (usually death, or at least financial ruin). If nothing was at stake, the story wouldn't pass the "so what" test. Also, the reordering now literally puts the antagonist between the protagonist, her action (which she hopes leads her to the goal), and her goal. In the example of John Wick, it's not mentioned but sort of implicit. What do you think is at stake when a retired hitman takes on an entire crime syndicate?

Bear with me. I know you're probably not writing a movie, and most probably you're not standing in an elevator, trying to sell a spec script to a Hollywood producer. So why bother? First, it's a fantastic exercise to learn how to boil down your story. You can do this at any stage during your writing process, to ensure you have fully grasped what your story is about. Journalism professor John Capouya makes a point of saying that as a journalist, you can use loglines in the newsroom. It's a pitching tool that helps you tell the gist of the story in two sentences. Narrative journalists like Ben Montgomery use it to sum up their stories before they write it, and then wrap facts around the logline like stripes on a barber pole (Capouya 2014).

Let's try another example, straight from a science story: "When a new astronomy student gets fired under false pretenses, she must expose her lovelorn supervisor's real motivation to restore her academic reputation." All the essential story elements are there. A protagonist, a new astronomy student (which hints at the difference in power between her and her supervisor), she just got fired under false pretenses (inciting incident), exposing the antagonist's motivation (action, that's her quest), restore her academic reputation (goal). In an earlier version, I was more expansive and had included what the false pretenses were (bad work morale) and I had included what the supervisor's real motivation (unrequited love, followed by fear). That would have been too much detail. This way, I'll let the audience wonder what those false pretenses and the supervisor's motivation were. That's just the right amount of tension. In fact, Sorkin and Capouya recommend not giving away too much detail. When writing loglines, you want to be specific enough to create some pictures in your audience's mind, but you don't want to be overly specific. It takes a bit of tinkering until the logline feels right. But this way, you could perfectly include it as the opener of your pitch. Or, if someone asks you at dinner what your story is about, that's what you can come up with. What you don't know is how it ends: the supervisor gets fired, his own reputation damaged. The student changes university, and the whole case is exposed by *BuzzFeed* journalist Azeen Ghorayshi.

Case study: Story Collider

Erin Barker is the artistic director of Story Collider. She's also a writer and an editor. Story Collider is a US-based nonprofit organisation that coaches scientists (and non-scientists) to tell their science-related stories on stage. The Story Collider team uses theatrical techniques to coach scientists, so I had to call them. Without further ado, I had a chance to talk with Barker via Skype and am going to share that conversation here. I've edited the interview for brevity and clarity.

Q: How did Story Collider start?

A: We're coming up on our ten-year anniversary next year. We've been around for almost ten years. We got started in 2010, here in New York. Essentially, I took a storytelling class here, and in that class I met a physicist named Ben Lillie, who had just decided to leave academia and try to do something in connection with science and theatre in New York City. He had this idea he wanted to start a storytelling show about science in New York. At the time, I didn't have any science connections at all, had barely taken any science classes in school. I thought this sounded like a terribly boring idea. I couldn't imagine how it would work out. But then he met another physicist named Brian Wecht, and they ended up putting a show together out here in Queens, in the basement of a bar. I went, and I just loved it. The stories were personal, they were real, they were funny, and they were moving. It was just not the way that I had ever experienced science before. So, I was totally excited about this idea after this. I went, overnight, from thinking it was a dumb idea to thinking like, "How can I get in on this? How can I be a part of this?"

Q: Let's assume I'm a scientist. Let's say I'm a biologist and I think I've got a story to tell. How would I approach Story Collider?

A: Normally, people will send us a pitch through our website, just a short synopsis of what they're interested in talking about, and if it feels like a good match for the show, we'll reach out. Sometimes we meet people who we think would be a great fit for the show and we want to explore different ideas with them, so we'll just talk on the phone with them and see if we can come up with a good story idea. What we really look for is an arc or, essentially, a change that takes place in the storyteller between the beginning and the end of the story.

Q: Where does the inspiration for your story coaching come from?

A: I think that we're influenced by a lot of ideas. We're influenced by Randy Olson's work, we're influenced by books like "Save the Cat!" by Blake Snyder, and we share some of Kurt Vonnegut's writing advice and his original thesis concept about story arcs. But when we're coaching, it really comes down to: what is that dramatic question? What is that question that's being asked at the beginning of the story, and is it answered by the end? Is that question threaded throughout every scene of the story? Is every line in every paragraph in service to that question?

Q: What about structure?

A: Early on in our workshops, we have an outline that we share from a book that I think is called something like "How to Improvise a Full-Length Play" (note: by Kenn Adams). But essentially it's just honing in on causality, so it's like, "In the beginning, the world was this way, until one day it wasn't. Then, because of that, this happened. Because of that, this happened. Because of that, this happened. Until, finally… and then every day after that the world was this way."

Q: Do you give your storytellers any stylistic advice?

A: Part of our aesthetic at Story Collider is that we really want everyone to sound conversational and to sound like themselves. At a certain point while we're working on the story, depending on the storyteller, we encourage them to step away from the script and start practicing it out loud so it sounds like them. We don't allow notes on stage at our show because we want it to come out sounding very natural.

Q: Theme being one of the most important story elements: do you define it beforehand?

A: The theme usually naturally emerges from the arc.

Q: What does a typical workshop look like?

A: We have all different formats that we work in, depending on what our client's interested in. We range from anything from a keynote and individual coaching to three-day workshop that we've done for a few clients. I would say, generally, we start out with a lecture period, and we talk about storytelling from the perspective of art and also of science. We talk about the neuroscience behind storytelling, why stories are an effective tool for reaching people. We like to speak to folks in both languages, in science and in art.

Q: Do you write a lot in your workshops?

A: The goal for most of our workshops, the longer ones, anyway, is for everyone to leave with a story, or at least the beginning of a story that they're working on. So we do some brainstorming exercises, and folks develop some ideas. We actually don't devote too much time in our workshops to writing and revising, because we don't want folks to get too much in their heads. We don't want them to get too caught up on individual words and phrases. I think of the nature of our medium, which is oral storytelling, and we want it to feel very natural and very in the moment.

Q: Are some scientists just reluctant to get in touch with storytelling techniques?

A: I would say for sure. That was something that really surprised me early on, not having really existed in the scientific world prior to my work with Story Collider. I had no idea that there was any kind of resistance to storytelling, which seemed to me like a very natural, intrinsic, human communication tool. It really took me off guard, especially because, as I started to learn more about science. As I started to learn that, for example, papers generally aren't written using first person. That took me off guard.

Q: And where do you think that comes from?

A: I think they are trained to think in a non-narrative way about their science. I think there's not a lot of rewarding in scientific culture for things like an engaging story as part of your talk. There's not a lot of reward for things like being vulnerable and sharing emotion, talking about failures. That's generally not rewarded a lot, so I think a lot of folks just get away from that in their everyday work. They're doing a different kind of writing and different kind of communication. I don't think it's that people with scientific minds don't have narrative communication skills or aren't natural communicators, I think it's just not a part of their culture.

Q: If you had a wish: in which direction would scientists ideally evolve in terms of communication?

A: That's a big question. I would like to see, I think, science get more comfortable with vulnerability. Get more comfortable with talking about themselves, with themselves as characters, and relating to the public on that level, because I think there's an appetite for that. We see, consistently, from our audience, this really sincere interest in understanding what takes place behind the scenes of science. I think there are so many stories that have never been shared that people are so hungry for and have such a genuine interest in. I would also like to see science get more comfortable listening, hearing stories from people about how science has impacted them, and incorporating that into their work, as well. I think it's definitely a two-way street, and I think there's lots of room for people to benefit on both sides.

Review questions

- How can screenplay structure help you outline science stories?
- Where can you get good dialogue from?
- How can you improve the style of dialogue through editing?
- What elements make a good scene?
- What is subtext?
- How can you use the different shot types to set scenes?
- Which techniques can you use to sneak in exposition?
- What does a good logline deliver, and why should you use them in journalism?

Links

"He Fell In Love With His Grad Student – Then Fired Her For It" (BuzzFeed): https://www.buzzfeednews.com/article/azeenghorayshi/ott-harassment-investigation

"Pixar in a box: The art of storytelling – film grammar" (Khan Academy): https://www.khanacademy.org/partner-content/pixar/storytelling#film-grammar

"Whale Hunters of the Warming Arctic" (*The New Yorker*): https://www.newyorker.com/magazine/2016/09/12/fossil-fuels-and-climate-change-in-point-hope-alaska

"John Yorke on Story Structure" (BBC Writers Room): https://www.youtube.com/watch?v=jsUNJ9OAbdk

"How the Parks of Tomorrow Will be Different" (*National Geographic*): https://www.nationalgeographic.com/magazine/2016/12/national-parks-climate-change-rising-sea-weather/

References

BBCWriters (2018) "John Yorke on story structure and common mistakes made by new writers," BBC Writers [Online Video]. Available at: https://www.youtube.com/watch?v=jsUNJ9OAbdk (date accessed 28 August 2019).

Benham, K. (2007) "Hearing Our Subjects' Voices: Quotes and Dialogue," in: Kramer, M. & Call, W. *Telling True Stories*. New York: Plume, 104–107.

Blake, M. & Bailey, S. (2013) *Writing the horror movie*. New York: Bloomsbury Publishing USA.

Capouya, J. (2014) "Want to write great narrative? Study screenwriting," NiemanStoryBoard [Online]. Available at: https://niemanstoryboard.org/stories/want-to-write-grea t-narrative-study-screenwritin/ (date accessed 23 August 2019).

Curran Bernard, S. (2004) *Documentary Storytelling Making Stronger and More Dramatic Nonfiction Films*. New York: Focal Press.

Draper, R. (2016) "Inside the Fight to Save One of the World's Most Dangerous Parks," *National Geographic* [Online]. Available at: https://www.nationalgeographic.com/maga zine/2016/07/virunga-national-parks-africa-congo-rangers/ (date accessed 25 August 2019).

Ephron, N. (2007) "What Narrative Writers Can Learn From Screenwriters," in: Kramer, M. & Call, W. *Telling True Stories*. New York: Plume, 98–102.

Ghorayshi, A. (2016) "He Fell In Love With His Grad Student – Then Fired Her For It," BuzzFeed [Online]. Available at: https://www.buzzfeednews.com/article/azeenghora yshi/ott-harassment-investigation (date accessed 23 August 2019).

Hart, J. (2011) *Storycraft: The Complete Guide to Writing Narrative Nonfiction*. Chicago: The University of Chicago Press.

Hochschild, A. (2007) "Reconstructing Scenes," in: Kramer, M. & Call, W. *Telling True Stories*. New York: Plume, 24–28.

Junger, S. (2015) "How PTSD Became a Problem Far Beyond the Battlefield," *Vanity Fair* [Online]. Available at: https://www.vanityfair.com/news/2015/05/ptsd-war-home-seba stian-junger (date accessed 22 August 2019).

Kaplan, J. (1987) "Tom Wolfe on How to Write New Journalism," *Rolling Stone* [Online]. Available at: https://www.rollingstone.com/music/music-features/tom-wolfe-on-how-to-write-new-journalism-90742/ (date accessed 22 August 2019).

Kramer, M. (2007) "Setting the Scene," in: Kramer, M. & Call, W. *Telling True Stories*. New York: Plume, 136–139.

Kizzia, T. (2016) "Whale Hunters of the Warming Arctic," *The New Yorker* [Online]. Available at: https://www.newyorker.com/magazine/2016/09/12/fossil-fuels-and-climate-change-in-p oint-hope-alaska (date accessed 25 August 2019).

McKee, R. (1997) *Story: Substance, Structure, Style, and the Principles of Screenwriting*. New York: ReganBooks.

Morell, R. (2018) "What Journalists Need to Know About Writing Screenplays," Nieman Storyboard [Online]. Available at: https://niemanstoryboard.org/stories/what-journa lists-need-to-know-about-writing-screenplays/ (date accessed 22 August 2019).

Nijhuis, M. (2016) "How the Parks of Tomorrow Will Be Different," *National Geographic* [Online]. Available at: https://www.nationalgeographic.com/magazine/2016/12/na tional-parks-climate-change-rising-sea-weather/ (date accessed 28 August 2019).

Pixar in a box (2015) "The Art of Storytelling: Film Grammar," Khan Academy [Online]. Available at: https://www.khanacademy.org/partner-content/pixar/storytelling#film -grammar (date accessed 25 August 2019).

Sorkin, A. (2019) "Screenwriting Tips: How to Write a Logline," Masterclass [Online]. Available at: https://www.masterclass.com/articles/screenwriting-tips-how-to-write-a -logline (date accessed 23 August).

Unitas, A.J. (2019) "How to Write a Logline Producers Won't Pass On [with Logline Examples]," StudioBinder [Online]. https://www.studiobinder.com/blog/write-comp elling-logline-examples/ (date accessed 23 August 2019).

Villarejo, A. (2007) *Film Studies: The Basics*. London: Routledge.

Yorke, J. (2013) *Into the Woods: How stories work and why we tell them.* London: Penguin Random House UK.

Walter, R. (2010) *Essentials of Screenwriting: the Art, Craft, and Business of Film and Television Writing.* New York: Plume.

Weingarten, M. (2010) *The Gang That Wouldn't Write Straight: Wolfe, Thompson, Didion, Capote, and the New Journalism Revolution.* New York: Crown.

8 Literary Techniques

What you will learn in this chapter:

- Crafting themes
- Status symbols in science
- Point of view
- Comparing: Metaphors and similes
- Literary devices
- Tension: More literary devices
- Comedy writing techniques
- Case study: The Hot Zone

Writing about science is difficult. Many readers shrug off science pieces as dry and boring. Science writing needs explanation and, alas, the occasional jargon word. That is why the New Journalists since the 1960s have been using literary techniques to make journalism more relatable. Science is also incredibly complex, which doesn't make your job as a science storyteller easier. No matter whether you are a science journalist or a scientist, or both. After having worked with so many scientists over the years, I claim one of the biggest dangers they run into is trying to give you a complete picture. When they explain their science, they throw in everything that you should know. But even if they do, science can never be an absolute truth. Many claims are valid only for a specific amount of time, until they're replaced or overturned by newer knowledge. For every study, every claim and every hypothesis you can find in academic writing, I challenge you to find the opposite. You will. The same is true of popular science writing. Whatever you can think of, chances are that a lot has been written about it already, regardless of which angle you take. What helps your story stand out, while limiting the amount of input that goes into it? Finding the story's theme. That's why I will start this chapter off with an immersion into how you can craft your own themes, when to look for them and how to find them. Themes are your story's universal truth, the golden thread that runs through it. If you find it, you'll find it easy to distinguish between useful reporting material and superfluous one. So theme is your first tool.

It is the abstract message of a story that glues together all of its elements. One of those, perhaps the most important element in storytelling is character. You'll see a number of techniques on how to reveal character detail by applying the "show don't tell" storytelling rule. How do you evoke empathic reactions for your characters? Give your audience character details they can connect with (like personality traits and forgivable flaws), and then let them draw their own conclusions. Your characters have also to be goal-driven. Although scientists are rooted in the same psychological principles as everybody else's, academia is a particular social system that fosters its very own status symbols. That's why I've dedicated an entire section to status symbols, their use in New Journalism and what status symbols scientists employ. This can be quite revealing, and in the storytelling workshops I run for scientists, connecting this technique with some acting exercises (like Susan Batson's brilliant need, public persona and tragic flaw) has caused some participants to deeply reflect on their practices – including myself!

In literary writing, you'll have to take decisions, decisions, decisions. Once you know your characters, you'll have to figure out which perspective you want to tell their story from. This could be their own, or you could narrate the story hovering above them high in the sky, knowing it all, like a deity. We'll look at an example of a science article by master storyteller Elizabeth Kolbert in order to illustrate this. And I will obviously not skip the opportunity to rant a bit of how point of view is framed in academic writing, and to hint at the potential for improvement in that area.

What scientists do employ are metaphors. They are indeed your primary weapon against jargon and help you write about science in a way that is actually relatable. That section includes some proven techniques on how you can come up with original images and avoid pitfalls like dead metaphors and clichés. This kind of writing requires a lot of effort, but it also strengthens your voice and will make your writing sound much more like you. Above all, it's fun and a playful way to experiment with language. That is also valid of the sections that follow, the first of which focuses on figures of speech that have been around for thousands of years. They are incredibly powerful tools to deliver messages to your audience that are guaranteed to stick. We'll also have a look at more high-concept techniques like foreshadowing and flashbacks. If you write longer stories, they are invaluable tools, both for structuring and keeping the tension high.

When you write really short stories, comedy writers' techniques could be worth looking into. Yes, puns are frowned upon. But if you invest enough time in crafting original ones that subvert your readers' expectations, then you'll see how effective can be. The section on comedy writing techniques contains a bucket full of advice on how to do that, and some funny examples from academic writing that illustrate those techniques.

The subject of this chapter's case study is a real gold nugget. We'll dissect the techniques journalist Richard Preston uses in one chapter of his 1994 bestseller *The Hot Zone*, unveiling step by step which literary techniques he used to write a page-turner. Make sure you read his entire first chapter before starting to read the case study. I promise, there won't be a moment when you'll want to stop reading. Then get back to this book and read the case study. Preston uses many techniques that you'll read about in this chapter, like foreshadowing and meta-phors, and he also uses many techniques that you've seen in previous chapters. I absolutely recommend that you read his piece again after finishing this chapter, and that you then go back to the previous three chapters, while observing which techniques to write about science. Off we go, let's start with crafting themes!

Crafting themes

Yes, we've talked about theme in previous chapters. But since it's so central to storytelling, let's unpack it again in more detail here, as a literary technique. Plot serves the theme (Hart 2011). The earlier you find the theme, the easier it will be to select and reject story events. It sounds simple and logical: if you know what you're looking for, you can easily chuck the events you don't need and keep those that support the theme. When writing fiction, this is perfectly fine. When writing nonfiction, it's dangerous in terms of selecting "evidence" that feeds into your possibly biased assumptions. The same is naturally true of all nonfiction writing and doesn't spare scientific writing at all. I will make another point about this in the appendix on the scientific method, but that much is clear: for most theories (heck, I'll go out on a limb and say *all*) you'll find somebody in the scientific community who supports it, and someone else who rebuffs it. That's just to say: if you can formulate a theme early in the process of writing, do so. It'll help you select story events. But stay critical of it. With every new fact you gather as part of your reporting, be prepared to challenge your theme. Or you take the approach of investigative journalists and, instead of proving your hypothesis, you try to disprove it. If you can't find any piece of evidence that refutes your hypothesis, then there are good chances it might be true (Hunter 2011). The other approach is to let the theme naturally emerge from the reporting, structuring and writing. It really depends on the amount of reporting you have done before you start outlining and writing. The more, the easier it is to identify patterns and a theme.

What makes themes work? In terms of form, we've seen playwright Lajos Egri's theme-finding in Shakespeare plays before in this book. "Love defies death" (*Romeo and Juliet*), or "blind trust leads to destruction" (*King Lear*), or "ruthless ambition leads to its own destruction". In fact, if you look at Hollywood, you can find a variation of the last theme in revenge films. In the 2007 film "Death Sentence", starring Kevin Bacon, everybody dies at the end, so "revenge destroys everybody" (including the protagonist) is a valid theme. In other revenge films, all the perpetrators but the protagonist dies, so the theme is essentially the same, like in "John Wick" (2014), "Payback" (1999) and "The Revenant" (2015).

I want to point out two important traits of themes. First, the term "theme" is often interchangeably used (and confused) with subject, or topic. That's wrong. When somebody claims the theme of their story is "love" or "respect", then that's not really the theme. It's the topic. This is also not a valid answer to what a story is about, and it certainly doesn't pass the "so what?" test. Louis Slotin's story is neither about "bravery" nor "negligence". It's about how negligence leads to deadly accidents. Or let's think about logician Walter Pitts' story from this book's first chapter. The story author, Amanda Gefter, hints at the story's theme at the beginning. The subtitle says: "Walter Pitts rose from the streets to MIT, but couldn't escape himself." It's almost a perfect "A leads to B" structure. You could even draw this using one of Kurt Vonnegut's story shapes. You cannot sum up a theme in one word alone. Pitts' story isn't just a story about alcohol. Or depression. These are subjects, but not the story's themes.

Good story themes convey change. In most cases, this change represents the protagonist's character arc. Gefter's description contains it all. The protagonist works his way up from the streets only to fail at the end. It's a full narrative arc in one short sentence. A theme tells you in three words whether the story is going from good to bad or vice versa. In Pitts' case, it even tells you that it goes from bad to good to even worse than at the beginning. In terms of style, your verb choice also reflects change. You don't form a theme using a linking verb. You could rewrite the previous revenge movies' themes as "revenge is bad". But that doesn't convey any kind of movement, action or change. Instead, it's static. Stasis is death. If you flatline, you die. If your theme flatlines, your story dies. Also, it expresses a mere opinion instead of a universal truth that the audience understands. A static theme tells your audience, but you need to show them. The static variant also won't work, because they can't see a cause and effect structure (unlike in Egri's "A leads to B" template). An "is" theme is like giving the audience an opinion without backing it. Choose strong action verbs, motion verbs and transitive verbs. Let your theme follow this structure: "state A / strong transition verb / state B". A final note: although a theme describes a character arc, you don't name or describe the actual character. Gefter did it, yes. But it's part of the story, not an actual theme statement. In a theme, the protagonist (or another character) is implied, but unlike in a logline, you don't articulate the protagonist's profession and name.

Among all themes (at least in movies), screenwriting professor Richard Walter has found a unifying thread: identity. We just go to the movies to find out who we are. "Who am I? How do I know what's real and what's not? Why should I stop at the red lights? Why should I pay my taxes? Why should I put up with the bumps and bruises that afflict all of us every day of our lives?" (Walter 2010:45). What the theme also reflects is your, the storyteller's, own value system. Your themes are your beliefs about how the world works. And master storyteller Jack Hart makes a point about themes and clichés. For living a good life, only a few principles exist, and yes, storytellers have repeated them over and over again. But children don't know those few basic plots, and grown-ups forget them over time and need to be reminded. "So don't worry if you come up with a theme that's been around the block. As Jon Franklin has pointed out, clichés may be an embarrassment at the sentence level, but they are at the heart of theme" (Hart 2011:140). So good themes are non-original but universal. Analyse existing stories and figure out which ones reflect your own values and the evidence you have for them. Reuse them.

Status symbols in science

In his manifesto "The New Journalism", Tom Wolfe established four devices New Journalists from the 1960s and 1970s used to tell literary but still factually true stories:

- **Scene-by-scene construction**
- **Realistic dialogue**
- **Third-person point of view**
- **Status symbols**

We've already seen much about writing scenes. Scenes are equally important in nonfiction writing as in screenwriting, because they both transport the audience into the story (through vivid descriptive writing), but they also lend the story structure by being logically connected. According to Lee Gutkind, narrative journalism teacher and editor-in-chief of *Creative Nonfiction*, scenes are *the* essential building blocks of literary journalism. Dialogue is part of scenes, and we've also seen that device in the previous chapter on screenwriting. It is what encounters traditional journalistic writing, which employ mostly quotes, from narrative writing. So when you spot actual dialogue in a nonfiction story, you bet the author tries to put you into narrative mode.

In this section, I would like to focus a little bit more on point of view, or perspective, and on status symbols. With his "New Journalism" manifesto, Wolfe tried to establish literary techniques as part of a new journalism movement. Instead of bare information, scenes became the unit of reporting (Witt 2018 on Tom Wolfe). But Wolfe, who was both a journalist and a novelist, was also fascinated by social status, its symbols and mechanics. He believed in full immersion in reporting and in collecting lots of details to describe the story characters' status in their social systems. I would like to say that his approach was new back then, but even that is disputed. Apparently, the idea of using literary techniques in journalism had existed before. What Wolfe's school of journalists did, however, was actually apply those techniques for the first time. In doing so, the New Journalists assumed more of a sociological and psychological role than traditional newspaper journalists before them. For the newer generation of narrative journalists, his approach didn't go deep enough, though:

> How one dresses or where one lives takes on near-theological significance for him [...] But Wolfe's status-fixated reporting so values fashion over substance that it robs much of his journalism (and similarly, many of the characters in his novels) of complexity and depth. Wolfe's writing is all about surface.
>
> (Boynton 2005)

What the next evolutionary step, namely the New New Journalists (not a typo) like Ted Conover criticise is that Wolfe was too focused on individuals' position in society. Current narrative journalists, on the other hand, rather focus on class, race (which they claim Wolfe largely ignored), and on subcultures. They are also more invested in how they get the story. Some of them follow their characters over the years and take on jobs to fully immerse themselves in their characters' surroundings. As for Wolfe, it's easy to spot the social status symbols in his stories. For example, have a look at the following *Esquire* story he has written about physicist Robert Noyce (check the "Links" section). Here are a few examples that show how concerned he was with status (Wolfe 1983):

- "Noyce drove a Porsche roadster, and he didn't mind letting it out for a romp."
- "Noyce also bought a 1947 Republic Seabee amphibious airplane [...]"
- "At Fairchild there were no hard-worsted double-breasted pinstripe suits and shepherd's-check neckties. Sharp, elegant, fashionable, or alluring dress was a social blunder. Shabbiness was not a sin. Ostentation was."

In his portrait of Noyce, Wolfe dug into his personal life, his marriages, his divorces, his portrayals in newspapers, his cars and his status in society. Although today's narrative journalists and the New Journalists take a different approach to portray status, both camps require similar skill sets. You need to meticulously record the details that make a person's status. How deep and where you start digging depends on the system you break into. Social status is only valid within clearly defined boundaries. It requires a surrounding system. This social circle could include your friends, family, the line of job you're working in. Science has its own status symbols. The ones Wolfe recorded about Noyce did not so much concern his social status within academia, but they are rather everyday symbols. But it's worth looking at academia's status symbols, as that can explain much on why, for example, misconduct exists. Status defines the pecking order. Status is power. Status buys you cars, yachts and mansions. Status gets you laid. It all boils down to the basic human needs (if you've ever been on a scientific conference, you know what I mean). Here are just a few of scientists' status symbols:

- h-index (higher is better)
- Absolute number of publications (higher is better)
- Publications in high-profile journals (where high-profile means a high impact factor)
- Degrees (more is better)
- Professional/scientific association memberships
- Universities attended (VIP factor)
- Conference participation (more is better, high-profile is better)
- Travel: countries visited (more is better, and more exotic is even better)
- Collaborations with rock star scientists (VIP factor)
- High-profile projects (for example, with funding from prominent institutions)
- News coverage received
- Awards / prizes

Now, I'm not saying having status symbols is good or bad. It's neither. It's just part of the system. I'm also not saying that every scientist responds equally to these symbols. But if you're a scientist, if you're part of academia, you can't just ignore them. The aforementioned scientific status symbols are on top of the everyday status symbols like the area you live in, the way you dress and what type of house you have. Those are also perfectly relevant to scientists. You can measure the symbols in the above list both in terms of quantity and quality, although the seesaw tips towards quantity. I've been working with scientists for more than a dozen years, and over the past few years I've started running workshops on science writing for scientists. What I found (and yes, that's probably purely anecdotal evidence or at least a very limited sample size, but still) is that the number one status symbol is their reputation. How do I know? I can tell by the amount of fear they express before starting to write. It seems hard for them to take a stand on their own opinions, because they fear it might damage their reputation. Some even told me. The importance of a status symbol and the amount of fear losing it are directly proportional. That is also why using status symbols in writing about science is a fantastic tool. It shows what is at stake for them. How strong the stakes are perceived and experienced depends on the culture a scientist works in. It reveals a great lot of the person behind the status symbols. In some cases, the stakes of losing one's reputation are too high. In 2014, a Japanese stem cell scientist took his own life after being shamed and criticised when scientific fraud under his oversight was exposed, despite being cleared from direct misconduct (Webb 2014).

Point of view

Every story is told from one or more perspectives. The point of view (POV) through which you deliver it influences how much your audience will feel immersed in it. Where do you, the narrator, stand when you tell the story? Do you hover over it, like an omniscient god? Or are you in the middle of the story and even participate in the dialogue that unfolds, turning yourself into a story character? The perspective from which you tell a story does not just have an effect on the audience in terms of how well they are immersed in the story. It also influences their opinion forming. It's much like photography or filmmaking. In a way, what you include in the frame is just as important as what you leave out of it. Because your audience cannot know what you omit. Once you change the perspective, opinions may change.

Literature professor Valerie Vogrin comes up with the example of a lovers' triangle. Imagine the story from the husband's perspective, who is left at home with their son, while his wife goes on a secret getaway with her lover. Who do you root for? Now imagine the same story, but from the perspective from the cheating wife, who says her husband hasn't talked to and loved her in years. Does your opinion change? How do you feel now? Now imagine the same story from the lover's perspective. He might not even know she's married. It feels different every time, and for good reason. Changing the point of view changes the audience's emotional reaction to a story. What a change in perspective also means is a change of tone and theme. The same story told through a different character's eyes just makes the audience feel different. So, use this device consciously, since changing it also changes the information, thoughts and emotions the audience has access to. These are the most common types of point of view (adapted from Vogrin 2003):

1   **First person**: tells the story from a story character's perspective. Perceptions and thoughts are the character's. In fiction, this is often the protagonist. But in nonfiction, this doesn't have to be the case (we'll see a science writing example in a minute). Pronouns used are "I", "we", "our". This point of view is closest to the audience. On the downside, digressions become more difficult; for example, when you try to slip out of narrative and into explanatory summary.

2   **Second person**: directly addresses the audience. Pronouns are "you" and "your". It's not as popular as first- or third-person point of view.

3   **Third person**: this is the most distant (towards the audience) and most popular point of view in fiction writing. Pronouns are "she", "her", "he", "his", "they", "their". Vogrin distinguishes between the following types:

   a   **Single vision**: the story is told through one character's eyes. Typically used in in short stories. The audience has only access to whatever that character knows.

   b   **Multiple vision**: the story is told through alternating characters' eyes. Typically used in novellas and novels. The audience has access to what all the POV characters know.

   c   **Omniscient**: the narrator is god and knows everything. This POV used to influence the narrators' voices: Dickens, Tolstoy and Austen sounded authoritative. Because you, the narrator, know things some characters don't, you can use this POV for creating suspense.

   d   **Objective**: the narrator knows nothing about the characters, but reports impartially through dialogue and action. Raymond Carver used this technique in short stories.

I would argue that most narrative science pieces' authors use third-person limited points of view. I haven't used the fully objective point of view yet but find that one most interesting. And science? Scientific papers' publishers unfortunately often neglect the power of POV. In a (vain) attempt to convey that science is fully objective, taking the actors out of papers, the copy becomes often passive and unreadable. But suggesting objectivity through language when the procedures are not, is misleading:

> Using this form of language conveys, and is intended to convey, an impression that the ideas being discussed have a neutral, value-free, impartial basis. Its universal use in academic writing is not justified unless the material being

presented is in fact underpinned by these qualities. I hope to demonstrate that this is rarely, if ever, the case.

(Webb 1992:748)

It feels like scientific authors are indeed trying to remove any kind of perspective from their papers. When they don't, by tradition, they prefer third person to first person POVs. Most of the researchers I work with write this way. They have been trained to. So it's no wonder. While Christina Webb conceded already in 1992 that writing first-person research articles is justified (she wrote her own paper this way), I found a recent article from *Enago Academy* that advises scientific authors to not use the first person perspective, because it is "often considered arrogant and self-serving" (this advice is, by the way, based on an exchange in an online forum). Another lowlight is this phrase: "when you want to persuade the reader, it is best to avoid personal pronouns" (Enago Academy 2019). No, Enago. Just no. And a third one: even though some journals allow the use of the first person in their abstracts, avoid the use of pronouns like "I". Give me a second to dry my eyes. My allergy against bullshit advice just struck really hard. How will science ever get rid of its ivory tower image when professional proofreaders churn out advice like that? Forgive me for thinking it's slightly ironic that the *Enago* article doesn't have a byline. And that the Enago tagline says "Author First. Quality First". Author first. Right. Unlike most academic authors, popular science writers and editors embrace the full point of view spectrum. Some writers use POV to slip in and out of different characters' perspectives, including their own as narrators. Let's have a look at how the fabulous Elizabeth Kolbert pulls this off in her piece on rising sea levels:

> Knowing the tides would be high around the time of the "super blood moon," in late September, I arranged to meet up with Hal Wanless, the chairman of the University of Miami's geological-sciences department.

(Kolbert 2015)

This happens in the first paragraph. The second one starts with scene setting, again from Kolbert's perspective:

> We had breakfast at a greasy spoon not far from Wanless's office, then set off across the MacArthur Causeway.

(Kolbert 2015)

Kolbert is a bystander, but she's also part of the story. The narrative that spans her story is both chronological and spatial, driving in a car with Wanless. All the action that takes place, all the dialogue that is spoken, Kolbert tells it from her perspective. She occasionally steps out of her perspective to digress into explanatory passages that provide background on how coastlines and ice sheets developed. In those passages, she becomes an omniscient narrator. Kolbert goes from narrative mode to explanatory mode in these sections, and some of them span several (comparatively longer than the narrative) paragraphs. Read her story (the link is you-know-where). After you read it, ask yourself in light of the *Enago* advice: has Kolbert persuaded you?

Comparing: Metaphors and similes

Conveying science is hard. You'll have to explain things the audience doesn't know. There's two problems you'll face: one, explanations are not entertaining. When they come alone, they don't stick. Two, science is complicated to understand. Jargon makes it even more complicated. Some people explain jargon by using more jargon, or worse, repeat the definition. My favourite quote in the 2006 film "Lucky Number Slevin" is this. Slevin: "I guess no one ever taught you not to use the word you're defining in the definition." Slevin gets suckerpunched in the face for that statement. But he has a point. In science, you can use metaphors and similes to come up with graspable examples that compare complex terminology to objects your audience is already familiar with. This gives them an "aha!" moment. One important property is that the object you are comparing your original one with has two meanings. An obvious trait (say, colour), and another, strongly implied one. For example, if you tell a girl her eyes shimmer like an emerald, the implied meaning is precious, not green (of course, they need to be green to match). If you say "green like mould" – that probably wouldn't be perceived as a compliment because of the second meaning of mould, which is harmful (adapted from Forsyth 2013).

The ideal simile and metaphor lets the audience either think of a new object in a familiar way, or think of a familiar object in a new way. That's why you should write only original ones, and that means comparing objects with the qualities of objects they haven't been compared to yet.

That is why before you get started choosing apt metaphors and similes, and before we even define what metaphors and similes are, you need to think about whom you're writing for. There is only one goal you can have when trying to explain something as complicated as science: getting it across. So let's have a look at these two literary devices. They're easy to distinguish. First, let's get the definition out of the way. When you use a simile, you compare two things by writing (or saying) they are "like" each other. When you use a metaphor, you say one thing "is" another, based on traits that connect them. You don't have to follow that exact structure. Sometimes it's sufficient to combine noun and adjective, or two nouns. For example, think of "pitch black" (yes, that's also a cliché, but it'll illustrate the point). You could write the simile as "black like pitch", but the contracted version is snappier (even for a cliché).

Screenwriting coach Jack Hart writes in his "Storyteller's Lexicon" that figurative language like similes and metaphors translate "unfamiliar aspects of a scene into the familiar" (Hart 2007:236). What similes and metaphors really are, are steps down on a lower stave of the ladder of abstraction. You take something abstract from the top of the ladder all the way down to make it tangible. At the lowest rungs, there is no ambiguity and no abstraction. The higher you get, the more abstract things get. Metaphors and similes connect the abstract with the concrete. They add clarity to your writing (Clark 2008). Let's have a look at them in action. Here's a simile John McPhee uses to illustrate with words what a tree's canopy looks like:

> Its trunk broke freakishly – about twenty feet up – and the crown bent all the way over and spread the upper branches **like** a broom upon the ground.
>
> (McPhee 2018)

McPhee could have also written the passage like this: "The crown is a broom", that is, as a metaphor. But his use of a simile is much more effective in creating a picture in readers' minds, because it contains strong motion verbs. That's no wonder. McPhee is a master at writing similes, metaphors and all sorts of comparisons (Malone 2019). Some terms or scientific concepts are particularly difficult to explain, because the very term you're trying to compare is abstract. For example, quantum theory. Sally Davis, science editor (*Aeon*, formerly *Nautilus*) shows impressive command of similes in explaining gravity:

> Gravity is rendered beautifully predictable by general relativity, which envisions it as an effect of how the four dimensions of space and time curve in response to matter, **like** a piece of tarpaulin bending under a bowling ball.
>
> (Davis 2016)

The dented tarp is now forever etched into my brain whenever I think about gravity. Gravity is not tangible. A tarpaulin is, and so is a bowling ball. Davis doesn't stop there. Comparing quantum theory with gravity, she comes up with another, sentence-long simile: "It's as if a soccer player and a tennis player were managing to carry on a game despite being ignorant of the opponent's rules". Davis' story packs a lot of story elements, and more great similes, too. Read it. I've included a link to in the "Links" section. As you can see, similes are not only good to compare objects, but behaviour, problems and much more. I tend to use similes more often than metaphors. Perhaps because I find metaphors too absolute.

In fiction, metaphors and similes are frequently used devices. If something is used very often, repetition looms. I've written about dead metaphors and clichés in the chapter on language and style. It's bad style in storytelling. But Lombardi (2003) makes a point saying that hackneyed similes and metaphors have their advantages on the street, because everybody knows them. But fiction (and I will add nonfiction here as well!) should use fresh similes and metaphors. Metaphors are heavier than similes. This can go as far as in Franz Kafka's novella *The Metamorphosis*, where the metaphor of the protagonist turning into a giant insect runs through the entire story (Lombardi 2003).

Metaphors are one of the most powerful literary devices to write about science, because they raise the audience's attention, because they are suggestive and because they stimulate the audience's imagination. Business psychology professor

Nikolas Westerhoff writes that metaphors equalise two terms. As such, metaphors are able to tear down boundaries between opposites. For example, the headline of a magazine article (German) reads "Head or gut: The intelligence of emotions". The underlying message is that emotions equal intelligence. He makes a valid point of saying that such metaphors can become entire story themes. On the downside, if the comparisons are inaccurate, the audience's associations will be wrong. As a nonfiction writer (Westerhoff refers to journalists), it's your job to unearth existing metaphors, even when they're hidden in jargon and loanwords, like "alexithymia", which by itself is a metaphor. Once you find such words, you should then formulate your own metaphors. One journalist reformulated it as "soul of ice" when writing about alexithymia for *Der Spiegel*.

I want to close this section with some advice on how to craft good metaphors. The advice isn't mine but Canadian poet's Daniel Tysdal. In a *TEDx* talk he gave a few years ago, he instructed the audience to write similes according a simple template: "Your image is like 'blank'. And to fill this blank, you may draw on anything from nature's animals, plants and environments to humankind's creations, communities and environs" (Tysdal 2015). It really is that simple to create a metaphor. "Compare. Connect. [...] A good simile or metaphor will possess some combination of surprise and aptness, of trueness and newness" (Tysdal 2015). Here is a simple process of how to get there: first, come up with an image and write it down (in Tysdal's example, the subject is a person who audience members lost). As a next step, ask yourself, which animal is that image like? Which season is it like? Then, expand the comparison and ask the questions why and how the image is like the season or animal you just came up with. In doing so, your metaphor or simile becomes more specific (Tysdal 2015). I use his technique in my storytelling workshops, and the results are remarkable. It takes a number of iterations and revisions, but most participants end up with metaphors that circumscribe abstract concepts as tangible, relatable examples.

Literary devices

Poetry. Dialogue. Movies. Political speeches. Novels. Newspaper headlines. Plays. What do they all have in common? People remember specific lines. Those lines are memorable for good reason. They are crafted in a way that "just works". The writer tinkered with them until they became memorable, and consciously chose a figure of speech that conveys the semantics also through its form. When I say form, I mean structure. There are so many one could write a book about, which, in fact, Mark Forsyth has done (have a look at it, the link is in the "References" section). So here's my take on what I deem some of the most important literary devices (sorry, but they're all Greek):

Let's start with an effective and simple-to-use figure of speech: ***alliteration***. It's essentially choosing words whose first letter sounds similar. "Curiosity killed the cat" is an example. It sticks not because of the apparently unprovable truth, but because of the way it sounds (Forsyth 2013). In that sense, the same initial letter alone is not enough to make a sequence of words sounds the same.

"Chocolate killed the cat" would be way less effective. You can find alliterations in newspapers, magazines, films, songs and on book covers. The 2005 movie "V for Vendetta"? That's one long alliteration in which everything V says starts with a "v". "Gone girl" (2014)? An alliteration. The cover of the 17–23 August issue of *New Scientist* reads "Bye-Bye, Big Bang" (the actual piece in the issue has a different title). Science writer Carl Zimmer's highly praised science book is titled as follows: "She Has Her Mother's Laugh: The Powers, Perversions, and Potential of Heredity". Power, Perversions, and Potential. This chapter's section on status symbols? "Status Symbols in Science". All of that is no accident. Alliterations emphasise, and they make lines more memorable. The twin sister of alliteration is **assonance**. If the former is all about similar-sounding consonants, the latter involves similar-sounding vowels. A true master of assonance is rapper Eminem. Consider this line:

> I sit **back** with this **pack** of Zig-**Zag**s and this **bag**
> / Of this **weed**, it gives **me** the shit **need**ed to **be**
> (Eminem 2000, from "The Way I Am")

I've highlighted the rhyming vowel combinations in the first line in bold, and in bold-italic in the second line. I'm not saying that you should write about science in rhymes or take Eminem as an example for word choice. But similar-sounding vowels, rhymes and rhythm have a place in headlines and enumerations. Whenever you want to emphasise something important for the reader, and whenever it needs to stick, you can use alliteration and assonance for effect.

One of prime literary devices is **irony**. In speech, it is just meaning the opposite of what you're saying. Imagine this scene: "Mom, can I touch the flatiron?" "Go try it, darling!" But children don't know irony right away. Yeah, that was how I learnt irony. She obviously didn't mean what she said. That's where irony is like subtext (we've looked at that in the chapter on screenwriting). It's the gap between what you say and what you mean (in my case, I would have preferred getting the on-the-nose answer). It's easier to not get irony when the ironic statements are written, because you miss out on the nonverbal cues. But generally, people who get irony faster have a higher degree of emotional intelligence (Jacob *et al.* 2016). I'm pretty sure you all know someone who just doesn't get irony, whether spoken or written. Irony requires that both parties, speaker and listener, are in the know of what's really going on. Irony also unfolds at the story level. In that case, it's called dramatic irony. Every horror movie ever made uses it. Most comedians use it. **Dramatic irony** is when the audience knows something the characters in the story don't. You know what's about to happen. The characters don't. Do you feel the itch when the knife-wielding killer pops up behind a film's protagonist but only you can see her? Juliet fakes drinks a sleeping potion and fakes her own death to escape an arranged marriage. The audience knows that Juliet isn't dead. But Romeo doesn't. So, when he arrives, thinking she has died, he drinks poison and kills himself. That's dramatic irony. It's also the ABT in action, in case you haven't noticed.

In that sense, an **antithesis** is also ironic. It raises expectations in readers by establishing a setup. This can be a simple declarative sentence in SVO-order. In its second part, the antithesis destroys the expectation and subverts readers' expectations. In terms of form, the second part can mimic the first one (parallelism), or it can invert its order (chiasmus). **Antithesis** contrasts something with its opposite. By simply adding its opposite, you can form an antithesis out of every declarative statement (Forsyth 2013). The general form (assuming it's parallelism) is: "X is Y", and "not X is not Y". Forsyth cites long passages from the bible that just contrasts things with their opposites and could be reduced to a single statement. He also makes a point of saying that modern pop culture employs antithesis, and he lists Katy Perry's "you're hot, then you're cold" song line (Forsyth 2013). "That's one small step for [a] man, one giant leap for mankind"? That's antithesis. "Hatred paralyzes life. Love releases it." (Martin Luther King Jr.) is another one. Science writer Mary Roach uses antithesis when in her book "Stiff" she writes about the human cadavers seen:

> They seemed sweet and well-intentioned, sometimes sad, occasionally amusing. Some were beautiful, some monsters. Some wore sweatpants and some were naked, some in pieces, others whole.
>
> (Roach 2003)

Another literary technique that is perhaps less playful than the previous one but highly effective in science writing is **zooming**. It's the implementation of the ladder of abstraction, which English professor Samuel Ichye Hayakawa formulated. The higher you climb the ladder in your writing, the more abstract you get. The lower you go, the more concrete and graspable your writing gets. Let me for once smack a truism in your face to illustrate this. "Not seeing the forest for the trees" is actually a fantastic example of zooming. Imagine hiking through a rainforest: You're macheting your way through shrubs. You smell the rotting leaves on the ground, feel the cold water around your ankles as you wade through it, you hear exotic birds chirping. You collect all these sensory details. If you write it as you experience it, low on the ladder of abstraction, you'll catapult readers right into the scene. But you can't see the larger issues the forest might suffer from. For that, you need to hop into a chopper and hover over the rain forest. Only then can you see the true extent of illegal logging and forest fires. Of course, up there, you miss out on all the details. This is what good science writers do very well, and we've actually looked at this structure several times throughout this book. You alternate between both modes. Zoom in, zoom out. It's very common, and based on Nijhuis (2013) (and because I'm a sugar addict, I will just continue calling it the "layer-cake" structure). You can typically find this technique right at the transition between a feature's lead (low on the ladder) and nut graph (high on the ladder).

I will honorably mention the **hendiadys**, which splits one word (an adjective or noun) into two, again for emphasis and joins them by the conjunction "and". Phrases that include "try and verb" are examples of hendiadys. They slow down the reading pace and emphasise the idea (it really is just one idea expressed by two different words). Shakespeare used it to great extent at the peak of his career (Forsyth 2013). **Litotes**, in contrast, is a bit like an understatement. Instead of "good", you say "not bad". For the logicians, if you want to say X, simply say "not not-X". And **anaphora**, that's when you start your sentences with the same words over and over again (Forsyth 2013). I've done this a few times in this chapter. Can you spot them?

Tension: More literary devices

When you use literary devices, you can employ them to persuade your readers at the sentence level, like many of the figures of speech in the previous section. For example, **diacopes** are persuasive in that they're word sandwiches that repeat one word that is interspersed with another one. You find them everywhere, for example in film: "Bond, James Bond" is one example (Forsyth 2013). But they're also used in songs. Think of Sheryl Crow's "Run, Baby, Run" or The Trammps' "Disco Inferno" that contains the lines "Burn, Baby, Burn" (which incidentally also is an alliteration). Or Diana Krall's "Bye bye, blackbird". But you can also use literary devices that support your structure and create tension. At the sentence level, if you want to give away the "what" only after the audience has reached the end of the sentence, because that's where the verb and hence the action of the sentence hides (or where the subject hides), then you can craft a **periodic sentence** (see also the chapter on language and style). They start with subordinate clauses and are often signalled by prepositions like "despite", "although", "because of" or "when". Neuroscientist Jordan Gaines Lewis defers her sentence's quintessence until the very last moment when writing about sleep habits in her former column "Brain Games" that ran at *The Conversation*:

> Despite my preaching – and despite being a sleep researcher myself – the last thing I do before I flip off the lights and snuggle into my bedsheets is play games on my iPhone.
>
> (Gaines Lewis 2015)

Her core statement is short: I play games on my iPhone before I go to bed. But because she wants you to read through all the little details, through all her rituals and through her self-reflections, she puts the main clause at the end.

Let's have a look at another powerful literary device that helps create tension, but at the structure level: **foreshadowing**. Exposition can be tricky to sneak into narrative, yes. But exposition is also the place that lets you foreshadow events to come. You can do that overly direct and actually announce what is going to happen. This often starts with "little did she know…" or "she had no idea what…". When you tell your audience a character did not expect the worst, then the audience will know that is exactly what the character is going to get (Hart 2011). Here's an example of on-the-nose foreshadowing:

"Having gone to college in the '60s myself, I thought it might be worth investigating," Abrams says. "Little did I know how difficult that would be."

(Ferro 2013)

In its structural form, this kind of foreshadowing is constructed like this: "little did protagonist know that conflict plus details was about to happen." This construct employs also dramatic irony: you know something the character in the story does not, at least not yet. This kind of foreshadowing, despite being direct, works, because it clearly says: "Hey audience, there's conflict ahead! The protagonist is going to be in trouble!" But you can do this in a subtler way. You could just write the protagonist's initial assumption, without the explicit subversion, and without giving away the actual conflict (Hart 2011). Another way is to use pronouns without the noun it refers to. Or a definite object without an antecedent. Since readers can't know, this means tension. Here's an example from the *New Yorker*:

The Kinderschreck. That's what the German man called him when he stole the gun and was caught and had to be banished.

(O'Brien 2002)

Who's the German man? What gun? O'Brien does this masterfully. She creates tension in the first sentence (okay, it's the second, if we count the ellipse "The Kinderschreck", which is another figure of speech). In fact, she creates it twice. Since you've just started reading the piece, you have no idea who "the German man" refers to, and you have no idea what the ominous gun is. You want, no, you need to know what happened with that gun. The author continues the next paragraph by still not giving away what it is or who used it for what: "He was ten when he took the gun" (O'Brien 2002). You get more information about the potential perpetrator called "Kinderschreck", but still no information about what actually happened. But what you do know is that something terrible must have happened. Of course, guns don't lead to anything positive. This goes on and on: "I didn't mean to kill anyone, only to frighten one man" (O'Brien 2002). By now, at the latest, you know somebody got killed. It's suspense at its best.

Foreshadowing also requires other literary techniques to function. For example, a third-person point of view. From a first-person perspective, this device won't work. The narrator has to be omniscient to pull off the "little did she know" trope. Another figure of speech you can use to deliver it is **Chekhov's gun** (Clark 2008). It stems from theatre and states that you should never throw a loaded rifle on stage if you have no intention of firing it. A single word can foreshadow events to come (Clark 2008).

When you use foreshadowing in a "medias res" opening like Hart (2011) suggests, the second scene that follows is probably a **flashback**. When you hop around in the timeline of events, you need to signal these time leaps to your audience. Tense is one way to do this subtly. If your main narrative is written in the simple present, your flashback could switch to the simple past. If you main narrative is written in the simple past, your flashback could switch to the past perfect. The audience will notice. Or you tell them explicitly, which date your narrative jumps to. Switching forth and back in science writing (especially in features) is quite common. Let's have a look at science journalist Lisa Parker's *Guardian* piece from 2016. It starts with a flashback scene:

> In the summer of 2005, Jeffrey Karp, a bioengineer at Brigham and Women's Hospital (BWH) in Cambridge, Massachusetts, was working late one night when he spotted a journal article on a colleague's desk.
>
> (Parker 2016)

Parker then jumps to the present day. Because it's a longform piece, and to make it clear, she indicates this often at the beginning of the paragraph. Note the changed tenses in the following examples – all of them are paragraph beginnings:

> Karp, who is now 40 and runs his own lab at BWH, is what is known in the business as a bioinspirationalist.
>
> (Parker 2016)

> Karp Lab, which opened in July 2007, is hidden behind a heavy white door on the third floor of an office building in Cambridge, near Massachusetts Institute of Technology.
>
> (Parker 2016)

Comedy writing techniques

Telling a good joke is a story. It has a setup and a payoff. It has protagonists and goals. It has a climax. Like many good stories, jokes have a surprise ending – a plot twist that subverts the audience's expectations. That's the payoff. Before that, the introduction of the joke guides the audience's attention in a different direction. In science writing, you don't have to be a comedy writer, but if you can season your pieces with a little humor, they'll be easier to remember. In fact, remembrance is one of the "three Rs" of humor writing (Helitzer 2005):

- **Respect**: humor draws attention (and in a healthy way), while enriching many things, including communication. It earns the speaker respectful attention. "It's psychologically impossible to hate someone with whom you've laughed" (Helitzer 2005).
- **Remember**: "Humor promotes learning and makes it memorable." Students who attend lessons that convey humor-infused lessons remember more and achieve higher test scores.
- **Reward**: if you can write humor, all sorts of job perspectives open up: business executives hire them, as well as US presidents. The downside? After one bad joke, the career might be over.

When you have a good time, your brain releases dopamine, which not only makes you happy but is also linked to learning and memorising facts. Mel

Helitzer's claim that students remember humorous lessons better than regular ones is backed by science. A large meta-analysis of more than 40 years of humor in education research confirms that humor helps students learn. It's most effective when used in between instruction and repetition (Banas et al. 2011). In statistics classes at university, students learnt and kept more of the content if the teacher conveyed it using humor (Garner 2006).

Comedians and nonfiction writers share one important part of their procedure: they have to produce regularly and can't rely on divine inspiration. Sure, ideas can come from everywhere. As Helitzer (2005) claims, as a comedy writer, you need to write jokes from scratch. One important technique to do so is called POW (play on words). More than half of humor is based on them. Base it on any familiar cliché (like aphorisms) or expressions, or book titles that you're sure the audience knows. Once you start formulating the cliché, the audience expects to know its outcome. That's when you add a twist and subvert the expectations. Here are a number of techniques you can use to write POWs (adapted from Helitzer 2005):

- **Cliché**: either interpret it or change it so it has a payoff that nobody expected. For example, you know the worn cliché "Laugh, and the world laughs with you; weep, and you weep alone." Helitzer cites Caryn Leschen's: "Laugh, and the world laughs with you. Cry, and the world laughs at you" (Helitzer 2005:64). Another technique that works is substituting similar-looking or -sounding words (homonyms) for words in the cliché.
- **Double entendre**: like a simile, this technique draws on the sometimes two meanings of the same word (or homonyms). Lots of versions use "it" or "to be in" and their second meanings (having sex) as the punchline. More sophisticated versions throw in irony and sarcasm.
- **Malapropism**: these are mostly unintentional errors. Similar-sounding words (with similar metrics and syllables) replace their originals and at first make listeners think they know what the speaker is saying but then subvert that expectation. For example, when former Prime Minister of Australia Tony Abbott said "No one is the suppository of wisdom" when he probably meant to say "repository" instead of "suppository". It's the superiority of knowing English better than the perpetrator that makes the audience laugh.
- **Oxymoron**: actually a rhetoric figure, an oxymoron is a contradiction, often combined by a conjunction. Oxymorons can be as short as one word. For example, bittersweet. Oxymorons can span multiple sentences, but you'll find them most often as word pairs. Here are some examples: living dead, open secret or Microsoft Works. Oxymoron itself is an oxymoron (oxys means sharp, moros means dull).
- **Pun**: an intentional confusion of the reader, puns are similar-sounding words that replace their originals. They work better when they are spoken than written (Helitzer & Shatz 2005). In fact, it takes the audience a moment to understand the double meaning and recognise the true meaning of the pun word. In 2015, comedian Leo Kearse won the UK pun championship, one of his puns being:

I was in hospital last week. I asked the nurse if I could do my own stitches. She said "suture self".

(Leo Kearse in Guardian Staff 2015)

You can use puns to reform clichés and surprise readers. One technique for that is switching words. For example: "Who am I to stone the first cast?" (Helitzer & Shatz 2005:77). Other ways are replacing letters in key words of a phrase, and using homonyms or homophones. Puns are often frowned upon, especially in journalism. But if you use original ones and use them sparingly, they have a surprising effect. Let's have a look at science writers utilise puns. Science writer Mary Roach is best known for writing about science employing humor. In her book *Stiff*, she uses a number of techniques. In one example, she writes a pun:

When I asked her why the eyes of the dead woman had no pupils, she did not answer, but reached up and closed the eyelids. As she slides back her chair, she looks down at the benapkined form and says, "May she rest in peace." I hear it as "pieces," but that's just me.

(Roach 2003)

But it's not just science writers who use humor writing techniques and POWs. In 2019, a biology paper became famous because of its word play on the title of J.K. Rowling's story *Fantastic Beasts and Where to Find Them*. The paper's title was: "Fantastic yeasts and where to find them: the hidden diversity of dimorphic fungal pathogens" (Van Dyke, Teixeira & Barker 2019). Or consider the following research paper title: "Actin' like actin?" (Mullins, Kelleher & Pollard 1996. It's a pun. In its first occurrence, actin' just means acting, the verb. In its second occurrence, actin means a particular protein. How can you write your own? What most comedy-writing trainers and comedians suggest is that you experiment. Choose your subject, one word (in the previous two examples, that word would have been "yeast" and "actin", respectively). Then play around with it. Write clichés, proverbs and double entendres. Don't worry about writing perfect English sentences. Humor tolerates linguistic flaws. Edit a lot (Herring and Caulfield 2008). Find homonyms, homophones and play around with those either.

Case study: The Hot Zone

So let's have a look at some of these techniques in action. The best science storytellers will give you hard facts while telling you a really compelling story. And you will never consciously notice you got those facts. One such writer is the *New Yorker* journalist Richard Preston. His 1992 article "Crisis in the Hot Zone" became the foundation for his 1994 nonfiction book on the Ebola virus, *The Hot Zone*. Preston writes in scenes, and he uses a lot of literary techniques in doing so. Many call his book a "nonfiction thriller". Let's see why. Preston starts the very first scene of his book by telling his audience the year and day. That's it. He then introduces a character, Charles Monet, from a third-person point of view. He describes what Monet looks like, where he lives, what he does. Then Preston uses a bit of foreshadowing to raise the tension: "So often in a case like this, it's hard to pin down the details". He then intensifies this tension, by writing about a hot agent's effects on a human being. Eventually, that's death. But the audience still wonders, what the case is Preston mentions. What did Monet contract? At this point, he only reveals that it is a Biosafety Level 4 hot agent. Preston keeps up the tension by comparing the (to the audience yet) unknown pathogen to HIV and AIDS, which, as he states is only a Biosafety Level 2 agent. He then tells how HIV cannot be transmitted from person to person. For example, you don't need a biohazard suit to handle it. It's not a direct comparison but a way of letting the readers add two plus two. Because of this indirect comparison, they can draw their own conclusion that the unknown pathogen is highly infectious. Also, in terms of style, Preston uses a simile to describe the spread of AIDS, by comparing it to a shadow that had fallen over the population. Preston sneaks in the background part on HIV/AIDS without readers noticing. At the beginning of the paragraph, he connects the chapter's protagonist Monet to the general problem and takes a few steps up the ladder of abstraction: "Monet came into the country in the summer of 1979, around the time that the human immunodeficiency virus, or HIV, which causes AIDS, made a final breakout from the rain forests of central Africa [...]" (Preston 1994). He then gives his audience a little anecdote, one that originates not from himself. Until this part, Preston has hinted several times that something terrible must have happened to Monet, and that he had had no chance to talk with him in person: "People who knew him recalled [...]", "They say that he spent most of his day [...]". All of this supports the initial dramatic question: what happened to Charles Monet? Preston then describes how Monet was in contact with monkeys and birds, possibly contracting a Biosafety Level 4 germ. But he still doesn't reveal which one it is. Instead, he uses this tension to slip in more expository information on who Monet was. He also describes the landscape, using only one or two adjectives to evoke vivid images in his readers' heads. For example: "[...] and so the fields were scorched and black", and "[...] the mountain turned silvery green". Preston's descriptions are scenic and sensory ("The air grew cool as they went higher [...]"), or when he writes that the volcanic roads were "as red as dried blood" – another simile. But he never overuses his techniques. What adds to the tension is that Preston frequently expresses uncertainty, using words like "probably" or phrases like "no one knows". Preston writes down Monet's and a friend's (who later turns out to be a prostitute, and that's not the first reference to sex for money in the chapter) journey to Mount Elgon and describes in a few paragraphs what the scenery looks like. He then again comes up with an anecdote of how Monet feeds a baboon. Until now, not much has happened in terms of action, but Preston manages to keep the story going via the journey and all the tension that he builds. His command of sensory language shows in particular in one sentence, where he uses "to scuffle", "to hum" and "huh-huh calls" (of a monkey species), all of which are onomatopoeic words. In Preston's words, pigeons don't fly, they "burst from trees". When he describes the landscape, his sentences get a bit longer. When he is in character mode, they tend to shorten. It's astonishing how clear his sentence structure is: most of them are declarative S-V-O sentences, starting with either a noun or a pronoun. This is the way he describes both characters going on, into a cave. There, they get in contact with fruit bats and a petrified forest. "Did he run his hands over the stone trees and prick his finger on a crystal?" Preston as the narrator asks. This again intensifies the dramatic question. His perspective may be third person, but he is not omniscient, which has been showing from the beginning of the chapter. He ends a later paragraph on a similar cliffhangeresque question, asking if Monet had put his hand in bat guano. Up until this point, readers must have developed two theories: either Monet contracted the unknown pathogen via animals, or via sexual intercourse with a woman. Preston builds more tension ("a Kenyan doctor who had investigated the Monet case") and ends Monet's journey as he returns home. Then he raises the tension by foreshadowing as I described in the section on tension-building techniques in this chapter.

> Meanwhile, something was making copies of itself inside Monet. A life form had acquired Charles Monet as a host, and it was replicating.
>
> (Preston 1994)

Two simple declarative sentences is all it takes Preston, and readers have lost their last chance to set the book aside. "Something" and "a life form" express uncertainty. It's what the horror filmmakers do. They don't reveal the antagonist in order to keep tensions high. Preston then describes in great detail how Monet's symptoms developed. That part is dominated by declarative sentences that most often start with the pronouns "he" and "his". Then, the action unfolds. Monet visits a doctor, who sends him to Nairobi. Preston weaves short expository paragraphs into the narrative, about how airlines ease the spread of viruses, and about viruses develop in the human body. He even explains jargon like "extreme amplification" throughout that process. And because of all the sensory description of vomit, blood and other body liquids, readers might actually be happy to get a break. Preston is a master in hinting at looming danger while letting readers draw their own conclusions. He describes how Monet vomits over and over again, and how the sick bag is about to leak. He also writes in an explanatory paragraph how many viruses a single drop of body liquid contains. Readers can connect these two pieces of information (and actually a third: how easy it is for viruses to travel on airplanes) by themselves. Tension, tension, tension. Here is another jargon word that Preston explains on the side. "His personality is being wiped away by brain damage. This is called depersonalization [...]". And he makes it even more graspable with a metaphor, likening the character to an automaton. All the gold coins (to use Roy Peter Clark's terminology) Preston has placed on the path, including reminding us how infectious a single drop of liquid is, now pay off. The chapter is nearing its climax: what happens to Monet? Will he survive? Will they save him? Before readers get an answer, more conflict hits Monet. After a taxi ride, where Preston again narrates how many people Monet came in contact with, Monet has to wait in the emergency room until it's his turn. Preston has introduced another metaphor, calling Monet a "human virus bomb". He keeps reusing it and makes clear that the bomb is about to explode. Tension is highest at the end of the chapter. I'll spare you the descriptive details. At the end, Monet falls over, bleeding. All the details make pretty sure readers get it that he doesn't survive. But they still don't know what infected him, or what happened to the other patients in the hospital, or to the airline crew, or to the taxi drivers. Preston's chapter ends on a cliffhanger. Does it have structure, a narrative arc, a character arc? Yes, absolutely. Just look at how Monet started and where he is at the end of his story. I absolutely recommend going back to the previous chapters of this book and analyse his chapter with an eye on structure and style. For me, Preston's book is one of the best pieces of nonfiction narrative science writing ever.

Review questions

- What was the theme of your last science story?
- How does a first-person POV change readers' perceptions?
- How do metaphors and similes differ?
- How would you explain nuclear fission using a metaphor or simile?
- How is zooming used in features?
- What is the difference between irony and dramatic irony?
- When should you employ periodic sentences?
- How do the two ways of foreshadowing differ?
- What is a double entendre?

Links

"This Physics Pioneer Walked Away from It All" (*Nautilus*): http://nautil.us/ issue/38/noise/this-physics-pioneer-walked-away-from-it-all

"The Tinkerings of Robert Noyce" (*Esquire*): https://classic.esquire.com/article/ 1983/12/1/the-tinkerings-of-robert-noyce

"The Siege of Miami" (*The New Yorker*): https://www.newyorker.com/magazine/ 2015/12/21/the-siege-of-miami

References

Banas, J.A., Dunbar, N., Rodriguez, D. & Liu, S.J. (2011) "A review of humor in educational settings: Four decades of research," *Communication Education*, vol. 60, no. 1, 115–144.

Becker, A.B. & Anderson, A.A. (2019) "Using humor to engage the public on climate change: the effect of exposure to one-sided vs. two-sided satire on message discounting, elaboration and counterarguing," *JCOM*, vol. 18, no. 04, A07 [Online]. Available at: https://jcom.sissa.it/archive/18/04/JCOM_1804_2019_A07?fbclid=IwAR0 EVoLWETTtoUzWtBtkc-xUV82pZynbA03i1SPJFx9dgLb15ORGgu0HjI (date accessed 30 August 2019).

Boynton, R. (2005) *The new new journalism: conversations with America's best nonfiction writers on their craft.* New York: Vintage.

Clark, R.P. (2008) *Writing Tools: 55 Essential Strategies for Every Writer.* London: Little, Brown.

Davis, S. (2016) "Why Fotini Markopoulou traded quantum gravity for industrial design," *Nautilus* [Online]. Available at: http://nautil.us/issue/38/noise/this-physics-pioneer-walked-away-from-it-all (date accessed 29 August 2019).

Egri, L. (1946) *The Art of Dramatic Writing.* New York: Simon and Schuster.

Enago Academy (2019) "We vs. They: Using the First & Third Person in Research Papers," Enago Academy [Online]. Available at: https://www.enago.com/academy/we-vs-they-using-first-or-third-person-in-a-research-paper/#comments (date accessed 30 August 2019).

Ferro, S. (2013) "Why It's So Hard For Scientists To Study Medical Marijuana," *Popular Science* [Online]. Available at: https://www.popsci.com/science/article/2013-04/why-its-so-hard-scientists-study-pot/ (date accessed 1 September 2019).

Forsyth, M. (2013) *The elements of eloquence: How to turn the perfect English phrase.* London: Icon Books Ltd.

Gaines Lewis, J. (2015) "Can wearing orange-tinted glasses before bed help you sleep? Only one way to find out...," *The Conversation* [Online]. Available at: https://theconversation.com/can-wearing-orange-tinted-glasses-before-bed-help-you-sleep-only-one-way-to-find-out-40684 (date accessed 1 September 2019).

Garner, R.L. (2006) "Humor in pedagogy: How ha-ha can lead to aha!," *College Teaching*, vol. 54, no. 1, 177–180.

GuardianStaff (2015) "That's punny: the winning puns at comedy championships," *The Guardian* [Online]. Available at: https://www.theguardian.com/stage/2015/feb/13/winning-puns-comedy-championships-leicester-leo-kearse (date accessed 13 September 2019).

Gutkind, L. (2012) *You can't make this stuff up: The complete guide to writing creative nonfiction – from memoir to literary journalism and everything in between.* Philadelphia: Da Capo Lifelong Books.

Hart, J. (2011) *Storycraft.* Chicago. Chicago University Press.

Hart, J. (2007) *Nurturing Narrative in the Newsroom*, in: Kramer, M. & Call, W. *Telling True Stories.* New York: Plume, 233–239

Helitzer, M. & Shatz, M. (2005) *Comedy Writing Secrets, 2nd ed.* Cincinnati: Writer's Digest Books.

Herring, R. & Caulfield, J. (2008) "The Comedian's Toolbox," *The Guardian* [Online]. Available at: https://www.theguardian.com/books/2008/sep/22/comedy4 (date accessed 5 September 2019).

Hunter, M.L. (2011) "Story-based inquiry: a manual for investigative journalists," UNESCO [Online]. Available at: https://unesdoc.unesco.org/ark:/48223/pf0000193078 (date accessed 3 September 2019).

Jacob, H., Kreifelts, B., Nizielski, S., Schütz, A. & Wildgruber, D. (2016) "Effects of emotional intelligence on the impression of irony created by the mismatch between verbal and nonverbal cues," *PloS one*, vol. 11, no. 10, e0163211.

Kolbert, E. (2015) "The Siege of Miami," *The New Yorker* [Online]. Available at: https://www.newyorker.com/magazine/2015/12/21/the-siege-of-miami (date accessed 30 August 2019).

Lombardi, C. (2003) *Description: To Picture in Words*, in: Steele, A. *Gotham Writers' Workshop: Writing Fiction.* New York: Bloomsbury.

Malone, T. (2019) "John McPhee: Seven Ways of Looking at a Writer," Literary Hub [Online]. Available at: https://lithub.com/john-mcphee-seven-ways-of-looking-at-a-writer/ (date accessed 29 August 2019).

McPhee, J. (2018) "Direct Eye Contact," *The New Yorker* [Online]. Available at: https://www.newyorker.com/magazine/2018/03/05/in-search-of-new-jerseys-wild-bears (date accessed 29 August 2019).

Mullins, R.D., Kelleher, J F. & Pollard, T.D. (1996) "Actin'like actin?" *Trends in cell biology*, vol. 6, no. 6, 208–212.

Nijhuis, M. (2013) "Sculpting the Story," in: Hayden, T. & Nijhuis, M (eds.) *The science writers' handbook: everything you need to know to pitch, publish, and prosper in the digital age*. Boston: Da Capo Press, 75–86.

O'Brien, E. (2002) "The Boy in the Forest," *The New Yorker* [Online]. Available at: https://www.newyorker.com/magazine/2002/02/04/a-boy-in-the-forest (date accessed 1 September 2019).

Parker, L. (2016) "Inspired by nature: the thrilling new science that could transform medicine," *The Guardian* [Online]. Available at: https://www.theguardian.com/science/2016/oct/25/bioinspiration-thrilling-new-science-could-transform-medicine (date accessed 1 September 2019).

Preston, R. (1994) *The Hot Zone*. New York: Random House.

Roach, M. (2003) *Stiff*. New York: Viking.

Talpos, S. (2016) "Science Writing as a Literary Art: What Are the Challenges?" *Kenyon Review* [Online]. Available at: https://www.kenyonreview.org/2016/10/sara-talpos-science-writing-literary-art-challenges/ (date accessed 29 August 2019).

Tysdal, D. (2015) "Everything you need to know to write a poem (and how it can save a life)," TEDxUTSC [Online Video]. Available at: https://www.youtube.com/watch?v=z0BUYzMypi8 (date accessed 29 August 2019).

Van Dyke, M.C.C., Teixeira, M.M. & Barker, B.M. (2019) "Fantastic yeasts and where to find them: the hidden diversity of dimorphic fungal pathogens," *Current opinion in microbiology*, vol. 52, 55–63.

Vogrin, V. (2003) *Point of View: The Complete Menu*, in: Steele, A. *Gotham Writers' Workshop: Writing Fiction*. New York: Bloomsbury.

Walter, R. (2010) *Essentials of Screenwriting: The Art, Craft and Business of Film and Television Writing*. New York: Plume.

Webb, J. (2014) "Stem cell scientist found dead in apparent suicide," BBC News [Online]. Available at: https://www.bbc.com/news/science-environment-28658269 (date accessed 30 August 2019).

Webb, C. (1992) "The use of the first person in academic writing: objectivity, language and gatekeeping," *Journal of Advanced Nursing*, vol. 17, no. 6, 747–752.

Witt, E. (2018) "On Being the Ideal Reader of Tom Wolfe's School of New Journalism," *The New Yorker* [Online]. Available at: https://www.newyorker.com/culture/cultural-comment/on-being-the-ideal-reader-of-tom-wolfes-school-of-new-journalism (date accessed 30 August 2019).

Wolfe, T. (1983) "The Tinkerings of Robert Noyce," *Esquire* [Online]. Available at: https://classic.esquire.com/article/1983/12/1/the-tinkerings-of-robert-noyce (date accessed 30 August 2019).

Westerhoff, N. (2006) *Beispiele, Metaphern, Vergleiche*, in: Göpfert, W. (ed.) *Wissenschafts-Journalismus: Handbuch für Ausbildung und Praxis*. Berlin: Ullstein Buchverlage GmbH, 133–143.

9   Writing and Revising

What you will learn in this chapter:

- Beginnings
- Explanatory writing
- Revising
- Verification
- Editing
- Endings
- An interview with Gloria Guglielmi

Writing about science is difficult. And it's been quite a journey so far. Throughout this book, we've seen theatrical techniques, screenwriters' tools, structures, literary devices and some style advice as well. I hope that in reading through all of this, you find a few useful techniques that you can apply. If you feel overwhelmed, choose a single technique, practice and hone it until you feel confident enough to use it in real life. Then move on and try the next one. The most important advice I can give you is to write. And of course read a lot, too. But seriously, write. As much as you can. Don't find excuses. As screenwriting professor Richard Walter puts it: there is no writer's block. Just write. This sometimes sounds easier than it is. A blank screen or sheet of paper can be terrifying. I know what I'm talking about. Lower your expectations until none are left. No first draft is perfect. It's totally fine to write lousy copy. What's the worst thing that can happen? You can always chuck it. But once a first draft has materialised on your page, you'll see the passages you can improve. Point being: if nothing is one your page, you can't revise it and make it better.

This chapter starts at the beginning. What types of leads do exist, and how are they crafted and to what effect? We'll have a look at both newspaper and magazine leads, and you'll see examples of real-life stories. While direct leads aim is to convey the gist of the story in one or two paragraphs, magazine leads must hook readers, grab their attention and lure them into reading a longer piece. There are different ways to do this, but the most interesting ones start on the lowest rungs of the ladder of abstraction. If you craft a compelling lead, you can get away with a lot of explanatory writing, which readers usually don't like that much. I once interviewed a journalism professor from Florida who told me that he absolutely hates the typical magazine story openers that zoom in on a protagonist and start off with a human touch. I can understand that he recognises the pattern, but that doesn't change the fact that a graspable lead with a protagonist and a complication always works. It's even better if you start it in the middle of the action. We are just wired for story, and we can't just switch that off.

What is more difficult to get across is the explanatory part. Science needs explanation, and there is no way around it. How we learn science, and everything else, resembles the Hegelian dialectic. You have some prior knowledge, then you absorb new knowledge, then you blend them together. You gain new insights. What finally emerges is the synthesis, a new state of knowledge. What about the research process? It just works the same way. But in terms of neuroscience, your brain goes out of narrative mode and into pragmatic mode when you digress from the story and branch out into explanations. It's easy to lose readers' attention in that mode. That's why we'll have a look at how to best sneak in explanatory parts into your science writing. The goal is that your readers never notice that you've just given them new information.

Once you've written something, anything at all, you should read it and revise it. And again. And again. In the section on revising, we'll see how editors and writers generally revise their texts. No first draft is good enough to be published right away. Each revision is a chance to improve your text and turn into a homogeneous piece instead of just loosely strung together bits of information. In screenwriting, no screenplay gets produced without revisions. The *Writers Guild of America* recommends assigning a colour to each revision. The first, unrevised draft is called white, the second becomes the blue revision, the third the pink revision. Sometimes, screenplays are revised for years and years. Sometimes, the screenplay writers are substituted with others. You usually don't have such extreme cases in nonfiction writing, but this should illustrate the importance of revising.

Unlike most fiction writers, you'll have to make sure that your information is absolutely correct. This includes tracing information back to its source, which can prove difficult when it comes from social media. The amount of imagery and documents you can obtain from the web is overwhelming. The problem with verification is not that there are no techniques to do so. We'll have a look at some of them in the verification section. The real problem is dwindling resources, newspapers laying off staff, including fact-checkers, and a lack of time when working on quick turnaround stories.

Time is also what you need when you edit stories. The editing section near the end of this chapter focuses on self-editing your work, by looking at how editors and writers edit. On top of time, what you need to edit your texts is a plan. Set up a process that includes some checklists. I have some for this book. What you're reading right now is an edited version of the initial draft. Those checklists will help you deliver consistent quality. Sure, editing won't make your writing perfect. But it will make it so much better and round out your stories. When you submit a self-edited, revised piece to an editor, its just makes it easier for her to work with you. I have never met an editor who loves completely rewriting a piece received by an author because it's a sloppy first draft. Especially not when it sports mistakes like bad spelling, grammar or inconsistently used proper names and section titles. All of these happen in unedited works.

Speaking of rounding out, every story has a beginning, a middle and an end. So a section on endings can't be missing in this chapter. If your write a news report using the inverted pyramid, your ending will in most cases be rather unspectacular, as that structure presents information in descending order of importance. But if you write a feature, then you should resolve the dramatic question in your ending. This will keep your audience reading until the very end. The ending is also the place where you can once again convey your story's theme, resolve all open questions and give readers a sense of satisfaction. There's more that goes into endings, after you've read through till the end of this chapter. As this book's final gem, US-Italian science writer Giorgia Guglielmi shares with you her writing and editing process. I met Giorgia at the 2019 World Conference of Science Journalists in Lausanne. She writes for all the high-profile science outlets, so make sure you don't miss her advice. But now, let's start at the beginning!

Beginnings

It's rather fitting that we begin this chapter with… beginnings. In journalism, they are called leads. Newspapers leads pack all the need-to-know information into their direct leads. Most of the journalistic questions (the five Ws and one H) get answered immediately, in the first paragraph of a story. This approach, typically found in news pieces that follow the inverted pyramid, has two effects: first, it gives readers the gist of the news item and in doing so, removes most if not all tension. Second, such a summary lead usually doesn't put readers' minds into story mode. You can recognise straight news stories by their title. They often start with "new study" or end with the clause "scientists find" or "study finds". Let's have a look at what a straight news lead typically look like.

> The "strange" anatomy of a family of giant marsupials that roamed eastern Australia and Tasmania for much of the past 25m years has been revealed in a new study.
>
> (Henriques-Gomes 2019)

This summary lead contains the gist. The *what* (the "strange anatomy of giant mar-supials), the *where* (Australia and Tasmania) and the *when* (25 million years ago). The who and how are missing, but the author delivers that later on in the text. This is typical for inverted pyramid-style articles. Where was the study published? Who exactly found it? How did they find out? All of that is secondary information in straight news items. In fact, Henriques-Gomes delivers the full answer to the *what* only in paragraph four. Generally, you give away most of the information in the lead, but you will expand on the details only later. Also, in this case, Henriques-Gomes manages to introduce a bit of tension using the word "strange". It's uncertain language that makes readers wonder what "strange" means. Now they have to know.

Longer stories like many magazine features start the story off low on the abstraction ladder. They are called indirect or delayed leads and don't give away the entire information in order to keep readers wondering what happens next, while putting them into narrative mode. Tom French advises to not give away everything in your opening scene if you want to build tension, but rather to "offer an experience that propels the reader forward through your story" (French 2007:143). Many magazine features will open like this, and indirect leads indeed contain a number of story elements, including a protagonist and a complication. They don't pay off the complication, though, because that's what the end of the story does. Journalism professor Melvin Mencher calls the direct (or summary) lead journalism's workhorse. The indirect or delayed lead is its showhorse (Mencher 2011). The delayed lead author consciously withholds facts from the readers. Science writer Michelle Nijhuis writes that magazine leads in the "Wall Street Journal style" can come at varying lengths and in many styles. They can include characters or quotes, they can be anecdotes, and they can be as simple as two words. But they all serve one purpose: to lure the readers into the story (Nijhuis 2013).

Whether you start writing your lead or your end first depends on you. Different writers do it differently. Some don't start writing the lead before the story is finished. Some can't write the story before they have the lead. Some need to write the end first. Some need to have both bookends, the lead and the end, before they write the story. Delayed leads are fantastic to foreshadow conflict and grip readers. When you withhold information, you need to hint at the hidden information. Have a look at astronomer Philip Plait's lead paragraph for his story "Alien Attack" from his book 2008 *Death from the Skies!*:

> Mindlessly – at least, lacking what we would call a mind as we know it – it examined the bright light of the star ahead of it. Employing a highly sophisticated complex of observational instrumentation, it patiently took data, examining each bit of information as it came in. After weeks of steadily staring at its target, the results were in.
>
> (Plait 2008)

Plait uses a simple technique we've seen in the previous chapter. It's foreshadowing. He uses the pronoun "it" to hint at the hidden information. Do you know what "it" is? No. Do you need to know what "it" is after reading the lead? Yes. Also, Plait opens in the middle of the action, which is good practice when writing scenes. Something happens right away. Jack Hart shows a similar example when he writes about "in medias res" openings. That means starting right in the middle of the climax, when the stakes are highest. That's especially smart, because tension is highest at this moment in the story. Whatever you start with you need to make sure that it is connected to your story's theme. So let's have a look at a few more ways to come up with leads. For example, this:

> Those fortunate enough to have a head of hair generally leave 50 to 100 strands behind on any given day. Those hairs are hardy, capable of withstanding years or even centuries of rain, heat and wind.
>
> (Murphy 2019)

What is *New York Times* reporter Heather Murphy writing about? This could be the opening for a piece on a hair salon. Or about hair loss. Instead, it's about how forensic scientists can sequence DNA from hair to catch culprits. It's clearly a delayed and not a direct lead. It's not an anecdote either, but it simply relates to readers by presenting a pile of facts. But not just any kind of facts. It's easy for readers to connect with. Everybody can relate to hair loss. But it's the final part of the lead, hair's sturdiness, that raises the question of why the author mentions this. Murphy makes sense of all of this in the following two paragraphs (the second one introduces detective work and is just one sentence long). The third paragraph is the nut graph, where Murphy gets to the larger issue. Forensic scientists can't use just any hair to extract DNA. Murphy's lead also shows: newspapers do run delayed leads (Mencher 2011). It's really just short news pieces that use direct summary leads (and even they are getting rather creative, as Mencher also mentions).

The following lead is also a delayed lead. It works similarly to Murphy's but adds a shock element on top:

> It was around 3 in the afternoon when Sherdrick Koffa spotted, in neatly written script, the name on the body bag that he was preparing to set ablaze.
>
> (Cooper 2015)

Suck shock leads are another type of delayed lead. They put readers right into narrative mode. Other types of leads start with startling facts that overturn established myths or common knowledge. But if you have a startling fact, that's always a good start. It's very important that the delayed lead's anecdote, fact or scene is relevant. That means it should highlight or illustrate the theme. So sometimes you'll find it difficult to come up with the lead and end first, especially if you haven't established the theme yet.

That's why, just like themes, leads don't have to (and probably won't) remain the same throughout the whole writing and revising process. The first lead you write is often just a catalyst that gets you into the writing process and leads you (no pun intended) to the final lead (Gutkind 2012). Gutkind is the editor of the literary journalism magazine *Creative Nonfiction*. In his narrative journalism book *You Can't Make This Stuff Up*, Gutkind writes how his editorial team revised three essays, eliminating the original leads and starting them paragraphs and pages later. Their goal? Catapult readers deeper into the story (Gutkind 2012).

I'll leave you with a final kind of lead. It's what Mencher calls the "combo lead". It sets a scene first and then puts a twist at the end of the lead. It's like a contained story with a final unexpected turn. The difference is that at the end of the lead, you need even more to know how the story goes on. Like a good joke or a good plot twist, you subvert readers' expectations. Apart from the structure and type of lead you run, keep in mind the stylistic rules (adapted from Mencher 2011):

- Reporting is your best way to find the details and start a beginning that's low on the ladder of abstraction. Ask for details.
- The *Associated Press* reporters cap leads at about 25 words.
- Write declarative sentences.
- Show don't tell: use active, sensory verbs.
- Eliminate compound sentences (signalled by conjunctions "and", "or").
- Throw away attribution and exact dates.
- A lead carries one idea. Like any good sentence and paragraph.

Explanatory writing

What distinguishes science journalism from other forms of journalism is that it needs more explanation. But many people don't like explanations. That is sort of unfair, because explanation lends depth to stories. Also, explanatory passages catapult the audience out of narrative mode. Much of journalism's output is news reports, because they are shorter, which in turn means faster and cheaper to produce. But they mostly don't stick, because your brain doesn't enter narrative mode without story. You won't remember most of the facts you read in plain news items. This seems almost ironic, because it's explanatory writings very purpose to get information across. Explanatory writing without storytelling may convey correct information, but it won't stick. On the other hand, stories need to give the audience essential need-to-know information (through explanation and exposition), or else the audience can't make sense of what is happening in the story and why. So it's fair to say that they mutually depend on each other.

The trick then is weaving in that information so skilfully that readers won't even notice. There are three ways to do it (Hart 2011). For example, you can use subordinate clauses to convey expository information in passing. They are most often signalled by relative pronouns. Take this sentence, for example:

> [...] his spleen, the delicate fist-sized organ that sits just below the ribs and which acts as a blood filter as part of the immune system, was ruptured.
>
> (Feinmann 2017)

Science writer Jane Feinmann tells readers what the spleen is, in passing, using a double relative clause that first starts with "that sits" to describe its location and then again at "which acts" to tell her readers what the organ does. The second way to convey expository information is to place it into appositives. Appositives are nouns that writers place near other nouns in order to specify them. Feinmann uses one in writing "his spleen, the delicate fist-sized organ [...],". I included the comma, because there are two rules for writing appositives. First, if the specification is not necessary for the sentence to be grammatically complete, you put the appositive between commas. In Feinmann's example, you could cut the whole part after the comma out of the sentence and it would still be a complete sentence: "his spleen was ruptured." The second case doesn't need commas, because the appositive can't be removed easily. You'll find direct appositives often in rulers' names, like "Peter the Great". Or you'll find it in fiction, like "Gandalf the Grey" in J.R.R. Tolkien's "Lord of the Rings". The first noun is the name, the second the determiner. You can also signal the appositive explicitly using markers like "like", "such as", "for example". Which is what I just did.

This works at a linguistic level, as does using metaphors and similes to explain complex issues. On a structural level, Hart (2011) distinguishes between fully-fledged story narratives and explanatory narratives. The former have a full narrative arc, while the latter contain only a few story elements. They are not full narratives that carry readers through the whole story. Instead, they digress frequently and switch forth and back between story and explanation. You can typically find these types of narratives in *The New Yorker*, written by authors like McPhee, Susan Orlean and David Grann (Pitzer 2011). What they do is digress, and some magazines and newspapers indicate such digressions visually by star lines, centred bullets or large capital letters at the beginning of a new section (Hart 2011). Does this structure sound familiar? Of course, we had a look at it several times in this book. It's what Michelle Nijhuis (2013) calls the layer-cake structure. It's what Germany's first journalism professor Winfried Göpfert (2006) calls the AB-structure (although I think he should have called it BA-structure, since he recommends starting with the story part "B"), and it's what Lee Gutkind (2012) calls the "creative nonfiction dance". This alternation between story and explanation also shows when you apply the zooming technique (see the chapter on literary techniques). In Gutkind's terms, you alternate between scenes and information. He adds that you can embed information (explanation, that is) in scenes. Hart (2011) introduces the "3+2 explainer", which is a narrative layer-cake that looks like this (adapted from Hart 2011):

Narrative 1: Protagonist introduced, explanatory (not dramatic) question posed
Digression 1: Necessary background and context established
Narrative 2: Protagonist followed as main action unfolds
Digression 2: Explanation completed
Narrative 3: Action logically stopped

To write the "narrative" parts, the scenes, you need to record vivid details or reconstruct them from existing material or interviews. But the reporting for the explanatory parts, the digressions, looks a bit different. What drives explanatory reporting is your curiosity about how the world works. Journalist Cynthia Gorney recommends taking a few steps back from the story and asking yourself questions like (Hart 2011):

- Why does this matter?
- Why here?
- Why now?

In order to find explanatory information, Gorney's advice is to talk with people, scour internet bulletin boards and chat rooms, browse specialised journals and spend time "in places where relevant things take place" (Hart 2011:191). And

Gorney has another list of questions that aim at revealing how the world works. Here it is (verbatim from Hart 2011):

- How do they *do* that?
- Where does that *come* from; where does that *go*?
- Who *is* that guy?
- How did this get to be such a *mess*?
- What's it *like* to be him or her?

Explanatory reporting is so important that is has its own Pulitzer Prize. Let's have a look at one example that won this prize in 2011. It's the second of three parts that ran in the Milwaukee Journal Sentinel in 2010. The story is not an explanatory narrative but a full-blown story with a few explanatory passages. The story is about doctors using genetic technology to save a four-year-old. After introducing the two main characters, the boy and the doctor who tries to save him, the journalists introduce the term "genetic script", which needs some explanation. They explain it in the following paragraph (which follows a very short story paragraph, which again is followed by another short story paragraph):

> Every human carries thousands of variations in the genetic script, the long chain of chemical bases that makes us who we are. These differences [...] determine everything from harmless diversity (brown hair vs. blond) to the defects that cause disease. Although some differences are harmful, most are not. Some are even beneficial.
>
> (Johnson & Gallagher 2010)

Although there is no real transition into this explanatory paragraph (and it is not signalled using one of the abovementioned markers), the transition to the next paragraph is smooth. It starts with "They could find 20,000 of these differences [...]", with "these differences" being the connector between the paragraphs.

Here's another technique, one we have seen in the section on character development: let a story character deliver the background information, exposition or, as in this case, the explanation. Unlike in fiction, as a nonfiction storyteller, you have to know in advance that you need to ask questions that aim at getting those explanations from your characters This, in turn, shows why structuring your piece early in the process and developing a reporting plan makes sense. Here is what this technique looks like in Johnson's and Gallagher's story:

> Mayer explains that a mutation on Nicholas' X chromosome has caused the illness in his gut. But there's more. The same mutation has also caused a second extremely rare disease called XLP. Only boys get this second disease, which leaves them unable to fight off one of the most common human viruses, Epstein-Barr.
>
> (Johnson & Gallagher 2010)

Revising

Narrative journalism guru Lee Gutkind has dedicated half of his book *You Can't Make This Stuff Up* to writing and editing. And he makes it clear from the outset: the two are inseparable. Once you have written something, read it out loud. But don't just read it from your own perspective as the author. Read it also from a reader's perspective and note which passages entice you most. If you were not the author, would you like the piece? This approach requires brutal honesty with yourself. Gutkind recalls how one of his editors simply drew lines down the side of the pages and passages where she felt her mind had wandered while reading them. She never changed a word, but he learnt a lot from her way to make him rethink his writing (Gutkind 2012). Typically, the passages where your mind strays are the ones that don't throw you into narrative mode. As an exercise, Gutkind lets his students highlight the scenes in texts with a yellow marker. In essays, magazines and nonfiction books, they will highlight between 50 and 70 per cent of the entire texts. You should try the yellow test also on your own writing. If there are not enough scenes, the yellow test will show it. The test is part of the second type of revision he suggests. Read like a writer. When you start rewriting, don't focus on style at first. Instead, focus on structure and getting that one right (Gutkind 2012). Which makes a lot of sense, if you think about it. Because restructuring doesn't mean just shuffling around paragraphs and sentences. It means rewriting them. So restyle afterwards. Also, when I revise my texts, rewriting is easier than just patching up passages. If you do that, you risk cutting previous connections to the rest of the copy. At the very least, read everything again to see if the passages still logically connect. What I usually do during the revision is rewrite entire passages and reconnect them to previous and later paragraphs. This, of course, means also rewriting parts of those, so essentially the amount of work triples. That is also the reason why I never underestimate how much time revising texts will take.

There's a little catch to Gutkind's approaches. You need to have written in order to revise. In his book *Writing Tools: 55 Essential Strategies for Writers*, and specifically in his chapter about procrastination and writer's block, writing coach Roy Peter Clark makes it clear that whatever you write has at least some value. On some days, you may write "many poor words", on others you may "write a few good words. The poor words may be the necessary path to the good words" (Clark 2008). In order to edit, to revise anything at all, you need to make sure to have put some sort of writing on an empty page. That is why Clark encourages writers to develop routines and start writing early in the day. To come up with a first draft, he advises them to lower their standards, as high standards may often be what causes writer's block. I know what he's talking about. I've been there, and I often am. As I wrote before, when I struggle to get started, I usually haven't done enough reporting yet. It's not fear of the empty page in front of me. I don't fear it. I am annoyed by it. I hate churning out the first letters. But the more I do it, the more I let my thoughts flow onto the page, the better it gets. Once I have written, I actually like it. But not the first draft. That's what distinguishes the professional from the amateur. The pro tinkers with words and letters and structure until she can't boil it down any further. It's literally cooking a ragout but not eating it right away, oh no. You'll let it simmer, stir and eventually boil it down until it's become the very essence of its ingredients. I've never been happy with a first draft, and neither should you be.

The best articles, as Jack Hart states in his book *Storycraft*, come to life when editors and writers work together, which usually means a back and forth between the two and multiple revisions. Revising means rewriting. It's not about removing single words and simply letting the structure be as it is. It means logical restructuring, detaching, re-attaching and reconnecting events until the cause-and-effect structure of a text makes sense. It's those discussions I had with my editors (thanks, Stephan Draf and Alan Niederer) that I learnt most from in terms of revising. But as an editor of a science blog network, I have also seen authors who are reluctant to accept any sort of suggested improvements. It's hard to grow from an arrogant attitude like that. You need to fail in order to learn. Yes, some writers (including scientists) are natural born storytellers. Most are not. My advice: embrace additional editing. It will make your texts better, and it lends a fresh perspective to your ideas. Learn from the suggestions and consider implementing them, even if you don't agree with them at first. Stow away your ego and focus on the text. There's only one goal: a well-flowing text that both entertains the audience and gets the theme across. As Clark claims, "quality comes from revision, not from speed writing" (Clark 2008).

Most newspaper reports don't get to the heart of the story, because of their distanced language, which doesn't convey the story from the character's point of view. "There are three ways to get to the heart of the story: reporting, thinking and rewriting" (Hull 2007:206). While thinking is the most underused skill in the newsroom, Hull dedicates the lion's share of her chapter to rewriting. Her first piece of advice is to get a good reader. Every journalist needs one. I've always had my texts read before they went to the editor, and for that I'm really grateful. The exact moment that editor/reader is needed, depends from writer to writer. Hull writes she needs to contact an editor to work with her on the structure when she hits the 30 per cent mark. And in her following statement you can actually recognise several story elements (protagonist, conflict, a turning point/insight):

> If you put yourself in a challenging environment and force yourself to stretch, you *will* improve. That means you must always be shifting your location slightly so that you are always around people who are better than you.
>
> (Hull 2007:207)

Revising is like sandblasting, and having a hard copy of your full draft and then going over it with a pen will elevate it from 70 per cent done to 90 per cent. Hull's advice is to set your ego aside, eliminate extra words and "cut to the bone". Also, cut out all familiar phrases (Hull 2007). That last piece of advice obviously targets clichés.

What all the writing coaches seem to agree on is that working with an editor is immensely valuable. I agree. I wouldn't say there is an upper limit for the amount of times that you and your editor play ping pong with your draft, but more is usually better. When I get texts back from editors with no edits suggested whatsoever, that's when I get suspicious. Have they even read it? Authors that I work with should get equally keen-eared when they get articles back from me with only minor edits (which usually doesn't happen). It's a moment of growth, and only when both author and editor have a feeling that the story flows, all questions are answered and the style is flush, then and only then the story is ready to be published.

The following is an extreme case of ordering and revising. Pulitzer Prize-winner Sonia Nazario had gathered 110 notebooks, several hundred hours of recorded interviews and written notes from phone interviews. Her story revolved around Enrique, a Honduran boy looking for his mother. Nazario's editor asked her to transcribe all her material and then to compress it into a rough draft. That first draft spanned a whopping 95,000 words. The editor then used a pencil to remove many sections, and the final piece still spanned about 35,000 words. The whole process took several months, and the series, which appeared in 2012, went through ten drafts. How could she reduce the first draft into a much more focused revised version? By focusing on the main character Enrique and turning the other characters into secondary ones, which required less description. The story's structure was chronological, but Nazario learnt that she could skip ahead and omit events that had happened in between two other events. She cut out similar events. For example, Enrique got robbed several times; Nazario only included one of these incidents. Once she had reduced the structure, she started doing the same at the sentence and word level. She did so with rhythm in mind, as short paragraphs add suspense. Nazario added details to slow readers down, and she deliberately removed them (the details, not the readers) to speed up the reading pace. At the very end, she questioned every fragment and word, asking whether they would be really needed. Can you see what's at the core of revision? Selection and rejection. Ditch whatever isn't part of your story's theme.

Verification

Narrative journalism, and narrative science journalism is a lot of fun, from finding ideas to reporting, to structuring stories to writing them. But it still is journalism, which means whatever you write must be verifiable facts. There is no room for speculation, but if you do, you should clearly point that out. Verification starts during reporting, and it ends when your piece is published. Verification means asking questions. Ask yourself questions. Ask your sources questions. Ask your data questions. At the heart of verification lies one question: how do you know that? It sounds simple and mechanical, but it isn't. *Der Spiegel* runs the largest fact-checking operation in the world with about 70 fact checkers employed (Schäfer 2011). Still, their department didn't detect the fabricated stories of then reporter Claas Relotius. And it increasingly becomes apparent that Relotius had fabricated more stories for many other outlets, none of which apparently detected his fraudulent practices. *Der Spiegel* fact checker Maximilian Schäfer has written an article on the publication's fact-checking practices. In it, he also makes clear that fact checking is a matter of resources. For example, it's impossible to apply the same rigorous fact-checking process to *Spiegel Online*, because the volume of published texts is much higher (Schäfer 2011). You should definitely read Schäfer's full article. I put a link to it in the "Links" section.

Reporter and writing coach Steve Buttry writes in the *Verification Handbook* that persistence is key. Hence, asking another question, "how else do you know that" is important. These three factors are crucial to verification (adapted from Silverman 2015):

1 A person's resourcefulness, persistence, skepticism and skill
2 Sources' knowledge, reliability and honesty, and the number, variety and reliability of sources you can find and persuade to talk
3 Documentation

Do you feel that science journalists apply these principles rigorously when reporting and writing their stories? Some do, and they're really good at it. Others don't. They drink the Flavor Aid and copy-paste claims, quotes and even entire formulations from press releases. There are a number of problems associated with the process. Fear of making mistakes is one such issue. If you simply parrot what the press officer feeds you, or if you just take repeat jargon because you fear boiling it down and going out on a limb when doing so, then you're not doing your job. Journalism is not for the fearful. Explanation is part of science journalism. Another issue is resource management. Many journalists are overburdened: I remember talking with one Australian science journalist for my previous book. He loves his job but has to cover lots of beats, not just science. He has little time for verification or challenging claims. Good writing takes time. Challenging claims takes time. Verification takes time, too.

The news cycle has become much faster, but so have the tools to verify (Buttry in Silverman 2015). People who accidentally witness a scene brandish their smartphones, shoot some footage and then upload it to the social media instead of forwarding it the traditional media for verification. This user-generated content (UGC) is often hard to verify. You can never ever assume that it is correct without verifying it. Which means you can't use unverified UGC content in your stories. Claire Wardle is an expert in UGC verification. She writes that UGC verification takes four steps (adapted from Wardle in Silverman 2015):

1 **Provenance**: is this the original piece of content? Twitter: the microblogging platform verifies accounts to ensure you know who runs them. Unverified profiles try to bypass this process by including a screenshot of the badge as part of their header image. How can you check if a profile has really been verified? Hover over the badge, it should display a popup message that says "verified account". If it doesn't, it's a fake-verified profile. If you want to go the extra mile, look at whom the profiles are following and who is following them. Images: you can find an image's provenance by using reverse image searches like Google Image or TinEye. Simply upload a

picture or insert a link to it, and these search engines will find out if it has been published anywhere else on the web before (Wardle in Silverman 2015). In summer 2019, I used this technique to expose a fake image that anti-wolf campaigners used in a local newspaper (they drank the Flavor Aid without verifying), declaring a wolf had killed a horse in a Northern Italian region. A couple of reverse image checks later, I could verify that the picture had already appeared two years before on a Spanish blog, claiming the horse had been eaten alive by hornets. It had been repurposed multiple times.

2   **Source**: who uploaded the content? Find out who the original uploader was and ask her where she was standing when she recorded the footage. You can cross check this information against EXIF data in pictures and by using Google Street View to assume the same vantage point. Do they match?

3   **Date**: when was the content created? This can be hard to verify. The You-Tube upload date is displayed using Pacific Standard Time, so this can be misleading if the event took place outside that time zone. What you can do with visual material is compare the weather in the footage with the recorded weather. For example, Wardle (Silverman 2015) recommends using the search engine Wolfram Alpha, because you can directly ask it about the specific weather conditions on a particular day.

4   **Location**: where was the content created? If your material is geo-tagged, this should be relatively easy to verify using online maps services. If that information is missing, you can try and pinpoint landmarks visually and then again cross check using maps services like Google Maps, Bing Maps or Wikimapia. An investigative journalism team at the European Investigative Journalism Conference in Mechelen revealed that they had been using high-resolution satellite imagery to determine warship models and verify that they were harbored in particular havens – against authorities' claims.

Video verification can be even more complicated. One way to do it is splitting it into its single frames and verifying, frame by frame, if the same content can be found in every frame. It's a tedious technical process that takes time. *Storyful* editor Malachy Browne provides an example of a video showing an eagle that attacks a baby in Montreal. Frame analysis showed that the eagle wasn't present in all of the video's frames. The video was created by Canadian students (Silverman 2015).

What about science journalism? If staff positions are dwindling, fact checking can't be doing well, either, right? Let's have a look at the facts. In 2018, freelance science journalist Brooke Borel ran a study for the MIT Knight Science Journalism Program. She conducted more than 300 surveys and more than 90 interviews among 80 English-language publications. This is what she found: a third of them employ independent fact checkers and researchers to verify content. A third employ no formal fact-checking processes, and 15 per cent rely on copy editors to verify the content (Borel 2018). This sounds grim, but at least longform narrative pieces have a higher chance of getting fact checked. In any case, verification should be a process, not a single yes or no statement.

In narrative nonfiction, the verification process really depends on what type of story you are producing. We've talked about reconstruction before. If you cannot observe events first-hand, you will have to rely on witness' statements and recorded documentation. This is true for all history writing, and you should trace every source to its origin. If witnesses exist, interview them, but challenge their answers. The aforementioned question "how do you know that" is a good start. Also, use digitised copies of historical documents (the "Library of Congress" and the "Web Archive" host lots of scanned historical documents). Trace them back to their source.

In science journalism, quotes are often subject for discussion. If you have recorded and correctly transcribed your quotes, and if they are on the record, then you don't need to check them with your source. Different publications have different policies about whether or not a journalist is allowed to let scientists review their quotes. For example, the *Washington Post, Discover* and *Nature* won't let their reporters share quotes or copy with their sources. *STAT News* allows it sometimes to verify accuracy, and *Undark* generally discourages it (Smith 2018). The discussion seems to revolve around the trade off between the hard rule of journalism not to let anybody review their quotes before publication and the quest for getting the facts right. In her *Undark* article, science reporter Dana Smith asks a number of science writers and scientists whether quotes should be checked before a piece gets published. What emerges is that it's mostly the scientists that would like to review their quotes (their motivations differ). Some of the interviewed science journalists are aware that they shouldn't let the scientists review their statements before they go out. They know they have to fact-check their pieces on their own. Others science journalists say they just want to get the facts right (Smith 2018). I champion the former approach, because it keeps our work independent. Some scientists may pursue an agenda that you don't know about.

Editing

As Jack Hart writes in his brilliant book *Storycraft*: the best articles result from writers working closely with editors. This process usually takes at least two rounds of editing, in some cases even just one. It's a back-and-forth. Editors ask writers clarification questions. They ask for sources that substantiate the stories' facts. Writers respond, editors respond to the response and ask new questions, and so on. How this back-and-forth between writers and editors unfolds varies from case to case. I've seen a number of cases. With one *Motherboard Germany* editor, we would regularly use shared Google Docs files, where we would both comment, ask questions and then answer the comments directly in the file. I rewrote the passages he asked me to directly in the file, so he could immediately see them. He would suggest, add or delete passages, but I could trace all his actions because of Google Docs' "history" and "review" functions. If he had a question, he inserted it as a comment. I sometimes answered it, but often I immediately amended the copy and put a note on it in that passage's comments. This was one of the fastest processes I had, and it works wonders for quick turnaround stories. I should add that these stories were rather short news reports, or news backgrounders, or short features. The longer a piece gets, the more important it is that you have an interactive process with your editor. I can't understand why some writers get offended when their editors come up with criticism. It's just stupid to reject their valuable advice. Those moments when they tell you "this passage doesn't really make sense to me – what are you trying to tell me here"? Those are the moments when you start rethinking it from another perspective. Indeed, most editors are much more audience-centred than their writers. They read your story from a reader's point of view. That's what's so valuable. When I submitted a magazine feature on online dating to an editor at *P.M. Magazin*, he sent me some questions but then asked for a phone call. On the phone, he told me that he wanted me to change a few passages, to shuffle around a few paragraphs and reorder them, so I could logically connect them. He thought we might eliminate one paragraph altogether, he had a few style questions and questioned some numbers. In particular, he asked me to put some of the numbers in clearer context and point out to readers whether those figures referred to a US or European audience, or both. He also made me double-check the figures I had extracted from studies. Most importantly, he asked questions from a reader's perspective. He bluntly told me that my text didn't really explain how Tinder works. Taking the stance from a typical reader of the magazine, he told me to rewrite that part. I did, and he was happy with it. So was I, because what would be worse than writing a text that your audience can't make sense of? If you write nonfiction professionally, your readers are the only party you should try to please.

Having an editor that interactively works with you is a luxury, no less. But sometimes you don't have that luxury. For example, if you run your own blog or if you self-publish a book. In those cases it is very tempting to just publish it after you've written a first draft. But it's cool, right? It saves time, right? No. Don't. Ever. No first draft is perfect, not even good. No editor would run a piece just as it is – exceptions prove the rule. That's why you should edit your own texts even if there is no editor between you and publishing the piece. Self-editing is always a good idea, especially considering that in some cases, editors are not the quality gatekeepers they're supposed to be. That's why you need to have an idea of how editors look at your texts. It starts with taking a reader's perspective, but in all successful cases, it includes a process that systematically reviews your text at multiple levels. Publishers distinguish between different types of editing. These are the five most important ones, taken from the boo "The Editor's Companion" (adapted from Dunham 2014):

1 **Substantive editing**: this includes rewriting, checking the copy for clarity, eliminating repetitions, rearranging the structure. Typical speed: about 375 words or 1.5 pages per hour.
2 **Copy editing**: this is more detailed editing and includes reviewing grammar, spelling, punctuation, capitalisation, consistency, as that's easier to read. Copy editors are usually the ones to get back to the author with content-related questions. Typical speed: about 750 words or three pages per hour.

3   **Technical editing**: this includes checks whether tables, figures and tables are accurate. Fact checking is done at this stage.
4   **Proofreading**: this means comparing the typeset copy against the correct original manuscript. Whatever can be lost in formatting needs to be checked by proofreaders. This includes quotes and mathematical formulas.
5   **Quality checks**: these are the final checks performed after the layout is complete. Quality assurance doesn't read the copy but rather ensures that the following elements are correct: table of contents, dates, illustrations and captions and the legibility of visual material.

Dunham recommends reading each piece at least twice. When you finish it, read it and mark everything that doesn't make any sense. After the first editing is done, read through it again. Most probably, a few errors slipped your attention in the first pass, which is quite normal. Dunham writes even when he edited texts a second or third time, he found lots of errors that he had missed before. You can't hunt them down by just having a random look at your copy. There would be just too many aspects you would have to pay attention to, so you need an editing system. Professional publications have internal style sheets and checklists for that reason. Editors follow these lists and tick them off as they edit, otherwise it would be overwhelming even for them, regardless of all the experience they've accumulated over the years. If you regularly write for the same publications, their editors will tell you what their house style is and what they expect from you. Some may even send you their checklists and style guides, so you can better understand what they expect in terms of quality. I remember the moment I was discussing a news piece with an editor at *Neue Zürcher Zeitung* on the phone. He had called me to figure out what I had meant exactly, because a term in my piece means the opposite in Swiss German than in other variations of German. Once we figured it out, we had a good laugh about it. I always tried to write for as many different publications as possible, in print and online, to stay in shape. That makes it rather difficult soaking up each single house style. In that sense, it's better to be a staff writer. You just develop a better feeling for the editorial team's needs because you're part of it. Some major publishers release their style guides commercially. This includes the *Associated Press* and the *New York Times*. But you can't buy their editing checklists. Dunham includes a sample checklist for copy-editing and proofreading, which includes checking the proof word for word against the original copy, reading straight through the proof without any comparisons, checking the date, page numbers, chapter titles, chapter and section numbers, figure and table numbers, proper names, captions quotations, parentheses and widow and orphans (Dunham 2014).

So here's a checklist I use before submitting every piece of writing, no matter if I write short or long. In the process of writing this book, I've extended it using pieces of advice I found (for example, William Zinsser's). Here is the current version of my checklist:

1 **Read out your text aloud**. Mark everything that strikes your attention, in terms of facts, grammar, style, spelling. If the text is reasonably long, I read it out to a friend, too.

2 **Does every paragraph convey one idea?** If not, split them into logical units.

3 **Are all ideas connected in a cause-and-effect style?** If not, connect them using transitions.

4 **Highlight all the facts in your copy**. Have you verified them? If not, do so. Either using the study you're referring to or secondary material. Conduct interviews, too.

5 **Do you provide context for all stats and relative figures?** If not, grab the study and secondary material and add that context.

6 **Have you double-checked all the quotes against your transcripts or other source documents?** If not, do so.

7 **Are all the people's names, their roles and institutions correct?** Are they spelled correctly and consistently? If in doubt, call them up and ask them about their current role and where they work at.

8 **Highlight all jargon words**. Have you explained them in plain English? If not, add explanations and/or come up with metaphors and similes.

9 **Are there any ambiguous words (even the non-jargon ones)?** If so, grab a dictionary, look for synonyms and replace them with clear words.

10 **Can you omit words or phrases?** If so, do so. Here's a test: try putting them between brackets, and read just that passage again. Does it still make sense? If so: hit the delete key.

11 **Are all of your sentences complete and as simple as they can be?** If not, reorder, split, combine, rewrite them.

12 **Are most of your sentences declarative?** If not: rewrite overly long periodic sentences, split loose sentences and turn the clauses into declarative ones.

13 **Where does your mind wander?** Read through the entire copy and draw a line near the passages where you feel you lose focus and/or concentration. Then consider rewriting those passages.

14 **Do you repeat any ideas?** If so, weed out the repetitions, no matter how eloquently you think you formulated them.

15 **Do you oversynonymise?** If so, replace the synonyms by the initial term. The clearest cat is the one that doesn't become a feline in the next paragraph.

16 **Read your copy aloud once again**.

17 **Go through this list over and over again until your copy reads pleasantly**.

We're nearly at the end of the book. I've written it more or less in the order the chapters are arranged. Once I'm through, guess what I'll be doing? Exactly. I'll start again. I'll read it. I'll take notes. I'll look for missing consistency, grammar, spelling and factual errors, repetitions, unneeded passages, expletives, stylistic glitches and much more. Then I'll correct them. And then read it again. The whole whopping 120,000 words. Until all items on my checklist are ticked off.

Endings

"Everything that has a beginning, has an end." Yep, that's right. Aristotle knew it. Shakespeare knew it. The Wachowski brothers (now sisters) knew it when they wrote the *Matrix: Revolutions* (not the best sequel, but still). Every story needs an end. And no, it's not the "conclusion" titled paragraph that simply repeats and "sums up" what your audience already knows. At least, that's not what story endings should look like. Instead, it should leave readers with a sense of closure. Endings are just as important as beginnings. For a scenic delayed lead, it's often a good idea to "come full circle" (heartfelt apologies for the truism) and pick up the narrative thread where you left it off at the beginning. Which, of course, you did for effect. Such endings can be very short. But if you started your lead with a non-narrative approach, you'll have to take a slightly different approach. For example, I started a story on rhino poaching in South Africa with a "startling facts" style lead, not a story or anecdote. My lead ends like this:

> No wonder rhino horn poaching is continuously increasing, with 333 poached South African rhino in 2010, 448 in 2011 and a total of 668 in 2012. The South African government's latest statistics show that alone this year until March 15, 158 white rhinos have already been poached.
>
> (Angler 2013)

I simply wanted to put numbers in context (the beginning of the lead compares rhino horn with gold and cocaine), and to raise readers' awareness about the phenomenon. So, how can you find closure at the end of such a story? For example, by giving a personalised outlook on how things might develop in the future. That's the logical bookend for a piece you start by highlighting what doesn't currently run right in the world. You provide an outlook, a comment. This is how I ended my piece:

> Anyway, no matter the anti-poaching technologies used: 2013 is on the way to hit a new poaching record high. Van Niekerk's anti-poaching treatment is simple yet impressive, but: in order to become fully effective, awareness must be raised among horn consumers. In late April, TRAFFIC launched a marketing campaign to sensitize cancer patients in Vietnam, claiming rhino horn powder is useless as medicine. I wonder what the next poaching statistics will look like.
>
> (Angler 2013)

So, I simply pick up on the statistics from the lead. I can't fully answer it (which is usually bad), but at least I give a graspable outlook of what others do to fight the problem. Also, and quite importantly, it's the ABT in action! Status quo established (we're hitting a new poaching record high AND Van Niekerk has this new treatment), BUT we need awareness to solve the problem. SO, TRAFFIC's marketing campaign tries to attack the problem from that angle. The best part about this? Back then, I had no idea what the ABT was. I wrote the story's end at the end of my writing process (it didn't change substantially during the self-editing). But I definitely revised the lead and made sure it was flush with the ending. The end is usually a bit more work, as it must transition from both its previous paragraph (the butlast in the story), and from the lead.

Freelance science writer Robin Meadows has written an article for *The Open Notebook*, where she distinguishes between three types of endings. She comes up with examples for each type and interviews both the editor and the writer on that ending. The first type is the one just mentioned, "coming full circle". Meadows (2015b) cites Nijhuis (2013) when she writes that kickers at the end of a story are the writer's last word to the reader, essentially their take-home message. In her full-circle example, the ending circles back to the beginning, summarises the main points, gives future directions and includes a pithy quote – all of which are building blocks of satisfying endings. On top of that, it includes a plot point, an epiphany, which elevates it further from typical "full-circle" endings. Meadows adds that the ending is a great moment to remind readers of a story's theme. The second type of ending, the "everything together", also circles back to the beginning and states the story's theme. It also hooks into the lead's preceding scenes, so it's best to use it with stories that open with an anecdote. The writer came up with the ending late in the process and he imagined the final scenes. The third type of ending is scenic and very descriptive. The story ends with the writer being in the middle of a stream, surrounded by salmon. What's more, the scene carries the take-home message of the story. For such endings, the writer usually looks for scenic story material, like vivid description and dialogue (Meadows 2015b).

What unites all types of endings is that they pull readers into narrative mode. In extreme cases, your lead and ending are bookends for your story. They are wrapped around a chunk of explanatory passages, draw the readers inside the story and then leave them with a sense of closure and a graspable take-home message. The story part is bait, and all the rest is explanation. Believe it or not, this is sufficient, even for longer pieces. Readers are likely to bear with the writer until the end, until the writer pays off the initial scene (Hart 2011). Writing coach Jack Hart calls this type of structure "bookend narrative." In such stories (and in general, very often), endings are scenes. But endings can come also come in other forms than vivid scenes (adapted from DeSilva 2007):

- An anecdote that encapsulates the story's theme
- A telling detail that symbolises something larger than itself or indicates how the story might proceed
- A conclusion that addresses readers and explicitly states the story's theme

DeSilva shares most of the other scholars' and writing trainers' view. But he makes another important point: don't overuse quotes in your endings. It is you, the writer, whose take-home message should emerge, not somebody else's. Apart from that, if you can come up with a plot twist or unexpected detail in your ending, go for it. In most cases, you can combine several of those endings' elements to craft your own. For example, science writer Kat Arney starts her story on job-threatening AIs with a clear statement:

Let's get one thing straight: robot teachers are not coming to your school and they are not going to steal your job.

(Arney 2017)

Part of her story's theme emerges, but not all of it. She ends her story letting one of the characters tell the story's theme through quotes:

But if that does happen, then Luckin says AI's future in education will depend on more than just that evidence. She describes the challenge as winning over "hearts and minds" – AI doesn't just need people to believe it works, it needs people to trust it […]

(Arney 2017)

The story doesn't quite end there; the ending stretches over a few more paragraphs. But Arney nails the ending in coming up with more quotes from the characters that repeat the theme, which proves to be quite effective. This is the final quote and the story's real kicker is the character's plead for letting AI into education after addressing the fears about it: "But that will be such a great shame because it can do so much" (Arney 2017). In this case, the writer remains more objective, and probably she has deliberately chosen this approach in order to remain in the background. It seems pretty obvious that the theme, although articulated by a story character's quote, resonates with Arney's own view. In the next and final section of this book, science writer Giorgia Guglielmi lets you in on her writing process.

An interview with Giorgia Guglielmi

Giorgia Guglielmi is a freelance science journalist covering the life science, science policy and the intersection of science and society. Her stories have appeared in publications including *Science, Nature* and *Scientific American*. Giorgia has a PhD in Biology from the European Molecular Biology Laboratory in Heidelberg, Germany, and a Master's in Science Writing from the Massachusetts Institute of Technology in Cambridge. She is currently based in Cambridge, Massachusetts. I got to know her as a prolific science writer at the 2019 World Conference of Science Journalists in Switzerland in 2019. So I asked her a few questions about her writing and editing process.

Q: How do you make sure you consistently deliver quality articles?

A: Thorough reporting, accuracy, and resourcefulness are key. For hard news stories about a scientific discovery, I read in depth the article(s) that detail the discovery, especially the results and discussion session, and I highlight any bit that is interesting, important or shady. This helps me to come up with specific questions to ask as I do the reporting and spot overblown claims or questionable statistics. If I need relevant background on the topic that I have to cover, I scour the reference list at the end of the article, which also helps me to figure out who I need to call for outside comment. Then I reach out to the study authors and at least four experts who have not been involved in the study. They help me to put the story in context and understand the importance and the implications of the discovery. For news features, I tend to talk to many more people – usually around 15–20 – to make sure I grasp all the nuances of an issue and get great quotes or interesting anecdotes that will provide some perking up for fatigued readers. If my sources make assertions about an individual or organization, I contact them to verify the information and get comment. This is crucial, especially for policy stories, and it's where resourcefulness comes into play. Sometimes it can be hard to get comments from public officials, and just sending off an email won't help: you have to be prepared to spend hours on the phone trying to reach someone or even track them down on social media. After doing the reporting and writing the article, I use an accuracy check-list to verify all factual assertions, names, titles, affiliations, dates, and numbers. Often I verify the details of a story with my sources, but I never share drafts or quotes prior to publication, as that would compromise my independence as a journalist.

Q: What does your writing process look like, from finding ideas to writing the first draft?

A: There are many ways of finding story ideas – press releases, scientific journals, government records, conferences. But most of the times, story ideas do not come to you, so I try to monitor social media and develop primary sources such as academics or staff at universities who know what is being done there. Once I find something interesting, I evaluate whether it could be a story and what kind of story it could be. Why is it interesting? Is it surprising? Funny? Controversial? A significant development in science? If other journalists have already covered it, can I find a new angle? Is it a straight news story, a Q&A, a feature? If I think a story might be a feature, I make some phone calls early on to find a good angle and a compelling narrative approach. When I have a story idea, I pitch it to the relevant editor at the publication where I'd like to publish it. If they're interested and assign me the story (yay!), I start reporting it. This can take anywhere between one day and two weeks, depending on the story. Once I've gathered all the information that I think I need, I make a plan for writing the story. I transcribe recorded interviews, read through my notes, and mark the information and the quotes I want to use. Then I start to make an outline with the essential information that I want to give in each paragraph or section of a story. The outline helps me to define a story structure, which generally follows the inverted pyramid, with an introductory section that engages the reader and summarizes what the story is about, followed by background and supporting details from most to least important. Once I'm happy with the outline, I finally start writing a first draft. As I write, I make sure to convey information in an accurate, balanced, and objective way. Quotes humanize the story, but I use them sparingly, only if a source says something in a particularly colorful or clear way.

Q: Would you share your editing workflow with us?

A: Before filing a story, I read it from beginning to end to check that it flows logically and doesn't leave the reader asking questions that could have been answered. Then I verify dates, factual assertions, and numbers, especially percentages or averages. I check spelling and typos, and I remove any passive verbs, jargon, and clichés that may have slipped in. I never file a story that is more than 10% longer than the assigned word-count, unless I have a good reason, which I'll discuss with my editor. So, if my first draft is too long, I try to make it tighter by cutting unnecessary words or quotes. When I get queries back from editors, I make a plan for editing. First I take care of queries that need additional reporting, then those that I can answer by reading through my notes. Finally, I address queries that relate to my writing, such as "is there a better way to describe this experiment?" Before filing a revised draft, I do a style-check and verify names, titles, and affiliations.

Q: What's the hardest part when self-editing your work?

A: I enjoy self-editing my stories, but the hardest part comes when I have to "kill my babies," which means cutting quotes, anecdotes or asides that I got attached to. Sometimes editors ask to ditch those bits because they're unnecessary or don't communicate an idea clearly. It's a painful job, but most of the times editors are right.

Q: You're a freelancer: How do you adapt to the different house styles?

A: I write on a regular basis for two or three publications, so I'm familiar with their house style. When I have to write for a new publication, I read stories that they've published before to study their style and content, and I ask my editor for the house-style guide.

Review questions

- How do summary leads and delayed leads differ?
- What ways can you start a delayed lead?
- How can you sneak in explanatory or expository information that the audience needs to know?
- What is a "3+2" explainer?
- What is a bookend narrative?
- What should be on an editing checklist?
- How do you verify a Twitter profile's authenticity?

- How do the five main editing stages differ?
- How would you end a feature that starts with an anecdote?

Links

"Science Journalism and fact checking" (JCOM): https://jcom.sissa.it/sites/defa ult/files/documents/Jcom1004%282011%29C02.pdf

"Self-Editing Tips for Journalists" (Investigative Journalists' Network): https:// ijnet.org/en/resource/self-editing-tips-journalists

Verification Handbook (European Journalism Centre): http://verificationha ndbook.com/downloads/verification.handbook.pdf

"TinEye Reverse Image Search" (TinEye): https://www.tineye.com/

References

Angler, M.W. (2013) "Dye and Poison Stop Rhino Poachers," Scientific American Guest Blog [Online]. Available at: https://blogs.scientificamerican.com/guest-blog/dye-and-poison-stop-rhino-poachers/ (date accessed 18 September 2019).

Arney, K. (2017) "Algorithm's Gonna Get You," TES.com [Online]. Available at: https://www.absw.org.uk/files/entry-1179-algorithm_tes_kat_arney.pdf (date accessed 18 September 2019).

Borel, B. (2018) "The State of Fact-Checking in Science Journalism," MIT Knight Science Journalism [Online]. Available at: https://www.moore.org/docs/default-source/defa ult-document-library/fact-checking-in-science-journalism_mit-ksj.pdf?sfvrsn=a6346e0c_ 2 (date accessed 19 September 2019).

Clark, R.P. (2008) *Writing Tools: 55 Essential Strategies for Every Writer.* London: Little, Brown.

Cooper, H. (2015) "They Helped Erase Ebola in Liberia. Now Liberia Is Erasing Them," *The New York Times* [Online]. Available at: https://www.nytimes.com/2015/12/10/world/africa/they-helped-erase-ebola-in-liberia-now-liberia-is-erasing-them.html (date accessed 17 September 2019).

DeSilva, B. (2007) "Endings," in: Kramer, M. & Call, W. *Telling True Stories.* New York: Plume, 116–121.

Dunham, S. (2014) *The Editor's Companion: An Indispensable Guide to Editing Books, Magazines, Online Publications, and More.* Blue Ash: F+ W Media, Inc.

Feinmann, J. (2017) "The little yellow box that's made thousands of operations safer," Mosaic [Online]. Available at: https://mosaicscience.com/story/safer-surgery-pulse-oximeter-m ongolia/ (date accessed 20 September 2019).

French, T. (2007) "Sequencing: Text as Line," in: Kramer, M. & Call, W. *Telling True Stories.* New York: Plume, 140–145.

Göpfert, W. (2006) "Reportage, Feature, Magazingeschichte," in: Göpfert, W. (ed.) *Wissenschafts-Journalismus: Ein Handbuch für Ausbildung und Praxis.* Berlin: Ullstein Verlage Gmbh, 104–116.

Gutkind, L. (2012) *You can't make this stuff up: The complete guide to writing creative nonfiction – from memoir to literary journalism and everything in between.* Boston: Da Capo Lifelong Books.

Hart, J. (2011) *Storycraft.* Chicago: Chicago University Press.

Henriques-Gomes, L. (2019) "Ancient Australia was home to 'strange' marsupial giants, scientists find," *The Guardian* [Online]. Available at: https://www.theguardian.com/sci

ence/2019/sep/14/ancient-australia-was-home-to-strange-marsupial-giants-scientists-find (date accessed 18 September 2019).

Hull, A. (2007) "Revising – Over and Over Again," in: Kramer, M. & Call, W. *Telling True Stories*. New York: Plume, 205–208.

Johnson, M. & Gallagher, K. (2010) "Sifting through the DNA haystack," *Milwaukee Journal Sentinel* [Online]. Available at: http://archive.jsonline.com/news/health/112248249.htm l (date accessed 20 September 2019).

Meadows, R. (2015a) "Good Beginnings: How to Write a Lede Your Editor – and Your Readers – Will Love," *The Open Notebook* [Online]. Available at: https://www.theop ennotebook.com/2015/07/14/good-beginnings/ (date accessed 17 September 2019).

Meadows, R. (2015b) "Good Endings: How to Write a Kicker Your Editor – and Your Readers – Will Love," *The Open Notebook* [Online]. Available at: https://www.theop ennotebook.com/2015/11/24/good-endings-how-to-write-a-kicker-your-editor-a nd-your-readers-will-love/ (date accessed 18 September 2019).

Mencher, M. (2011) *News Reporting and Writing*. New York: McGraw Hill.

Murphy, H. (2019) "Why This Scientist Keeps Receiving Packages of Serial Killers' Hair," *The New York Times* [Online]. Available at: https://www.nytimes.com/2019/09/16/sci ence/hair-dna-murder.html (date accessed 17 September 2019).

Nazario, S. (2007) "Transforming One Hundred Notebooks into Thirty-five Thousand Words," in: Kramer, M. & Call, W. *Telling True Stories*. New York: Plume, 208–212.

Nijhuis, M. (2013) "Sculpting the Story," in: Hayden, T. & Nijhuis, M (eds.) *The science writers' handbook: everything you need to know to pitch, publish, and prosper in the digital age*. Boston: Da Capo Press, 75–86.

Pitzer, A. (2011) "Jack Hart on "Storycraft" and narrative nonfiction as an American literary form," Nieman Storyboard [Online]. Available at: https://niemanstoryboard.org/stories/ jack-hart-storycraft-narrative-nonfiction-interview/ (date accessed 20 September 2019).

Plait, P.C. (2008) *Death From the Skies! These are the Ways the World Will End*. New York: Viking Penguin.

Schäfer, M. (2011) "Science journalism and fact checking," *Journal of Science Communication*, vol. 10, no. 4, C02.

Silverman, C. (2015) "Verification Handbook," European Journalism Centre [Online]. Available at: http://verificationhandbook.com/downloads/verification.handbook.pdf (date accessed 19 September 2019).

Smith, D. (2018) "Scientists and Journalists Square Off Over Covering Science and 'Getting it Right'," *Undark* [Online]. Available at: https://undark.org/article/science-journa lism-fact-checking-quotes/ (date accessed 14 October 2019).

The Scientific Method

For to every one who has will more be given, and he will have abundance; but from him who has not, even what he has will be taken away.

(Matthew 13:12)

What you will learn in this chapter:

- Origins
- Essential elements
- Limitations
- Peer review
- Metrics
- How to read a scientific paper
- Scientific method, meet story

It's funny: either you meet people who blindly believe in science, or you meet people who blindly reject it. Both camps are wrong. Science doesn't produce absolute truth, and its methods and quality assessments are sometimes questionable. You could assume that a blueprint exists that determines how scientists formulate hypotheses, design experiments, run those experiments, collect data, apply statistical methods to analyse their data, draw conclusions, confirm or reject their hypotheses and assess the quality of data and significance of their findings. This scientific process would of course also include clear guidelines on how to produce papers, disseminate them and ensure the results are fairly easy to repeat by other scientists. Alone, there exists no such unequivocal process. Science is far from being perfect. Results are often not reproducible. For example, a nature survey of 1,576 scientists showed that more than 70 per cent of the participants were unable to reproduce findings in their respective scientific fields. Most prominently, chemistry, biology and physics papers could not be reproduced. The surveyed scientists named "selective reporting", "pressure to publish" and "low statistical power or poor analysis" as the top reasons for why they couldn't reproduce reported results. While 34 per cent of the respondents claimed their labs had no established procedures to guarantee reproducibility, nearly 90 per cent said "more robust experimental design", "better statistics" and "better mentorship" (Baker 2016).

One of the reasons why reproducibility differs from scientific discipline to discipline: they fundamentally differ in how their scientists formulate hypotheses, design experiments, how they collect data and which statistics methods they apply. Even the exact same words of jargon differ from discipline to discipline, as a scientific method teacher from the Free University of Bozen-Bolzano told me in an interview (Scandellari 2018). A single definition of the scientific method that is valid across all fields does not exist. Or, if one exists, it must be formulated rather vaguely to fit all disciplines. This obviously leaves a lot of leeway for how science in those disciplines is conducted. This is not necessarily a flaw, but rather by design. So in this chapter, we'll take a look at the elements that unite most disciplines and how and when science started wrapping a structured process around its observations, theories and experiments.

I will also expand a bit on the publishing industry, their incredible profit margins and the inherent selection bias and respective pressure to publish in high-profile journals. That's often down to using metrics that are often used by scientific institutions to assess a single paper's quality, while instead being totally unsuitable for that purpose. They're neither precise nor apt for the purpose they're being employed. And Jesus do the scholars game those systems sometimes. In this chapter, we will examine how scientific research is assessed, the reviewers' quality standards and their (that is, the methods') limitations.

An important part of this quality assessment is scientific peer review, a process that is meant to anonymously and independently ensure the quality of research papers before they are published. Peer review is far from being perfect. All of the aforementioned stakeholders (save intentional fabricators) involved in the acquisition of scientific knowledge assume once results are published, they are true. Full stop. This includes science reporters and editors. But that assumption is a shortcoming. Many of your science articles will either revolve around single studies (short news items) or a number of studies that you will cite from. Your audience will take your word for it, because it (rightfully) assumes you double-checked all the caveats. The value at stake here is trust. People will take life decisions based on your advice, no matter whether you write about a novel cancer treatment or an upcoming investment opportunity. Let's face it: under the premise that a paper delivers non-controversial, positive results, as soon as it's published, few people will question it. The newspapers will hail the researchers for their findings and often interview them in an attempt to obtain trivial explanations that further cement their findings. As a science reporter, it's your job to question all of that.

Don't let that depress you. Science is an important, yet sometimes flawed process. That's natural, because everywhere humans are involved, values are at stake. Sometimes these values oppose each other and conflict arises. That's also the very fabric of story. So who could possibly deny that science and story don't match? To make your life a bit easier, I've also included a short section on how to read a scientific paper. This can be really daunting, especially when papers are dozens of pages long. But if you apply a focused approach, you can pinpoint the most important elements for your reporting immediately and then dig deeper whenever you need it. The very final section of this book is my personal plea: let's weave story into the scientific method. And let's encourage scientists and journalists, you, to tell the story of science. It's our best bet against fake news.

Origins

Attempts to observe and understand the natural world are probably as old as humankind. Describing these scientific inquiries using a rigorous methodological process can be traced back to the ancient world. Aristotle was neither the first nor the last philosopher to wrap his mind around what approach could best structure scientific inquiries. The scientific method has been developed across a variety of cultures, eras and disciplines. This includes Aristotle (300 BC), Ibn Sina (1,000 AD) René Descartes (17th century). The latter is often considered the founder of the scientific method (Voit 2019). Over time, all approaches have tried to explain observations in nature, for example by drawing on rationalism, or the two prevalent types of logical reasoning, either inductive inference (generalisation) or deductive reasoning (from premise to conclusion): Plato's dialogues about fellow philosopher Socrates are an example of inductive reasoning, that is developing common truths from specific instances. In contrast, Aristotle's syllogisms showcase his deductive reasoning, which works vice versa: drawing specific conclusions from a general assumption. Here's a simple example: all humans are mortal. Socrates is human, too. Hence, Socrates must be mortal. As if to prove his point, Socrates drank the poison cup and died.

Aristotle liked the idea better that knowledge and truth stems from trusting your eyes (and other sensory organs) and must hence be observable and measurable. While strict empiricism has its quirks (like rejecting the idea that humans have innate ideas), it does emphasise that experiments should help scientists gather evidence. To this day, experiments are one of the cornerstones of the scientific method. The introduction of scientific experiments, along with scientific paradigms and theories in order to observe and describe nature are also the pivot point that turns nature from an unobservable, superstitious and religious world into a measurable and graspable realm. Physicist Frederick Betz pinpoints that revolution to the 1600s, when six scientists contributed "all the component ideas of scientific method came together and operated fully as empirically grounded theory" (Betz 2011:22):

1 A scientific model that could be verified by observation (Copernicus)
2 Precise instrumental observations to verify the model (Brahe)
3 Theoretical analysis of experimental data (Kepler)
4 Scientific laws generalized from experiment (Galileo)
5 Mathematics to quantitatively express theoretical ideas (Descartes and Newton)
6 Theoretical derivation of an experimentally verifiable model (Newton)

On a side note, the term "scientist" did not even exist until polymath William Whewell coined it in 1834. Since then, the scientific method exists in its current hypothetico-deductive form (Voit 2019). In the early 1900s, a group of intellectuals held regular meetings in Vienna ("Wiener Kreis", or Vienna Circle). These philosophers of science called themselves logical positivists and championed the idea that objects and events in science must be observable (still popular) and that scientific theory can only be constructed through inductive inference from experiments (not exactly popular any more). The group had many sympathisers, and among them was the Austro-American philosopher of science Karl Popper. In his groundbreaking 1934 book *The Logic of Scientific Discovery*, he introduced the idea that scientific hypotheses cannot be verified but only falsified. His falsification theory is the basis of the null hypothesis, that is proving the opposite of the initial hypothesis (Wilkinson 2013). Inductive inference as a source for constructing scientific theories is largely rejected, perhaps most notably by Popper. Theories formulated through inductive reasoning are never true with certainty, because you can only run so many experiments:

> No matter how many instances of white swans we may have observed, this does not justify the conclusion that all swans are white.
>
> (Popper 2002:4)

Sure, they may be true with a certain probability, but who guarantees that tomorrow no other scientist shows up with an experiment that contradicts the theory? There is not even consensus on whether a universally valid scientific method exists at all. Initially agreeing with Popper, fellow Viennese science philosopher Paul Feyerabend argued that there is no such thing as objective rationality, so no logical method to conduct science can exist (Gauch 2003:4). In his essay "Against Method", Feyerabend rejects the idea of a method that contains strict and immutable rules for conducting science. He writes that every single epistemological rule has been violated at some time, and for good reason. Indeed, such violations are necessary for scientific progress and presents the Copernican revolution and quantum theory as examples that "occurred only because some thinkers either *decided* not to be bound by certain 'obvious' methodological rules, or because they *unwittingly broke* them" (Feyerabend 1993:14). Consequently, Feyerabend proposes his famous "anything goes" principle that according to him does not inhibit progress. But Feyerabend was not opposed to a scientific method, as his interviewer John Horgan points out in several articles for *Scientific American*. Instead, he feared the abuse of a strict and universal scientific approach that is agenda-driven:

> Scientists are not content with running their own playpens in accordance with what they regard as the rules of scientific method, they want to universalize these rules, they want them to become part of society at large and they use every means at their disposal – argument, propaganda, pressure tactics, intimidation, lobbying – to achieve their aims.
>
> (Feyerabend 1993:163)

While Popper argued in favour of a single scientific method, and while Feyerabend not only adamantly argued against it but outright refused it, Hugh Gauch, reader of scientific method courses at Cornell University, finds the truth must lie somewhere in between in his book *Scientific Method in Practice*, he writes:

> The thesis of this book [...] is that there exist general principles of scientific method that are applicable to all sciences, but excessive specialization often causes scientists to neglect the study of these general principles, even though they undergird science's rationality and greatly influence science's efficiency and productivity.
>
> (Gauch 2003:XV)

Gauch, too, rejects the notion of the scientific method as a fixed sequence of rigid steps that can be automated and repeated across all scientific disciplines. That said, Gauch's book focuses on the general underlying principles (not the specific techniques to conduct science that are uniquely linked to their corresponding fields). Following these general principles allows, despite all criticisms, a definition of basic elements of the scientific method, as the next section will outline.

Essential elements

The scientific method is our current gold standard, a (more or less) structured and systematic approach to acquire new knowledge. In using it, scientists observe, ask questions, formulate hypotheses, run empirical experiments to find out whether these hypotheses are true, make predictions and apply logical reasoning to make conclusions and gather new knowledge. We can boil this complex process down to three essential elements that all scientific conclusions must consider: presuppositions, evidence and logic. Similarly, in his introduction to the scientific method for students, logician Stephen Carey likens the scientific method to a three-step process, consisting of observing, proposing explanations and testing explanations.

Here's an attempt to answer what the scientific method is, and I'm going to start with a rather intuitive definition of what it isn't: it is not a universal recipe according to which all science across all disciplines is carried out. That would be nonsense. The disciplines vary so much alone in terms of experiments. What sort of experiments do they design? Most disciplines don't carry out experiments at all, Scandellari (2018) tells me. How are they designed? A single way of doing every bit of research across all disciplines can't exist, although, as Gauch notes, there are overlaps. That means, if you drew a cross section across all definitions out there, the following list of steps would be sort of a common denominator that contains the following elements (based on my previous book, see Angler 2017):

1 Observe a natural phenomenon
2 Formulate a hypothesis
3 Make predictions using your hypothesis
4 Design and run experiments, and collect empirical data
5 Analyse your data

6   Draw conclusions

7   Communicate your results

This might look like a rigid, numbered structure, but it helps if you see this process more like guidelines and a way to develop a scientific mindset, rather than an immutable and rigid workflow. In fact, many of the steps are cyclically repeated. You can see this repetition in Eberhard Voit's (2019) depiction of the traditional scientific method in Figure A.1.

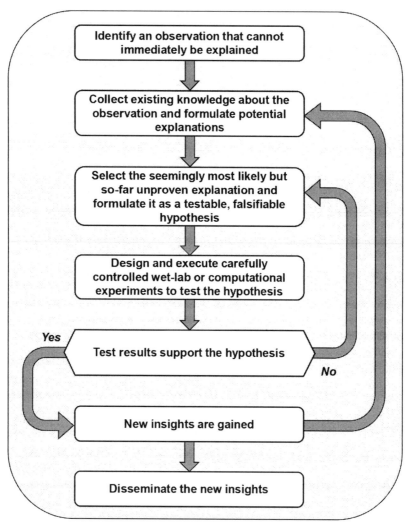

Figure A.1 The traditional scientific method: Hypothesis-based deduction
Source and License: Eberhard O. Voit (Voit 2019). License: CC BY 4.0.

These steps should be generally acceptable by most disciplines. In his book, Gauch draws a Venn diagram that shows the principles of scientific method as the overlapping core of psychology, astronomy, chemistry, geology and microbiology. The iterative nature of the scientific method reflects in its output. That's step seven in the above list, "communication of results", which translates to journal paper publication. Step one is often the creative part that sparks scientists' curiosity and motivates them to invest considerable effort in a specific research project in the first place. This generally leads to specific research questions, the ones you see denoted as "RQ1" through "RQx" in many research project and PhD proposals. Of special interest is step two, formulating the hypothesis, where scientists attempt to find a generalised answer to the initial research questions and hence establish a correlation, or causation, between two or more phenomena they observed. In modern science (especially after Karl Popper), the hypothesis must not only be measurable and testable, it must be falsifiable. That's why, alongside the initial hypothesis, modern research formulates a null hypothesis, which is virtually the negation of the initial hypothesis, hence stating that the phenomena are not connected in any way. The goal of the research itself becomes then to reject the null hypothesis instead of proving the initial hypothesis true (which goes back to Popper's falsification theory). If you think about that for a moment, the approach makes a lot of sense. If your hypothesis is that feeding a specific hormone lets male piglets grow faster than female ones, you cannot possibly test all piglets in the world to prove your theory. But what you can do is disprove the theory that it has no effect (the null hypothesis, that is): in fact, one case seems to philosophically justify rejecting that null hypothesis. But that's just a thought experiment. In actual science, your results have to be statistically significant in order to reject a null hypothesis. Statistically significant means that your data is (in probability speak) unlikely to be under the null hypothesis. The conventional threshold for rejecting a null hypothesis is a p-value lower than 0.05. In recent years, p-values have come under fire, as statistics professor Regina Nuzzo prominently points out in her 2014 *Nature* article. In it, she argues that the p-value nowadays is often used as the sole indicator of sound science and absolute truths, while initially it was intended to be only one piece of the science puzzle (Nuzzo 2014). You can read similar criticism in Wasserstein and Lazar's (2016) paper on p-values, in which they address the dangers of misusing p-values:

> Statistical significance is not equivalent to scientific, human, or economic significance. Smaller p-values do not necessarily imply the presence of larger or more important effects, and larger p-values do not imply a lack of importance or even lack of effect.
>
> (Wasserstein & Lazar 2016:10)

As you can see, just looking for p-values lower than 0.05 in a paper and claiming the results have an important effect is not going to cut it. Instead, if you're unsure about what the results means in terms of significance, importance and effect size, you should take the time and discuss the findings with one of the researchers involved and another, independent researcher. Especially with statistics, whenever

I am in doubt, I ask those who know the most about it: statisticians. The statistical significance (p-value) threshold of 0.05 has a number of problems. If the p-value is higher than said threshold, then that's no proof of the null hypothesis. If the value is higher, you can't discard a possible link or association between two phenomena, like the efficiency of a drug. The statistical significance tells if there is an effect. When you test a drug on two different groups, it will tell you how high the probability is that the observed difference is due to chance. But only when you complement it with the effect size, that's the "by how much" factor whereby you have a complete picture of how well the drug works:

> The effect size is the main finding of a quantitative study. While a P value can inform the reader whether an effect exists, the P value will not reveal the size of the effect. In reporting and interpreting studies, both the substantive significance (effect size) and statistical significance (P value) are essential results to be reported.
>
> (Sullivan & Feinn 2012:279)

When a null hypothesis can't be rejected and the data just doesn't confirm the initial assumptions, it may be necessary to re-formulate and adapt the hypotheses. Interestingly, this whole process is where the scientific method and investigative journalism overlap. You can see that in Gauch's graph of the scientific method (Figure A.1). This is also what investigative journalists do. They formulate hypotheses in the early stages of a project and then, instead of trying to prove them, they find evidence against their hypothesis and try to disprove it (Hunter 2011).

But before p-value and effect size are determined, data must be collected and recorded. In order to do that, scientists design and run experiments. There are quantitative and qualitative research methods, like surveys, focus groups, round tables, case studies, observational trials, narrative inquiry, questionnaires, (unstructured, semi-structured and structured) interviews and many more methods through which they gather and record data. Which method is most suitable depends on the scientific discipline. The handling of the data itself (storage, security, processing) can be complex and depends, among other factors, on its size. The nature of the data (quantitative or qualitative) also determines which analytical methods scientists can use to analyse it and draw deductive conclusions from it. Personal and sensitive data requires special attention in terms of privacy and data security. Before any data is collected, scientists design experiments and draw data samples. Again, the type of experiment depends on the scientific discipline, but comparative experiments are frequent. For example, when testing a new medication, one group of patients (the experimental group) receives medication that contains the actual agent, while another group (the control group), equal in size, receives medication without the agent, a placebo. After running the experiment, the agent's effect in one group is compared against the effect in the other. The hypothesis of such studies usually assumes that the expected effect of the medication containing the agent is bigger than the one without. In the latter case, it is almost never zero, due to the placebo effect. If the study participants don't know which group they belong to, the experiment is called a blinded experiment. If on top of that neither the scientists know which subjects receive the agent and which one the placebo, the study is called a double-blinded experiment, currently the gold standard in medical research. This is supposed to eliminate bias and lower the placebo effect. But bias can also occur when scientists draw their samples. Since they can't test entire populations (for example, "all of humankind"), they need to draw a finite sample that represents the entire population. If, in order to represent all of humanity, scientists chose only 100 male white Germans, that would not be a representative sample, as it does not reflect the world's diversity. Representative samples mirror the population in the distribution of the examined variables.

All steps of the scientific method, from posing the research questions to the formulation of the hypothesis, to the experiment design to drawing samples, and all the way through to communicating the results, serve one purpose: the reproducibility of the findings. But, as Baker (2016) has shown, many scientific studies' results are not reproducible. Sometimes even the original researchers themselves are unable to reproduce their findings. Most prominently, the social sciences are affected. Hence, an additional question we as science writers should think of asking is: if you had to reproduce your own results right now, would you be able to? Have you tried it? If so, how many times? We should also and especially ask independent researchers those same questions. While it is clear that nobody could reproduce the results in the course of an interview, if the study contains evident methodological errors, or if it fails to include the necessary data to verify, they would be able to give you an initial indication of whether the study might be generally reproducible or not. As medical researcher Stefan Schmidt notes in his 2009 paper, replication is indeed at the core of all empirical science and of utmost importance. Only if the steps and results of research are repeatable (Schmidt draws on science philosopher Karl Popper's seminal work *The Logic of Scientific Discovery*) can we assume that the findings can become common knowledge and distinguish them from coincidental events. Paradoxically, and this view is widely acknowledged, Schmidt claims there is little literature about replication in science. In his paper, he focuses on how the social sciences deal with replication and promptly finds that replication studies are essentially non-existent in that area. The closest type of study that he could find in the social studies are follow-up studies (Schmidt 2009). But why does nobody publish replication studies in the social sciences? Schmidt finds a culprit: only new findings are acknowledged and credited, so there is very little incentive to produce such studies, because there is no reputation to be earned, and "anything that reduces the chances of getting published will be avoided" (Schmidt 2009:95). This is not the only problem associated with academic publishing. Schmidt also cites a survey among 79 social sciences journal editors that found 94 per cent of respondents would not encourage the submission of replication studies to their journals. Many scientists simply have to keep publishing (after all, it's still "publish or perish"!) and will not want to risk putting in the time to write replication studies but then not getting published because their papers are unwanted by journal editors. It's not hard to see why this sort of publication pressure and bias is a disservice to science and society.

The publication of results is usually considered the final step in the acquisition of scientific knowledge. This usually includes conference presentations, conference proceedings and the obligatory journal papers. But this isn't where scientific dissemination should stop. In fact, I would encourage scientists to actively do additional outreach, like writing blog posts and engaging on social media. While still frowned upon by many scientists and not recognised by their superiors, true public outreach (i.e. not just for scientific peers) does have an increasing societal impact of studies. The main problem is that the public dissemination is often not integrated into the actual scientific process, hence from a "business" perspective scientists lack the support (in a word: the time) their superiors should grant them so they can plan for this sort of activity. If (and that's a big if) you manage to put in the time: what's in it for you as a scientist? The answer is societal impact, which is increasingly measured by many journals in the form of so-called Altmetrics, that is metrics that consider how many times your study was picked up by the media, social media and blogs. You'll find a bit more about Altmetrics in a later section of this chapter. But first, let's have a look at some of the scientific method's known limitations.

Limitations

Nobody can claim or expect that science is a perfect process that's always correct and sells absolute truths. But it should produce reliable and reproducible results. Science has certain standards, some of which are the best currently available; but some of these standards need improvements. If the scientific method is our state-of-the-art method for acquiring new knowledge, how can it be that our verified body of knowledge is so often not reproducible? How and why can we base our life decisions on such weak evidence?

We have already seen that the scientific method is not perfect, but there are more limitations that are inherent to the way scientific research is carried out. For example, as Gauch argues, science cannot possibly gather all the knowledge about every object in the physical world. Even if all the world focused on knowing everything about an object as simple as a pebble, that would be impossible. In fact, every resolved scientific question raises ten more new questions. Such an increase in precise and productive questions, however, is not a shortcoming but possibly the clearest evidence that we are making scientific progress (Gauch 2003).

Second, and this is where Gauch brings the scientific endeavour full circle, is the fact that research needs specific ethical guidelines. What Gauch means is that the scientific priorities must reflect the goals of society, which in turn enables and finances science (for example, through taxes). In turn, the funded science projects reflect what society considers as good (Gauch 2003). If this is true, then it becomes all the more evident that the aforementioned dissemination part of the scientific method must be expanded in a way that society gets repaid and its investment amortised. Why should the societal benefit only be implicit? The general public should not only benefit from science's findings but also have a right to be educated about what the science it funds means, about its limitations and misconceptions. After all, science is part of an enabling circle that, as Gauch correctly states, is not just funded by the public, but the general public also elects the political representatives that set the course for supporting and fostering science. While it is true that this task is in part covered by the media, the media can't cover all the research nor are they as close to the lab benches as the actual researchers are.

Gauch also addresses presuppositions as one of science's limitations. He points out that on the one hand, science's presuppositions must be true in order to exist at all. On the other hand, science is unable to prove its presuppositions. "Consequently, a striking limitation of science is that it cannot provide its own foundation. Science is based on non-science" (Gauch 2003:369). We cannot possibly know why nature exists in the first place and fully explain its how and why, even if we (and at that point, we should) employ other disciplines like religion, philosophy and worldview (although science cannot explain worldview issues like the question of whether god exists or not). Drawing on Edward Caldin, Gauch writes that the "method of science is an imperfect means of investigating matters that lie outside of its scope, and leads to false conclusions if the attempt is made to apply it to them; so that its limitations ought to be explained as carefully as its merits" (Caldin 1949:172, 130 in Gauch 2003:370).

Personal rewards are another limitation inherent in the scientific method. Sometimes, science is self-serving, benefitting predominantly those who conduct it. One such reward is status, in the form of perceived rationality and wisdom; another one is the cultivation of discipline, character, realism and humility. This could lead to blind faith in science as the panacea for every problem (Gauch 2003). That said, reality is showing that the effects of science are not as romantically beneficial as often portrayed. Agendas and interests are at stake. The current publication system with its often wrongly applied metrics, outdated academic quality assessment and a precarious academic career system fosters the rise of narcissistic scientists, mental illnesses (for example, in those who work for the narcissists) and scientific misconduct. No other (legal) system has higher profit margins than the scholarly publishing industry. Its profit margins approach 40 per cent routinely. Elsevier alone claims to produce 25 per cent of all scientific papers in the world, earning £900 million in 2018 (Guardian 2019). Libraries spend millions to enable their researchers to access scientific knowledge. Researchers have to pay high fees in order to consult single articles if their institution doesn't have that specific subscription. In turn, they don't get paid for writing articles. They don't get paid to do peer reviews. This is, in all honesty, a ridiculous system of publication capitalism and pure exploitation. Nowhere else in the publishing industry do you have to pay serious publishers.

What's more, it's really hard to climb the academic career ladder. Compared to the general population, graduate students are six times as likely to experience depression and anxiety. In a 2014 report, 43 to 46 per cent of graduate students of the University of Berkeley were found to be depressive. One of the reasons might be the academic work-life balance, which typically involves long working hours, but also the relationship between the principal investigator (PI) and the trainees turns out to be of significant influence (Evans *et al.* 2018). In informal talks with PhD students and early career researchers, I found that most don't mind putting in many unpaid overtime hours. I know some who spent holidays and their vacation time to finish academic work that doesn't fit into their regular schedule (which is already going overtime). Those who did told me they liked doing that. Cases of cognitive dissonance? Possibly. In any case, I will claim that this phenomenon is due to bad management practices and again, exploitation. If you don't get paid for half or even a quarter of the time you put into, it's a bad deal. After all, science or not, getting paid for work is business. A survey among 4,000 university employees at three Norwegian universities has shown that academic staff suffer more from workaholism and related work-family conflict. The survey authors also argue that recent changes in academic governance and management are changing the environment for the worse (Torp, Lysfjord & Midje 2018). Gemma Ahearne, lecturer at the University of Liverpool, has written about her own experience with workaholism. When her husband, also an academic, woke up from a three-week coma in the ICU, he worried more about his work than about his health.

> Yet in academia, workaholism is rife. It is normalised and dare I say it revered. If you loved your work enough you would answer emails whilst on annual leave/ at a funeral/ on maternity leave/ sick in hospital. You love your work, so why not do it 7 days a week?
>
> (Ahearne 2017)

Ahearne writes about her previous point of view, where she would work endless overtime hours and immediately return to her desk after undergoing an operation. Her attitude has changed since. She now works 40 hours a week (at peak times more, but that's not the rule), and she sees spending time for oneself and with the family as a basic right that keeps one healthy, not a privilege (Ahearne 2017). A group of occupational health researchers has conducted a survey among 410 academics in order to find out how prevalent workaholism is among Irish academics and what that means in terms of work-life fit (does the work schedule fit with the home schedule?), work-life conflict, psychological well-being and other factors. Half of the respondents were either workaholics or enthusiastic workaholics. Unsurprisingly, the workaholics experienced lower job satisfaction and a lower work-life fit (Hogan, Hogan & Hodgins 2016).

When academics work long hours, work-life conflict is more likely to occur, and Irish academics show the longest working hours across Europe (with a median of 47 hours per week, compared to US academics with 55 hours per week). British academics regarded their workload as unmanageable. The reason why they work longer hours is that they have too much to do in too little time. The effects, including psychological strain, were higher in men (Hogan *et al.* 2014).

Does it stop here? Of course not. The metrics, science's assessment system with its "incentives", fosters a culture of scientists who chase accolades, instead of focusing on providing societal benefits, as one anonymous academic describes in a 2018 article for *The Guardian*. She states that instead of providing meaningful work, she has seen scholarly articles that were artificially inflated to make it into prestigious journals. She has even peer-reviewed such articles herself. "This ultimately leads to showboat science that under-investigates less eye-catching – but ultimately more useful – areas" (Anonymous 2018). She concludes her statement with the following paragraph:

> I worry that the KPI-driven impact culture increasingly means that careful, meticulous and incremental science is anathema in the academy, especially for those at the early stages of their careers. There are many who are so attracted by the prospect of success that they are willing to obfuscate, mystify and perhaps falsify research to game the system and reap the plentiful rewards.
>
> (Anonymous 2018)

(Note: Key Performance Indicators (KPIs) are performance measurements, or measurable goals. For example, a research institute head might demand that its scientific collaborators produce two scholarly publications per year, plus two blog posts. "Number of publications per year" might then be the name of one of the KPIs. At the end of the year, the institute could then easily evaluate whether its collaborators met their goals or not.) Another limit of the scientific method is that it's carried out by humans. This includes misconduct, fabrication but also psychological traits like (non-pathological) narcissism. In fact, this trait is fostered by the current way that academia assesses research quality. If you think all scientists are altruistic with just societal benefits in mind, then you're wrong. They're not. In fact, some of them only care about themselves, their academic profile and career. Swiss biology professor Bruno Lemaitre claims: "Power struggles and ego battles are, for instance, quite prevalent in the academic world, notably in our so-called elite institutions" (Lemaitre 2017:875). He also identifies two factors that contribute to the development of narcissism in science: the high demand for attention for status, which often manifests as a quest for visibility, and the influence narcissistic people have on their research environments. Up to a certain degree, that hunger for visibility in order to climb the social ladder is understandable and a behaviour that we share with many other animal species. Status is a thing in every social system (that's why Tom Wolfe's status-observing technique is so exciting in science). Scientists seek attention through the publication of papers, Lemaitre further claims, and they prefer top-tier journals to low-ranked journals for doing so. He also argues that scientists not only actively seek to influence their social status by travelling and networking but are also transformed by achieving a higher social status among their peers. In fact, early peer recognition apparently contributes to the development of dominant personalities as opposed to scientists who receive little recognition from the outset and hence rather exhibit subordinate personality traits. This, in turn, means that established scientists might prevent emerging, potentially creative scientists from building their careers. Consequently, "the passing of a 'famous professor' is often positive for the field since it allows the emergence of new alternative leaders" (Lemaitre

2017:876). In science, like in the military, apparently visibility is more important to climb the career ladder. Ironically, the exaggerated self-confidence of narcissistic individuals is often mistaken for competence:

> We all know that certain scientists (usually lower in self-esteem) will need to work hard to impress in a public presentation while others (usually high in self-esteem) will bluff us with just two pieces of preliminary data.
>
> (Lemaitre 2017:877)

I have been teaching science blogging, social media and science storytelling workshops for the past couple of years at a European research institution. The participants were almost exclusively scientists. What has informally emerged as the primary motivation for a considerable number of the participants is that they want to gain more visibility online. Yes, some researchers have idealistic goals like educating the public about their scientific disciplines, project progress. But some higher-ranking scientists in leading roles simply put "visibility" as their primary goal they want to achieve. This is worrying, to say the least, and it makes me question whether I should be supporting this sort of behaviour and give them the tools to do it or whether I myself am part of this malfunctioning system.

And we haven't talked about scientific misconduct and fraud yet. Assuming that scientists always act ethically and in a morally correct way is just nonsense. Especially when careers are at stake and a publishing system in the background that actually pressurises them to publish as often as possible in high-profile journals is a factor that can cajole scientists into fabricating data. It's a quest for fame, and some people would do anything and everything for social recognition. Sometimes, this quest is fatal. For example, the case of the Italian surgeon Paolo Macchiarini, who, at the time, worked at the Swedish Karolinska Institute. He had transplanted bioengineered windpipes, but despite claiming the operations successful, almost all of his patients died. Investigations started, and Macchiarini was found guilty of scientific misconduct, including data fabrication. Six of his papers were retracted – they had been published in high-profile science journals like *Nature Communications* and *The Lancet*. This shows not just some rockstar scientist's thirst for power, it also exposes that the control mechanisms (like peer review) that should assess scientific advances and guarantee high-quality papers are sometimes deeply mistaken.

Peer review

Writing science news reports is pretty simple. Here's an easy recipe. Find a peer-reviewed article in a good or high profile journal. Find two interviewees, one involved in the study, the other independent. Write the piece using the inverted pyramid and weave in the interviews as supporting quotes. Done. I bet nobody will question the validity of the study's findings prior to its publication. Nor the methodologies. Nor whether the study came from a predatory journal that just claims to offer some sort of peer review. Peer review is a quality label. It's the magic word. It means: good. It means: trust me. In its ideal, innocent form, peer review is an anonymous assessment of a study's quality (including the quality of the sample, the methodologies and so on), done by independent reviewers who have no conflicts of interest. It's actually the best method we have to assess scientific validity. But it's not without flaws. Paleontologist Jon Tennant and journalist Paul D. Thacker published an article in the *Washington Post* to address these issues. Let's start with gender bias. Women are underrepresented as peer reviewers, and scientific journal editors prefer choosing their own kind because of a principle called "inbreeding homophily", a natural tendency to choose those who have similar traits to you. And not everything that goes through peer review has been thoroughly tested. "Peer reviewers often fail to detect bad research, conflicts of interest and corporate ghostwriting" (Thacker & Tennant 2019). I mean, if it was, there would be no retractions, right? Instead, there are lots of retractions. Not all of them because of scientific misconduct, but fake peer review is one of the larger issues (Brainard & You 2018). Fake peer review is when a scientist forwards an email addresses to the journal that she controls. It's essentially self-peer review. Computer science professor Chen-Yuan Chen had set up a fake peer-review ring that included fake and real scientists' identities that he had assumed. In at least one case, he reviewed his own publication. *Sage Publications* then retracted 60 of his publications they suspected Chen had at least partially reviewed himself. In a comment on the case for the *New York Times*, biologist Michael B. Eisen said that this sort of misconduct is unsurprising and fostered when academia offers promotions based on the number of publications (Fountain 2014). Some research institutions also promote their researchers based on authorship and where in the authors' list they appear. Women again score lower as first authors in medical journals. Kin co-authorship is an issue, for example, when spouses publish together. This gets even more bizarre. In Korea, authors add their middle- and high-school kids as inappropriate co-authors. And believe it or not, there is a black market for authorship. You can pay to get a publication under your belt without actually contributing anything to it (Rivera 2018). Speaking of contributions, here's a bummer:

> In fact, an analysis of 12,772 articles with 2 to 14 authors published in PLoS ONE during 2007–2011 by 79,776 researchers disclosed a 47.66% rate of undeserved authorship.
>
> (Rivera 2018)

That's almost half of them. And part of why this is happening is journal regulations. The authors admitted allowing themselves to be put on the author list just for the sake of fulfilling journals' submission requirements. It's perhaps important to address what "contribution" means. Here's a clear distinction from researchers working in the medical sciences:

> An author is considered someone who has made an "intellectual contribution" to the work. Intellectual contributions include things like determining questions to investigate and deciding the main ways to do this, planning

experiments, writing code, interpreting data, performing analyses, and so on. However, not all contributions are intellectual contributions, e.g., copy editing or providing samples and data that have already been used for a publication or where acquisition did not involve any input or understanding of the research project.

(Zauner *et al.* 2018)

Again, biased authorship is down to questionable incentives. While gift authorship and the pharma's influence in terms of ghost authorship is a known phenomenon, so-called paper mills have appeared over recent years. In China, companies have been exposed that produce ghostwritten papers. The aim is to position them in top journals, because authorship of papers in journals in the Science Citation Index is worth a lot of money: Chinese funders will reward publications in top journals with up to $165,000. In turn, the production of such a paper "merely" costs $10,000 (Zauner *et al.* 2018). So how could this be fixed? The researcher's proposal: the incentive system must be changed, and at the same time, co-authorship should be changed into contributorship.

Conflicts of interests can occur at every level. Thacker and Tennant point out the journal *Energy & Environment*, which had published climate skeptics' contributions. The journal has a peer review process. Editors choose the peer reviewers during the process. *Energy & Environment*'s editor-in-chief is a climate change skeptic and encourages the submission of skeptic material (Thacker & Tennant 2019). It's not hard to believe that industries and interest groups that fund research can and will have an influence on it. For example, take the Sugar Research Foundation who secretly funded research looking into health issues that are linked to sugar, and then hid undesirable outcomes (Kearns, Apollonio & Glantz 2017).

The criticism doesn't end here. Richard Smith, former *British Medical Journal* editor-in-chief, points out that there are a number of what he coins "defects" of the peer review process. He also writes that the mechanisms journals use to review papers can be hazy and likens them to a black box, in whose muddy inner clockwork there may be big gains and big losses alike. This is the list of defects the former editor addresses:

- **Slow and expensive**: from submission to publication, it takes a year or more. Since journals do not pay their peer reviewers, the actual cost of peer review is hard to estimate. But accessing a paper costs the community about $5,000.
- **Inconsistent:** reviews are subjective. Different reviewers may arrive at very different assessments of the same paper. Smith cites an example where reviewer A gauged the same paper to contain "a large number of deficits", while reviewer B found the same paper to be "written in a clear style".
- **Biased**: there is strong evidence that women are discriminated against in the process of awarding grants. Moreover, Smith cites a study that found journal editors to be biased against submitted papers from authors working at

seemingly insignificant institutions. Incidentally, the authors of said study also found that when re-submitting the same papers (with only minor changes), in most of the cases the reviewers did not find that the papers had been already published. Smith himself admits to almost have turned down a paper by Karl Popper but eventually was cajoled into publishing it because of his big name.

- **Abusive**: reviewers could steal ideas or purposely reject papers in order to block out competitors from publishing work in the same field. As Smith points out, this has already happened, citing a case from the *New England Journal of Medicine*.

As for that last part, the *New England Journal of Medicine* case is not the only one. When endocrinologist Michael Dansinger's paper was turned down by *Annals of Internal Medicine*'s peer review, he was unsuspecting. When his paper appeared six months later under the name of one of the peer reviewers, that changed. The journal never disclosed the identity of the plagiarist. But Dansinger later published a letter addressing the plagiariser (Dansinger 2017). I have personally talked to one doctor who has suffered a very similar case in which a journal editor was involved.

The problem with all these problems is not only that they exist. Media reports mask and veil all their flaws. Once a media report on a paper is published, boiling down (some would say: dumbing down) its takeaways and encapsulating them in graspable, relatable headlines, these claims become common truths. Readers assume (and rightfully so), that some quality checks carried out by journalists and/or fact-checkers should have occurred that assess the paper's methodologies and conclusions. They would assume (if they knew what to look for and what that means) that the findings are statistically significant and have a relevant effect size, that the results are reproducible, that the scientists were honest, that no vested interests were at stake and that the journal has independently proof-read the results and ensured that all claims are bulletproof. Alas, that is not what reality looks like.

Metrics

Peer review may not be perfect (actually, it's far from it), but some ideas to improve it are underway. One attempt is open peer review, which has been around for a while now. It generally means reviewers know whose paper they are reviewing, and also the author knows who has reviewed his paper. But open peer review can take many forms, depending on how a journal implements it. Some disclose the reviewers, other publish entire peer review reports. A whopping 122 different definitions for open peer review exist. They can be boiled down to a core of seven definitions (Tennant 2018):

1 **Open identities**, where authors and reviewers are reciprocally identified
2 **Open reports**, where the review reports themselves are published

3　**Open participation**, where the wider community can contribute to the process
4　**Open interaction**, where review takes the form of a discussion
5　**Open pre-review manuscripts**, where manuscripts are available prior to any formal review process
6　**Open final-version commenting**, where the final published manuscript can be reviewed further
7　**Open platforms**, where reviews are facilitated by a service external to the journal itself

　　Some of the advantages seem clear: reviewers have to be more respectful when their identity is disclosed. Constructive criticism is more likely to occur under these circumstances. It would also be easier to reveal reviewers with conflicts of interest that just block publication of a manuscript, at least not without fearing backlash. What's more, if journals published the reviewers' names in their papers' footnotes, that might be an incentive for the reviewers to work thoroughly. When bad papers get published, both authors and reviewers may be responsible (DeCoursey 2006). But not all peer reviewers appreciate open peer review, and some fear the aforementioned repercussions in case of unfavourable reviews. It's totally happening that the tables are turned, and today's reviewers become tomorrow's reviewed scientists and vice versa. The real-life effects of open peer review are not fully clear yet.

　　We also need to talk about what quality in science means. Do you remember when we discussed recording status symbols as a journalistic practice? We're right in the middle of science's status symbols. One of the highest and most controversial is a journal's "Impact Factor" (IF). The impact factor was established by chemist Eugene Garfield in the 1960s, when he founded the Institute for Scientific Information (ISI), which created the Science Citation Index (SCI). Citation indices show how and how often publications cite each other (there are more indices than the SCI, for example, the Social Sciences Citation Index SSCI). Ownership for these indices went to Thomson Reuters and eventually to Clarivate Analytics. Online databases like "Web of Science" and "Scopus" provide access to these citation indices. But back to the IF. The IF is calculated based on the number of citations. To be exact, a journal's IF is the ratio of the preceding two years' citations to the number of publications. For example, to calculate a journal's 2018 impact factor, you calculate the sum of its citations in 2017 and 2016, and then you divide it by the sum of its publications in 2017 and 2016. This means: the higher the number of citations in relation to its publication is higher and hence better the IF. In other words, the IF is the average number of citations each publication gets. The IF is used to compare journals in the same index (it doesn't make much sense to compare the ranking between an SCI-indexed and an SSCI-indexed journal). In the "Journal of Citations Reports", an annual report released by Clarivate Analytics, you can see the journal ranking. It's integrated in the Web of Science. Other online tools to find and compare journals' IF are "Eigenfactor" and "SCImago Journal and Country Rank". There are many methodological caveats with the IF. The citable articles make a difference. What is the material that counts as citable? That depends on who calculates it. That's also the reason why IFs differ from Google Scholar to Web of Science to Scopus. It's obvious that the fewer citable items you consider, the higher the IF grows (PloS Medicine Editors 2006). Also, since the citable items do not distinguished between types of articles, the IF is influenced by that factor, too. For example, review articles tend to get more citations than others. Also, there's a language bias. All the top-ranking journals (in terms of IF) are English-speaking journals. This phenomenon apparently feeds back into science itself, introducing bias. For example, regional and local research outside English-speaking countries, and publishing in languages other than English is at a disadvantage. The SCI, for example, is also not exhaustive, since it covers a mere quarter of the world's peer-reviewed publications. Add to that the fact that the majority of highly cited papers get published in very few but highly renowned journals, and the bias should become evident. Here's a list of other biases connected to the IF (Dong, Loh & Mondry 2005):

- Coverage and language preference of the SCI database
- Procedures used to collect citations at the ISI
- Algorithm used to calculate the IF
- Citation distribution of journals
- Online availability of publications
- Citations to invalid articles
- Negative citations
- Preference of journal publishers for articles of a certain type
- Publication lag
- Citing behavior across subjects
- Possibility of exertion of influence from journal editors

But where it really gets bad is when the IF is misused as an indicator of quality that in reality it isn't. For example, it can't assess the quality of a single paper (Dong, Loh & Mondry 2005). The IF lumps all articles into the same quality drawer. That makes it impossible and impractical to derive the quality of a single article or author from the IF (PloS Medicine Editors 2006, Dong, Loh & Mondry 2005, Caon 2017, Larivière & Gingras 2010). The higher a journal's reputation the more people will cite your work. So, publishing in glossy high-impact journals like *Science* or *Nature* automatically increases the likelihood of being cited, at least according to sociologist Robert K. Merton who coined the term "Matthew effect" after the Gospel of Matthew (see the beginning of this appendix).

Another factor that influences the IF are scientists' self-citations (Dong, Loh & Mondry 2005). Let's see why. Academic careers are story material, with protagonists, complications and resolutions. When research institutions start using quantitative measures like the IF to decide on scientists' careers, then they manipulate an important story factor. They raise the stakes. If climbing the academic ladder depends on the IF of the journals she publishes in, then this system will invite her to game her IF a little bit. It's absurd that research institutions decide on promotions, tenure and recruitment using the IF. It just doesn't deliver that kind of individual information. Instead, it's become a status symbol, a measure of prestige, by which careers are made or broken. In an analysis of more than 800 review, promotion and tenure documents, researchers found that 87 per cent of the institutions that mention the IF are supportive of it. Only 13 per cent are cautious about it in their tenure processes. No institution criticise it or prohibit its use. More than 60 per cent associate the IF with quality. Around 40 per cent of the sample associate it with impact, importance or significance; 20 per cent associate it with prestige, status or reputation (McKiernan, Alperin & Fleerackers 2019). Other universities or research institutions even use the IF in their recruitment processes and to determine researchers' salaries. It's easy to see that such systems invite gaming. One well-known way to do that are self-citations and citation rings. That's groups and small networks of researchers that cite each other, as well as individual researchers frequently citing their own work. Science communication scholar Phil Davis, who specialises in citations, points out that there are indeed citation cartels (although Thomson Reuters refuses to call them like that because the term implies intent).

Other metrics, like the h-index (Hirsch index, after the physicist who introduced) it, are author-based but gameable nonetheless. Why? Because they're still based on the number of citations. It's obvious that once the stakes are known, as well as the flaws in the assessment systems, fraudsters show up. Predatory journals increasingly approach scientists, and those who are gullible enough or simply look out for more citations, no matter where, fall into their traps. We could go on and on about the problems with how science is currently assessed. Two patterns emerge. First, quantitative, incentivised measures invite gaming. That's not a new phenomenon. But as long as the most important players acknowledge those outdated assessment methods as "gold standards", change will be difficult. Second, change is possible, but it can only occur gradually. The biggest shortcoming of the current science quality measure systems that are in place is that they cater to a self-adulating and self-congratulating science bubble that leaves out the general public. But alternative metrics are on the rise. Providers like Altmetric.com and Plum Analytics scour the web for the DOIs of research artefacts that include material beyond the traditionally cited scholarly work (like presentations and images) and assign a (again quantitative, so equally gamable) score based on how often said artefacts are mentioned in online newspapers, magazines, on the social media etc. The difference is not that Altmetrics are flawless (they're not), but that they provide a potential pathway that goes beyond academia and extends to the public. They're not exactly a one-to-one mapping of how much of science reaches the public, but it's far closer than traditional metrics. Just like open peer review can't overcome all of peer review's shortcomings, Altmetrics are also not a silver bullet against the IF's flaws. But that's not the point. They're gradual improvements, and things are moving forward. What some institutions (around 1,500, to date) and individual researchers (around 15,000, to date) now do is sign the San Francisco Declaration on Research Assessment (SF DORA). In doing so, they vow to abolish the IF and instead base their hiring and tenure decisions on individual assessment, ideally introducing internal peer reviews that look at scientists' work also from a qualitative perspective.

How to read a scientific paper

It's astonishing how many storytelling elements you can find in academic papers, if you just look for the right elements. Let's have a look at the essential elements of a scientific paper. Their naming and position differs from discipline to discipline, and depending on that, some are omitted and others added. But the following list nonetheless contains the most prominent sections:

- Title
- Authors' list
- Abstract
- **Introduction**
- **Methods**
- **Results**
- **Discussions**
- Acknowledgments
- Disclosure statement for conflicts of interest (funding etc.)
- References

The sections highlighted in bold are journal articles' substantial quintessence. We've already seen those sections previously: it's the familiar **IMRAD** (**I**ntroduction, **M**ethods, **R**esults **a**nd **D**iscussion) structure, which typically follows an hourglass shape and is symmetrical from top to bottom. Introduction and discussion get equal weight and breadth, while the central section, which consists of methods and results, is usually less broad and gets less weight. Every section fulfills a different purpose:

- **Introduction**: research questions and researchers' hypotheses, as well as the motivation of why the researchers conducted the research. It's this research story's setup.
- **Methods**: samples, data, study and experiment design: this section answers the question how the study was conducted, what tools the researchers used. It's usually complex, so asking an expert from the field is advisable.
- **Results**: answers to the research questions and either confirmation or rejection of the hypotheses. Here the researchers pay off the setup.
- **Discussion**: how and where do the findings fit into the existing body of knowledge? What are the findings' implications?
- **Abstract**: a brief summary of the paper that contains a condensed version of the previous sections. Abstracts usually run no longer than 300 words.

When you read papers, you should employ each section specifically to fulfil a purpose. What most scholars recommend is to not read papers in a linear fashion. Instead, you should skim title, keywords and abstract to determine if the papers is relevant at all. This is a low-effort/high-value approach that requires only a small amount of time. There is no need to linearly read a scientific paper from start to finish, as they don't follow any story logic. Unlike a good story, academic papers start their introductions with lots of material on background, why the study was conducted, how the field evolved over recent years and what the challenges and non-challenges are. Lots of this information is, although historically and scientifically correct, alas not relevant in terms of theme and story structure. You will often just exclude that. With one exception, as scientific method teacher Francesca Scandellari of the Free University of Bozen-Bolzano told me during an interview: When she reads an academic paper, her first section of interest is always the final paragraph of the introduction, as that part most often highlights the researchers' explanation of why they put in the time to study that specific problem. She is not alone: in a guide on how to read scientific literature, author Elisabeth Pain interviewed a dozen scholars on how they read scientific literature. Several respondents replied they read the introduction to understand the research question and the researcher's motivation. If they want to delve deeply into a paper and assess the scientific rigor, they put more focus on reading the sections on methodology and results (which requires a considerable higher amount of time). Some interviewees responded they first take a good look at the main figures and try to interpret them in order to grasp the paper's gist (Pain 2016). A somewhat opportunistic skimming approach is also what Natalia Rodriguez recommends in an infographic for *Elsevier*. She outlines four steps, skimming, re-reading, interpreting and summarizing in order to understand the paper (Rodriguez 2015). As a journalist, your purpose is usually not to determine whether a paper is scientifically relevant to your work, but to answer the journalistic questions, the five Ws and one H. That means you should not completely skip any of the sections but use a focused approach to dig up the answers to the journalistic questions. "Work smarter, not longer", a friend told me. For short news reports, you will always have to find the research question, the motivation, the results, implications for the public and also an explanation of how the studies were conducted, including a description of the experiments. In the Methods section, you will also find the limitations of the experiment design, which will narrow down the scope and validity of the study. When interpreting a paper, be very careful to not transcend the objective description of what is written in the study. Don't ever think about implying or suggesting that a treatment that worked in mice could work in humans when it doesn't. So what about the abstract? The abstract rarely gives you what you need to understand the story's relevance and answer any of the journalistic questions. The abstract is good for indexing articles, but not for writing stories about them.

This is also what Craig Cormick, the president of the Australian Science Communicators, recommends: first, start with the "Introduction", not the abstract. Once you've got the picture, skip the other sections and go directly to the Discussion or Conclusion sections. You'll find the paper's findings here. Next, if you need more information, go to the Results section, which is "often cluttered with graphs full of error bars and statistics" (Cormick 2018). Cormick lists error bars (a measure of uncertainty), confidence intervals (a range of values with a particular certainty, usually 95 per cent, to contain your real values) and N (sample size) as typical elements of the Results section. I would definitely add that you should look at both the statistical significance and the effect size in order to determine the validity of the results. Also, don't miss the Limitations section (sometimes, it's not an actual section but a mere subsection of Results). They often contain important caveats that substantially relativise your statements in terms of clarity. Where I absolutely don't agree with Cormick is that looking at the IF as "they are assumed to be proxies for journal integrity. The higher the number, the better the publication." No. Just no. On the other hand, his tip to check for self-citations in the References section is fantastic advice.

A final remark: if you are an investigative science journalist (actually, even if you're not!), you should also closely look at the disclosure of conflicts of interest and funding schemes the researchers. You'll often find this kind of information at the very end of the paper. Even more interesting, if you can't find such a statement, it is often worth specifically inquiring about any such affiliations and/or conflicts of interest. The first papers you read will be painful, and this section is a mere starting point. Don't get daunted by their dozens of pages. If you have a quick turnaround story, you simply don't have the time to thoroughly read all the sections. But if you take a focused approach, starting from simple to complex, you'll get a good idea.

Scientific method, meet story

While the scientific method and its output, journal papers and conference proceedings and their formats are widely accepted for disseminating science among peers, it is by no means the best format to convey information to a broad audience. Scientific peers accept the standards, because, you know, it is established and all. It's a working system, true, but it only works within the science bubble. As soon as you leave that bubble and turn towards the general public, the status symbols don't count anymore, and the way you convey information in academia is invalid in the real world. Why is it so hard to convey science to the public? Certainly not because scientific experts need to fill in reluctant people's knowledge gaps. It's no wonder that this attitude is being perceived as arrogant, and that usually has the opposite effect. Most people don't want to be explained stuff. All of them want to be entertained. Even scientific experts struggle to decipher studies. The hard truth is: the scientific method currently ends with Dissemination. But dissemination currently just means submitting a paper to a journal, surviving peer review and then getting it published (and obviously hoping for lots of citations). That's where dissemination most often ends. Yes, sometimes, conference proceedings and presentations (and cluttered posters!) get thrown in, but those rarely leave the academic bubble. Scientist-turned-storyteller Randy Olson is a bit rough in his assessment of the current situation:

> Science is a profession that is permeated with narrative structure and process, yet scientists are so blind to the importance of narrative that they don't even make use of this established label.

> (Olson 2015:8)

I don't think it's too bad. On the contrary, it's really good to see that the outreach seems to be gradually changing. YouTuber-scientists reach out to the real world and boil down complex science for lay audiences, like evolutionary biologist and science communicator Valentine Delattre of *Sciences et Avenir* (who also runs the YouTube channel "Science de comptoir"), and mathematician Tom Crawford from Oxford University who is otherwise known as "The Naked Mathematician", both of whom I got to know at the World Conference of Science Journalists in 2019. More outreach is happening. Scientists are taking the stage in TED (and TEDx) talks, they are becoming increasingly active on the social media, and they participate in Story Collider events. All of these formats require storytelling skills. Improvisation theatre techniques training helps them hone their outreach skills. The storytelling workshops I run aim at the same. I use improv theatre exercises and lots of active interaction, but most importantly story structures to get them out of their shells and tell them stories. And they're getting really good at it.

These skills are badly needed in times of fake news. Why is it so difficult to persuade anti-vaxxers and flat-earthers even though all the scientific evidence speaks against their conspiracy theories? We shouldn't blame technology. True, fake news has never spread faster than today, "thanks" to social media. But it's also true that much of the spreading is done by humans clicking on "share" and not by bots. It's also true that the work may seem complex (there are a number of factors), but eventually this boils down to good storytelling. My point is: science can no longer afford not to tell stories. There is nothing bad about telling stories if you're not making up anything. Although papers carry plenty of storytelling elements in them, the scientific method doesn't imply scientists should go beyond scholarly publication in the communication of their results. So this is my plea to expand the scientific method, especially the Dissemination part and require scientists to interact with the public. It's not only a right, it's a duty. After all, the public elects the politicians who enable (or sometimes, hinder) scientific advances. The public throws in its tax money to fund research. And the public is: all of us. Including all scientists. So let's tear down those ivory towers.

There are already enough scientists who employ stories in the form of anecdotal evidence and other inductive fallacies to persuade the public of vaccines-lead-to-autism horror stories, like Andrew Wakefield. Or think of the patient narratives of Paolo Macchiarini, the surgeon who carried out scientifically unsound trachea transplants (almost all of his patients died). Or Dario Spinedi, the Swiss doctor who came up with advertising for his clinic in Switzerland, subtly implying that his clinic could cure with homeopathy. He later distanced himself from this (Hehli 2017). I would assume that you know how homeopathy works (or better: doesn't), but I'm always astonished at how many scientists and journalists believe in the healing power of those little sugar globules. They don't work beyond the placebo effect. There is no scientific method verification technique in the world that can distinguish different homeopathic globules from each other. There is just no active ingredient that can be found. That is why essentially, it's fraud. The sheer "logic" behind it is asinine, to be friendly: the more you dilute tiny active ingredients (followed by shaking), the higher the final product's potency, which implies higher efficacy. Producers sell the overpriced sugar balls as remedies, but there is no scientific proof whatsoever for an efficacy that goes beyond the placebo effect. So what gives? Why do people still buy it, despite knowing the truth? An inductive fallacy. Here's an example: "it worked for me. I know for sure", somebody told me once. "How can you know? It could have been just the placebo effect", I say. "You're not listening. I was a child. I didn't know about the placebo effect" was the answer I got. I then usually go on explaining the placebo-by-proxy effect that works even in kids and dogs, despite them obviously not knowing. But the fallacy is there. People tell their "success" stories and others assume this is always the case. But it's not. They then pass those stories on. Word-of-mouth recommendations are still super powerful. I've seen this happening, passed on from mother to daughter who takes it at face value. Ironically, what I just said is anecdotal evidence, too.

You cannot persuade anti-vaxxers, flat-earthers and homeopathy fans with scientific facts. Whatever studies find, they won't give a damn about the facts. We've seen this early in this book. Facts and stats and figures don't arouse anybody's emotions but rather appeal to the rational part of our brains. Anti-vaxxer stories like the ones from Ian Gromowski's parents are highly effective. But there are ways to counter this sort of storytelling. The remedy is: again, storytelling. But with news values in mind. Most fake news stories embody the strongest news value, negativity. Most vain attempts to counter them are positive stories that say: "oh no, this doesn't happen. It's all good." That won't work. Instead, former anti-vaxxer parents have written stories about how their children almost died (describing the "how" in detail), having a moment of insight and changing their attitude (Shelby & Ernst 2013). These stories are a good means. They too draw on negativity, but this time for a good cause, and most importantly, in factually correct stories. Conversion stories work wonders. Just take the example of Edzard Ernst, who was trained in homeopathy but now has become one of the most outspoken objectors.

If science wants to convert fake news believers or at least prevent more people from drinking the Flavor Aid, scientists and journalists alike need to tell the story of science. And the scientific method needs to acknowledge that outreach and storytelling beyond current dissemination practices is a must, not just an option. Equally, scientists should get credit for those additional activities. Most importantly, they should get the resources (time and money) to do them. These are not side activities that one does in her spare time, while walking the dog. This is a full-blown job with a lot of responsibility. Let's take it seriously, while having fun.

Review questions

- What elements must the scientific method have?
- What kinds of logic exist, and how do they differ?
- How is the quality of a journal determined?
- How does the human factor influence the scientific method?
- Which metrics measure societal impact?

- Which methods exist to game journal metrics?
- What limitations does peer review have?
- How would you approach reading a journal article?
- How many globules do you need to cure the flu?

Links

Wellcome Trust Quality Criteria: https://wellcome.ac.uk/funding/guidance/open-access-policy

Retraction Watch Database: https://retractiondatabase.org

"San Francisco Declaration on Research Assessment" (DORA): https://sfdora.org

Conflicts of Interest Statement (template, Elsevier): https://www.elsevier.com/__data/promis_misc/asjsur_coi.pdf

"How to read a scientific paper": https://www.elsevier.com/connect/infographic-how-to-read-a-scientific-paper

Story-Based Inquiry by Mark Lee Hunter: https://unesdoc.unesco.org/ark:/48223/pf0000193078

Open Science MOOC: https://opensciencemooc.eu/

References

Adam, D. (2019) "Reproducibility trial publishes two conclusions for one paper," *Nature* [Online]. Available at: https://www.nature.com/articles/d41586-019-01751-0 (date accessed 11 October 2019).

Ahearne, G. (2017) "The Workaholic and Academia: in defense of #AcaDowntime," *Academia Obscura* [Online]. Available at: http://www.academiaobscura.com/the-workaholic-and-academia/#comment-17459 (date accessed 10 October 2019).

Angler, M.W. (2017) *Science Journalism: an introduction.* London: Routledge.

Alberts, B. (2013) "Impact Factor Distortions," *Science*, vol. 340, no. 6134, 787.

Amrhein, V., Greenland, S. & McShane, B. (2019) "Scientists rise up against statistical significance," *Nature Comment* [Online]. Available at: https://www.nature.com/articles/d41586-019-00857-9 (date accessed 10 October 2019).

Anonymous, A. (2018) "Performance-driven culture is ruining scientific research," *The Guardian* [Online]. Available at: https://www.theguardian.com/higher-education-network/2018/feb/16/performance-driven-culture-is-ruining-scientific-research (date accessed 17 January 2019).

Baker, M. (2016) "1,500 scientists lift the lid on reproducibility," *Nature News*, vol. 533, no. 7604, 452–454.

Beall, J. (2016) "Predatory journals: Ban predators from the scientific record," *Nature*, vol. 534, no. 7607, 326.

Betz, F. (2011) "Origin of Scientific Method," in: *Managing Science. Innovation, Technology, and Knowledge Management.* New York: Springer.

Birkenkrahe, M. (2014) "Using storytelling methods to improve emotion, motivation and attitude of students writing scientific papers and theses." Cognitive Informatics & Cognitive Computing (ICCI* CC), 2014 IEEE 13th International Conference, 140–145.

Blachowicz, J. (2016) "There Is No Scientific Method," *The New York Times* [Online]. Available at: https://www.nytimes.com/2016/07/04/opinion/there-is-no-scientific-method.html (date accessed 12 January 2019).

Brainard, J. & You, J. (2018) "What a massive database of retracted papers reveals about science publishing's 'death penalty'," *Science* [Online]. Available at: https://www.scien cemag.org/news/2018/10/what-massive-database-retracted-papers-reveals-about-scien ce-publishing-s-death-penalty (date accessed 12 January 2019).

Caldin, E.F. (1949) *The Power and Limits of Science: A Philosophical Study.* London: Chapman & Hall.

Caon, M. (2017) "Gaming the impact factor: where who cites what, whom and when," *Australasian Physical & Engineering Sciences in Medicine*, vol. 40, no. 2, 273–276.

Carey, S. (2014) *A Beginner's Guide to Scientific Method*, 3rd edition Belmont, California: Wadsworth.

Cormick, C. (2018) "Checking the source: how to read a scientific paper," *Cosmos magazine* [Online]. Available at: https://cosmosmagazine.com/technology/check ing-the-source-how-to-read-a-scientific-paper (date accessed 11 October 2019).

Dansinger, M. (2017) "Dear plagiarist: a letter to a peer reviewer who stole and published our manuscript as his own," *Annals of internal medicine*, vol. 166, no. 2, 143.

DeCoursey, T. (2006) "Should authors be told who their reviewers are?" *Nature* [Online]. Available at: https://www.nature.com/nature/peerreview/debate/nature04991.html (date accessed 11 October 2019).

Dong, P., Loh, M. & Mondry, A. (2005) "The 'impact factor' revisited," *Biomedical Digital Libraries*, vol. 2, no. 1, 1–8.

Evans, T.M., Bira, L., Gastelum, J.B., Weiss, L.T. & Vanderford, N.L. (2018) "Evidence for a mental health crisis in graduate education," *Nature Biotechnology*, vol. 36, no. 3, 282–284.

Ferguson, C., Marcus, A. & Oransky, I. (2014) "The peer-review scam," *Nature*, vol. 515, no. 7528, 480–482.

Feyerabend, P. (1993) *Against Method*, 3rd ed., New York: Verso.

Fountain, H. (2014) "Science Journal Pulls 60 Papers in Peer-Review Fraud," *The New York Times* [Online]. Available at: https://www.nytimes.com/2014/07/11/science/science-journal-pulls-60-papers-in-peer-review-fraud.html (date accessed 10 October 2019)

Gauch, H.G. (2003) *Scientific Method in Practice.* Cambridge: Cambridge University Press.

Glänzel, W., Moed, H.F., Schmoch, U. & Thelwall, M. (2018) *Springer Handbook of Science and Technology Indicators*, Cham: Springer.

Goldacre, B., DeVito, N.J., Heneghan, C., Irving, F., Bacon, S., Fleminger, J. & Curtis, H. (2018) "Compliance with requirement to report results on the EU Clinical Trials Register: cohort study and web resource," *British Medical Journal*, no. 362, k3218 [Online]. Available at: https://www.bmj.com/content/362/bmj.k3218 (date accessed 13 January 2019).

Guardian (2019) "The Guardian view on academic publishing: disastrous capitalism," *The Guardian* [Online]. Available at: https://www.theguardian.com/commentisfree/2019/ma r/04/the-guardian-view-on-academic-publishing-disastrous-capitalism (date accessed 10 October 2019).

Haug, C.J. (2015) "Peer-Review Fraud – Hacking the Scientific Publication Process," *New England Journal of Medicine*, vol. 373, no. 25, 2393–2395.

Hehli, S. (2017) "Homöopathie-Klinik krebst zurück," *Neue Zürcher Zeitung* [Online]. Available at: https://www.nzz.ch/schweiz/angebliche-tumorheilung-homoeopathie-klinik-krebst-zur ueck-ld.1296092 (date accessed 12 October 2019).

Hill, T.E., Martelli, P.F. & Kuo, J.H. (2018) "A case for revisiting peer review: Implications for professional self-regulation and quality improvement," *PLoS One* [Online]. Available at: https://journals.plos.org/plosone/article/file?id=10.1371/journal.pone. 0199961&type=printable (date accessed 12 January 2019).

Hogan, V., Hogan, M. & Hodgins, M. (2016) "A study of workaholism in Irish academics," *Occupational Medicine*, vol. 66, no. 6, 460–465.

Hogan, V., Hogan, M., Hodgins, M., Kinman, G. & Bunting, B. (2014) "An examination of gender differences in the impact of individual and organisational factors on work hours, work-life conflict and psychological strain in academics," *The Irish Journal of Psychology*, vol. 35, no. 2–3, 133–150.

Hunter, M.L. (2011) "Story-based inquiry: a manual for investigative journalists." Paris: UNESCO [Online]. Available at: https://unesdoc.unesco.org/ark:/48223/pf0000193078 (date accessed 3 September 2019).

Hutson, M. (2018) "Artificial Intelligence faces reproducibility crisis," *Science*, vol. 359, no. 6377, 725–726.

Jones, M. & Crow, D. (2017) "How can we use the 'science of stories' to produce persuasive scientific stories?" *Palgrave Communications*, vol. 3, no. 1, 1–9.

Kearns, C.E., Apollonio, D. & Glantz, S.A. (2017) "Sugar industry sponsorship of germ-free rodent studies linking sucrose to hyperlipidemia and cancer: An historical analysis of internal documents," *PLoS Biology*, vol. 15, no. 11, e2003460.

Kristof, N. (2009) "Nicholas Kristof's Advice for Saving the World," Outside [Online]. Available at: https://www.outsideonline.com/1909636/nicholas-kristofs-advice-saving-world (date accessed 14 January 2019).

Larivière, V. & Sugimoto, C.R. (2018) "The Journal Impact Factor: A brief history, critique, and discussion of adverse effects," arXiv preprint [Online]. Available at: https://arxiv.org/pdf/1801.08992.pdf (date accessed 12 January 2019).

Larivière, V. & Gingras, Y. (2010) "The impact factor's Matthew Effect: A natural experiment in bibliometrics," *Journal of the American Society for Information Science and Technology*, vol. 61, no. 2, 424–427.

Lemaitre, B. (2017) "Science, narcissism and the quest for visibility," *The FEBS journal*, vol. 284, no. 6, 875–882.

McKiernan, E., Alperin, J.P. & Fleerackers, A. (2019) "The 'impact' of the Journal Impact Factor in the review, tenure, and promotion process," LSE Impact Blog [Online]. Available at: https://blogs.lse.ac.uk/impactofsocialsciences/2019/04/26/the-impact-of-the-journal-impact-factor-in-the-review-tenure-and-promotion-process/ (date accessed 11 October 2019).

Medoff, M.H. (2006) "Evidence of a Harvard and Chicago Matthew effect," *Journal of Economic Methodology*, vol. 13, no. 4, 485–506.

Nair, P.K.R. & Nair, V. (2014) "Organization of a Research Paper: The IMRAD Format," in: *Scientific Writing and Communication in Agriculture and Natural Resources*, Cham: Springer, 13–26.

Noseda, M. & McLean, G.R. (2008) "Where did the scientific method go?" *Nature Biotechnology ("To the editor")*, vol. 26, no. 1, 28–29.

Nuzzo, R. (2014) "Scientific Method: Statistical Errors," *Nature*, vol. 506, no. 7487, 150–152.

Olson, R. (2015) *Houston, we have a narrative: why science needs story.* London: The University of Chicago Press.

Pain, E. (2016) "How to (seriously) read a scientific paper," *Science* [Online] Available at: https://www.sciencemag.org/careers/2016/03/how-seriously-read-scientific-paper (date accessed: 13 January 2019).

PloS Medicine Editors (2006) "The Impact Factor Game," [Online]. Available at: https://journals.plos.org/plosmedicine/article?id=10.1371/journal.pmed.0030291 (date accessed 11 October 2019).

Polka, J.K., Kiley, R., Konforti, B., Stern, B. & Vale, R.D. (2018) "Publish peer reviews," *Nature Comment* [Online]. Available at: https://www.nature.com/articles/d41586-018-06032-w (date accessed 11 October 2019).

Popper, K. (2002) *The Logic of Scientific Discovery*. London: Routledge Classics.

Rekdal, O.B. (2014) "Academic urban legends," *Social Studies of Sciences*, vol. 44, no. 4, 638–654.

Rivera, H. (2018) "Fake peer review and inappropriate authorship are real evils," *Journal of Korean Medical Science*, vol. 34, no. 2, e6.

Rodriguez, N. (2015) "Infographic: How to read a scientific paper," Elsevier.com [Online]. Available at: https://www.elsevier.com/connect/infographic-how-to-read-a-scientific-paper (date accessed 14 January 2019).

Scandellari, F. (2018) Face-to-face interview 6 June 2018.

Schmidt, S. (2009) "Shall we really do it again? The powerful concept of replication is neglected in the social sciences," *Review of General Psychology*, vol. 13, no. 2, 90–100.

Shelby, A. & Ernst, K. (2013) "Story and science: how providers and parents can utilize storytelling to combat anti-vaccine misinformation," *Human vaccines & immunotherapeutics*, vol. 9, no. 8, 1795–1801.

Smith, R. (2006) "Peer review: a flawed process at the heart of science," *Journal of the Royal Society of Medicine*, vol. 99, 178–182.

Sorokowski, P., Kulczycki, E., Sorokowska, A. & Pisanski, K. (2017) "Predatory journals recruit fake editors," *Nature*, vol. 543, no. 7646, 481.

Sullivan, G.M. & Feinn, R. (2012) "Using effect size – or why the P value is not enough," *Journal of Graduate Medical Education*, vol. 4, no. 3, 279–282.

Tennant, J. (2018) "Dr. Jon Tennant on an Introduction to Open Peer Review Process," Eurodoc [Online]. Available at: http://www.eurodoc.net/news/2018/jon-tennant-on-an-introduction-to-open-peer-review (date accessed 11 October 2019).

Thacker, P.D. & Tennant, J. (2019) "Why we shouldn't take peer review as the 'gold standard'," *The Washington Post* [Online]. Available at: https://www.washingtonpost.com/outlook/why-we-shouldnt-take-peer-review-as-the-gold-standard/2019/08/01/fd90749a-b229-11e9-8949-5f36ff92706e_story.html (date accessed 10 October 2019).

Torp, S., Lysfjord, L. & Midje, H.H. (2018) "Workaholism and work – family conflict among university academics," *Higher Education*, vol. 76, no. 6, 1071–1090.

Tucket, A.G. & Kangasniemi, M. (2017) "Why we need a golden rule for peer review," *Nursing Ethics*, vol. 24, no. 8, 875–877.

Van Raan, A.F.J. (2004) "Measuring science, " in: *Handbook of quantitative science and technology research*. Dordrecht: Springer. 19–50.

Voit, E.O. (2019) "Perspective: Dimensions of the scientific method," *PLoS Computational Biology*, vol. 15, no. 9.

Wasserstein, R.L. & Lazar, N.A. (2016) "The ASA's statement on p-values: context, process, and purpose," *The American Statistician*, vol. 70, no. 2, 129–133.

Wilkinson, M. (2013) "Testing the null hypothesis: The forgotten legacy of Karl Popper?" *Journal of Sports Sciences*, vol. 31, no. 9, 919–920.

Wilson, K.J. & Rigakos, B. (2016) "Scientific Process Flowchart Assessment (SPFA): A Method for Evaluating Changes in Understanding and Visualization of the Scientific Process in a Multidisciplinary Student Population," *CBE-Life Sciences Education*, vol. 15, no. 4, ar63.

Zauner, H., Nogoy, N.A., Edmunds, S.C., Zhou, H. & Goodman, L. (2018) "We need to talk about authorship," *GigaScience*, vol. 7, no. 12, (December) giy122.

Index

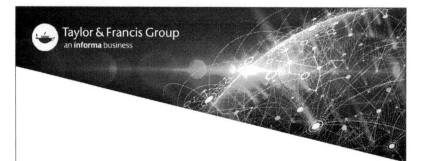